INJUSTICE

GODS AMONG US: YEAR TWO

VOLUME 2

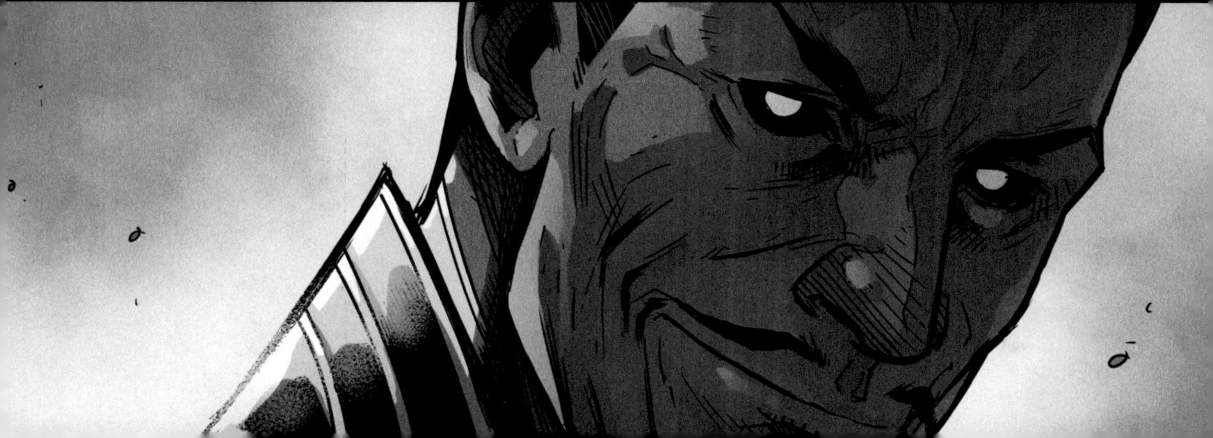

INJU
GODS AMON

Tom Taylor Marguerite Bennett
Writers

Bruno Redondo Thomas Derenick Mike S. Miller
Julien Hugonnard-Bert Vicente Cifuentes Daniel HDR
David Yardin Jheremy Raapack Xermanico Juan Albarran
Artists

Rex Lokus J. Nanjan (NS Studios)
Colorists

Wes Abbott
Letterer

Jheremy Raapack & David Lopez and Santi Casas of Ikari Studio
Cover Artists

STICE

US: YEAR TWO

VOLUME 2

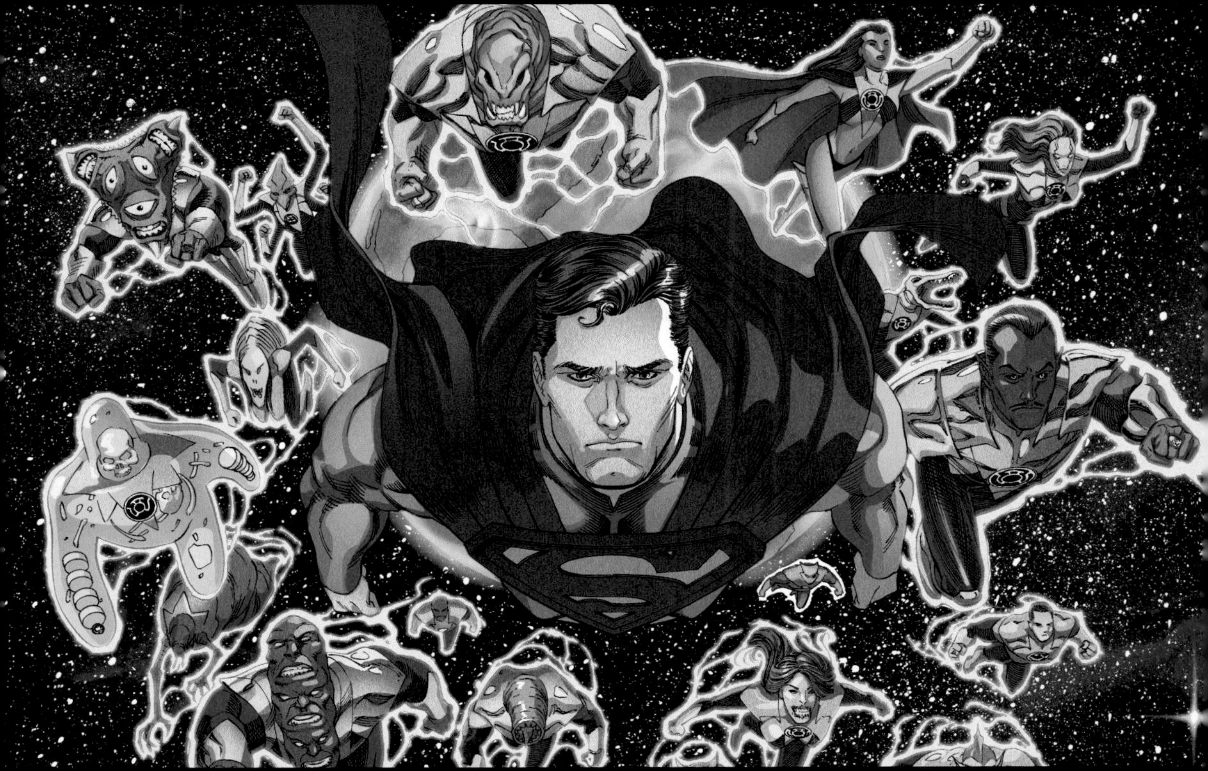

SUPERMAN Created by JERRY SIEGEL and JOE SHUSTER.
By Special Arrangement with the Jerry Siegel Family.

BASED ON THE VIDEOGAME INJUSTICE: GODS AMONG US

Jim Chadwick Editor – Original Series
Aniz Ansari Assistant Editor – Original Series
Rachel Pinnelas Editor
Robbin Brosterman Design Director – Books
Louis Prandi Publication Design

Hank Kanalz Senior VP – Vertigo & Integrated Publishing

Diane Nelson President
Dan DiDio and Jim Lee Co-Publishers
Geoff Johns Chief Creative Officer
Amit Desai Senior VP – Marketing & Franchise Management
Amy Genkins Senior VP – Business & Legal Affairs
Nairi Gardiner Senior VP – Finance
Jeff Boison VP – Publishing Planning
Mark Chiarello VP – Art Direction & Design
John Cunningham VP – Marketing
Terri Cunningham VP – Editorial Administration
Larry Ganem VP – Talent Relations & Services
Alison Gill Senior VP – Manufacturing & Operations
Jay Kogan VP – Business & Legal Affairs, Publishing
Jack Mahan VP – Business Affairs, Talent
Nick Napolitano VP – Manufacturing Administration
Sue Pohja VP – Book Sales
Fred Ruiz VP – Manufacturing Operations
Courtney Simmons Senior VP – Publicity
Bob Wayne Senior VP – Sales

INJUSTICE: GODS AMONG US: YEAR TWO VOLUME 2

Published by DC Comics. Compilation Copyright © 2015 DC Comics.
All Rights Reserved.

Originally published in single magazine form in INJUSTICE YEAR
TWO 7-12 and INJUSTICE YEAR TWO ANNUAL 1. Copyright © 2014
DC Comics. All Rights Reserved. All characters, their distinctive
likenesses and related elements featured in this publication are
trademarks of DC Comics. The stories, characters and incidents
featured in this publication are entirely fictional. DC Comics does
not read or accept unsolicited ideas, stories or artwork.

DC Comics, 1700 Broadway, New York, NY 10019
A Warner Bros. Entertainment Company.
Printed by RR Donnelley, Salem, VA, USA. 3/13/15.
First Printing.

ISBN: 978-1-4012-5341-7

Library of Congress Cataloging-in-Publication Data

Taylor, Tom, 1978- author.
  Injustice : Gods Among Us Year Two Volume 2 / Tom Taylor, writer ;
Bruno Redondo, artist.
    pages cm
  "Based on the videogame Injustice: Gods Among Us"
  ISBN 978-1-4012-5341-7 (hardback)
 1. Graphic novels. I. Redondo, Bruno, 1981- illustrator. II. Title. III. Title:
Gods Among Us Year Two Volume 2.
  PN6727.T293I59 2015
  741.5'973—dc23
                                        2014049027

SUSTAINABLE
FORESTRY
INITIATIVE

Certified Chain of Custody
20% Certified Forest Content,
80% Certified Sourcing
www.sfiprogram.org
SFI-01042
APPLIES TO TEXT STOCK ONLY

"The Quiver" **Bruno Redondo Julien Hugonnard-Bert** Artists
"Resistance" **Thomas Derenick Mike S. Miller** Artists **Rex Lokus** Colorist
Cover Art by **Stephane Roux**

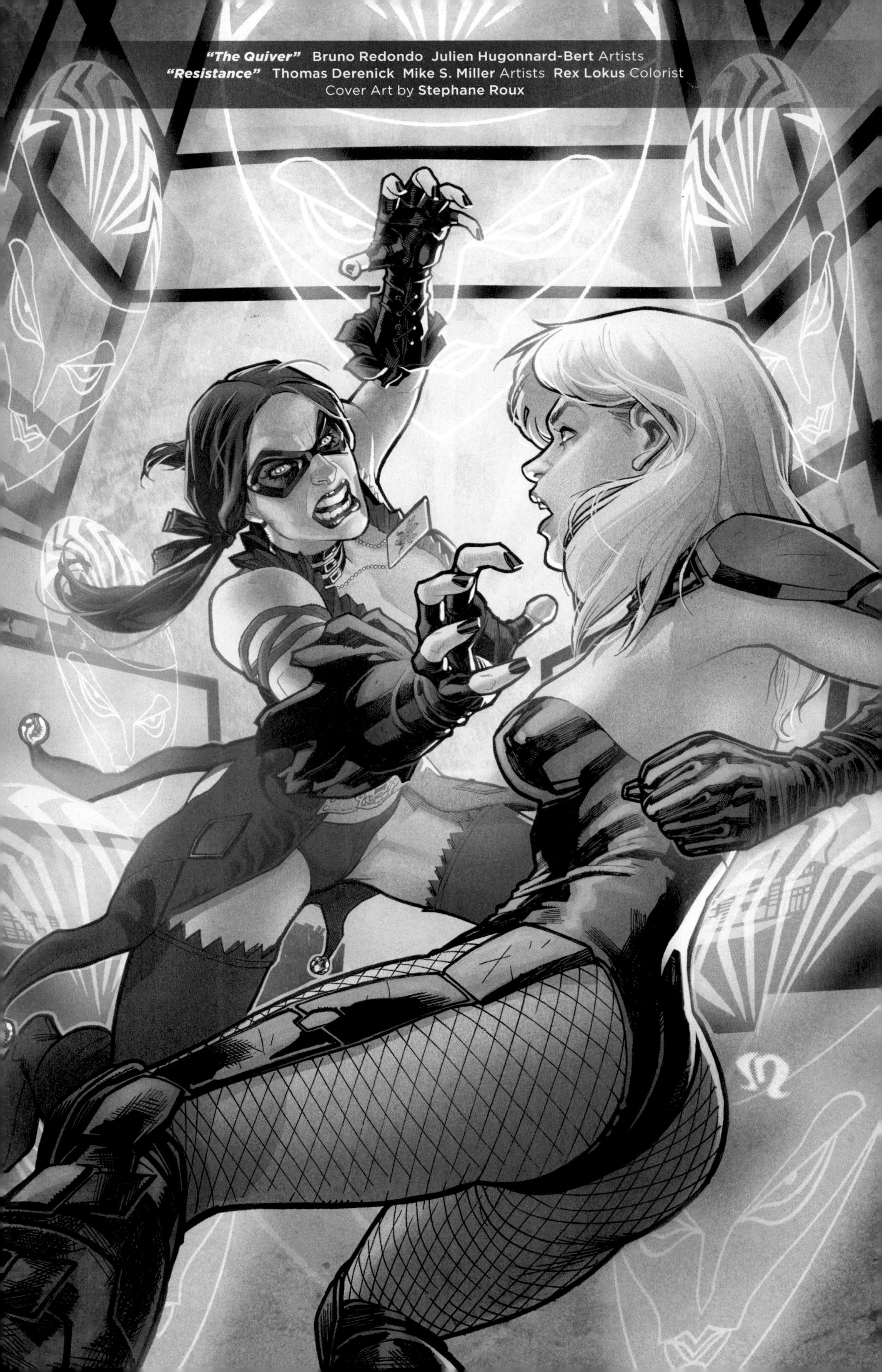

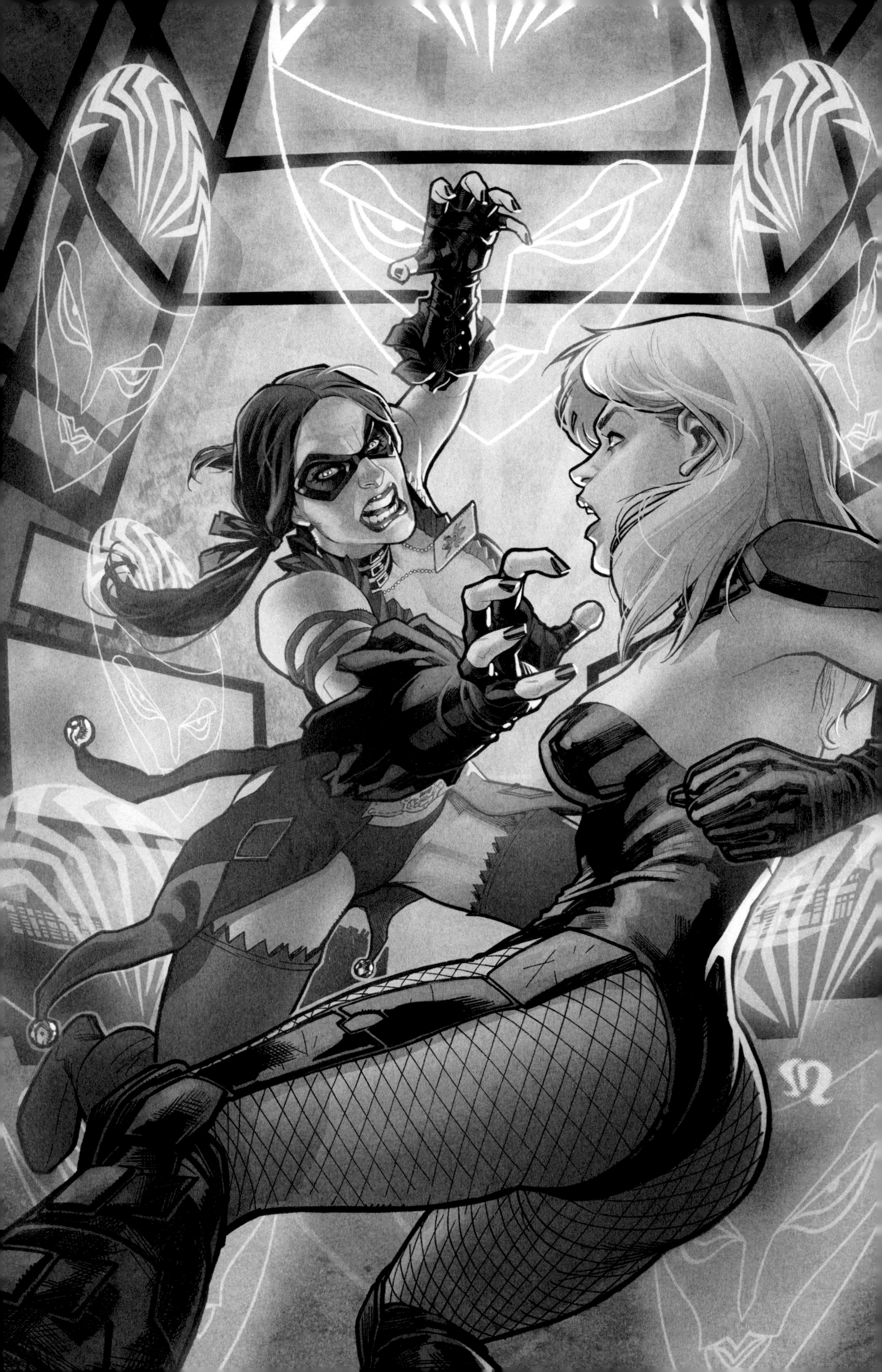

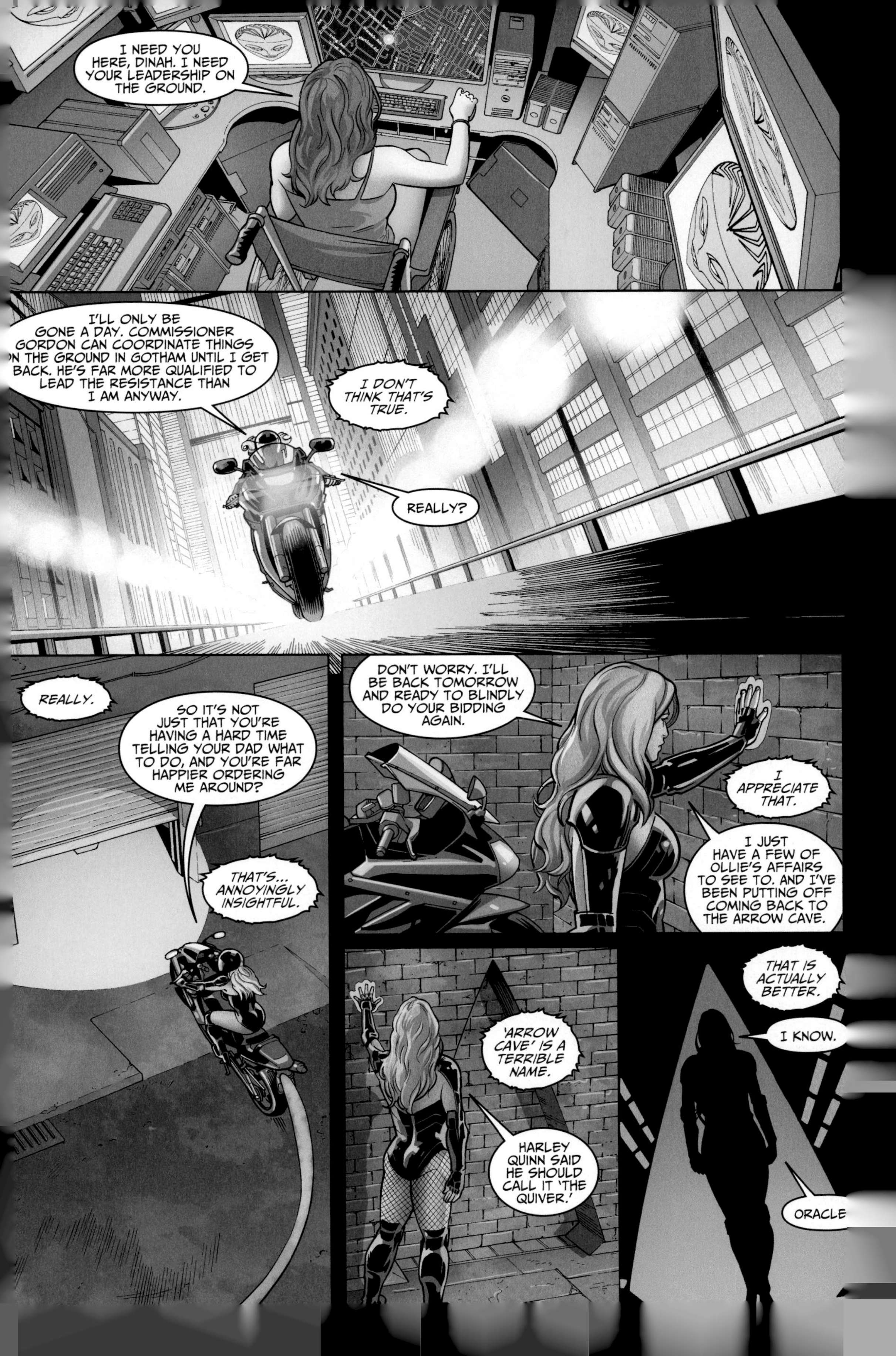
I NEED YOU HERE, DINAH. I NEED YOUR LEADERSHIP ON THE GROUND.
I'LL ONLY BE GONE A DAY. COMMISSIONER GORDON CAN COORDINATE THINGS ON THE GROUND IN GOTHAM UNTIL I GET BACK. HE'S FAR MORE QUALIFIED TO LEAD THE RESISTANCE THAN I AM ANYWAY.
I DON'T THINK THAT'S TRUE.
REALLY?
REALLY.
SO IT'S NOT JUST THAT YOU'RE HAVING A HARD TIME TELLING YOUR DAD WHAT TO DO, AND YOU'RE FAR HAPPIER ORDERING ME AROUND?
THAT'S... ANNOYINGLY INSIGHTFUL.
DON'T WORRY. I'LL BE BACK TOMORROW AND READY TO BLINDLY DO YOUR BIDDING AGAIN.
I APPRECIATE THAT.
I JUST HAVE A FEW OF OLLIE'S AFFAIRS TO SEE TO. AND I'VE BEEN PUTTING OFF COMING BACK TO THE ARROW CAVE.
'ARROW CAVE' IS A TERRIBLE NAME.
HARLEY QUINN SAID HE SHOULD CALL IT 'THE QUIVER.'
THAT IS ACTUALLY BETTER.
I KNOW.
ORACLE

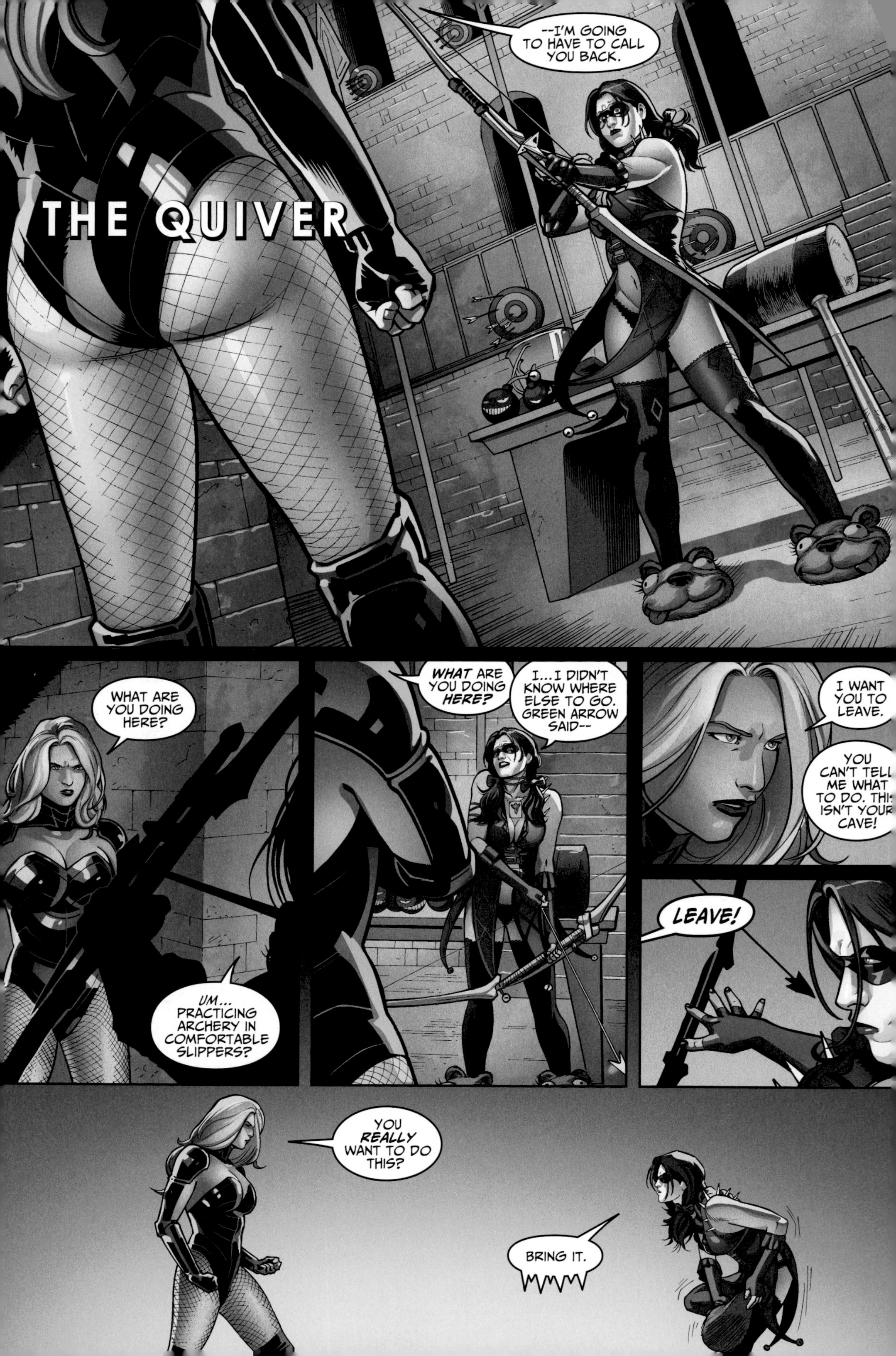
THE QUIVER
--I'M GOING TO HAVE TO CALL YOU BACK.
WHAT ARE YOU DOING HERE?
UM... PRACTICING ARCHERY IN COMFORTABLE SLIPPERS?
WHAT ARE YOU DOING HERE?
I...I DIDN'T KNOW WHERE ELSE TO GO. GREEN ARROW SAID--
I WANT YOU TO LEAVE.
YOU CAN'T TELL ME WHAT TO DO. THIS ISN'T YOUR CAVE!
LEAVE!
YOU REALLY WANT TO DO THIS?
BRING IT.

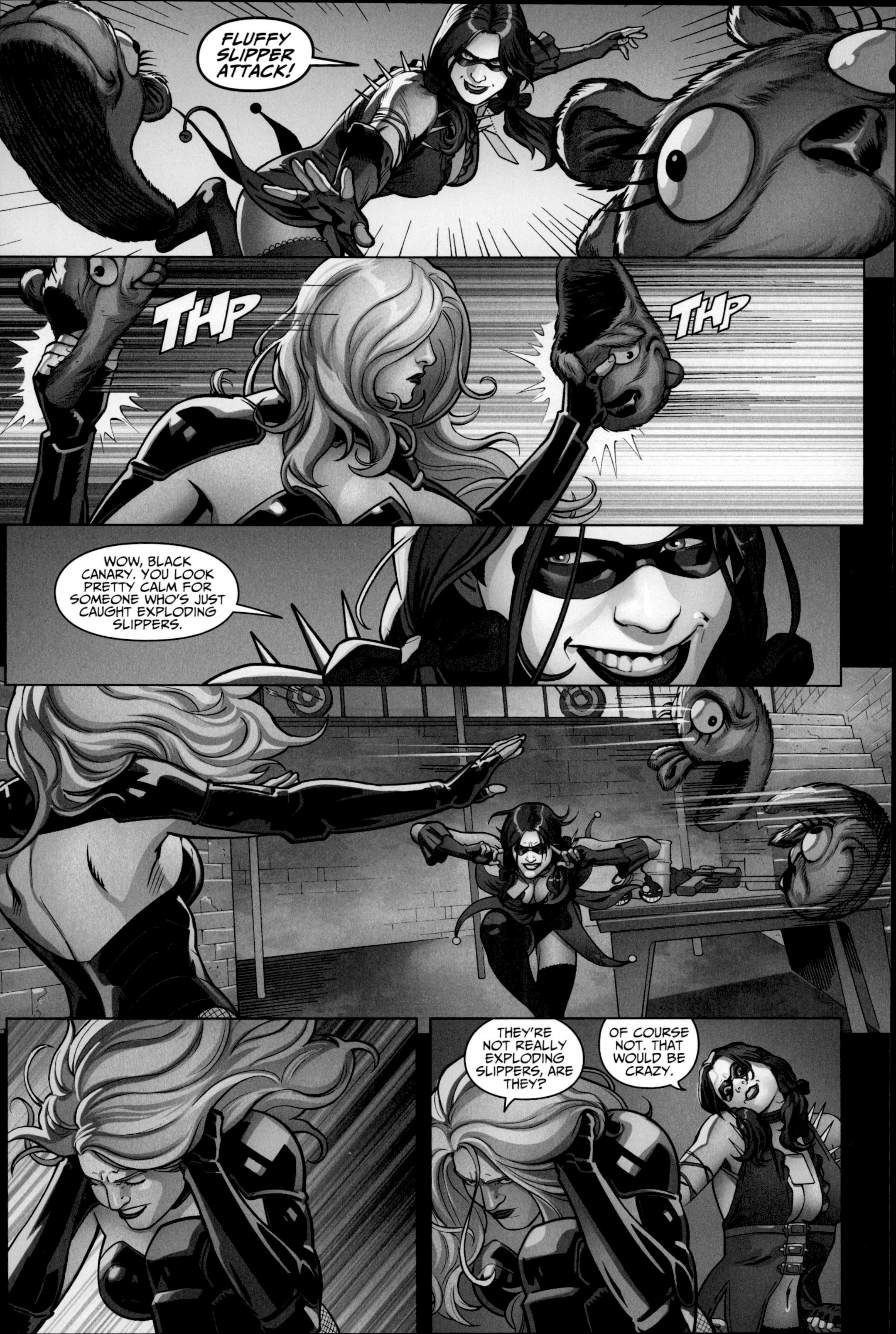
FLUFFY SLIPPER ATTACK!
THP
THP
WOW, BLACK CANARY. YOU LOOK PRETTY CALM FOR SOMEONE WHO'S JUST CAUGHT EXPLODING SLIPPERS.
THEY'RE NOT REALLY EXPLODING SLIPPERS, ARE THEY?
OF COURSE NOT. THAT WOULD BE CRAZY.

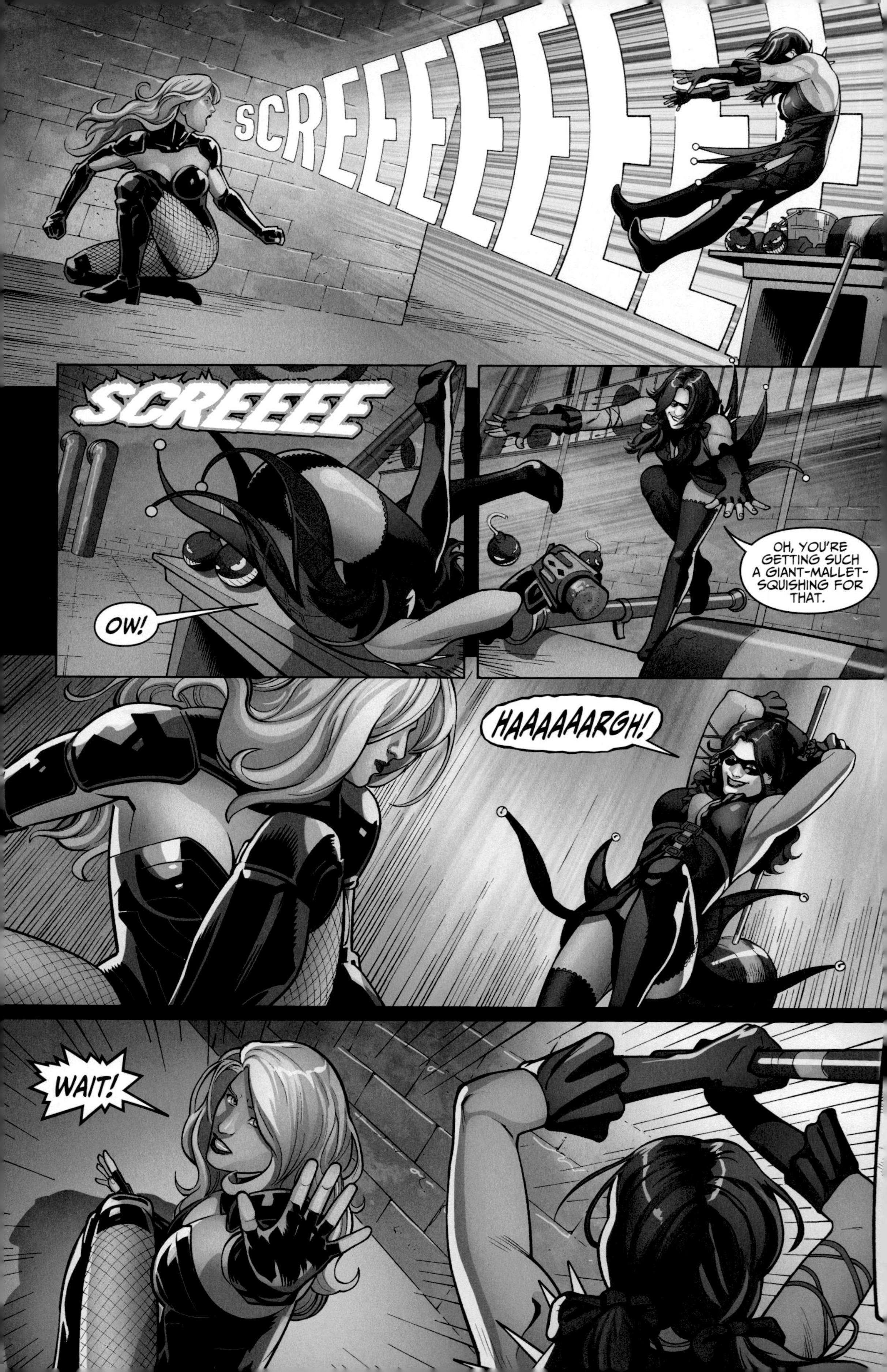
SCREEEEEEEEEE
SCREEEEE
OW!
OH, YOU'RE GETTING SUCH A GIANT-MALLET-SQUISHING FOR THAT.
HAAAAAARGH!
WAIT!

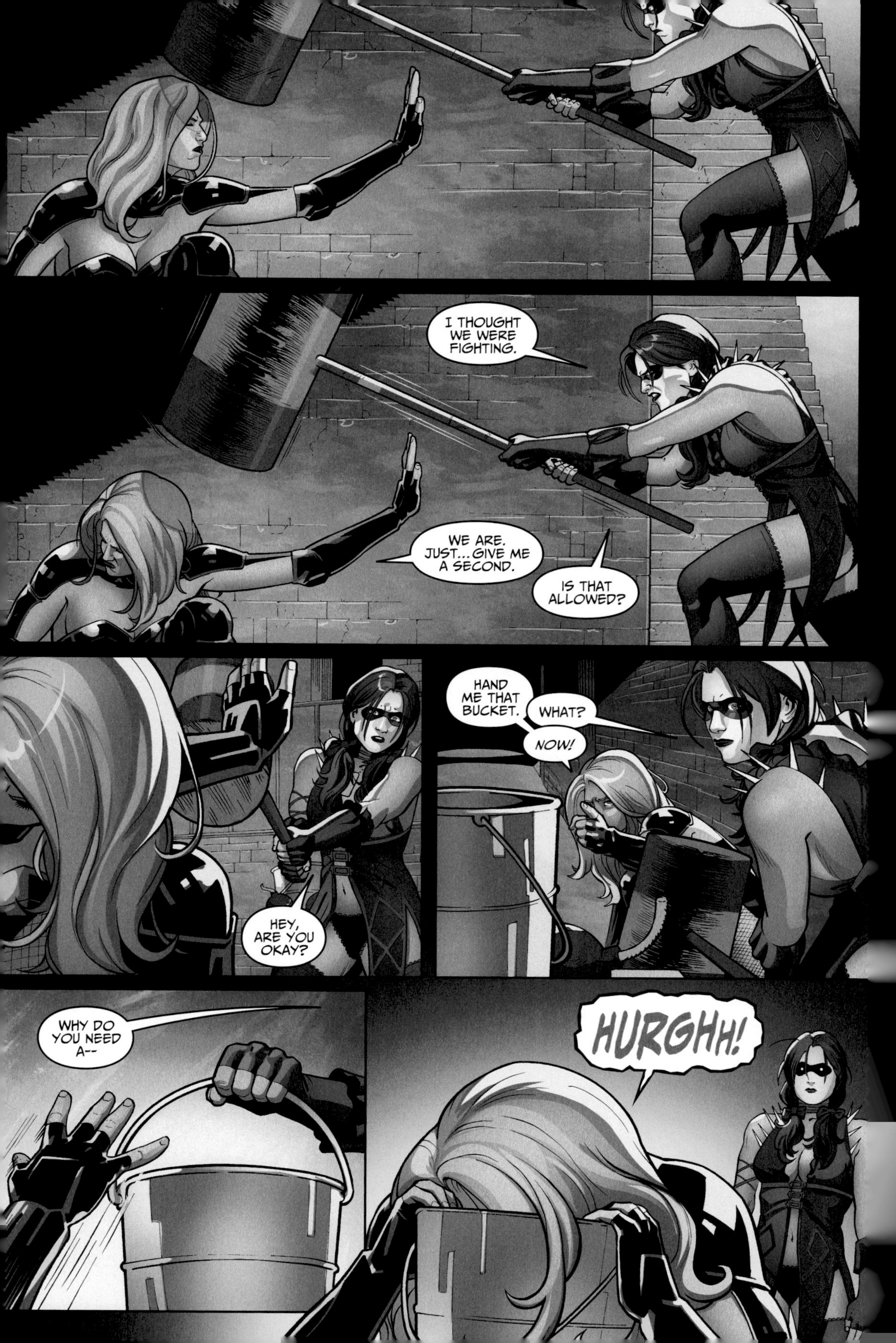

I THOUGHT WE WERE FIGHTING.
WE ARE. JUST...GIVE ME A SECOND.
IS THAT ALLOWED?
HEY, ARE YOU OKAY?
HAND ME THAT BUCKET.
WHAT?
NOW!
WHY DO YOU NEED A--
HURGHH!

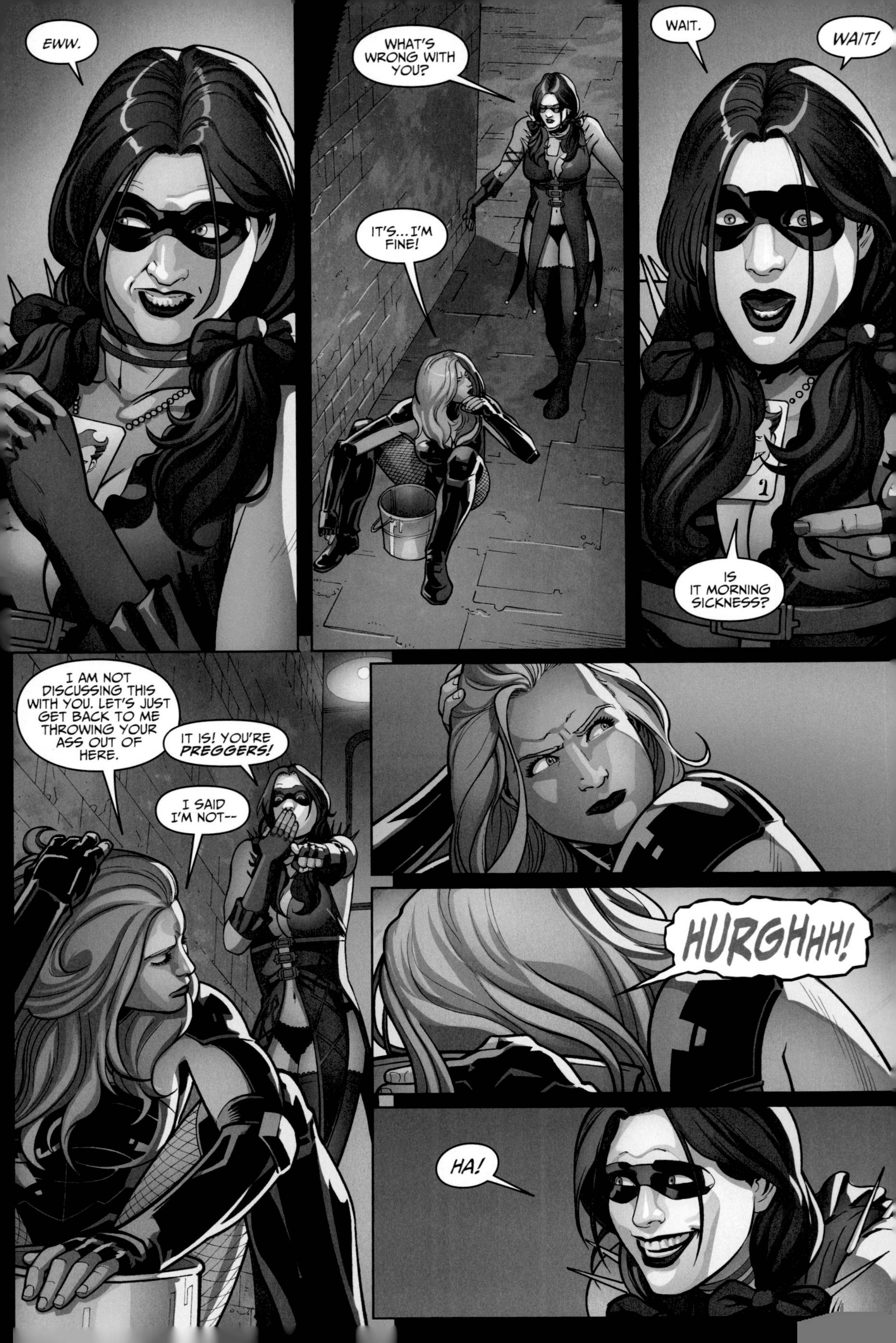
EWW.
WHAT'S WRONG WITH YOU?
IT'S... I'M FINE!
WAIT.
WAIT!
IS IT MORNING SICKNESS?
I AM NOT DISCUSSING THIS WITH YOU. LET'S JUST GET BACK TO ME THROWING YOUR ASS OUT OF HERE.
IT IS! YOU'RE PREGGERS!
I SAID I'M NOT--
HURGHHH!
HA!

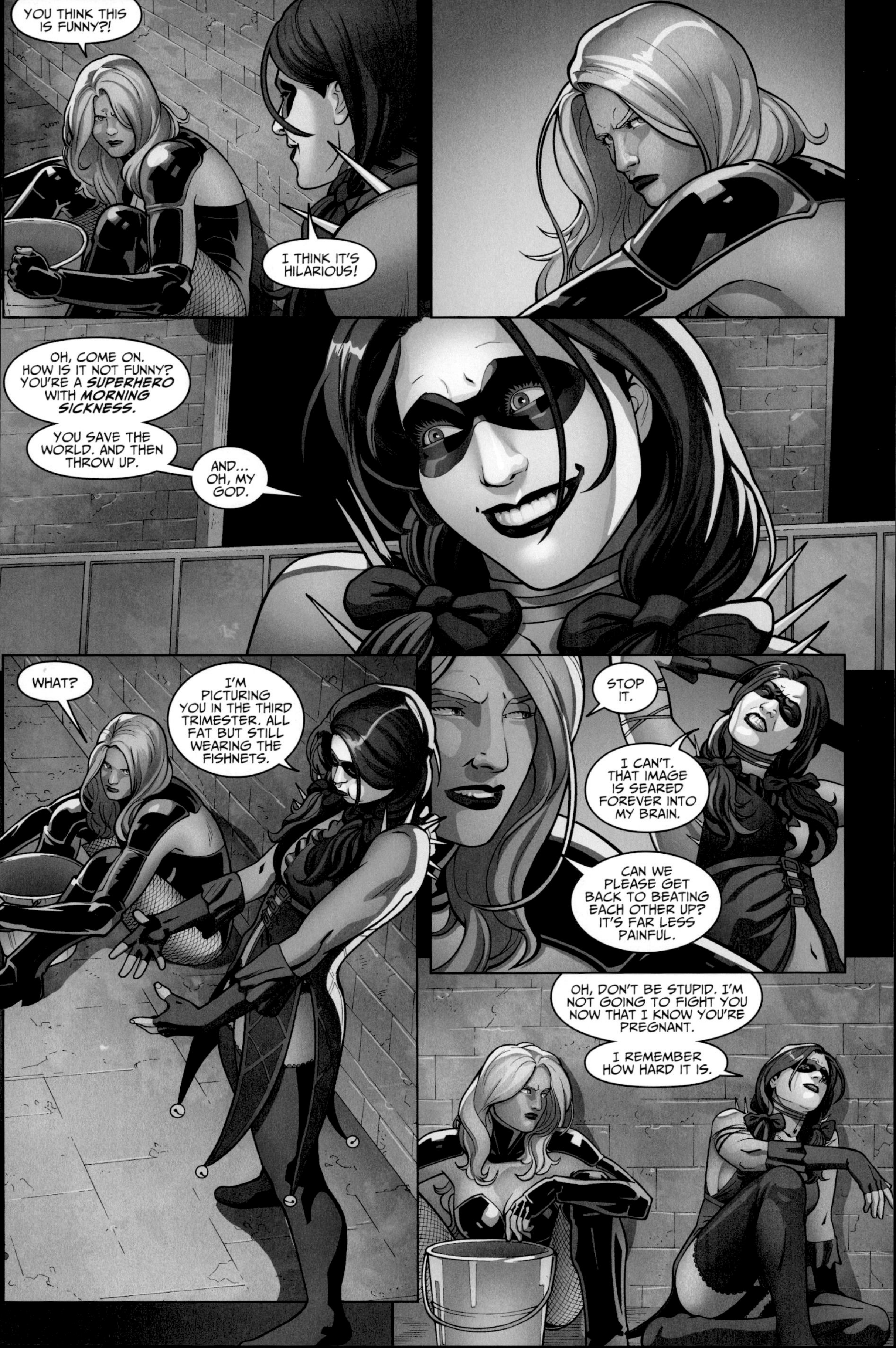
YOU THINK THIS IS FUNNY?!
I THINK IT'S HILARIOUS!
OH, COME ON. HOW IS IT NOT FUNNY? YOU'RE A *SUPERHERO* WITH *MORNING SICKNESS.*
YOU SAVE THE WORLD. AND THEN THROW UP.
AND... OH, MY GOD.
WHAT?
I'M PICTURING YOU IN THE THIRD TRIMESTER. ALL FAT BUT STILL WEARING THE FISHNETS.
STOP IT.
I CAN'T. THAT IMAGE IS SEARED FOREVER INTO MY BRAIN.
CAN WE PLEASE GET BACK TO BEATING EACH OTHER UP? IT'S FAR LESS PAINFUL.
OH, DON'T BE STUPID. I'M NOT GOING TO FIGHT YOU NOW THAT I KNOW YOU'RE PREGNANT.
I REMEMBER HOW HARD IT IS.

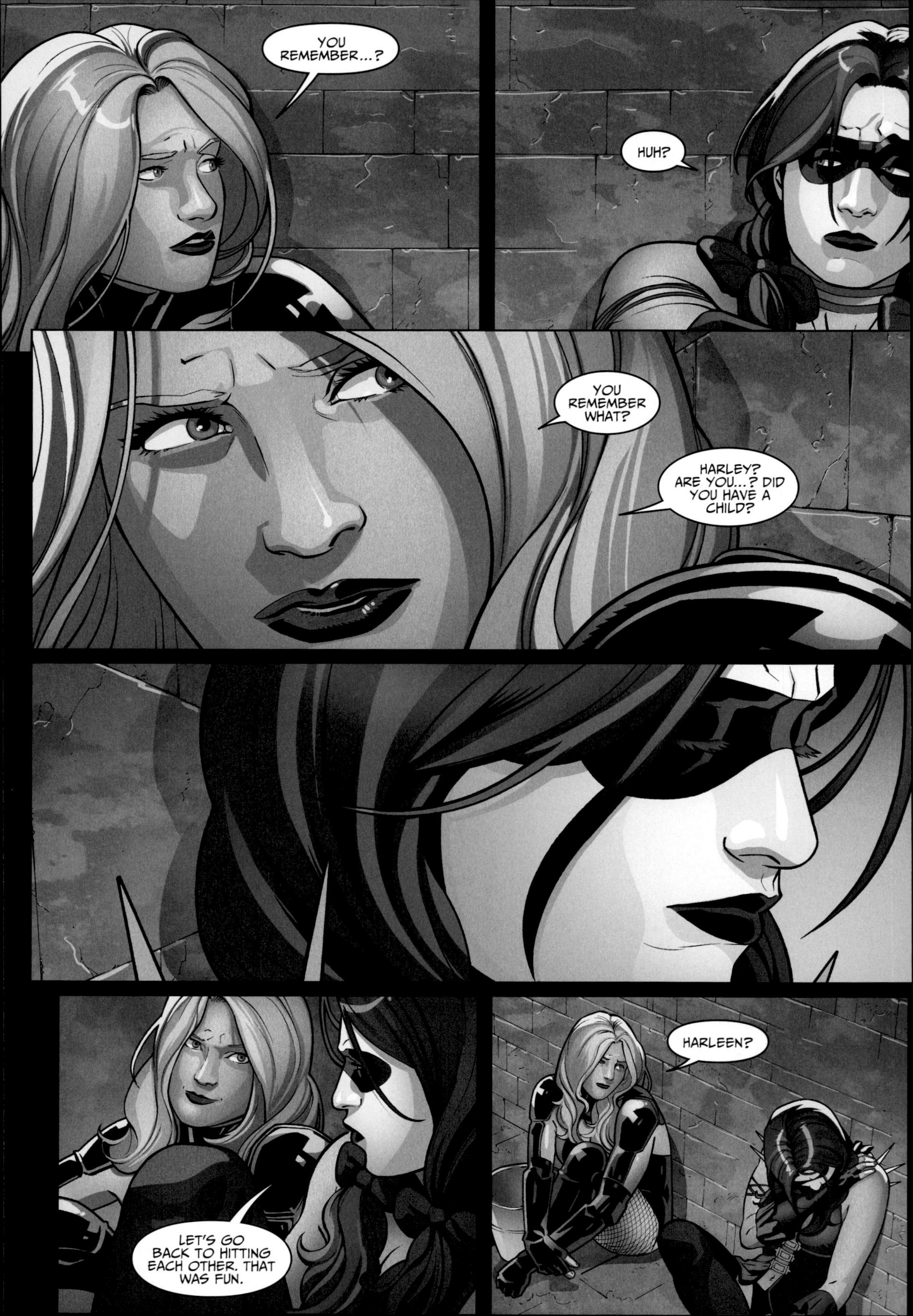
YOU REMEMBER...?
HUH?
YOU REMEMBER WHAT?
HARLEY? ARE YOU...? DID YOU HAVE A CHILD?
LET'S GO BACK TO HITTING EACH OTHER. THAT WAS FUN.
HARLEEN?

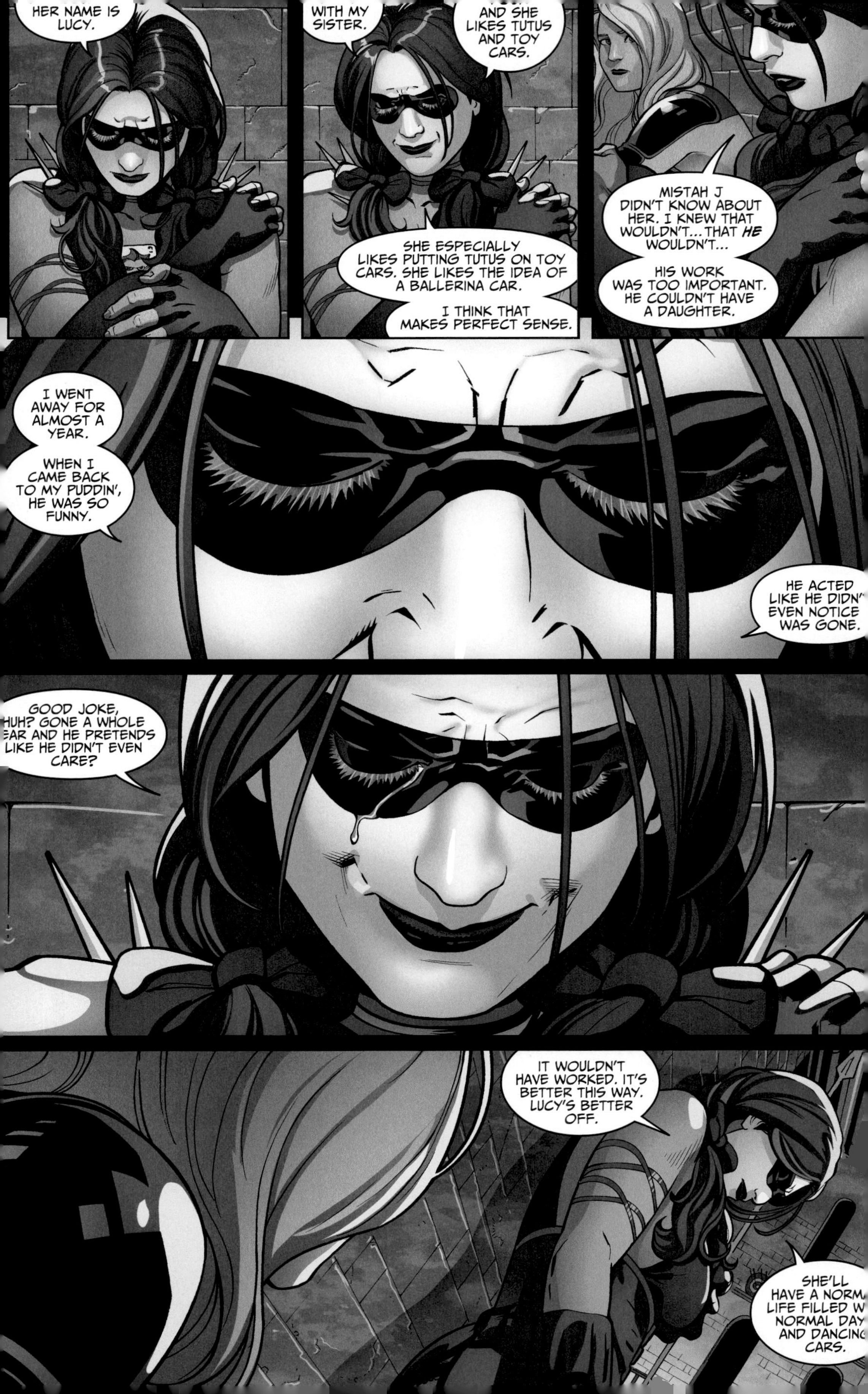
HER NAME IS LUCY.
WITH MY SISTER.
AND SHE LIKES TUTUS AND TOY CARS.
SHE ESPECIALLY LIKES PUTTING TUTUS ON TOY CARS. SHE LIKES THE IDEA OF A BALLERINA CAR.
I THINK THAT MAKES PERFECT SENSE.
MISTAH J DIDN'T KNOW ABOUT HER. I KNEW THAT WOULDN'T... THAT *HE* WOULDN'T...
HIS WORK WAS TOO IMPORTANT. HE COULDN'T HAVE A DAUGHTER.
I WENT AWAY FOR ALMOST A YEAR.
WHEN I CAME BACK TO MY PUDDIN', HE WAS SO FUNNY.
HE ACTED LIKE HE DIDN' EVEN NOTICE WAS GONE.
GOOD JOKE, HUH? GONE A WHOLE EAR AND HE PRETENDS LIKE HE DIDN'T EVEN CARE?
IT WOULDN'T HAVE WORKED. IT'S BETTER THIS WAY. LUCY'S BETTER OFF.
SHE'LL HAVE A NORM LIFE FILLED W NORMAL DAY AND DANCIN CARS.

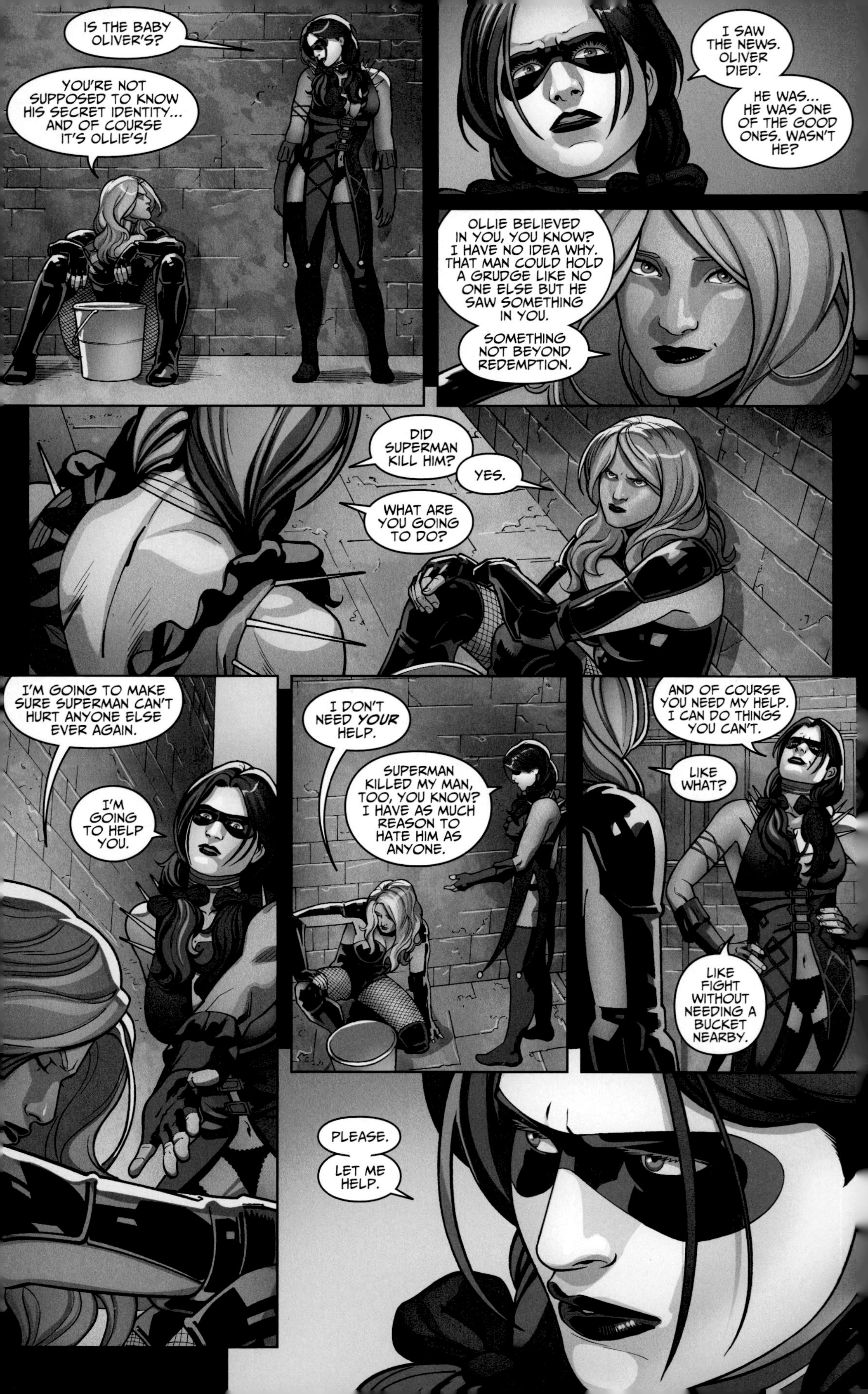
IS THE BABY OLIVER'S?
YOU'RE NOT SUPPOSED TO KNOW HIS SECRET IDENTITY... AND OF COURSE IT'S OLLIE'S!
I SAW THE NEWS. OLIVER DIED.
HE WAS... HE WAS ONE OF THE GOOD ONES. WASN'T HE?
OLLIE BELIEVED IN YOU, YOU KNOW? I HAVE NO IDEA WHY. THAT MAN COULD HOLD A GRUDGE LIKE NO ONE ELSE BUT HE SAW SOMETHING IN YOU.
SOMETHING NOT BEYOND REDEMPTION.
DID SUPERMAN KILL HIM?
YES.
WHAT ARE YOU GOING TO DO?
I'M GOING TO MAKE SURE SUPERMAN CAN'T HURT ANYONE ELSE EVER AGAIN.
I'M GOING TO HELP YOU.
I DON'T NEED *YOUR* HELP.
SUPERMAN KILLED MY MAN, TOO, YOU KNOW? I HAVE AS MUCH REASON TO HATE HIM AS ANYONE.
AND OF COURSE YOU NEED MY HELP. I CAN DO THINGS YOU CAN'T.
LIKE WHAT?
LIKE FIGHT WITHOUT NEEDING A BUCKET NEARBY.
PLEASE.
LET ME HELP.

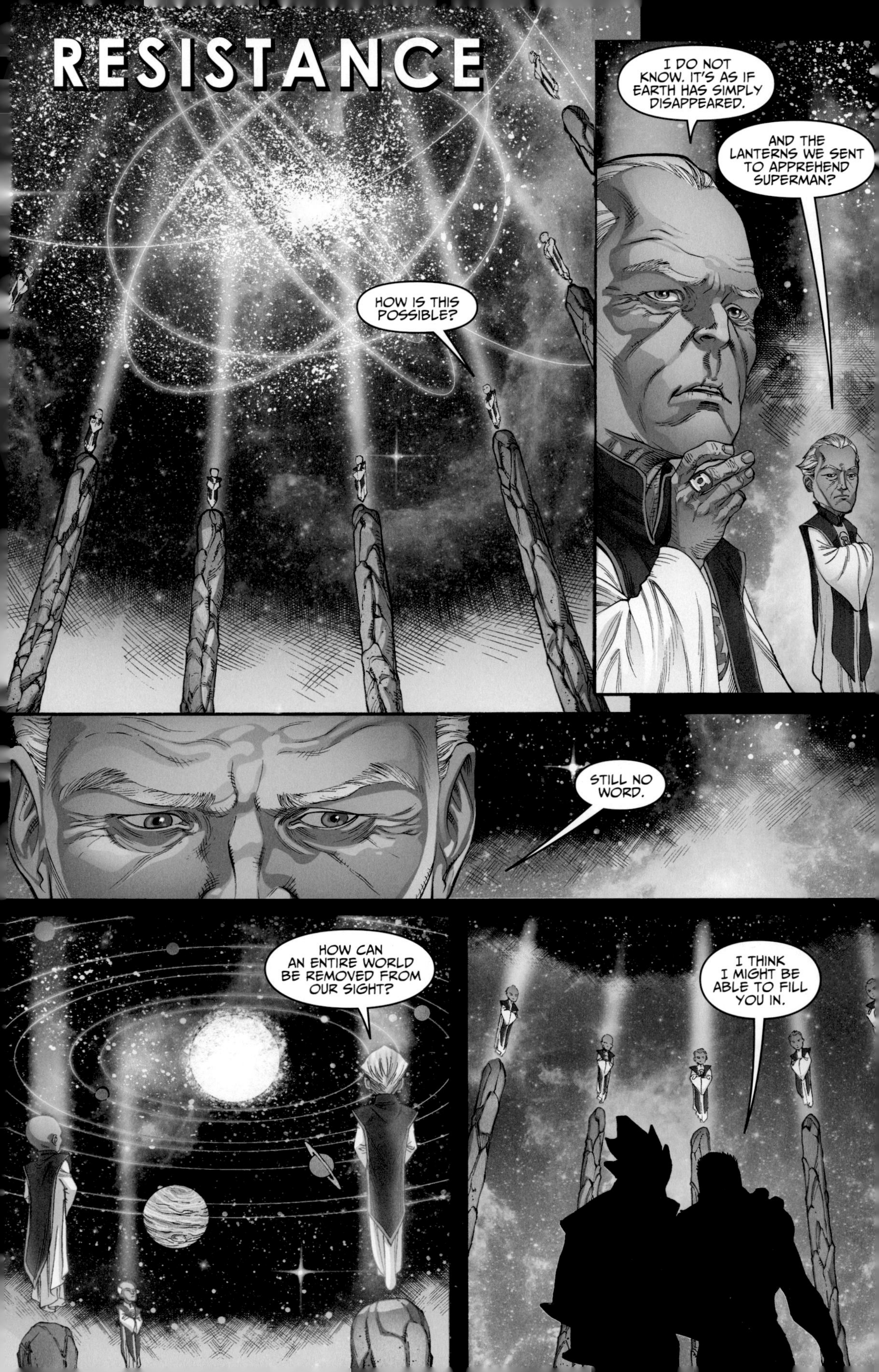
RESISTANCE
HOW IS THIS POSSIBLE?
I DO NOT KNOW. IT'S AS IF EARTH HAS SIMPLY DISAPPEARED.
AND THE LANTERNS WE SENT TO APPREHEND SUPERMAN?
STILL NO WORD.
HOW CAN AN ENTIRE WORLD BE REMOVED FROM OUR SIGHT?
I THINK I MIGHT BE ABLE TO FILL YOU IN.

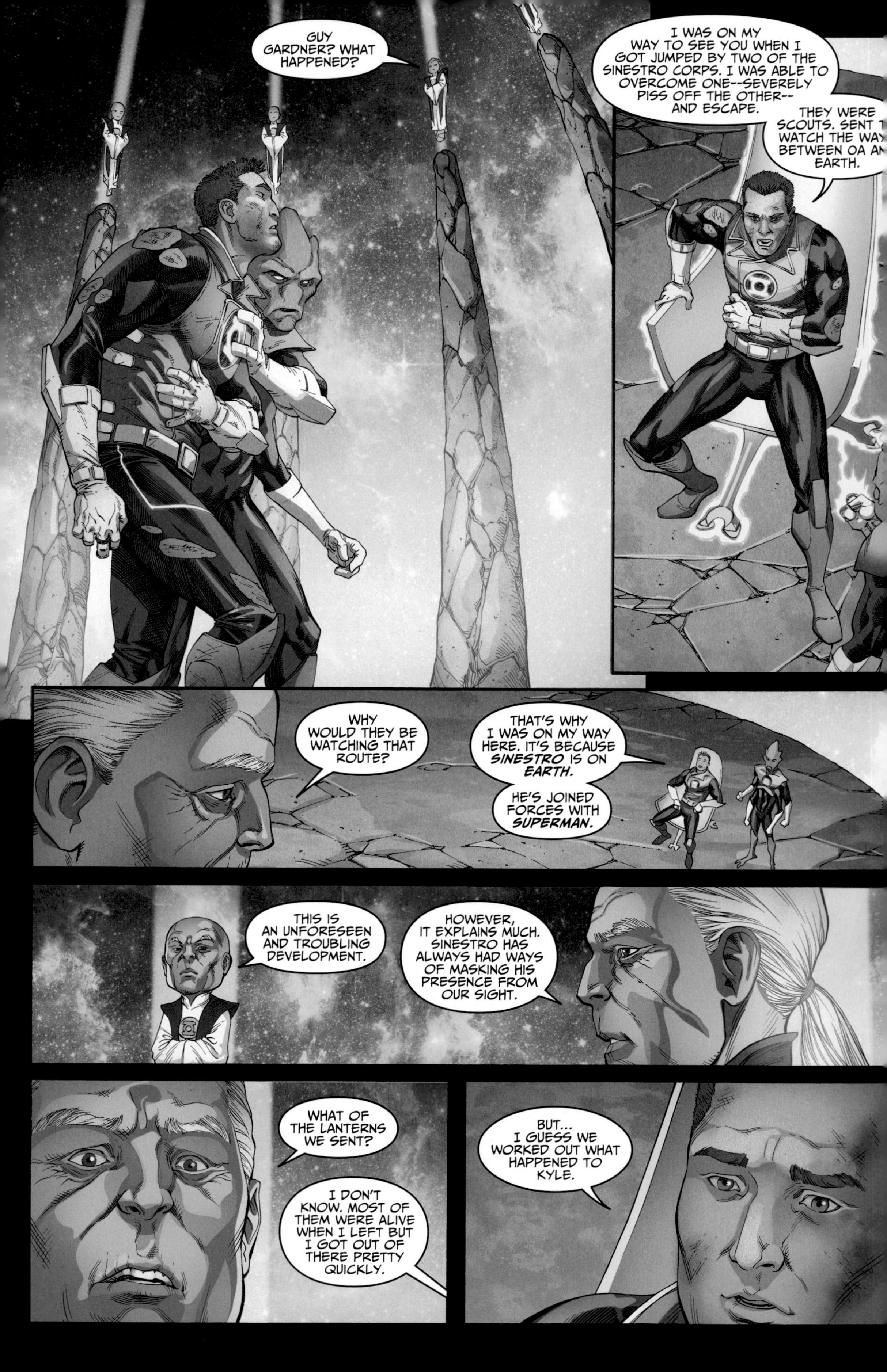
GUY GARDNER? WHAT HAPPENED?
I WAS ON MY WAY TO SEE YOU WHEN I GOT JUMPED BY TWO OF THE SINESTRO CORPS. I WAS ABLE TO OVERCOME ONE--SEVERELY PISS OFF THE OTHER--AND ESCAPE.
THEY WERE SCOUTS. SENT T WATCH THE WAY BETWEEN OA AN EARTH.
WHY WOULD THEY BE WATCHING THAT ROUTE?
THAT'S WHY I WAS ON MY WAY HERE. IT'S BECAUSE *SINESTRO* IS ON *EARTH.*
HE'S JOINED FORCES WITH *SUPERMAN.*
THIS IS AN UNFORESEEN AND TROUBLING DEVELOPMENT.
HOWEVER, IT EXPLAINS MUCH. SINESTRO HAS ALWAYS HAD WAYS OF MASKING HIS PRESENCE FROM OUR SIGHT.
WHAT OF THE LANTERNS WE SENT?
I DON'T KNOW. MOST OF THEM WERE ALIVE WHEN I LEFT BUT I GOT OUT OF THERE PRETTY QUICKLY.
BUT... I GUESS WE WORKED OUT WHAT HAPPENED TO KYLE.

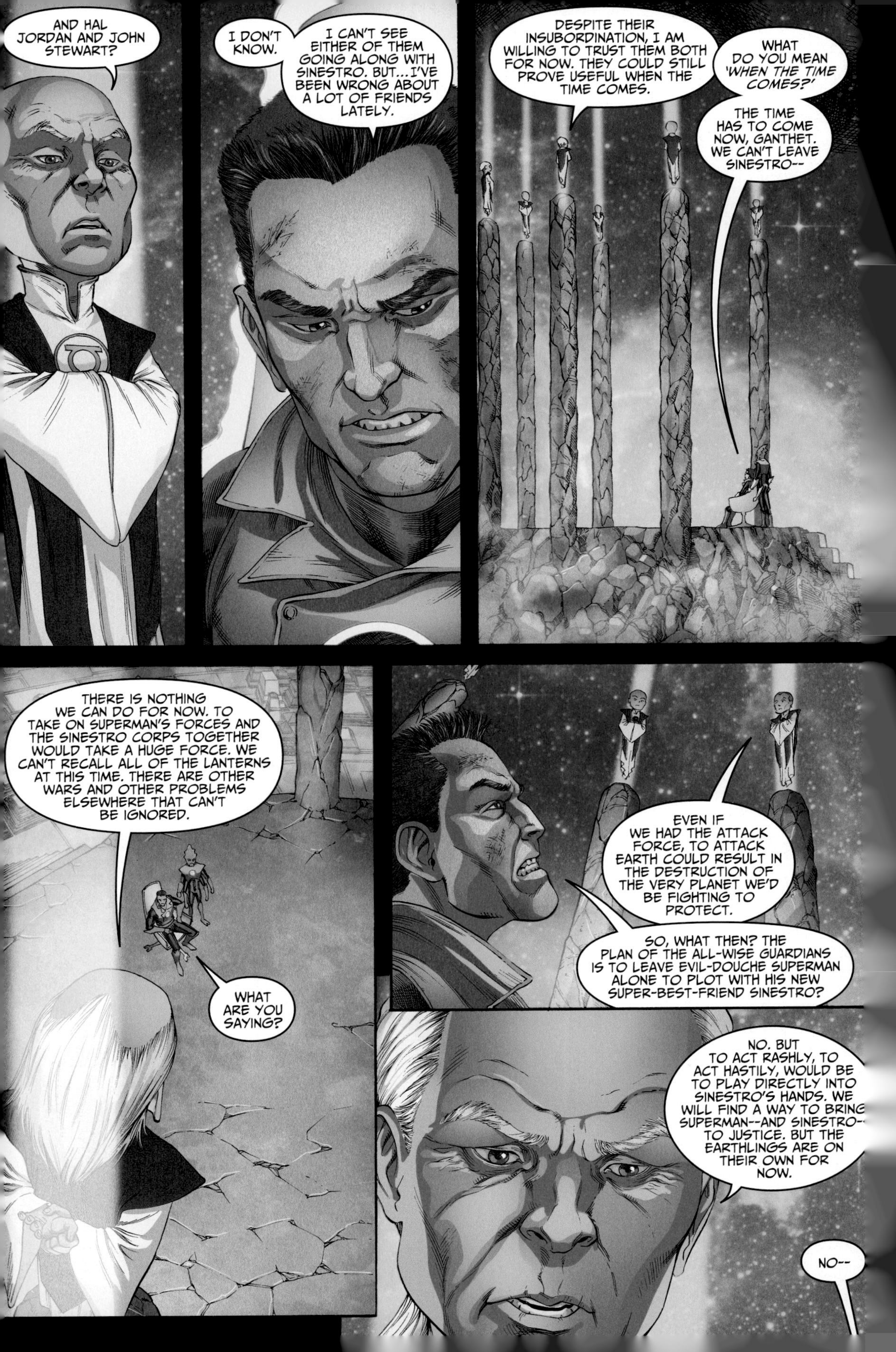
AND HAL JORDAN AND JOHN STEWART?
I DON'T KNOW.
I CAN'T SEE EITHER OF THEM GOING ALONG WITH SINESTRO. BUT...I'VE BEEN WRONG ABOUT A LOT OF FRIENDS LATELY.
DESPITE THEIR INSUBORDINATION, I AM WILLING TO TRUST THEM BOTH FOR NOW. THEY COULD STILL PROVE USEFUL WHEN THE TIME COMES.
WHAT DO YOU MEAN *'WHEN THE TIME COMES?'*
THE TIME HAS TO COME NOW, GANTHET. WE CAN'T LEAVE SINESTRO--
THERE IS NOTHING WE CAN DO FOR NOW. TO TAKE ON SUPERMAN'S FORCES AND THE SINESTRO CORPS TOGETHER WOULD TAKE A HUGE FORCE. WE CAN'T RECALL ALL OF THE LANTERNS AT THIS TIME. THERE ARE OTHER WARS AND OTHER PROBLEMS ELSEWHERE THAT CAN'T BE IGNORED.
WHAT ARE YOU SAYING?
EVEN IF WE HAD THE ATTACK FORCE, TO ATTACK EARTH COULD RESULT IN THE DESTRUCTION OF THE VERY PLANET WE'D BE FIGHTING TO PROTECT.
SO, WHAT THEN? THE PLAN OF THE ALL-WISE GUARDIANS IS TO LEAVE EVIL-DOUCHE SUPERMAN ALONE TO PLOT WITH HIS NEW SUPER-BEST-FRIEND SINESTRO?
NO. BUT TO ACT RASHLY, TO ACT HASTILY, WOULD BE TO PLAY DIRECTLY INTO SINESTRO'S HANDS. WE WILL FIND A WAY TO BRING SUPERMAN--AND SINESTRO--TO JUSTICE. BUT THE EARTHLINGS ARE ON THEIR OWN FOR NOW.
NO--

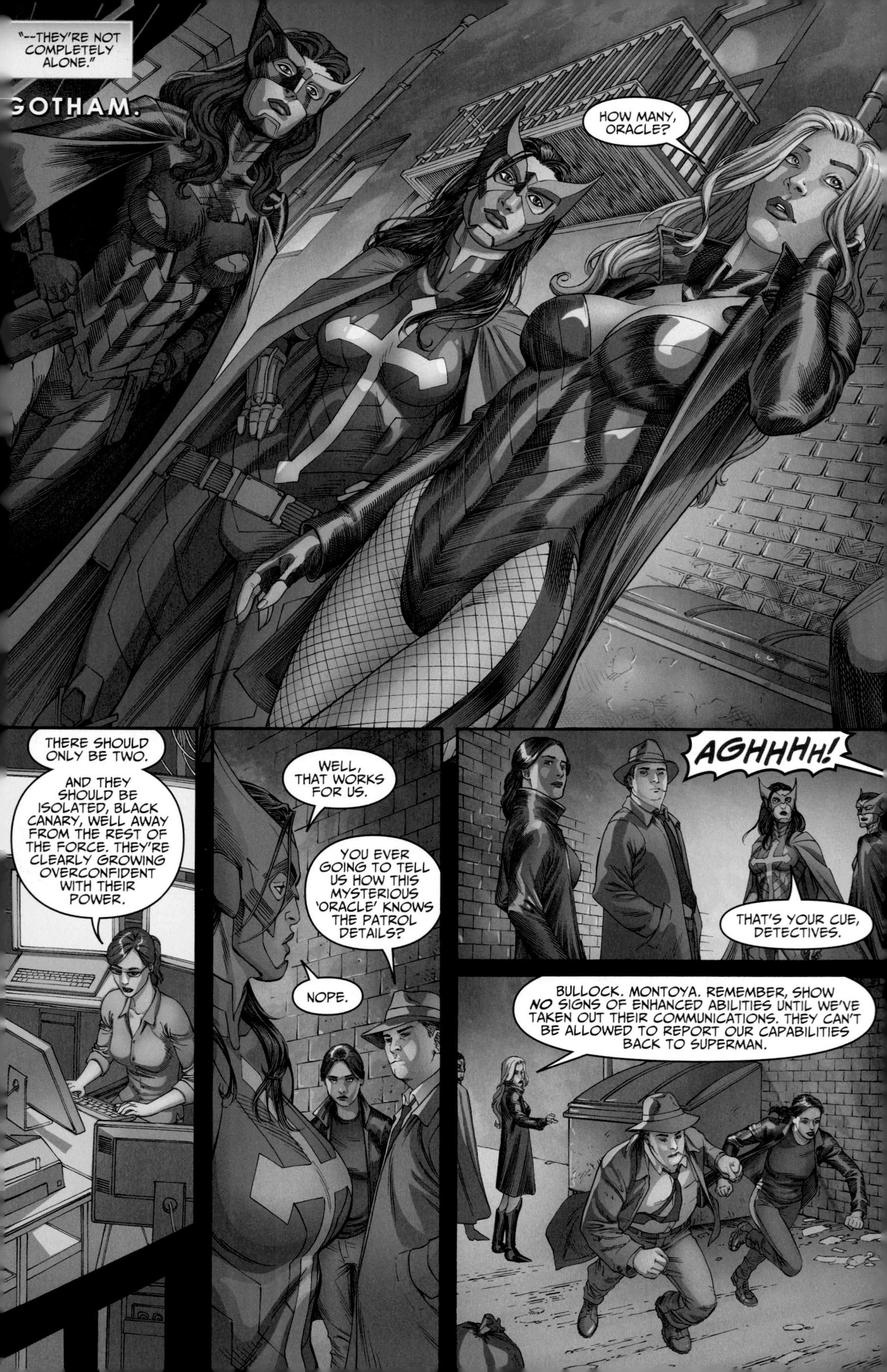
"--THEY'RE NOT COMPLETELY ALONE."
GOTHAM.
HOW MANY, ORACLE?
THERE SHOULD ONLY BE TWO.
AND THEY SHOULD BE ISOLATED, BLACK CANARY, WELL AWAY FROM THE REST OF THE FORCE. THEY'RE CLEARLY GROWING OVERCONFIDENT WITH THEIR POWER.
WELL, THAT WORKS FOR US.
YOU EVER GOING TO TELL US HOW THIS MYSTERIOUS 'ORACLE' KNOWS THE PATROL DETAILS?
NOPE.
AGHHHH!
THAT'S YOUR CUE, DETECTIVES.
BULLOCK. MONTOYA. REMEMBER, SHOW NO SIGNS OF ENHANCED ABILITIES UNTIL WE'VE TAKEN OUT THEIR COMMUNICATIONS. THEY CAN'T BE ALLOWED TO REPORT OUR CAPABILITIES BACK TO SUPERMAN.

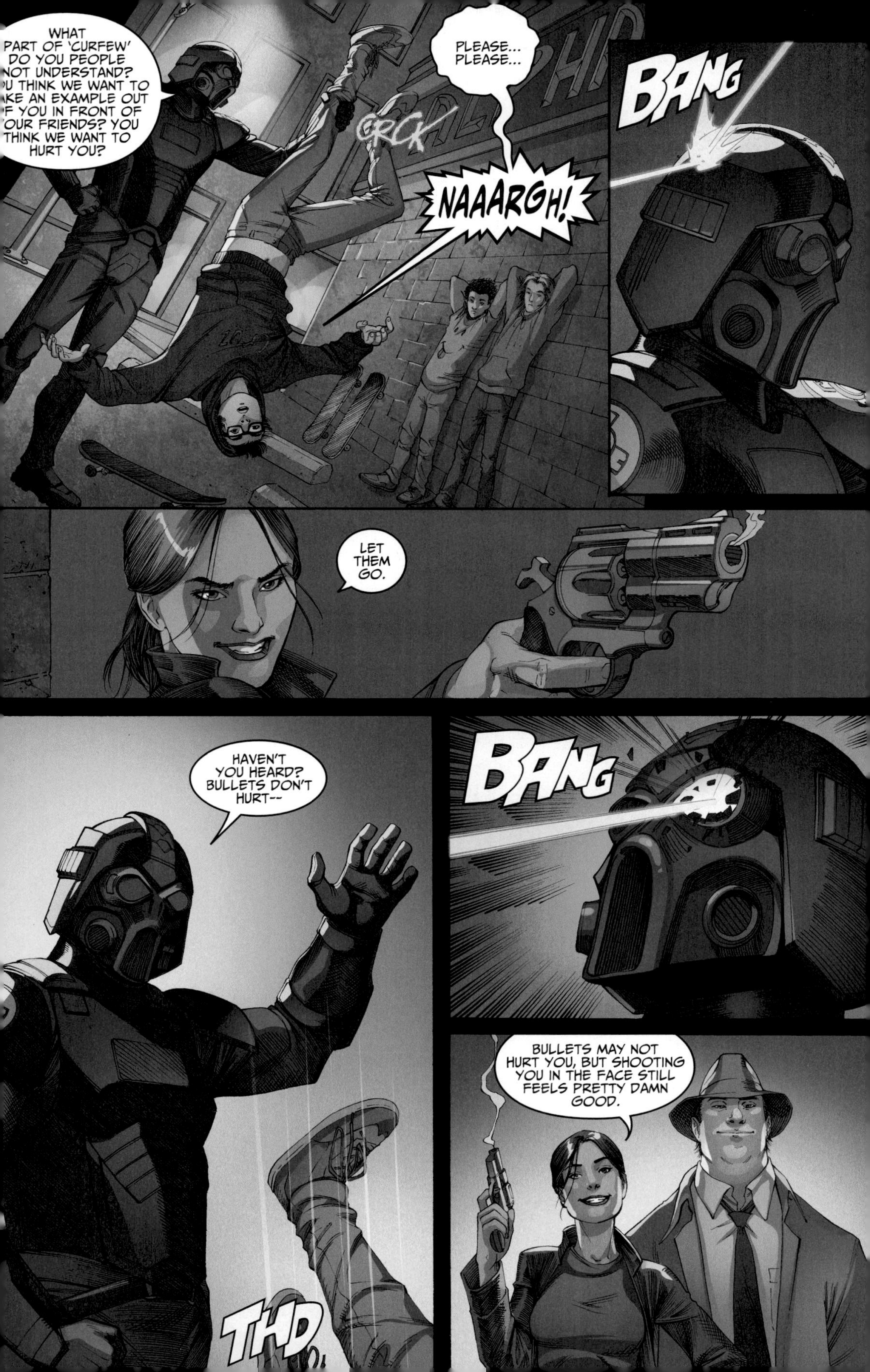
WHAT PART OF 'CURFEW' DO YOU PEOPLE NOT UNDERSTAND? U THINK WE WANT TO AKE AN EXAMPLE OUT F YOU IN FRONT OF OUR FRIENDS? YOU THINK WE WANT TO HURT YOU?
CRCK
PLEASE... PLEASE...
NAAARGH!
BANG
LET THEM GO.
HAVEN'T YOU HEARD? BULLETS DON'T HURT--
THD
BANG
BULLETS MAY NOT HURT YOU, BUT SHOOTING YOU IN THE FACE STILL FEELS PRETTY DAMN GOOD.

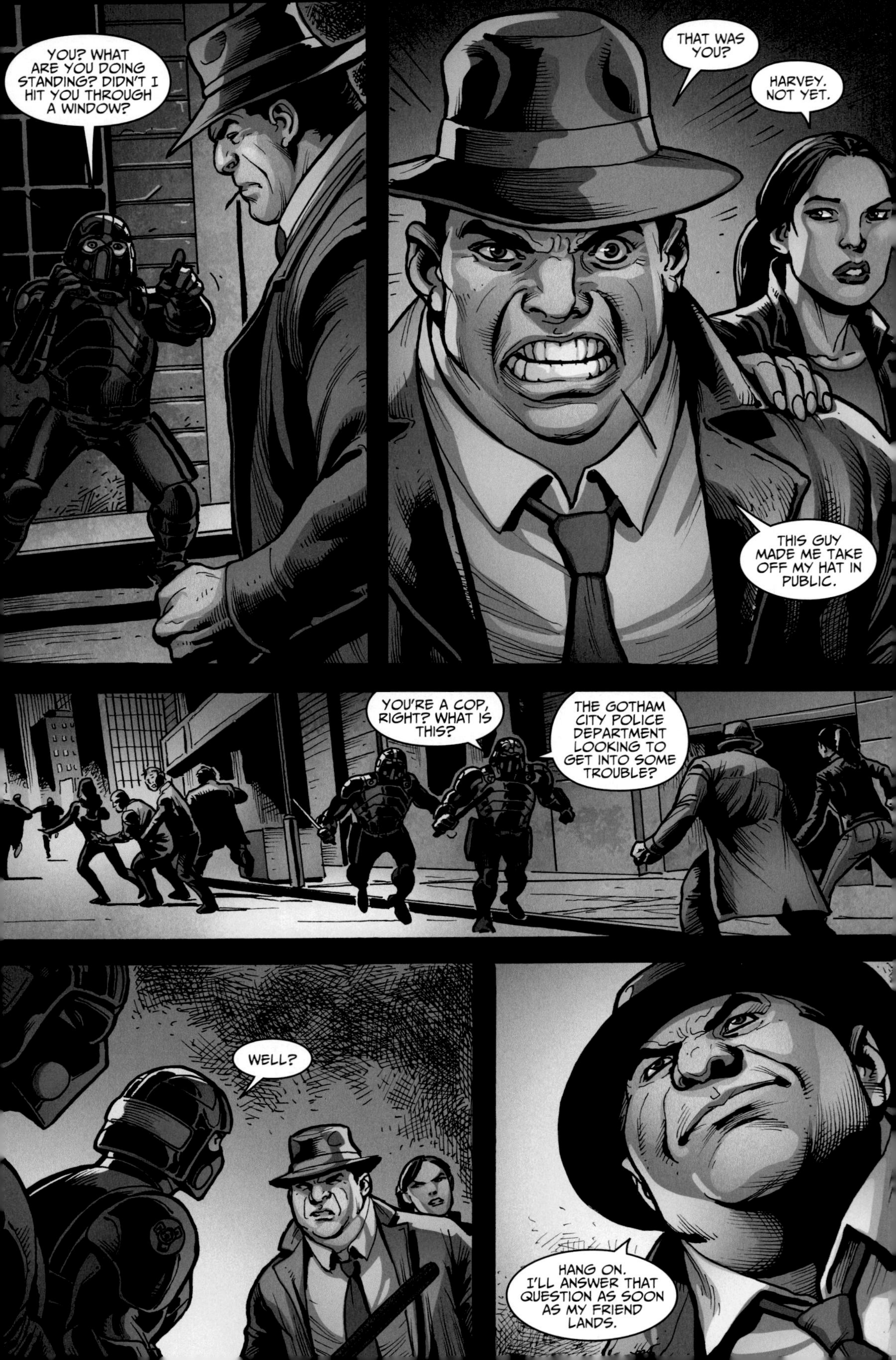
YOU? WHAT ARE YOU DOING STANDING? DIDN'T I HIT YOU THROUGH A WINDOW?
THAT WAS YOU?
HARVEY. NOT YET.
THIS GUY MADE ME TAKE OFF MY HAT IN PUBLIC.
YOU'RE A COP, RIGHT? WHAT IS THIS?
THE GOTHAM CITY POLICE DEPARTMENT LOOKING TO GET INTO SOME TROUBLE?
WELL?
HANG ON. I'LL ANSWER THAT QUESTION AS SOON AS MY FRIEND LANDS.

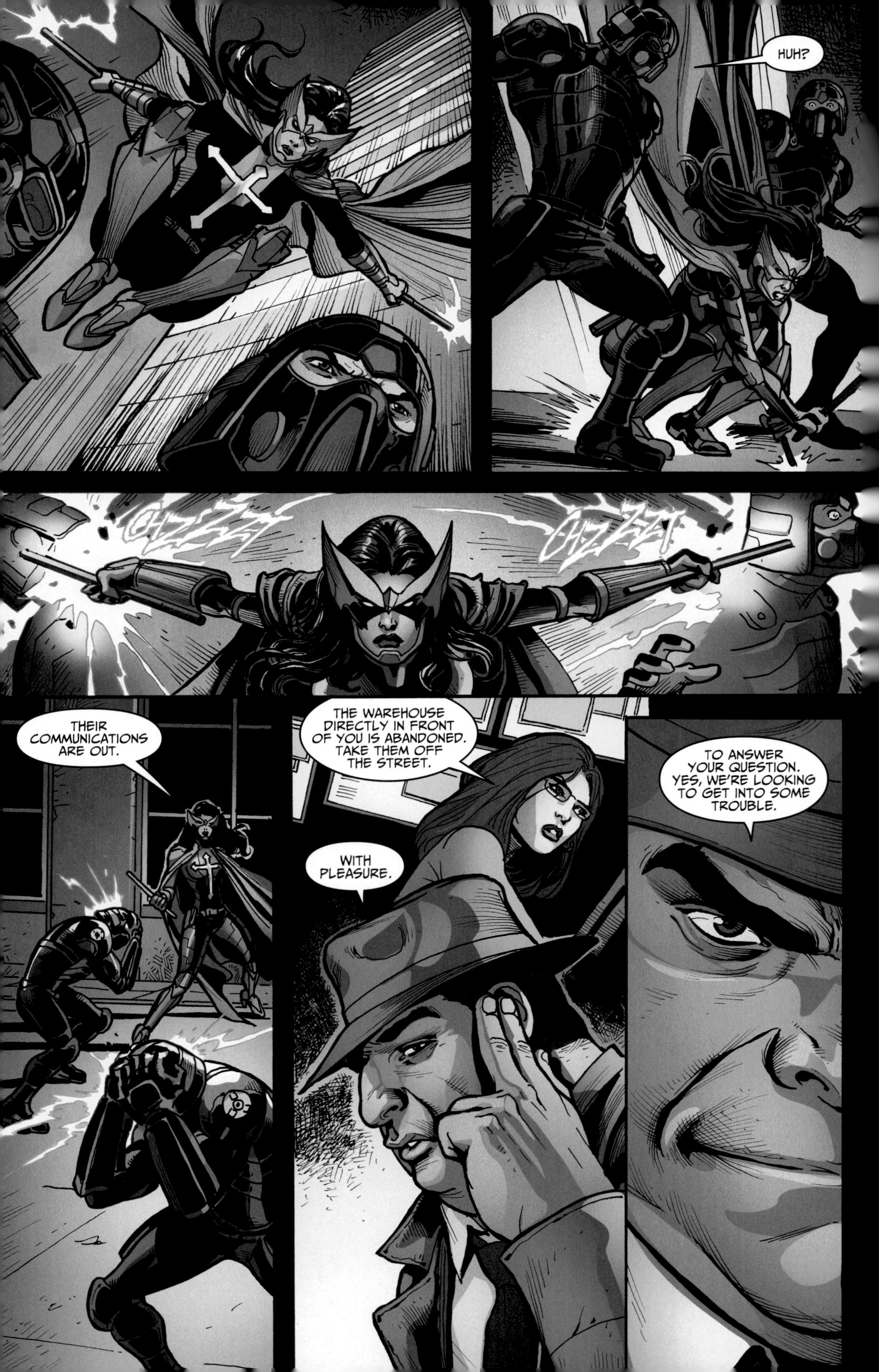
HUH?
CHZZZT
CHZZZT
THEIR COMMUNICATIONS ARE OUT.
THE WAREHOUSE DIRECTLY IN FRONT OF YOU IS ABANDONED. TAKE THEM OFF THE STREET.
WITH PLEASURE.
TO ANSWER YOUR QUESTION. YES, WE'RE LOOKING TO GET INTO SOME TROUBLE.

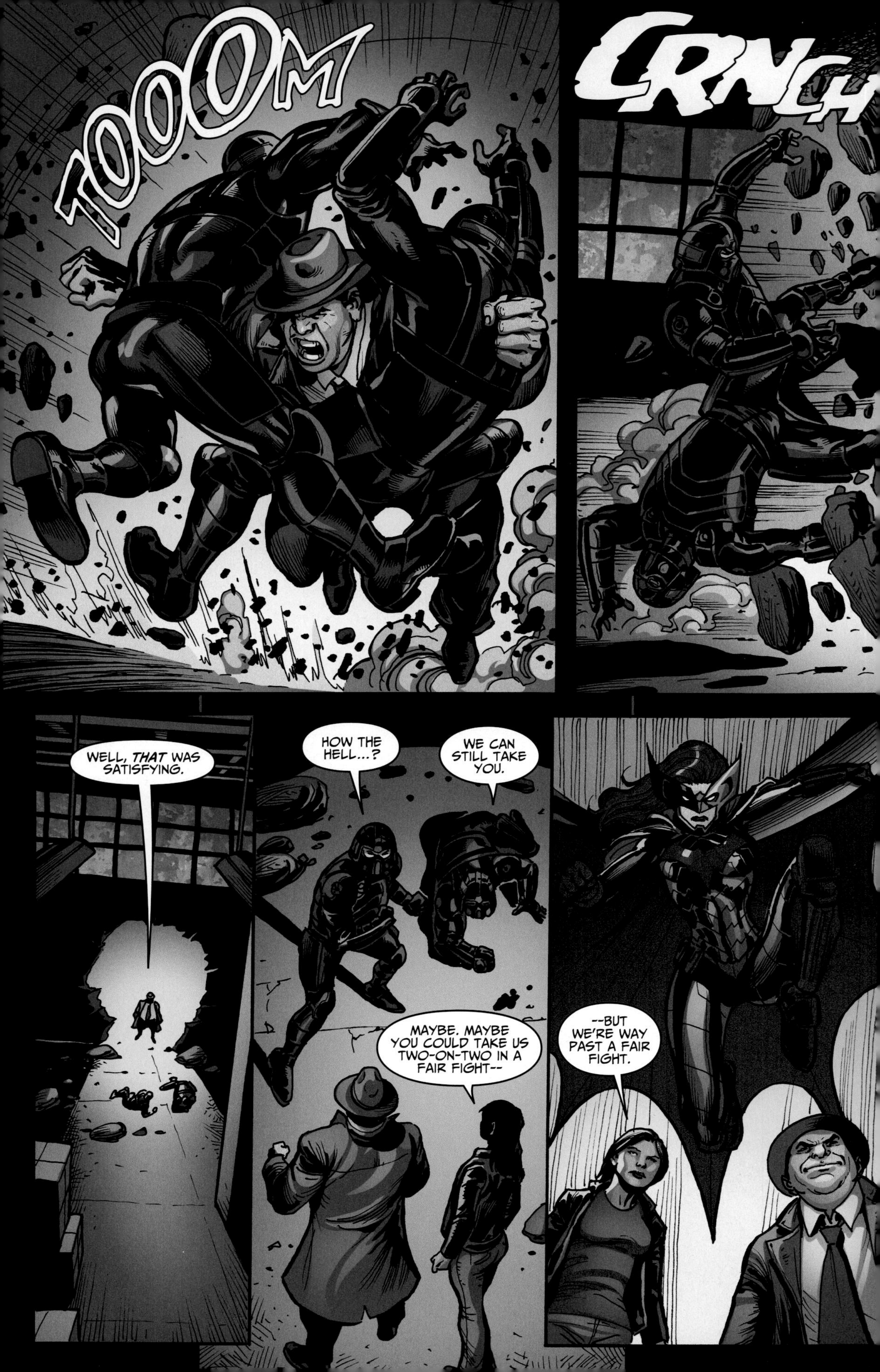
TOOOOM
CRNCH
WELL, *THAT* WAS SATISFYING.
HOW THE HELL...?
WE CAN STILL TAKE YOU.
MAYBE. MAYBE YOU COULD TAKE US TWO-ON-TWO IN A FAIR FIGHT--
--BUT WE'RE WAY PAST A FAIR FIGHT.

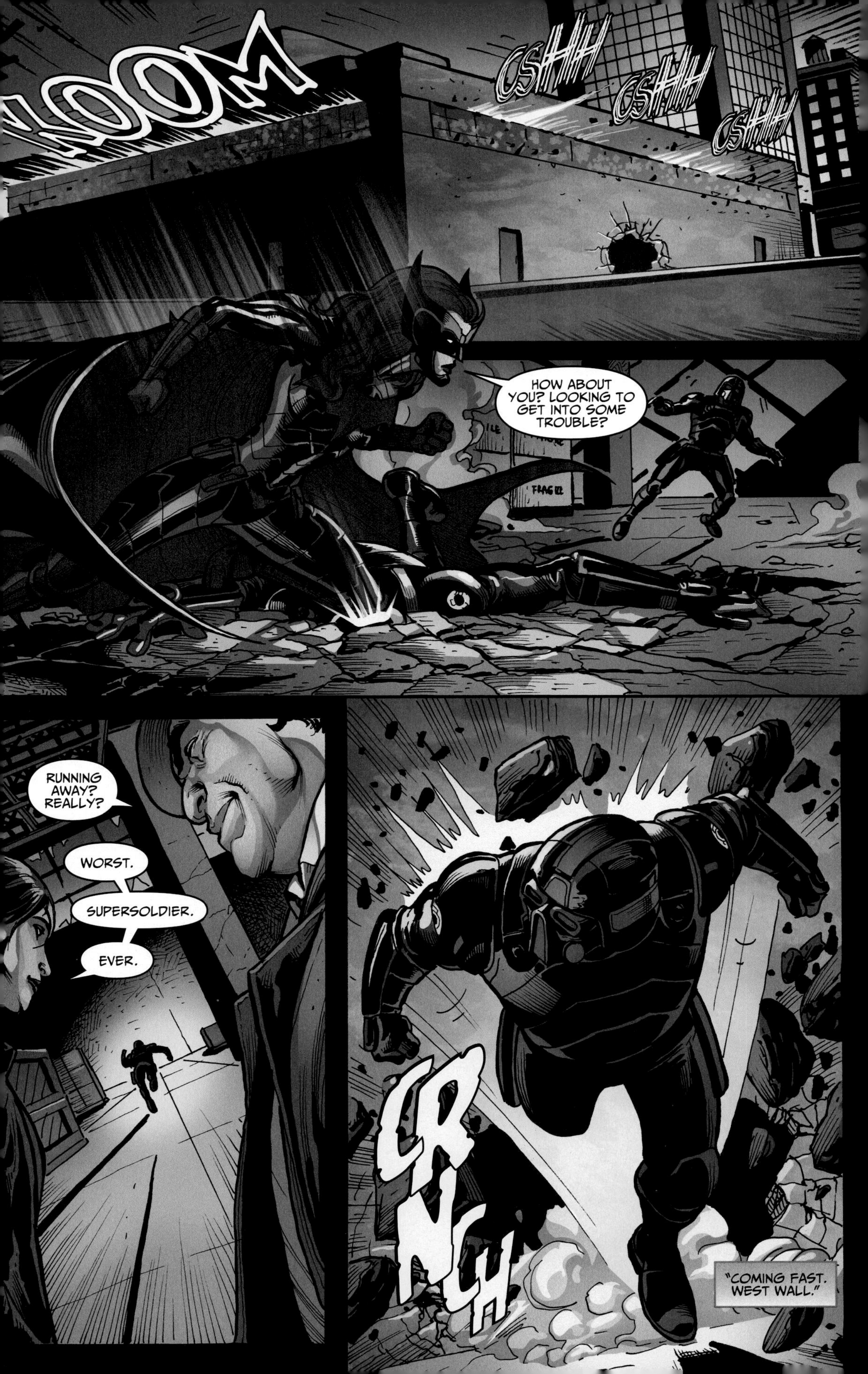
KOOM
CSHH CSHH CSHH
HOW ABOUT YOU? LOOKING TO GET INTO SOME TROUBLE?
RUNNING AWAY? REALLY?
WORST.
SUPERSOLDIER.
EVER.
CRNCH
"COMING FAST. WEST WALL."

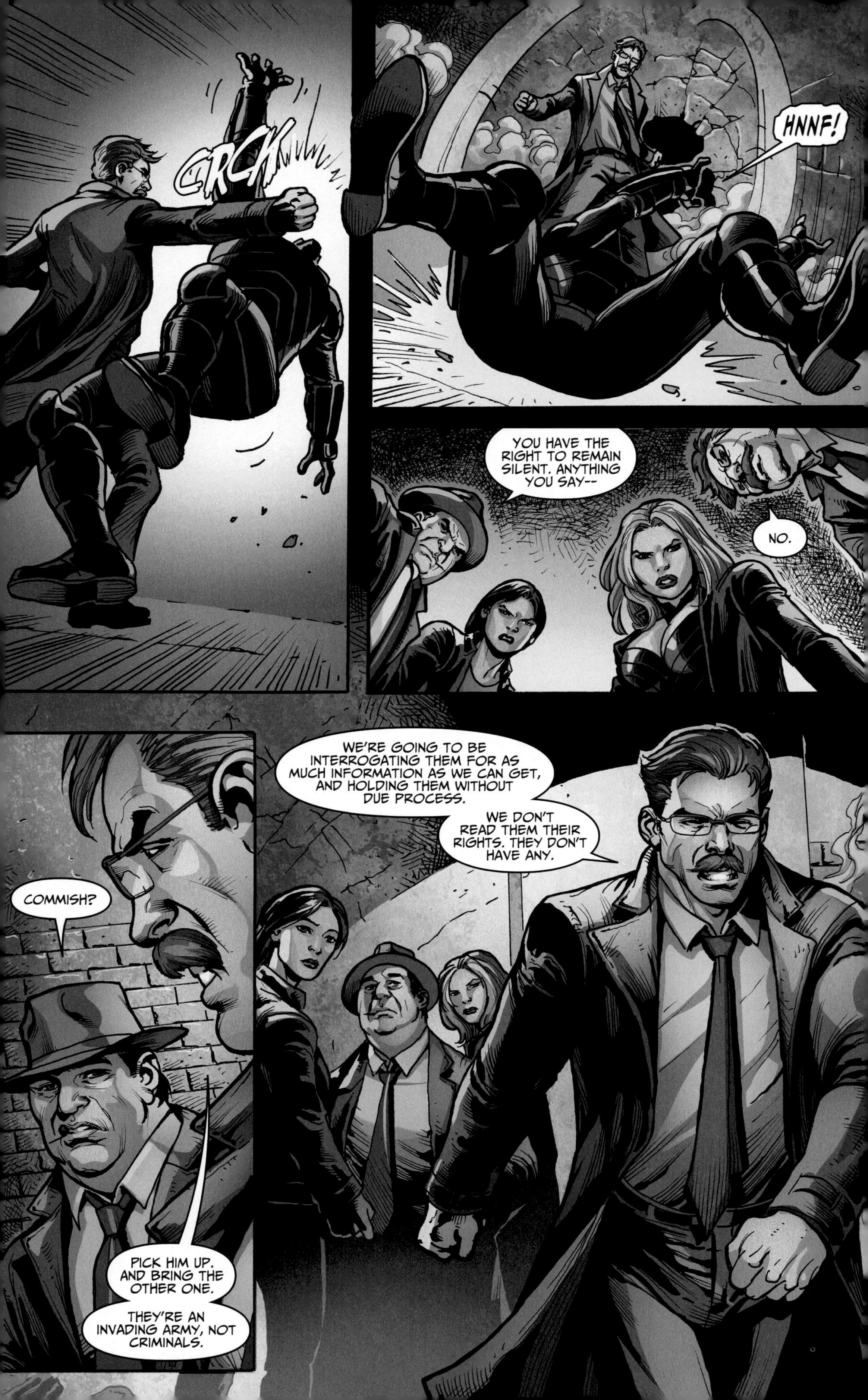
CRCK
HNNF!
YOU HAVE THE RIGHT TO REMAIN SILENT. ANYTHING YOU SAY--
NO.
COMMISH?
PICK HIM UP. AND BRING THE OTHER ONE.
THEY'RE AN INVADING ARMY, NOT CRIMINALS.
WE'RE GOING TO BE INTERROGATING THEM FOR AS MUCH INFORMATION AS WE CAN GET, AND HOLDING THEM WITHOUT DUE PROCESS.
WE DON'T READ THEM THEIR RIGHTS. THEY DON'T HAVE ANY.

Marguerite Bennett & Tom Taylor Writers
"Closing Time" Vicente Cifuentes Daniel HDR Mike S. Miller David Yardin Artists Rex Lokus Colorist
"The Ur-Forge - An Untold Injustice Tale" Jheremy Raapack Artist David Lopez & Santi Casas of Ikari Studio Colorists
Cover Art by Jheremy Raapack & Mark Roberts

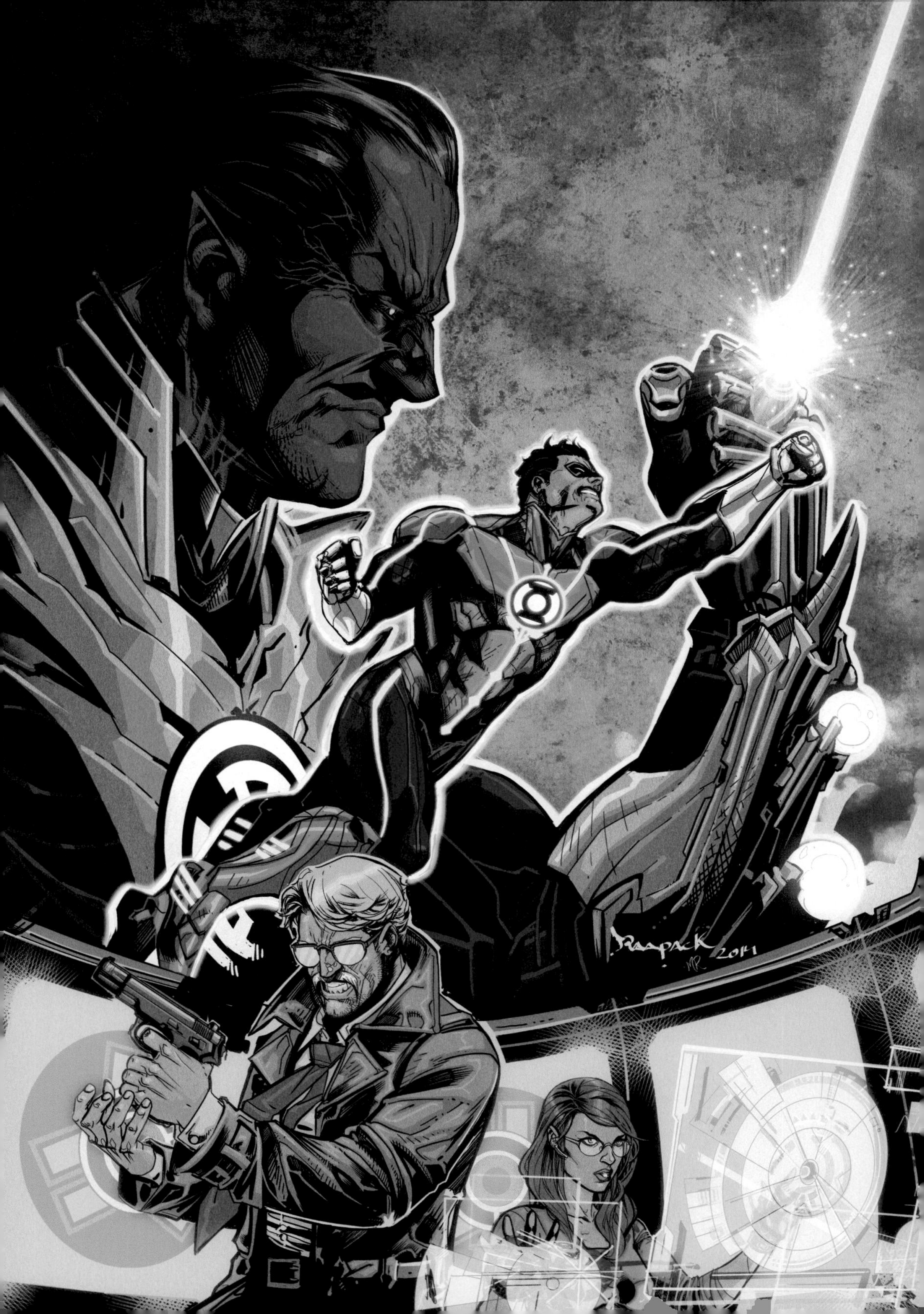
RAAPACK 2014
MR

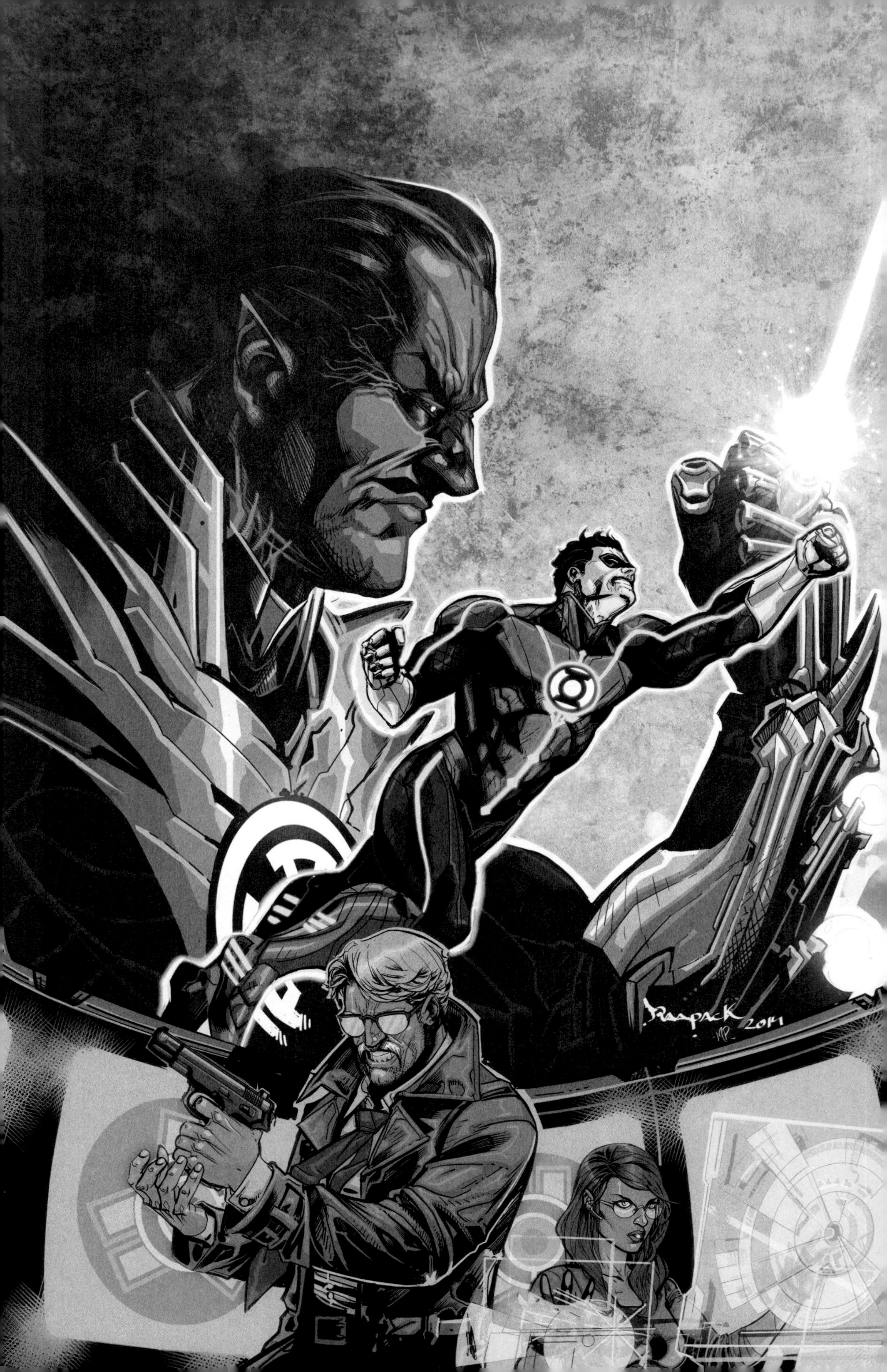
RAAPACK 2014
MP

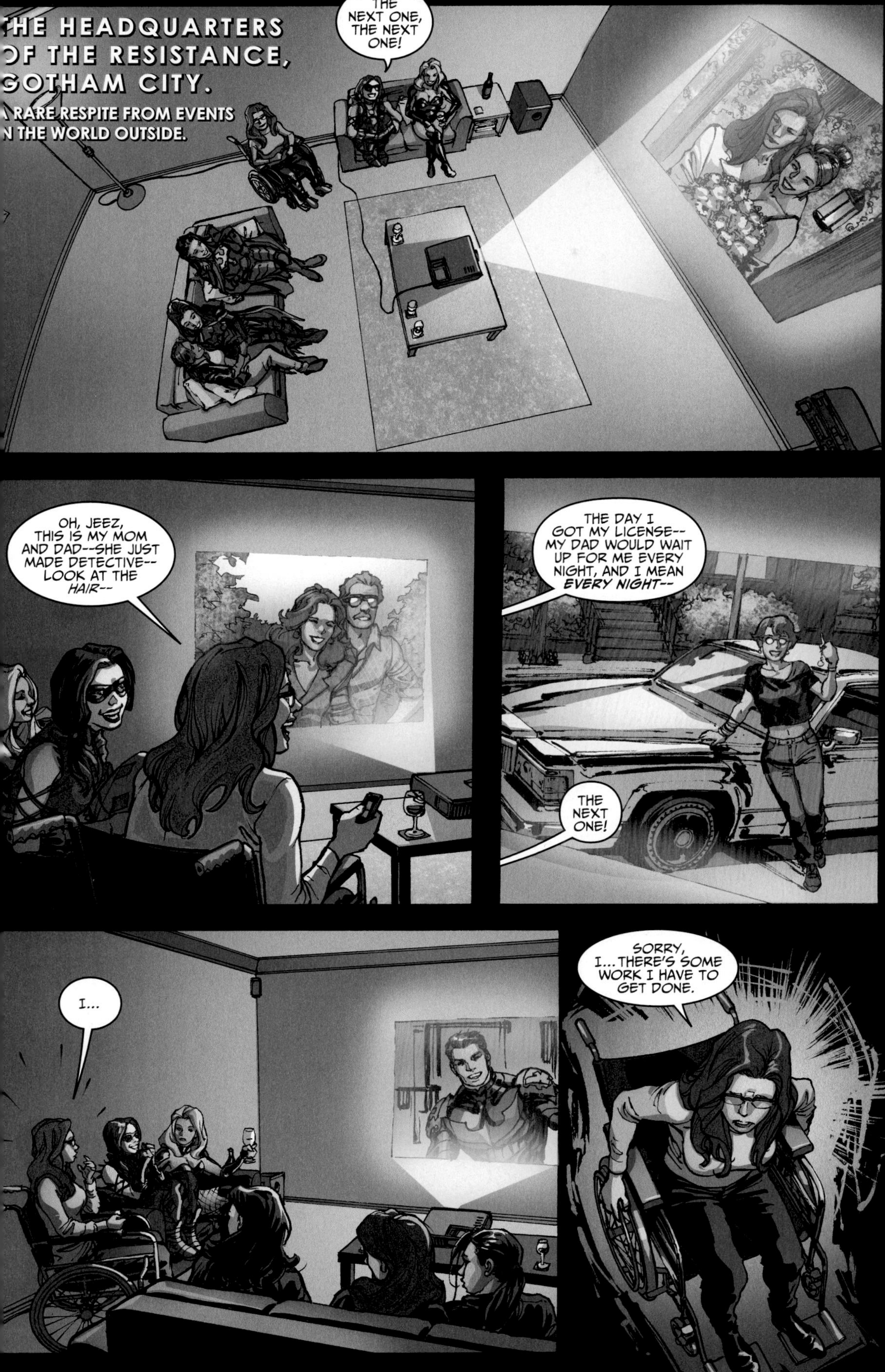
THE HEADQUARTERS OF THE RESISTANCE, GOTHAM CITY.
A RARE RESPITE FROM EVENTS IN THE WORLD OUTSIDE.
THE NEXT ONE, THE NEXT ONE!
OH, JEEZ, THIS IS MY MOM AND DAD--SHE JUST MADE DETECTIVE--LOOK AT THE HAIR--
THE DAY I GOT MY LICENSE--MY DAD WOULD WAIT UP FOR ME EVERY NIGHT, AND I MEAN EVERY NIGHT--
THE NEXT ONE!
I...
SORRY, I...THERE'S SOME WORK I HAVE TO GET DONE.

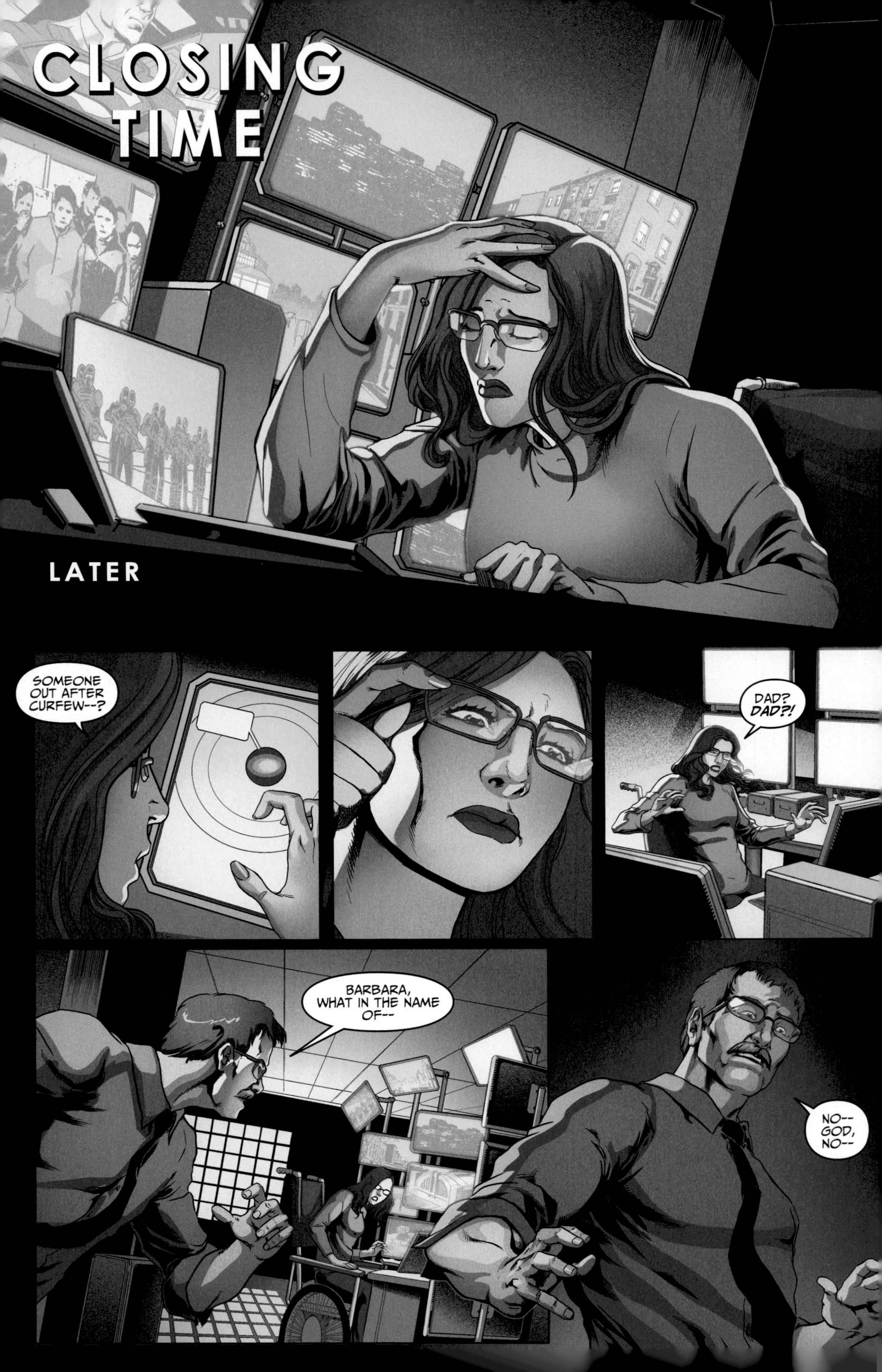
CLOSING TIME
LATER
SOMEONE OUT AFTER CURFEW--?
DAD? DAD?!
BARBARA, WHAT IN THE NAME OF--
NO-- GOD, NO--

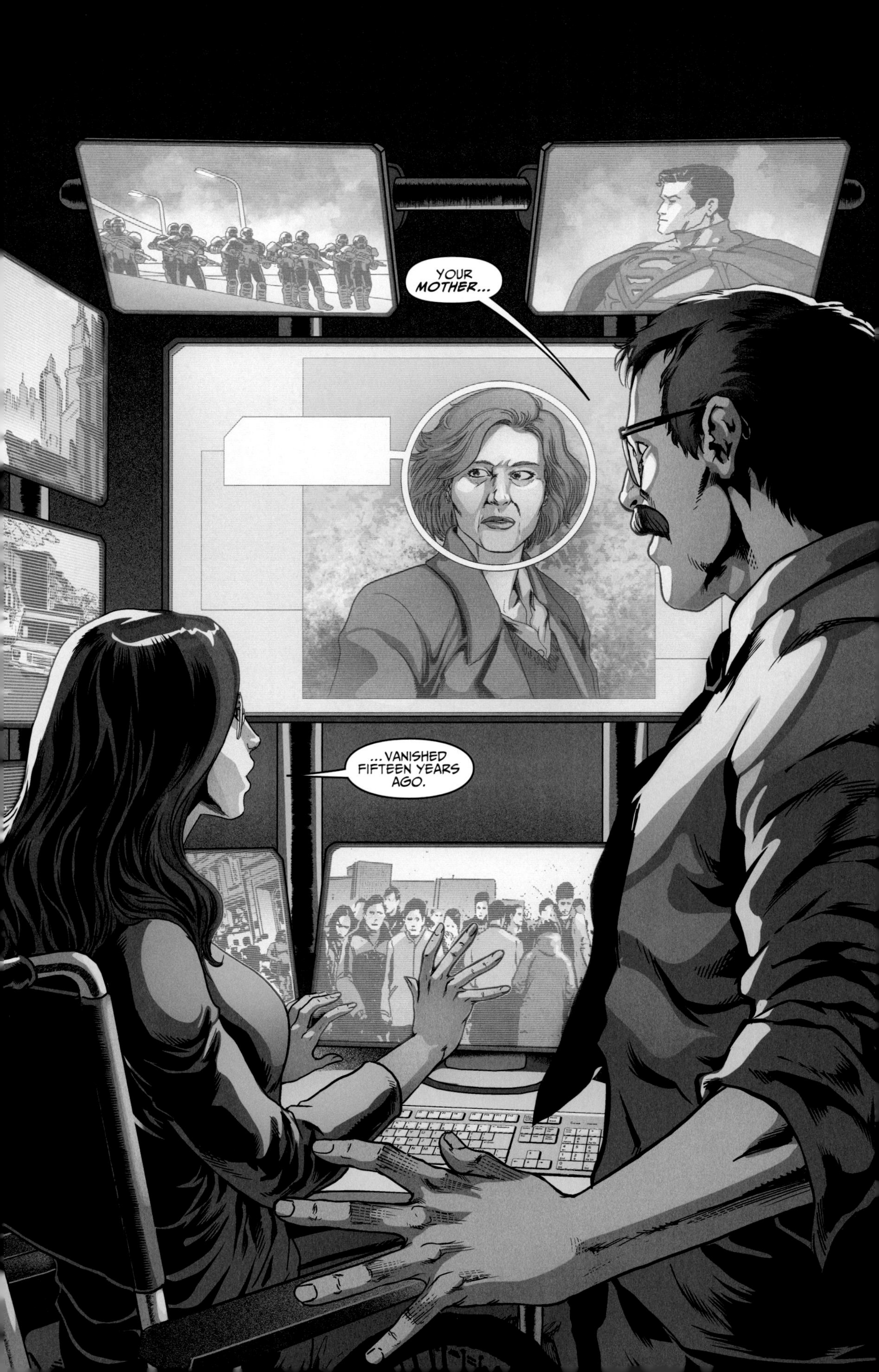
YOUR MOTHER...
...VANISHED FIFTEEN YEARS AGO.

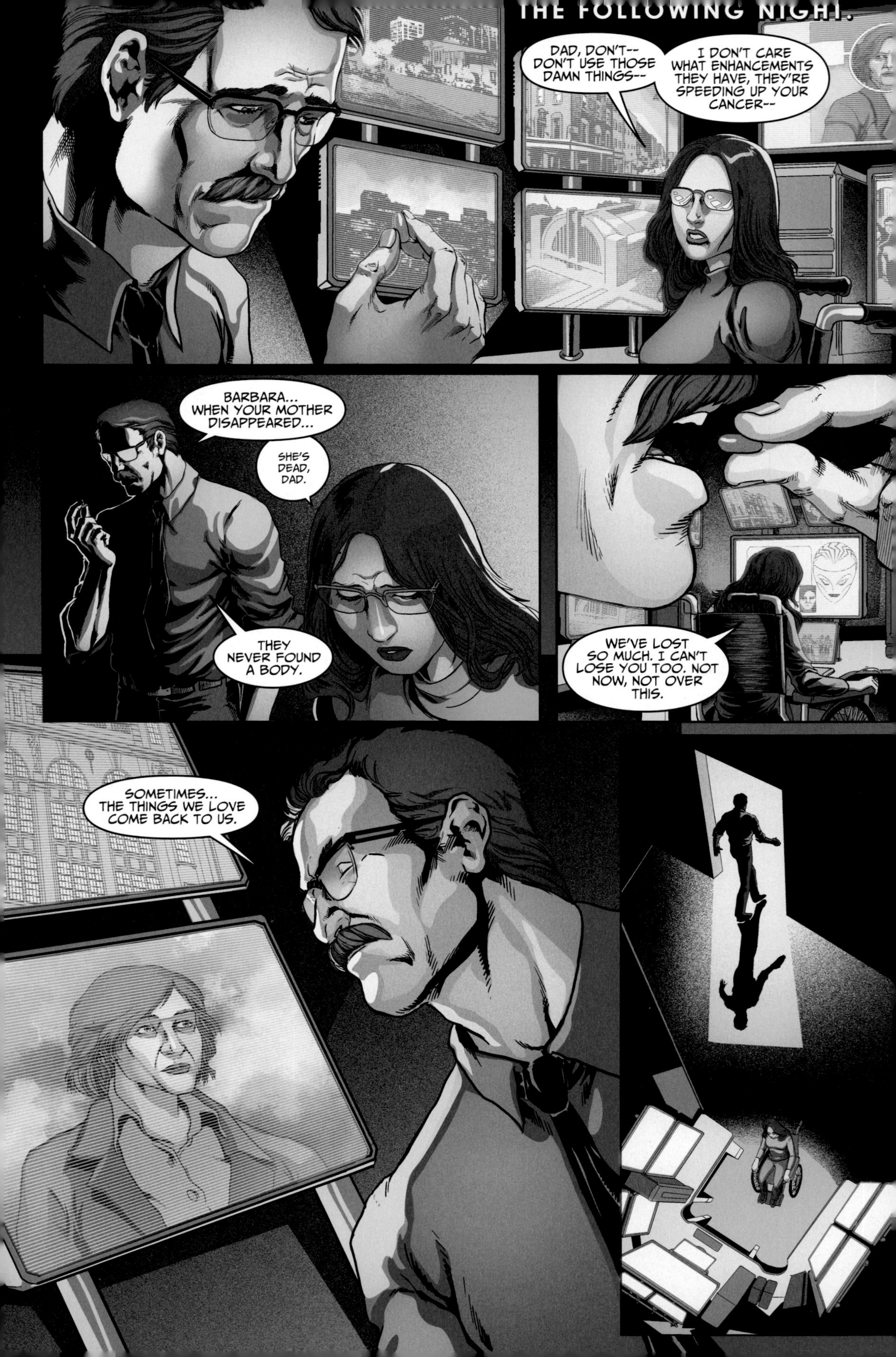
THE FOLLOWING NIGHT.
DAD, DON'T-- DON'T USE THOSE DAMN THINGS--
I DON'T CARE WHAT ENHANCEMENTS THEY HAVE, THEY'RE SPEEDING UP YOUR CANCER--
BARBARA... WHEN YOUR MOTHER DISAPPEARED...
SHE'S DEAD, DAD.
THEY NEVER FOUND A BODY.
WE'VE LOST SO MUCH. I CAN'T LOSE YOU TOO. NOT NOW, NOT OVER THIS.
SOMETIMES... THE THINGS WE LOVE COME BACK TO US.

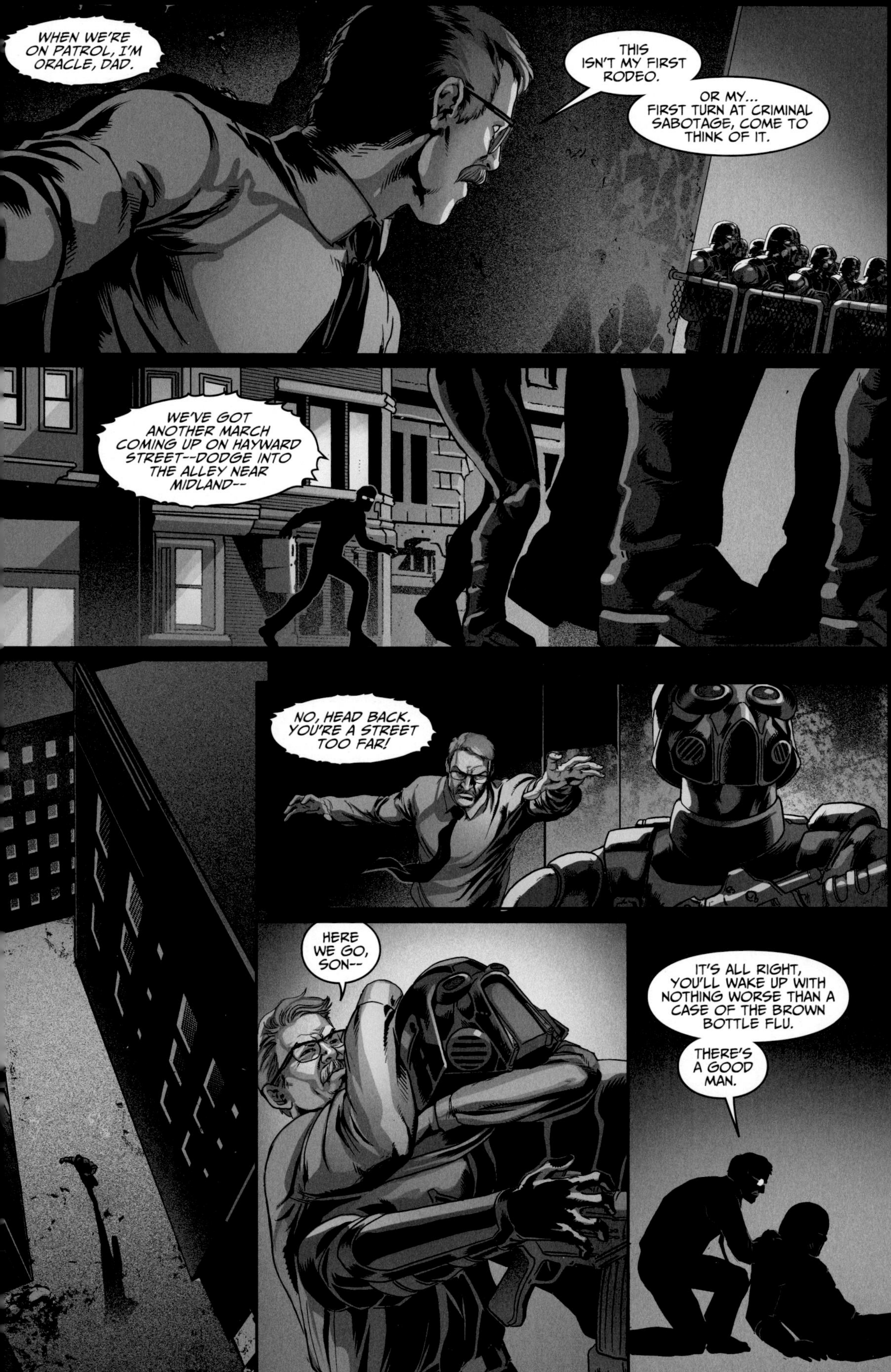

WHEN WE'RE ON PATROL, I'M ORACLE, DAD.
THIS ISN'T MY FIRST RODEO.
OR MY... FIRST TURN AT CRIMINAL SABOTAGE, COME TO THINK OF IT.
WE'VE GOT ANOTHER MARCH COMING UP ON HAYWARD STREET--DODGE INTO THE ALLEY NEAR MIDLAND--
NO, HEAD BACK. YOU'RE A STREET TOO FAR!
HERE WE GO, SON--
IT'S ALL RIGHT, YOU'LL WAKE UP WITH NOTHING WORSE THAN A CASE OF THE BROWN BOTTLE FLU.
THERE'S A GOOD MAN.

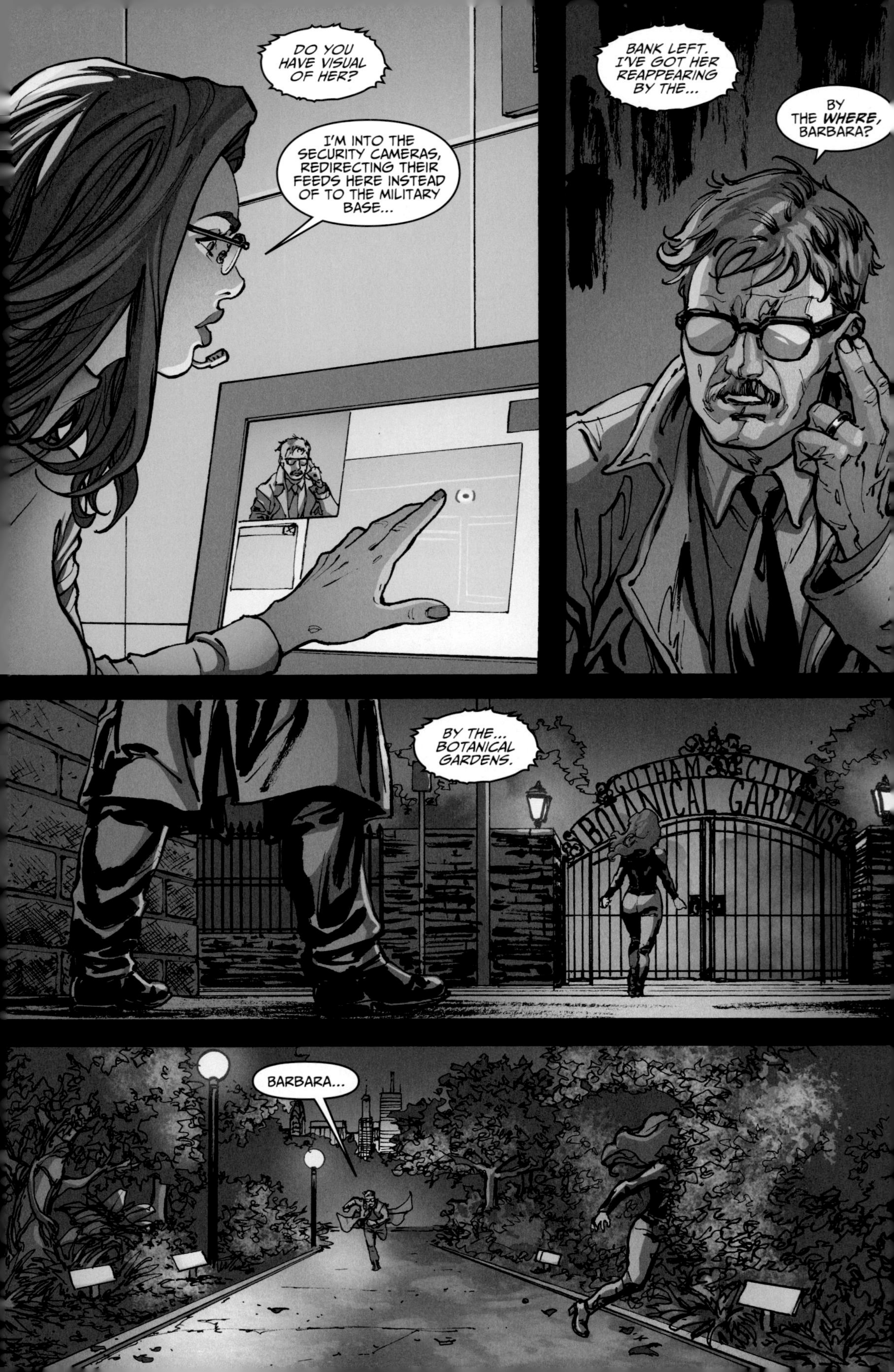
DO YOU HAVE VISUAL OF HER?
I'M INTO THE SECURITY CAMERAS, REDIRECTING THEIR FEEDS HERE INSTEAD OF TO THE MILITARY BASE...
BANK LEFT. I'VE GOT HER REAPPEARING BY THE...
BY THE *WHERE*, BARBARA?
BY THE... BOTANICAL GARDENS.
GOTHAM CITY BOTANICAL GARDENS
BARBARA...

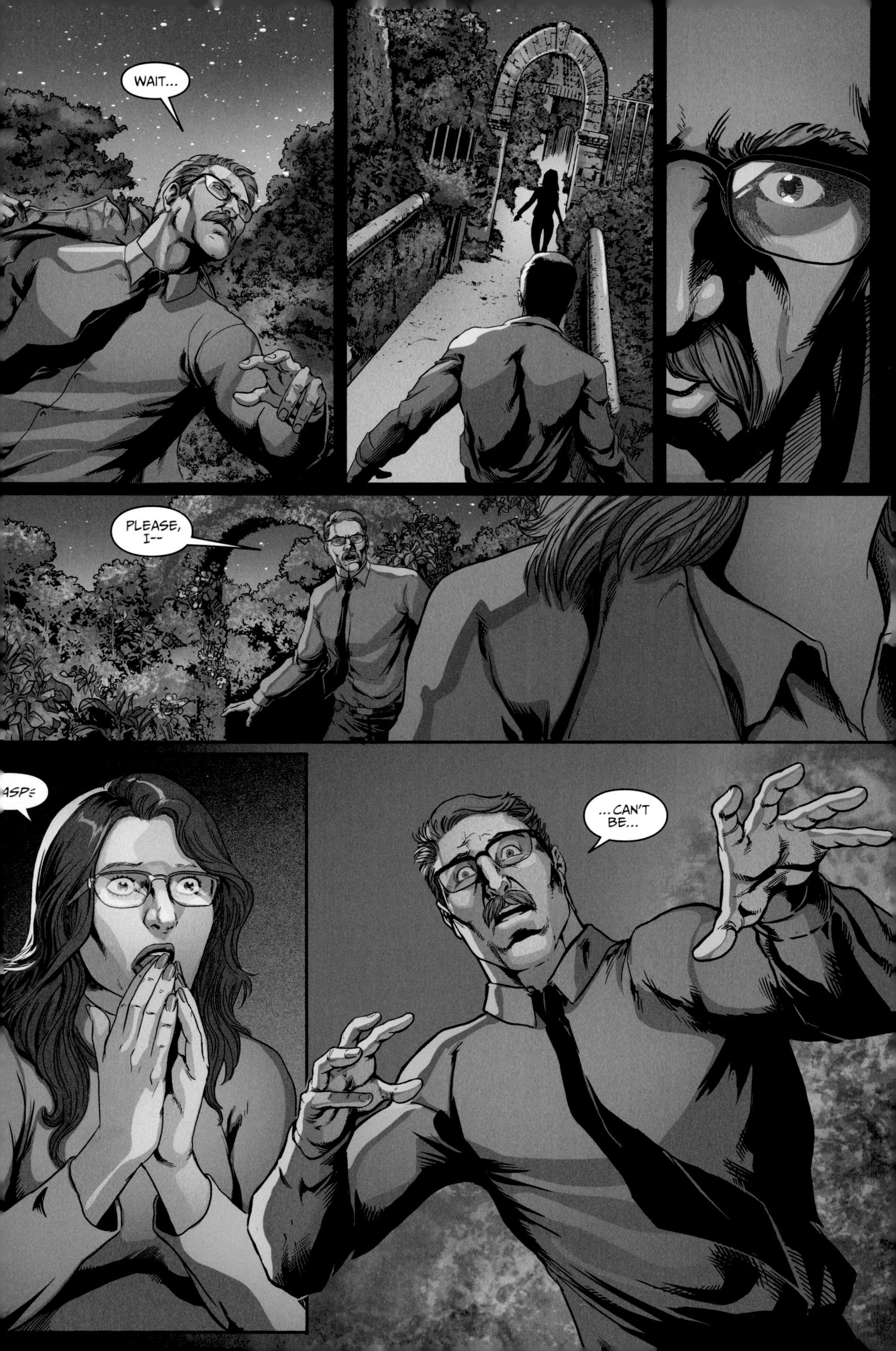
WAIT...
PLEASE, I--
...CAN'T BE...

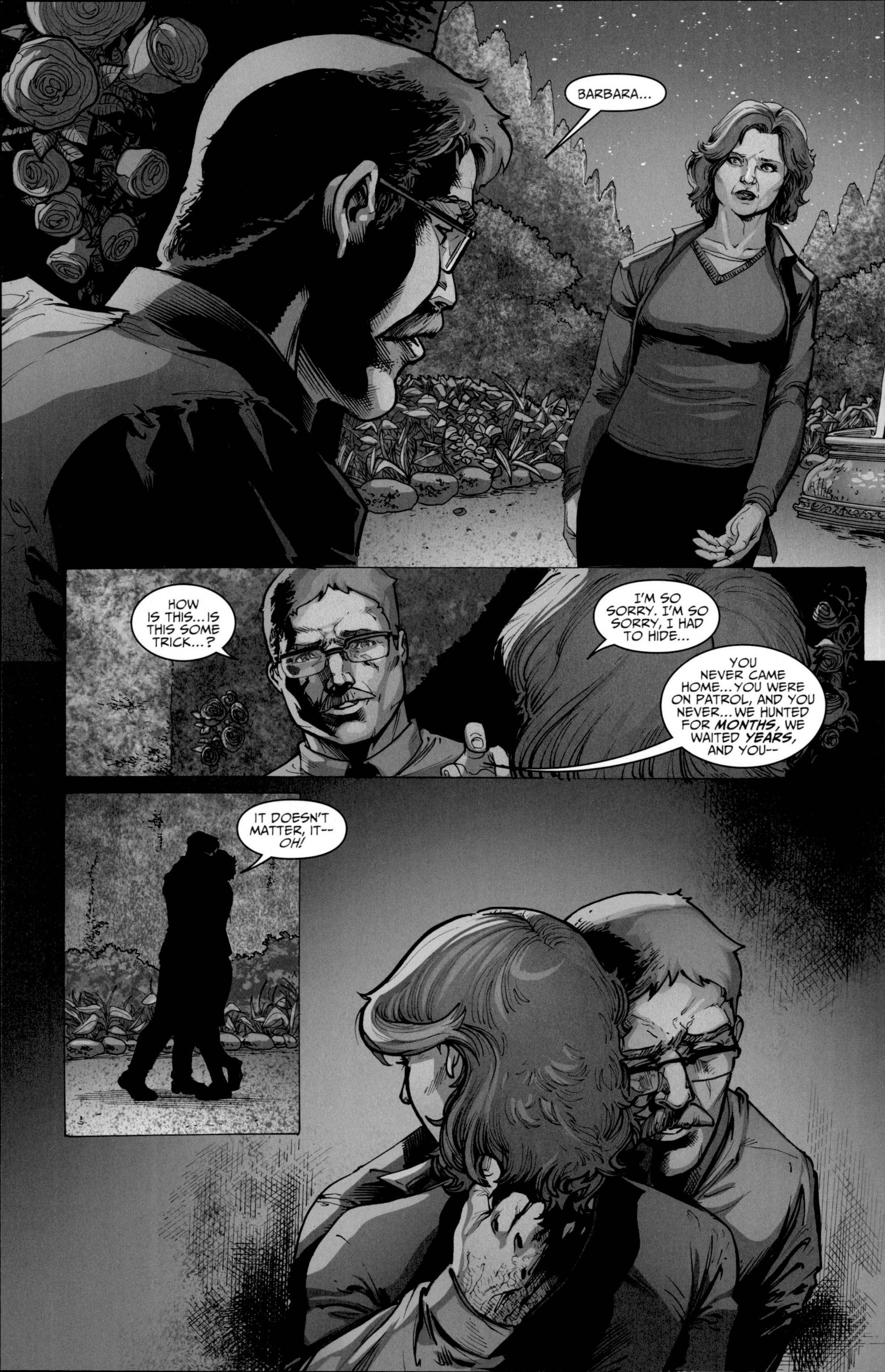
BARBARA...
HOW IS THIS...IS THIS SOME TRICK...?
I'M SO SORRY. I'M SO SORRY, I HAD TO HIDE...
YOU NEVER CAME HOME...YOU WERE ON PATROL, AND YOU NEVER...WE HUNTED FOR *MONTHS,* WE WAITED *YEARS,* AND YOU--
IT DOESN'T MATTER, IT-- *OH!*

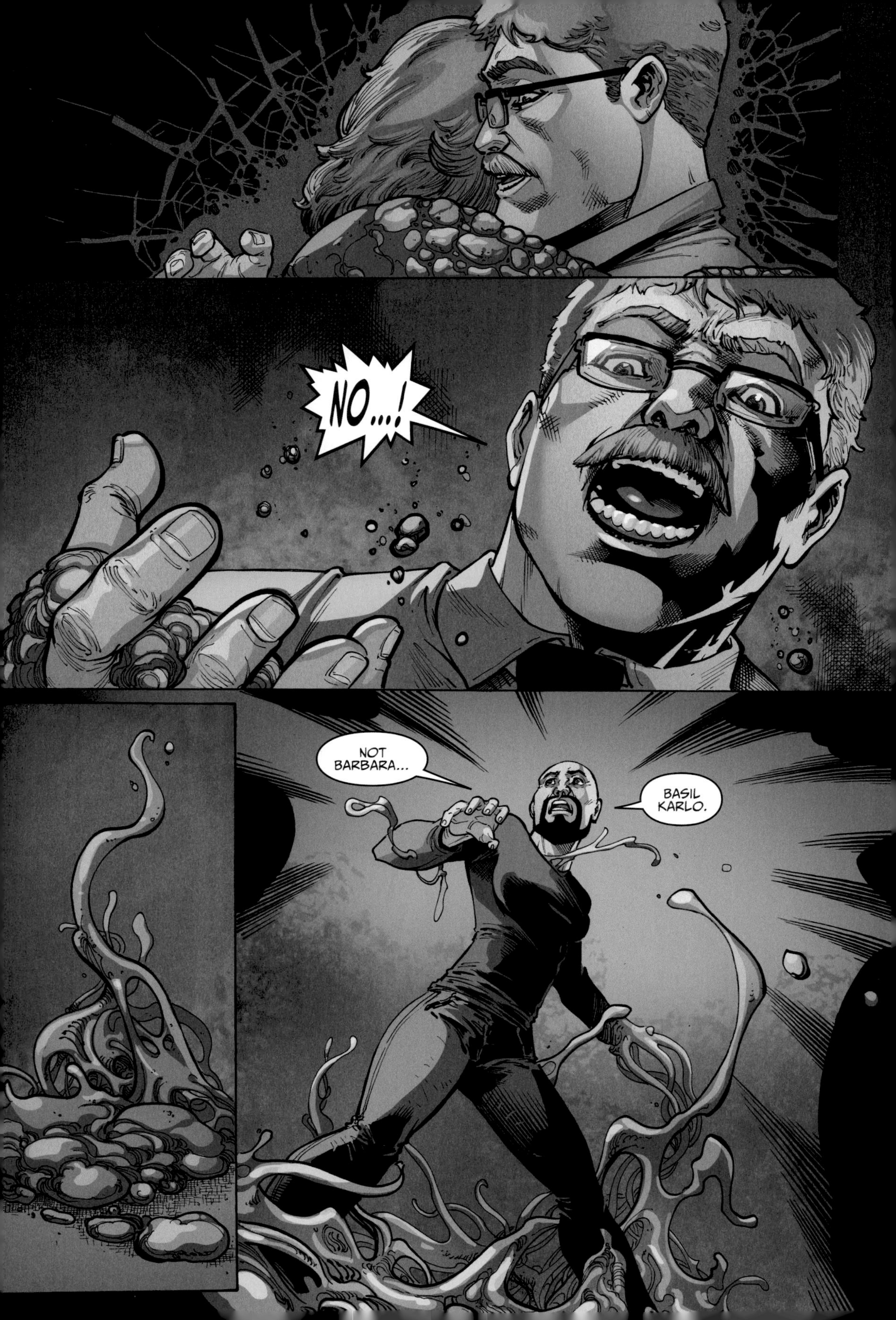
NO...!
NOT BARBARA...
BASIL KARLO.

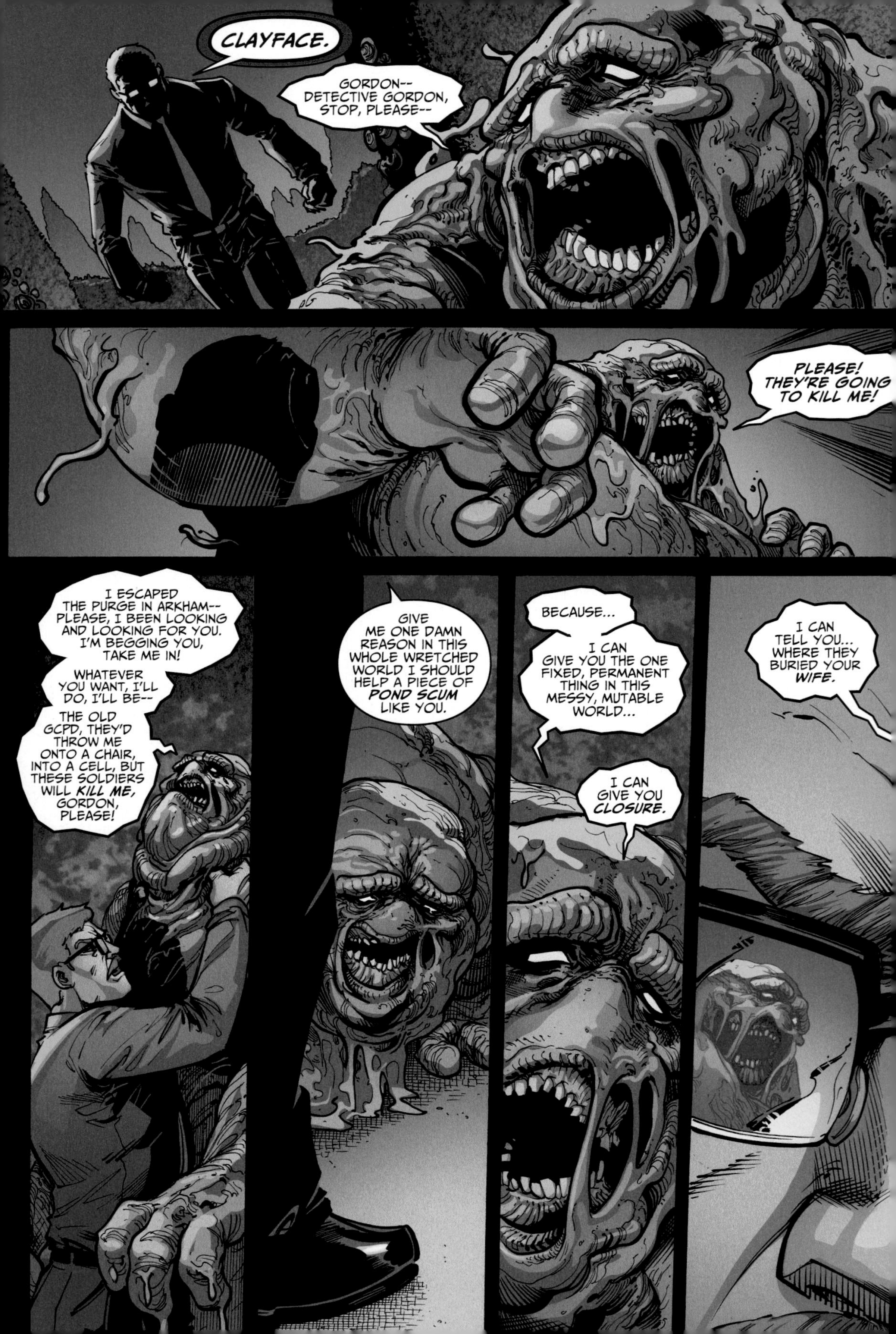

CLAYFACE.
GORDON-- DETECTIVE GORDON, STOP, PLEASE--
PLEASE! THEY'RE GOING TO KILL ME!
I ESCAPED THE PURGE IN ARKHAM-- PLEASE, I BEEN LOOKING AND LOOKING FOR YOU. I'M BEGGING YOU, TAKE ME IN!
WHATEVER YOU WANT, I'LL DO, I'LL BE--
THE OLD GCPD, THEY'D THROW ME ONTO A CHAIR, INTO A CELL, BUT THESE SOLDIERS WILL KILL ME, GORDON, PLEASE!
GIVE ME ONE DAMN REASON IN THIS WHOLE WRETCHED WORLD I SHOULD HELP A PIECE OF POND SCUM LIKE YOU.
BECAUSE...
I CAN GIVE YOU THE ONE FIXED, PERMANENT THING IN THIS MESSY, MUTABLE WORLD...
I CAN GIVE YOU CLOSURE.
I CAN TELL YOU... WHERE THEY BURIED YOUR WIFE.

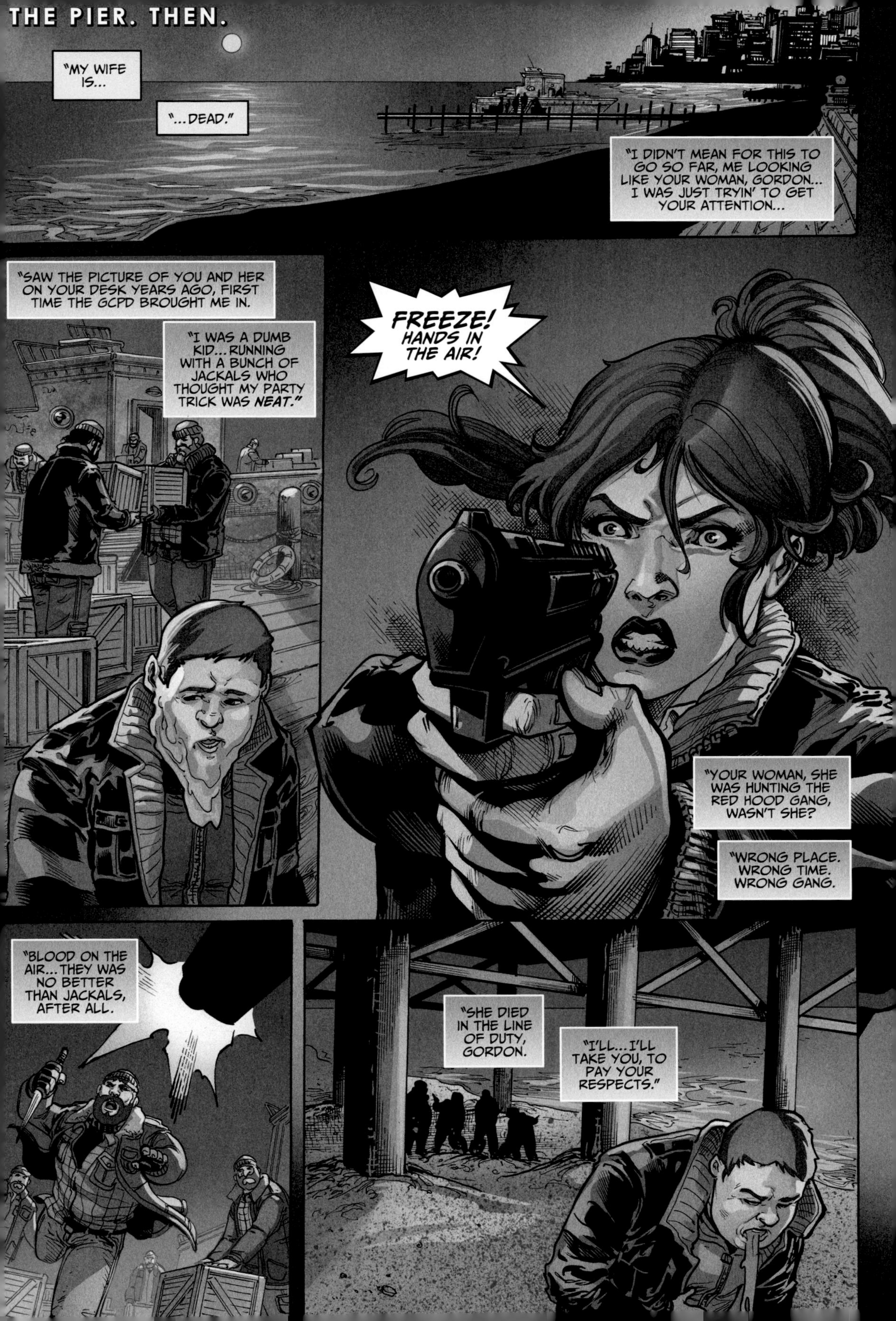
THE PIER. THEN.
"MY WIFE IS...
"...DEAD."
"I DIDN'T MEAN FOR THIS TO GO SO FAR, ME LOOKING LIKE YOUR WOMAN, GORDON... I WAS JUST TRYIN' TO GET YOUR ATTENTION...
"SAW THE PICTURE OF YOU AND HER ON YOUR DESK YEARS AGO, FIRST TIME THE GCPD BROUGHT ME IN.
"I WAS A DUMB KID...RUNNING WITH A BUNCH OF JACKALS WHO THOUGHT MY PARTY TRICK WAS NEAT."
FREEZE! HANDS IN THE AIR!
"YOUR WOMAN, SHE WAS HUNTING THE RED HOOD GANG, WASN'T SHE?
"WRONG PLACE. WRONG TIME. WRONG GANG.
"BLOOD ON THE AIR...THEY WAS NO BETTER THAN JACKALS, AFTER ALL.
"SHE DIED IN THE LINE OF DUTY, GORDON.
"I'LL...I'LL TAKE YOU, TO PAY YOUR RESPECTS."

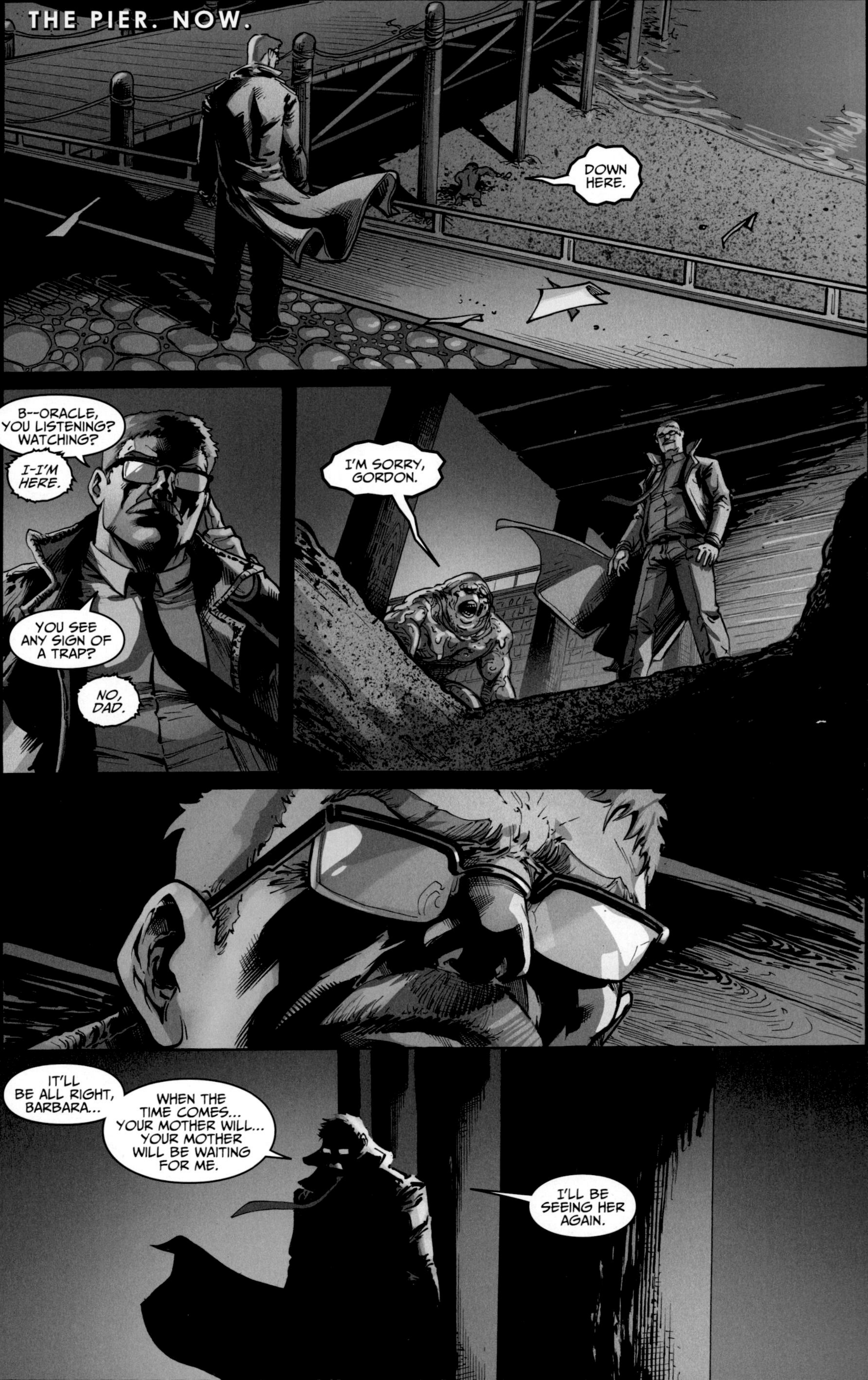
THE PIER. NOW.
DOWN HERE.
B--ORACLE, YOU LISTENING? WATCHING?
I-I'M HERE.
YOU SEE ANY SIGN OF A TRAP?
NO, DAD.
I'M SORRY, GORDON.
IT'LL BE ALL RIGHT, BARBARA...
WHEN THE TIME COMES... YOUR MOTHER WILL... YOUR MOTHER WILL BE WAITING FOR ME.
I'LL BE SEEING HER AGAIN.

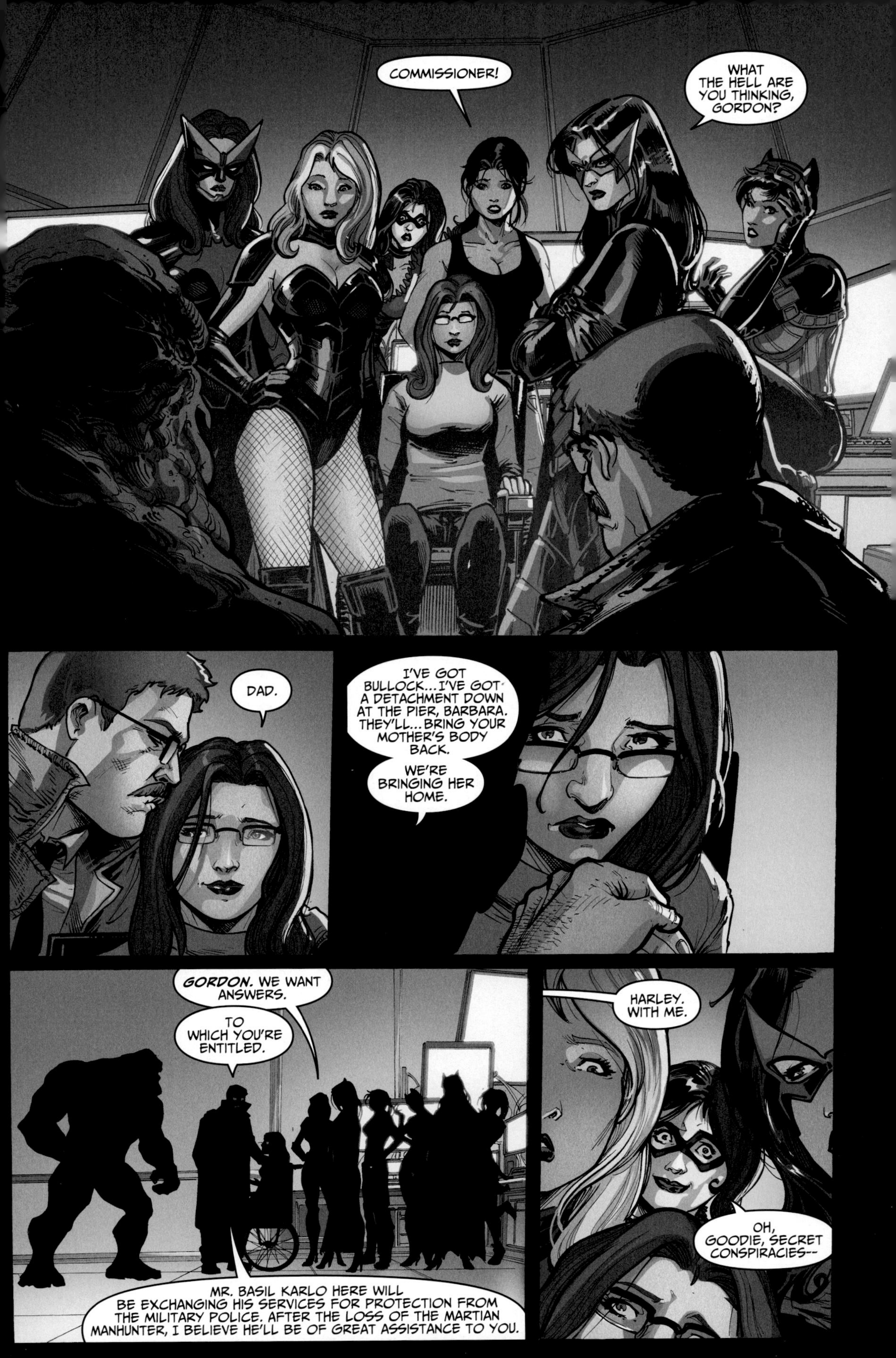
COMMISSIONER!
WHAT THE HELL ARE YOU THINKING, GORDON?
DAD.
I'VE GOT BULLOCK... I'VE GOT A DETACHMENT DOWN AT THE PIER, BARBARA. THEY'LL... BRING YOUR MOTHER'S BODY BACK.
WE'RE BRINGING HER HOME.
GORDON. WE WANT ANSWERS.
TO WHICH YOU'RE ENTITLED.
MR. BASIL KARLO HERE WILL BE EXCHANGING HIS SERVICES FOR PROTECTION FROM THE MILITARY POLICE. AFTER THE LOSS OF THE MARTIAN MANHUNTER, I BELIEVE HE'LL BE OF GREAT ASSISTANCE TO YOU.
HARLEY. WITH ME.
OH, GOODIE, SECRET CONSPIRACIES--

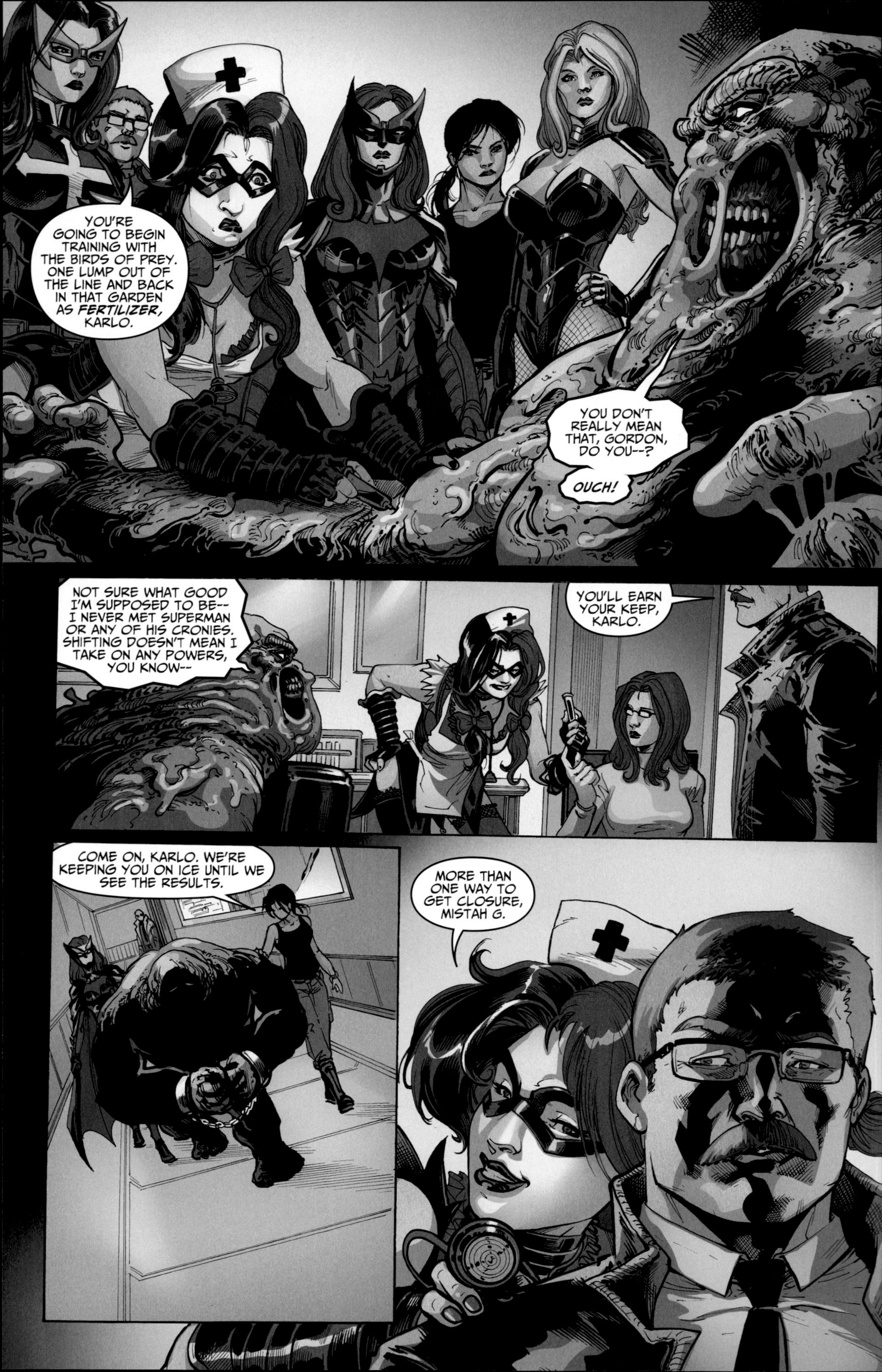
YOU'RE GOING TO BEGIN TRAINING WITH THE BIRDS OF PREY. ONE LUMP OUT OF THE LINE AND BACK IN THAT GARDEN AS *FERTILIZER,* KARLO.
YOU DON'T REALLY MEAN THAT, GORDON, DO YOU--?
OUCH!
NOT SURE WHAT GOOD I'M SUPPOSED TO BE-- I NEVER MET SUPERMAN OR ANY OF HIS CRONIES. SHIFTING DOESN'T MEAN I TAKE ON ANY POWERS, YOU KNOW--
YOU'LL EARN YOUR KEEP, KARLO.
COME ON, KARLO. WE'RE KEEPING YOU ON ICE UNTIL WE SEE THE RESULTS.
MORE THAN ONE WAY TO GET CLOSURE, MISTAH G.

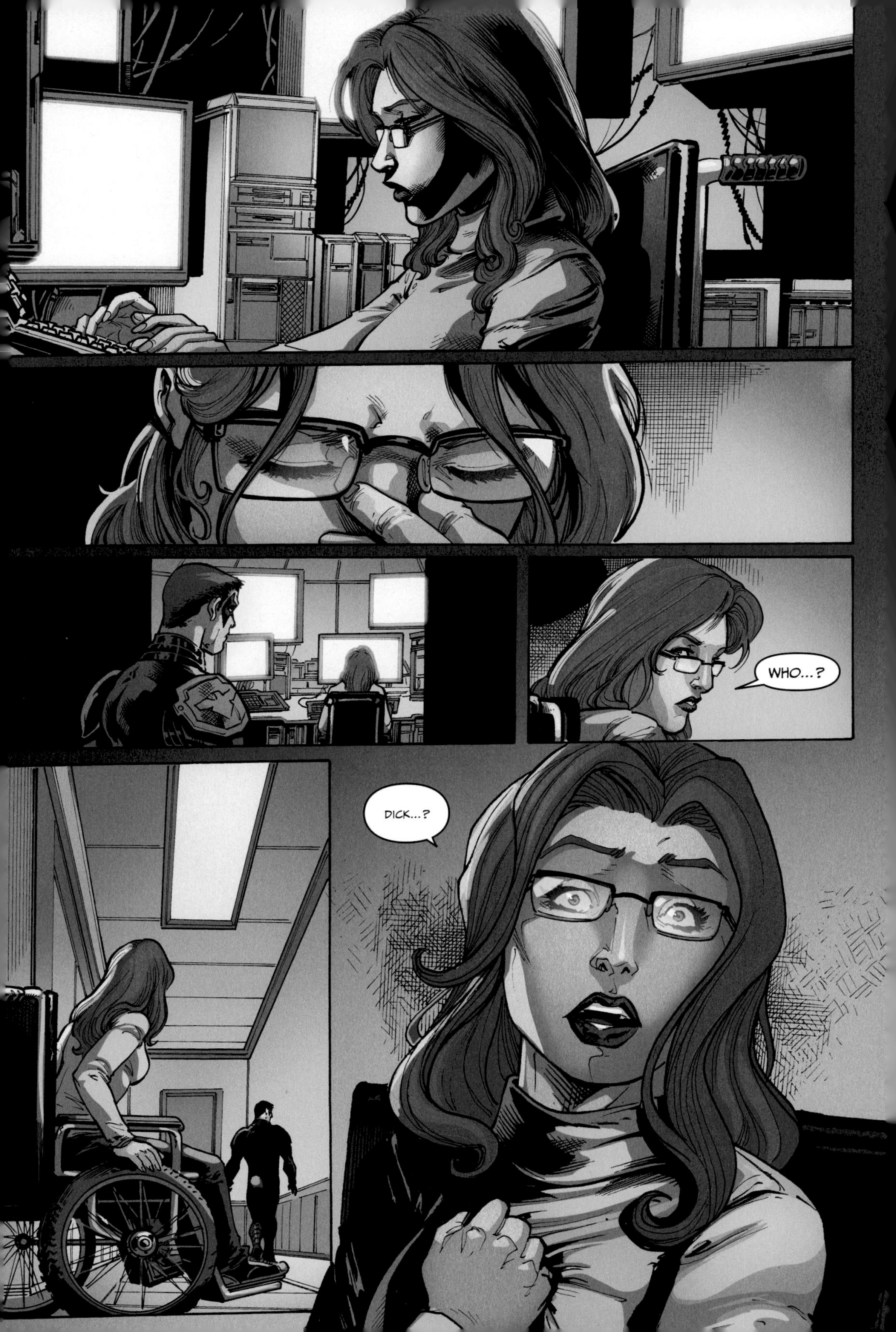
WHO...?
DICK...?

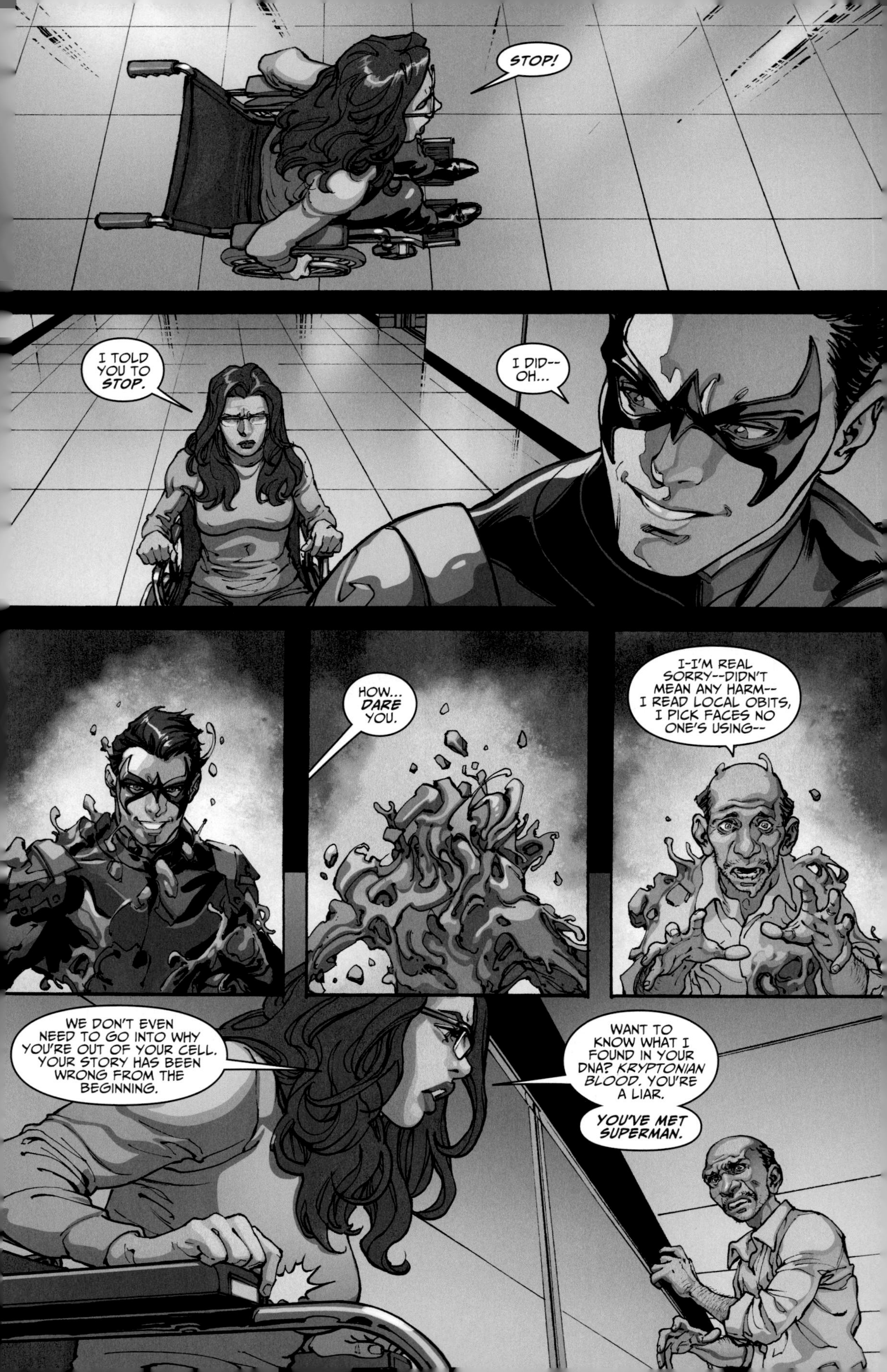
STOP!
I TOLD YOU TO STOP.
I DID-- OH...
HOW... DARE YOU.
I-I'M REAL SORRY--DIDN'T MEAN ANY HARM-- I READ LOCAL OBITS, I PICK FACES NO ONE'S USING--
WE DON'T EVEN NEED TO GO INTO WHY YOU'RE OUT OF YOUR CELL. YOUR STORY HAS BEEN WRONG FROM THE BEGINNING.
WANT TO KNOW WHAT I FOUND IN YOUR DNA? KRYPTONIAN BLOOD. YOU'RE A LIAR.
YOU'VE MET SUPERMAN.

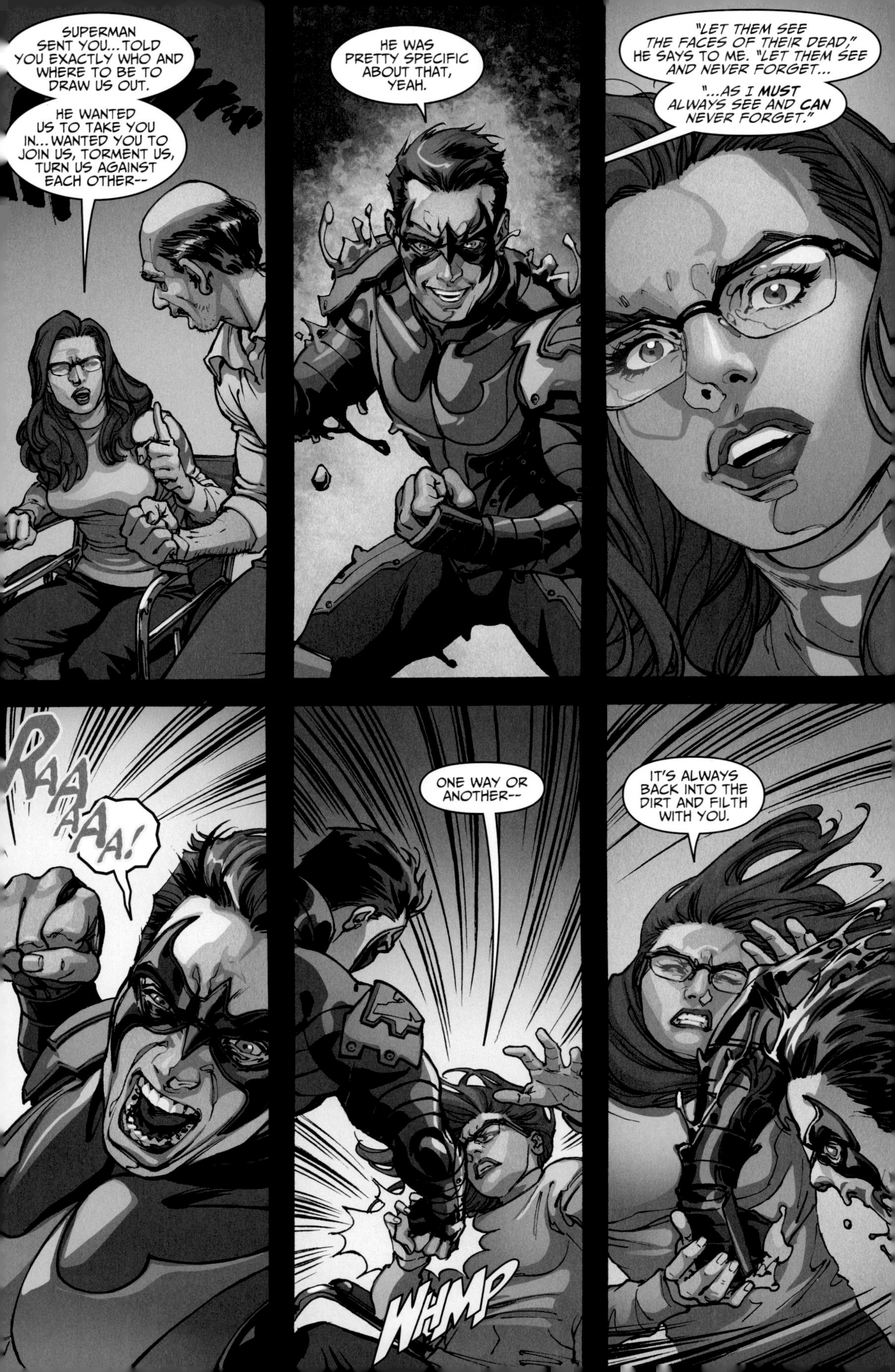
SUPERMAN SENT YOU...TOLD YOU EXACTLY WHO AND WHERE TO BE TO DRAW US OUT.
HE WANTED US TO TAKE YOU IN...WANTED YOU TO JOIN US, TORMENT US, TURN US AGAINST EACH OTHER--
HE WAS PRETTY SPECIFIC ABOUT THAT, YEAH.
"LET THEM SEE THE FACES OF THEIR DEAD," HE SAYS TO ME. "LET THEM SEE AND NEVER FORGET...
"...AS I MUST ALWAYS SEE AND CAN NEVER FORGET."
RAAAAAA!
ONE WAY OR ANOTHER--
WHMP
IT'S ALWAYS BACK INTO THE DIRT AND FILTH WITH YOU.

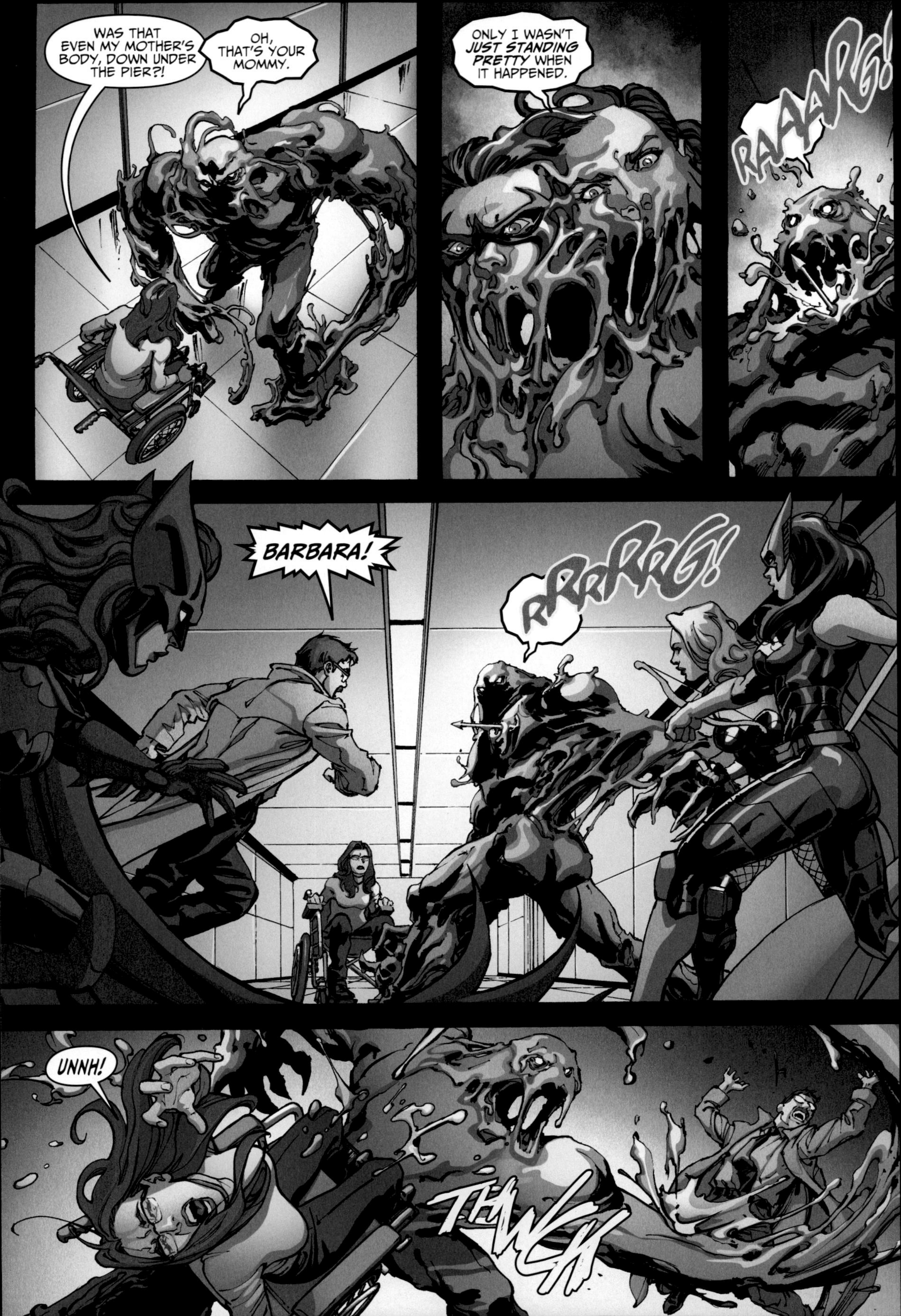

WAS THAT EVEN MY MOTHER'S BODY, DOWN UNDER THE PIER?!
OH, THAT'S YOUR MOMMY.
ONLY I WASN'T *JUST STANDING PRETTY* WHEN IT HAPPENED.
RAAAARG!
BARBARA!
RRRRRG!
UNNH!
THWCK

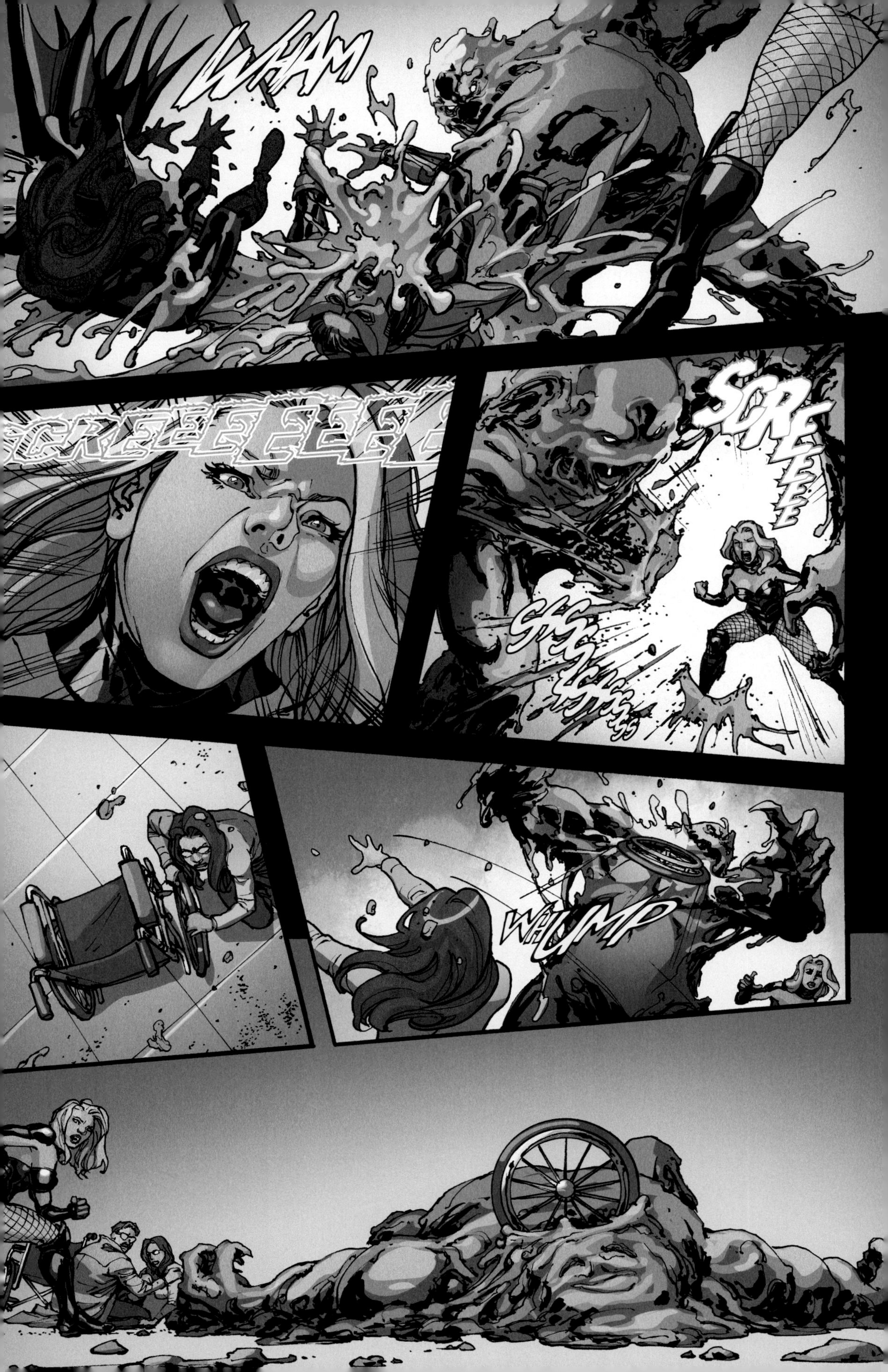
WHAM
SCREEEEEEE
SCREEEEE
SSSSSSS
WHUMP

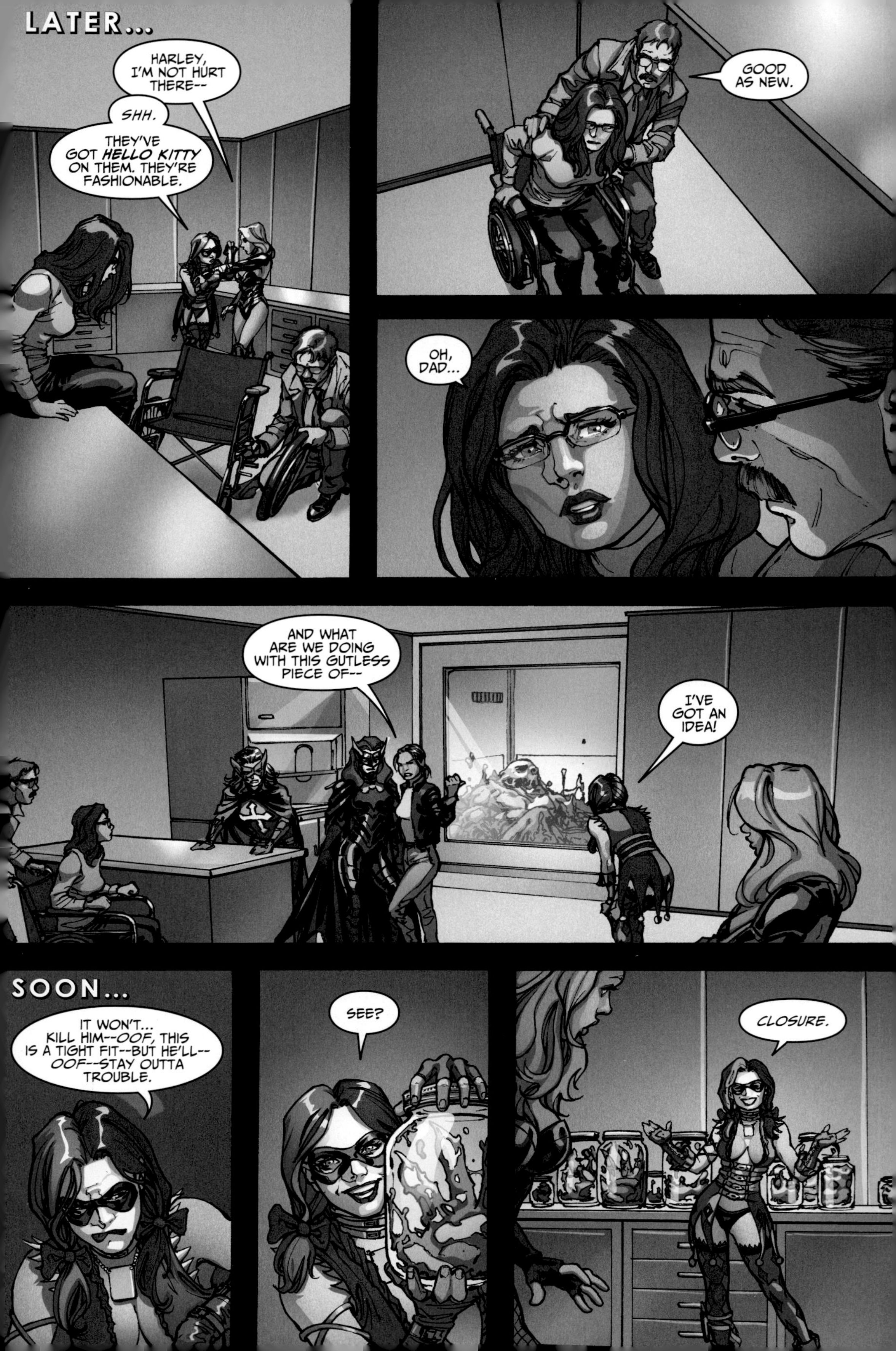
LATER...
HARLEY, I'M NOT HURT THERE--
SHH.
THEY'VE GOT HELLO KITTY ON THEM. THEY'RE FASHIONABLE.
GOOD AS NEW.
OH, DAD...
AND WHAT ARE WE DOING WITH THIS GUTLESS PIECE OF--
I'VE GOT AN IDEA!
SOON...
IT WON'T... KILL HIM--OOF, THIS IS A TIGHT FIT--BUT HE'LL-- OOF--STAY OUTTA TROUBLE.
SEE?
CLOSURE.

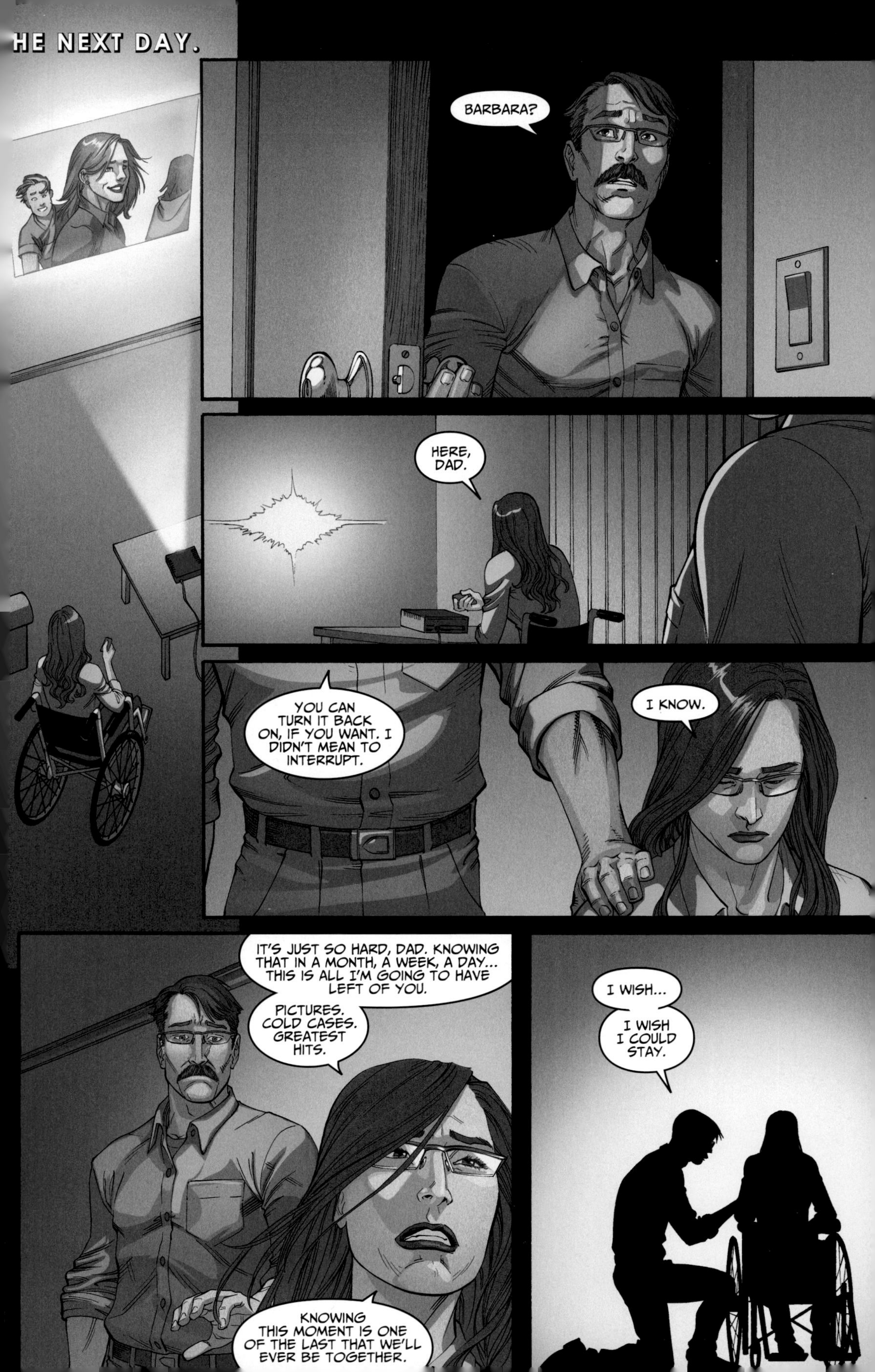
HE NEXT DAY.
BARBARA?
HERE, DAD.
YOU CAN TURN IT BACK ON, IF YOU WANT. I DIDN'T MEAN TO INTERRUPT.
I KNOW.
IT'S JUST SO HARD, DAD. KNOWING THAT IN A MONTH, A WEEK, A DAY... THIS IS ALL I'M GOING TO HAVE LEFT OF YOU.
PICTURES. COLD CASES. GREATEST HITS.
KNOWING THIS MOMENT IS ONE OF THE LAST THAT WE'LL EVER BE TOGETHER.
I WISH...
I WISH I COULD STAY.

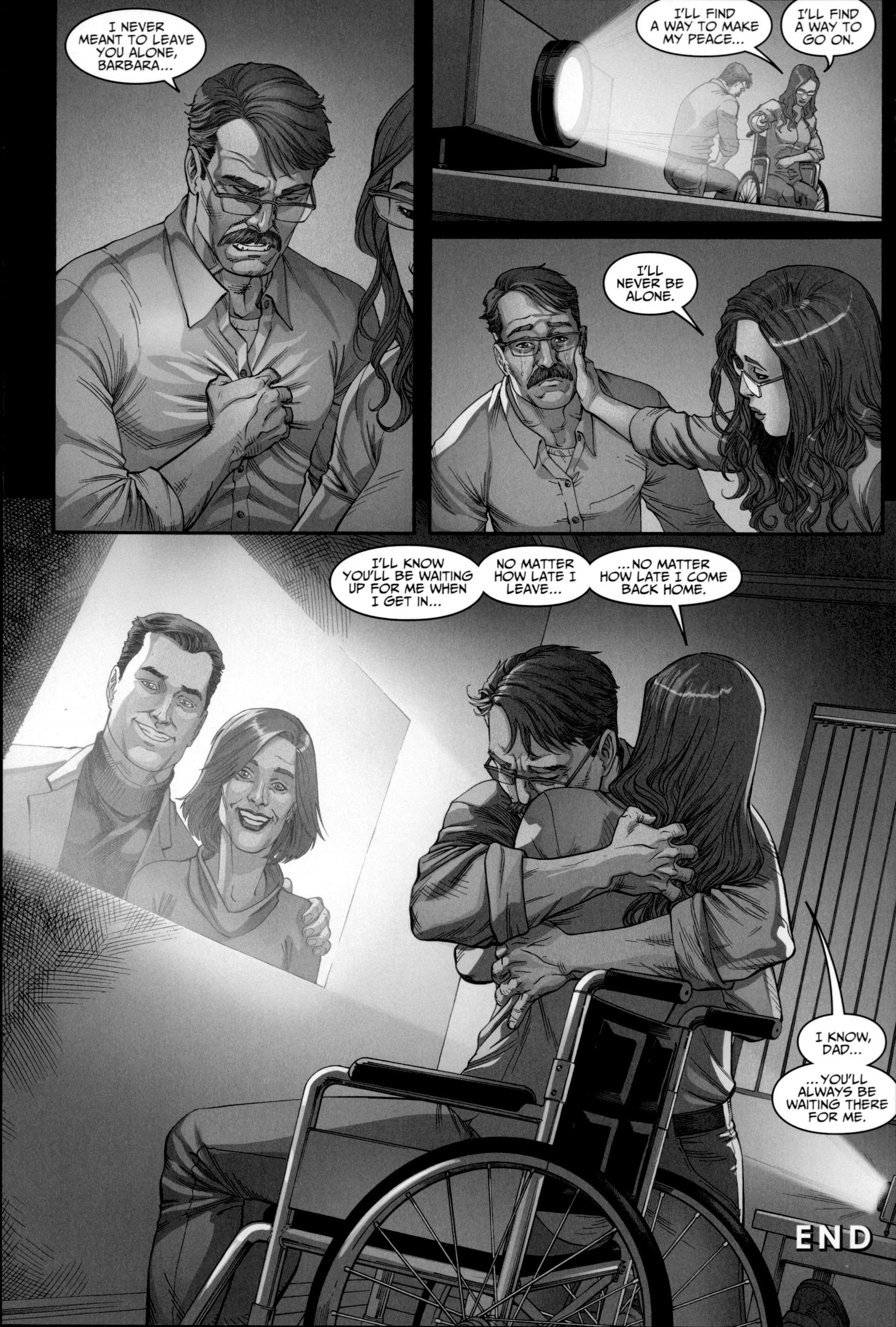
I NEVER MEANT TO LEAVE YOU ALONE, BARBARA...
I'LL FIND A WAY TO MAKE MY PEACE...
I'LL FIND A WAY TO GO ON.
I'LL NEVER BE ALONE.
I'LL KNOW YOU'LL BE WAITING UP FOR ME WHEN I GET IN...
NO MATTER HOW LATE I LEAVE...
...NO MATTER HOW LATE I COME BACK HOME.
I KNOW, DAD...
...YOU'LL ALWAYS BE WAITING THERE FOR ME.
END

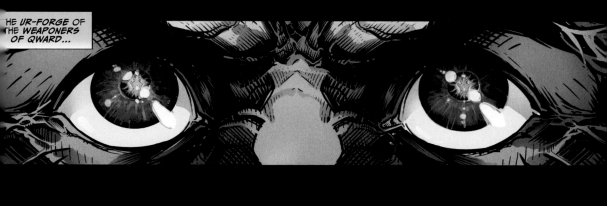

THE UR-FORGE OF THE WEAPONERS OF QWARD...

PRIMAL AND ANCIENT... ROOT OF VIOLENCE, WOMB OF DEATH...

"PLAYTHING OF THE GOD GONE MAD..."

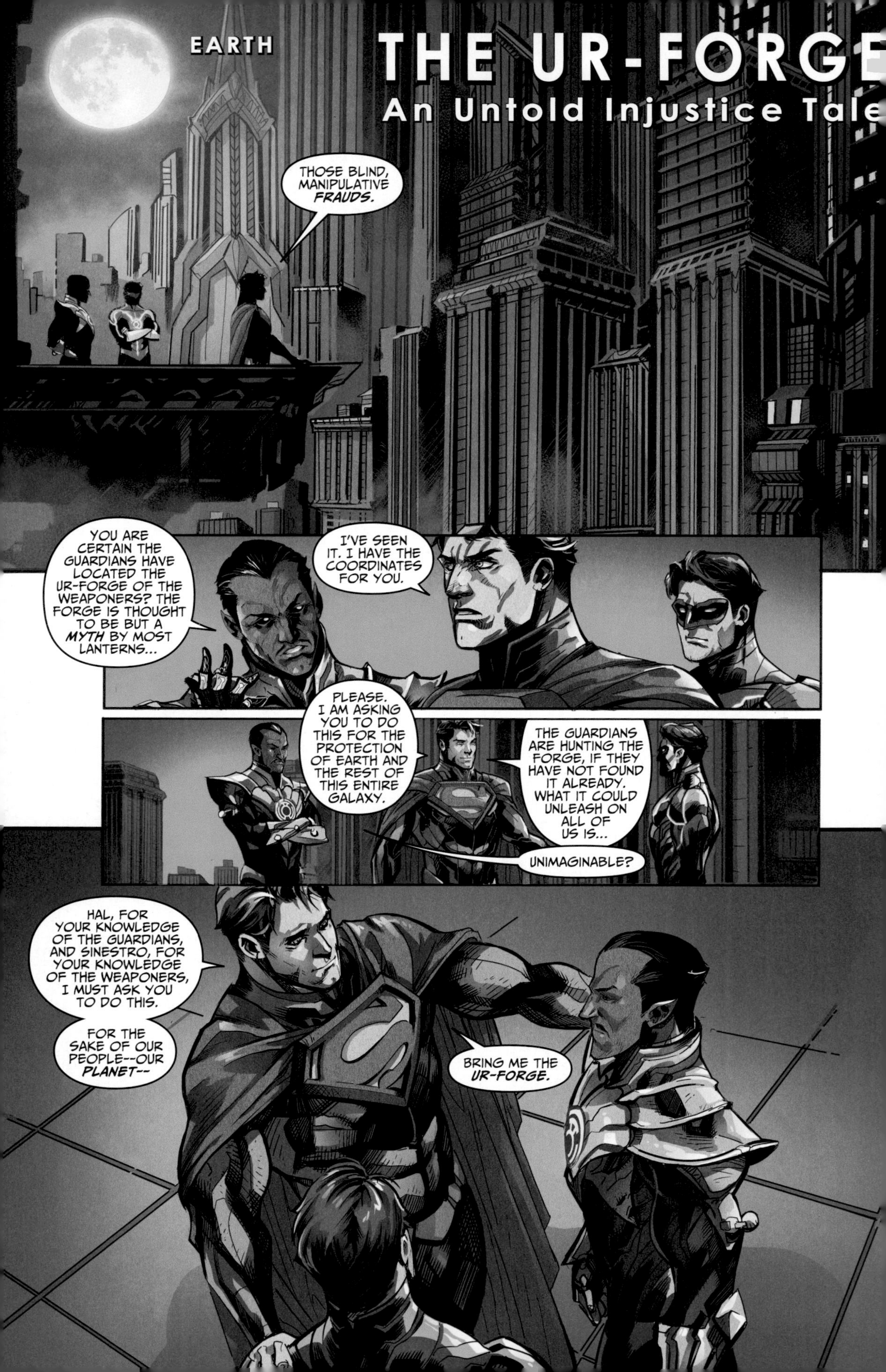
EARTH
THE UR-FORGE
An Untold Injustice Tale
THOSE BLIND, MANIPULATIVE FRAUDS.
YOU ARE CERTAIN THE GUARDIANS HAVE LOCATED THE UR-FORGE OF THE WEAPONERS? THE FORGE IS THOUGHT TO BE BUT A MYTH BY MOST LANTERNS...
I'VE SEEN IT. I HAVE THE COORDINATES FOR YOU.
PLEASE. I AM ASKING YOU TO DO THIS FOR THE PROTECTION OF EARTH AND THE REST OF THIS ENTIRE GALAXY.
THE GUARDIANS ARE HUNTING THE FORGE, IF THEY HAVE NOT FOUND IT ALREADY. WHAT IT COULD UNLEASH ON ALL OF US IS...
UNIMAGINABLE?
HAL, FOR YOUR KNOWLEDGE OF THE GUARDIANS, AND SINESTRO, FOR YOUR KNOWLEDGE OF THE WEAPONERS, I MUST ASK YOU TO DO THIS.
FOR THE SAKE OF OUR PEOPLE--OUR PLANET--
BRING ME THE UR-FORGE.

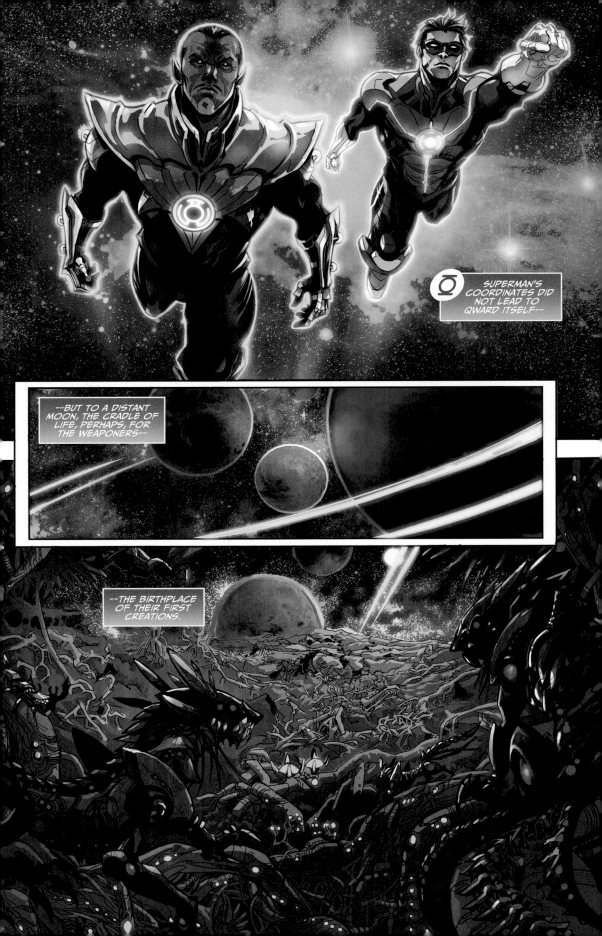

SUPERMAN'S COORDINATES DID NOT LEAD TO QWARD ITSELF--

--BUT TO A DISTANT MOON, THE CRADLE OF LIFE, PERHAPS, FOR THE WEAPONERS--

--THE BIRTHPLACE OF THEIR FIRST CREATIONS.

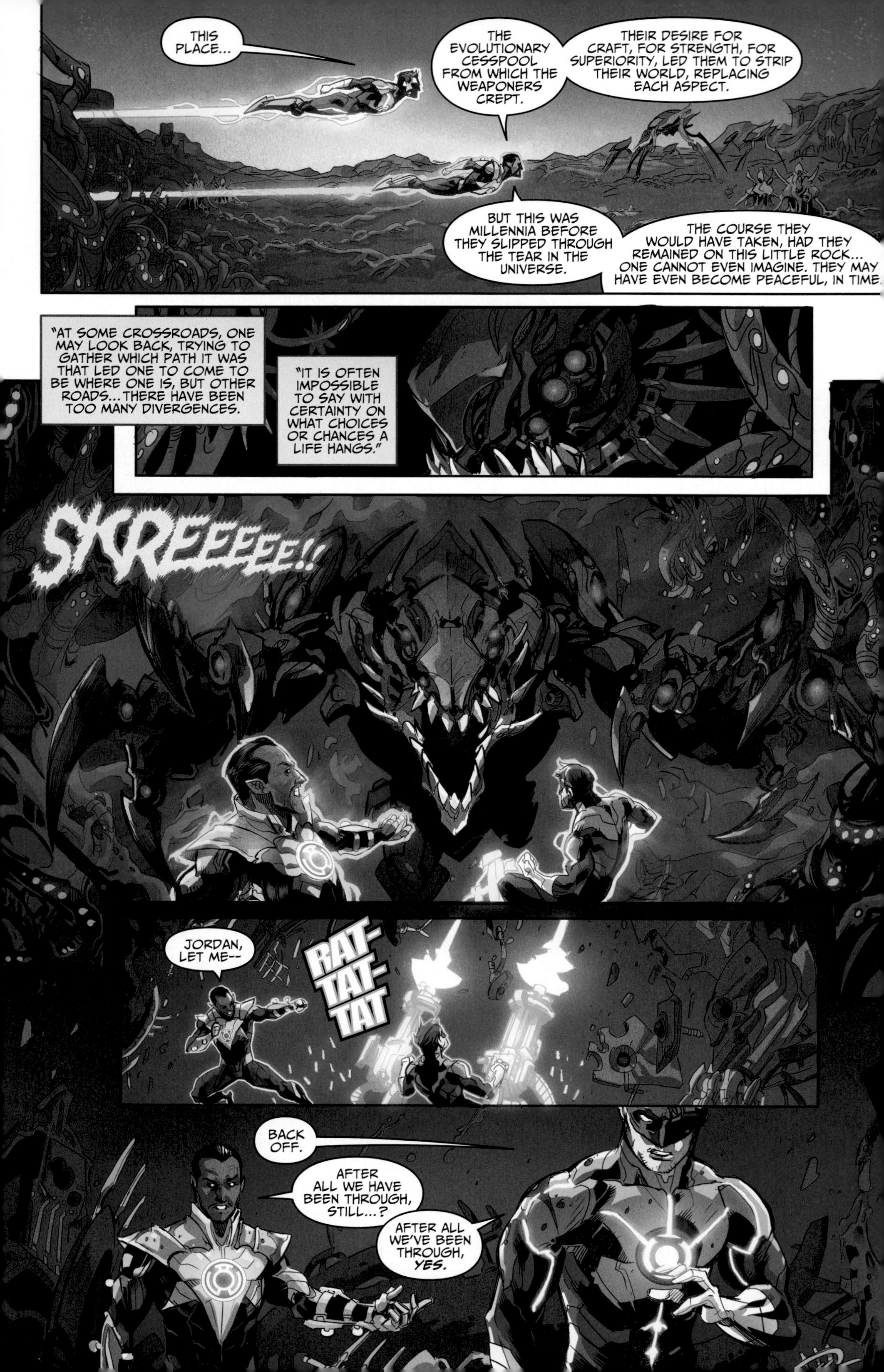
THIS PLACE...
THE EVOLUTIONARY CESSPOOL FROM WHICH THE WEAPONERS CREPT.
THEIR DESIRE FOR CRAFT, FOR STRENGTH, FOR SUPERIORITY, LED THEM TO STRIP THEIR WORLD, REPLACING EACH ASPECT.
BUT THIS WAS MILLENNIA BEFORE THEY SLIPPED THROUGH THE TEAR IN THE UNIVERSE.
THE COURSE THEY WOULD HAVE TAKEN, HAD THEY REMAINED ON THIS LITTLE ROCK... ONE CANNOT EVEN IMAGINE. THEY MAY HAVE EVEN BECOME PEACEFUL, IN TIME.
"AT SOME CROSSROADS, ONE MAY LOOK BACK, TRYING TO GATHER WHICH PATH IT WAS THAT LED ONE TO COME TO BE WHERE ONE IS, BUT OTHER ROADS... THERE HAVE BEEN TOO MANY DIVERGENCES.
"IT IS OFTEN IMPOSSIBLE TO SAY WITH CERTAINTY ON WHAT CHOICES OR CHANCES A LIFE HANGS."
SKREEEEEE!!
JORDAN, LET ME--
RAT-TAT-TAT
BACK OFF.
AFTER ALL WE HAVE BEEN THROUGH, STILL...?
AFTER ALL WE'VE BEEN THROUGH, *YES.*

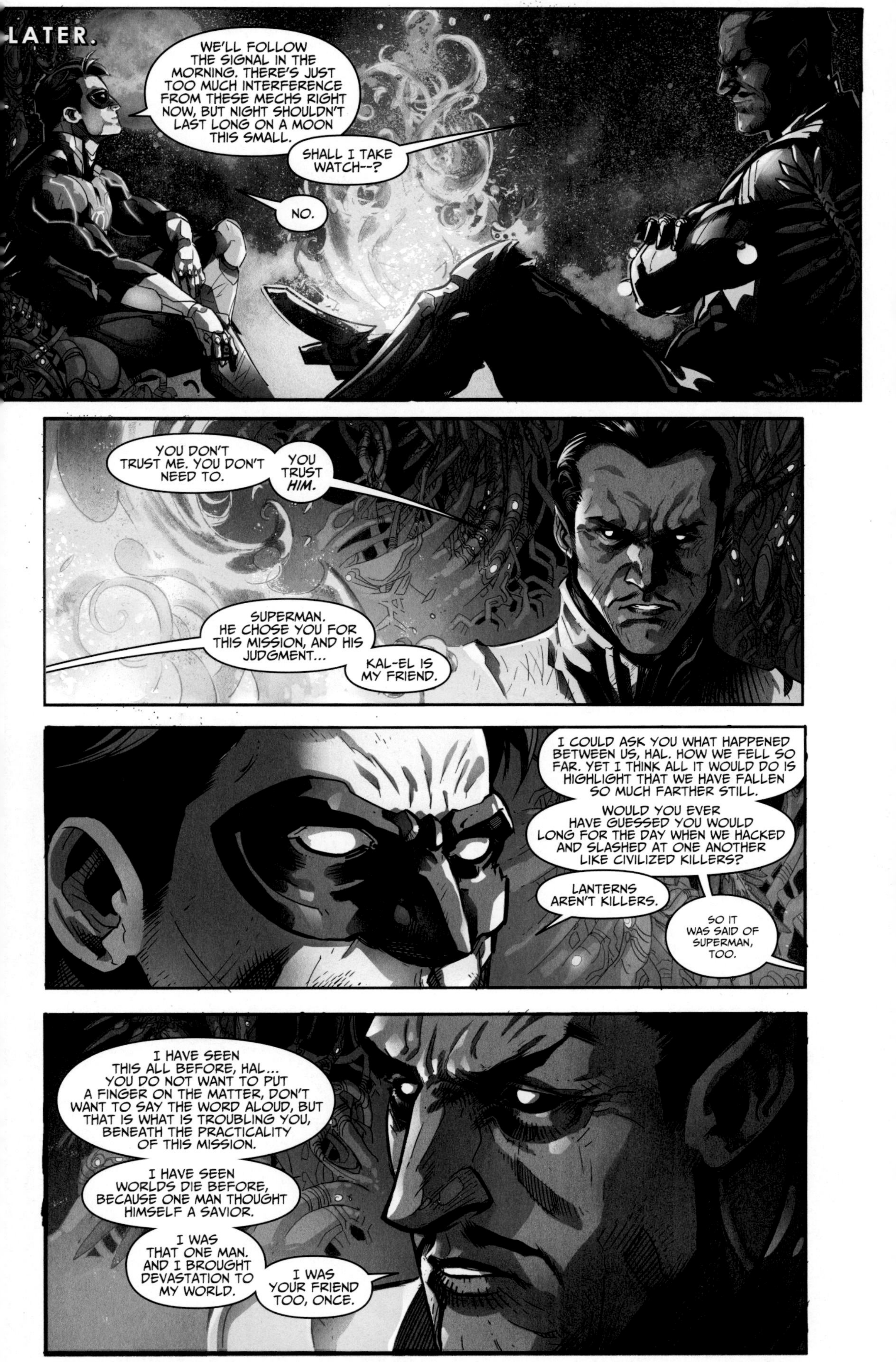
LATER.
WE'LL FOLLOW THE SIGNAL IN THE MORNING. THERE'S JUST TOO MUCH INTERFERENCE FROM THESE MECHS RIGHT NOW, BUT NIGHT SHOULDN'T LAST LONG ON A MOON THIS SMALL.
SHALL I TAKE WATCH--?
NO.
YOU DON'T TRUST ME. YOU DON'T NEED TO.
YOU TRUST *HIM.*
SUPERMAN. HE CHOSE YOU FOR THIS MISSION, AND HIS JUDGMENT...
KAL-EL IS MY FRIEND.
I COULD ASK YOU WHAT HAPPENED BETWEEN US, HAL. HOW WE FELL SO FAR. YET I THINK ALL IT WOULD DO IS HIGHLIGHT THAT WE HAVE FALLEN SO MUCH FARTHER STILL.
WOULD YOU EVER HAVE GUESSED YOU WOULD LONG FOR THE DAY WHEN WE HACKED AND SLASHED AT ONE ANOTHER LIKE CIVILIZED KILLERS?
LANTERNS AREN'T KILLERS.
SO IT WAS SAID OF SUPERMAN, TOO.
I HAVE SEEN THIS ALL BEFORE, HAL... YOU DO NOT WANT TO PUT A FINGER ON THE MATTER, DON'T WANT TO SAY THE WORD ALOUD, BUT THAT IS WHAT IS TROUBLING YOU, BENEATH THE PRACTICALITY OF THIS MISSION.
I HAVE SEEN WORLDS DIE BEFORE, BECAUSE ONE MAN THOUGHT HIMSELF A SAVIOR.
I WAS THAT ONE MAN. AND I BROUGHT DEVASTATION TO MY WORLD.
I WAS YOUR FRIEND TOO, ONCE.

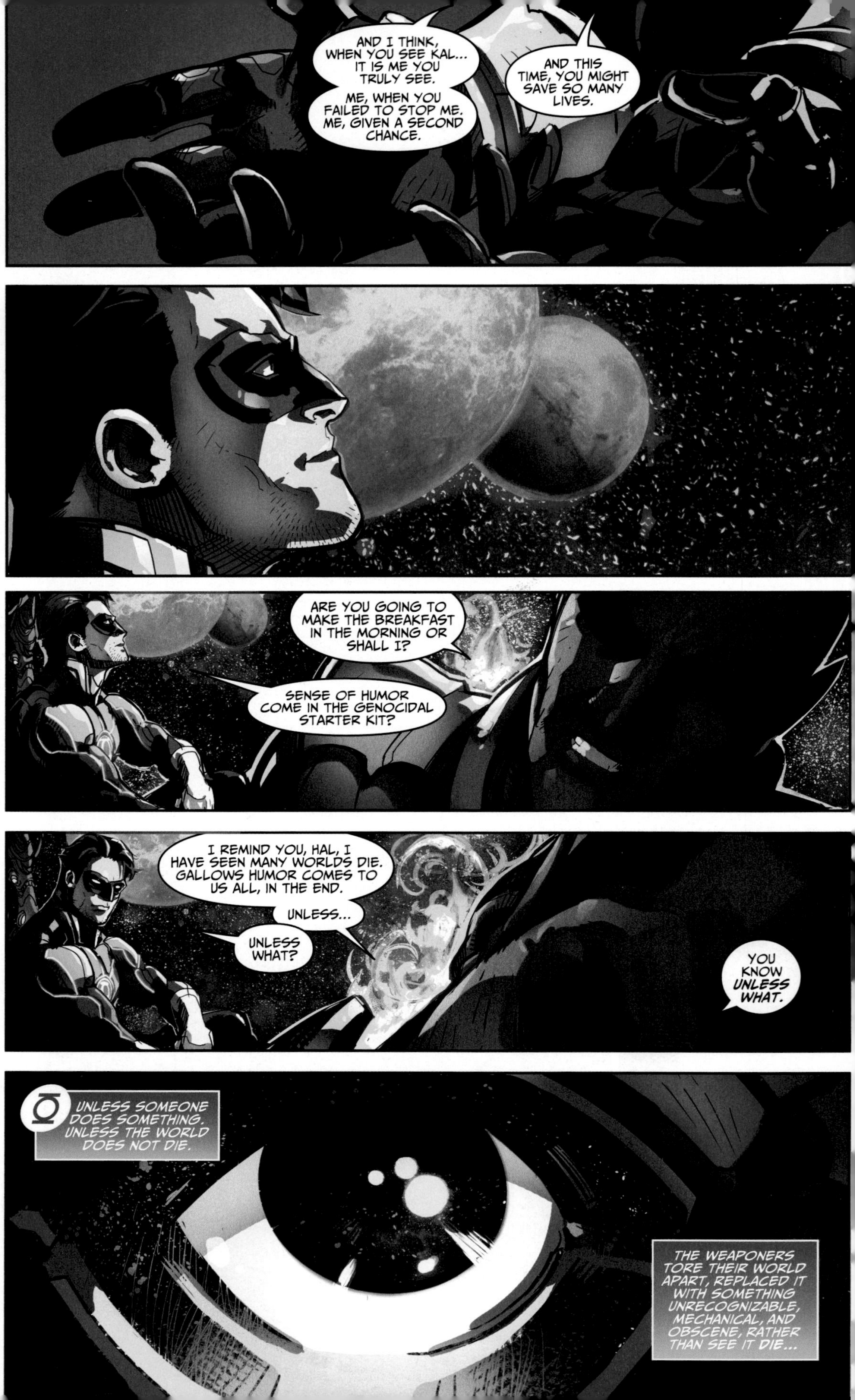
AND I THINK, WHEN YOU SEE KAL... IT IS ME YOU TRULY SEE.
ME, WHEN YOU FAILED TO STOP ME. ME, GIVEN A SECOND CHANCE.
AND THIS TIME, YOU MIGHT SAVE SO MANY LIVES.
ARE YOU GOING TO MAKE THE BREAKFAST IN THE MORNING OR SHALL I?
SENSE OF HUMOR COME IN THE GENOCIDAL STARTER KIT?
I REMIND YOU, HAL, I HAVE SEEN MANY WORLDS DIE. GALLOWS HUMOR COMES TO US ALL, IN THE END.
UNLESS...
UNLESS WHAT?
YOU KNOW UNLESS WHAT.
UNLESS SOMEONE DOES SOMETHING. UNLESS THE WORLD DOES NOT DIE.
THE WEAPONERS TORE THEIR WORLD APART, REPLACED IT WITH SOMETHING UNRECOGNIZABLE, MECHANICAL, AND OBSCENE, RATHER THAN SEE IT DIE...

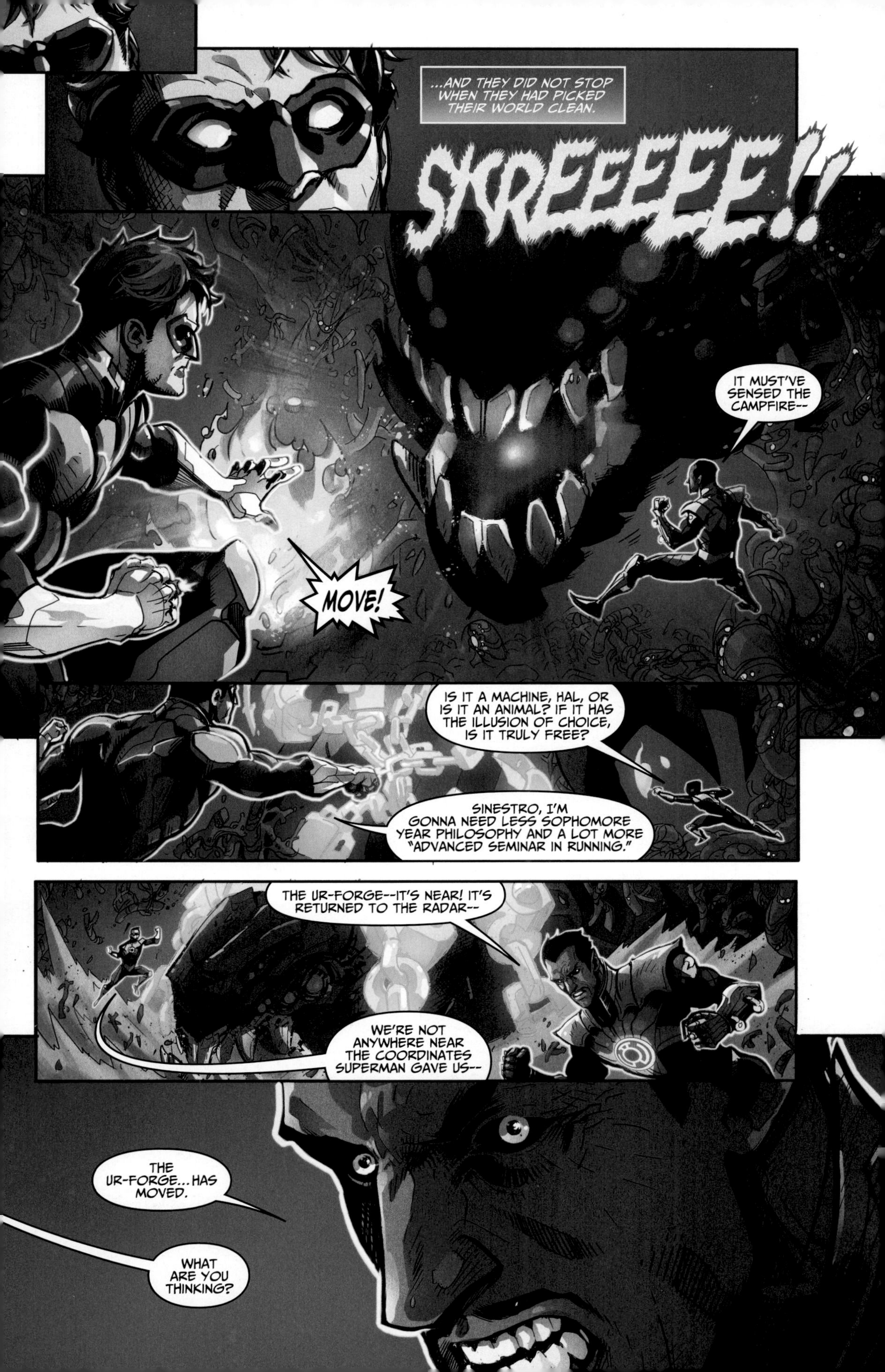
...AND THEY DID NOT STOP WHEN THEY HAD PICKED THEIR WORLD CLEAN.
SKREEEEEE!!
IT MUST'VE SENSED THE CAMPFIRE--
MOVE!
IS IT A MACHINE, HAL, OR IS IT AN ANIMAL? IF IT HAS THE ILLUSION OF CHOICE, IS IT TRULY FREE?
SINESTRO, I'M GONNA NEED LESS SOPHOMORE YEAR PHILOSOPHY AND A LOT MORE "ADVANCED SEMINAR IN RUNNING."
THE UR-FORGE--IT'S NEAR! IT'S RETURNED TO THE RADAR--
WE'RE NOT ANYWHERE NEAR THE COORDINATES SUPERMAN GAVE US--
THE UR-FORGE... HAS MOVED.
WHAT ARE YOU THINKING?

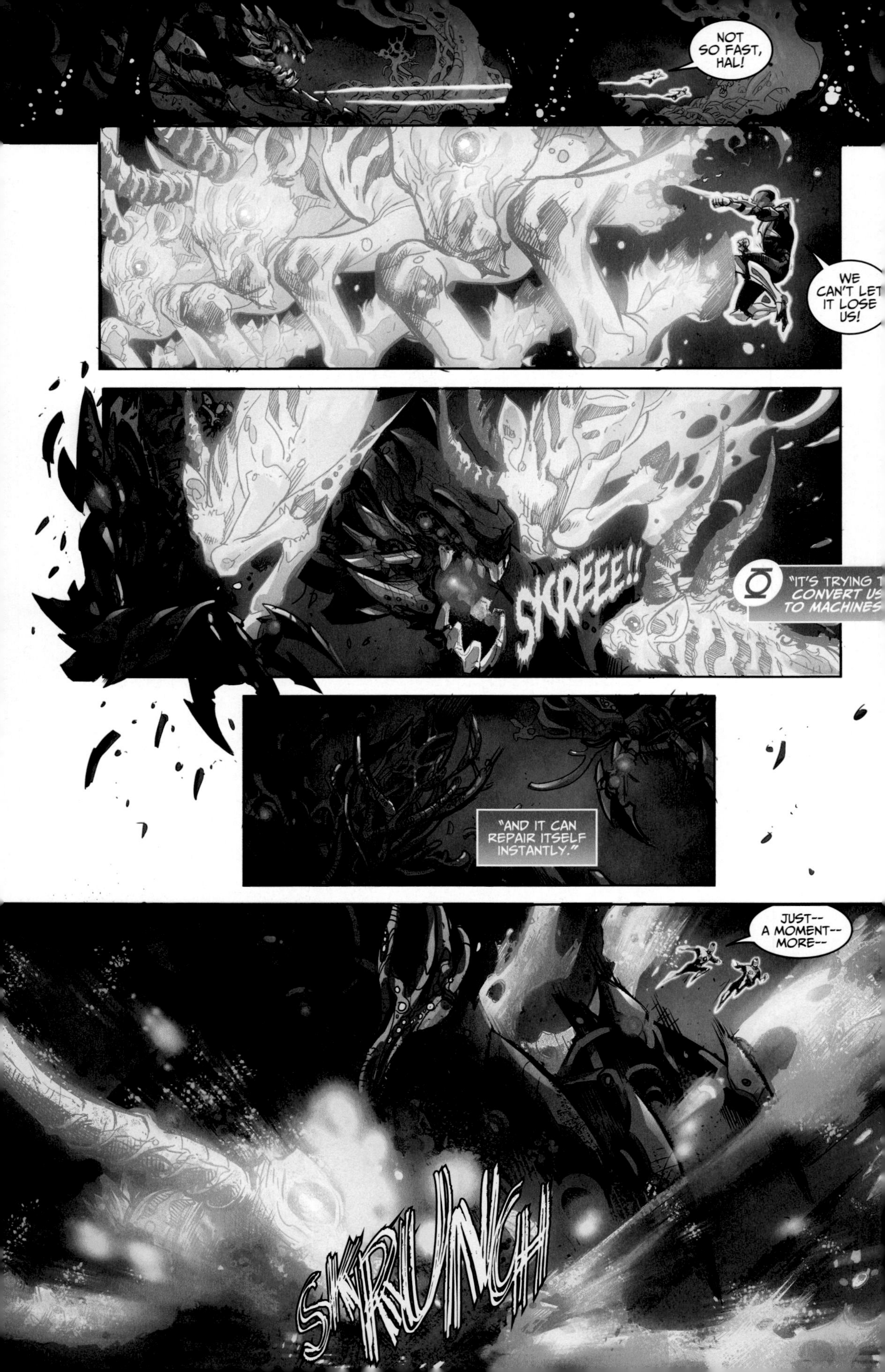

NOT SO FAST, HAL!
WE CAN'T LET IT LOSE US!
SKREEE!!
"IT'S TRYING T CONVERT US TO MACHINES
"AND IT CAN REPAIR ITSELF INSTANTLY."
JUST-- A MOMENT-- MORE--
SKRUNCH

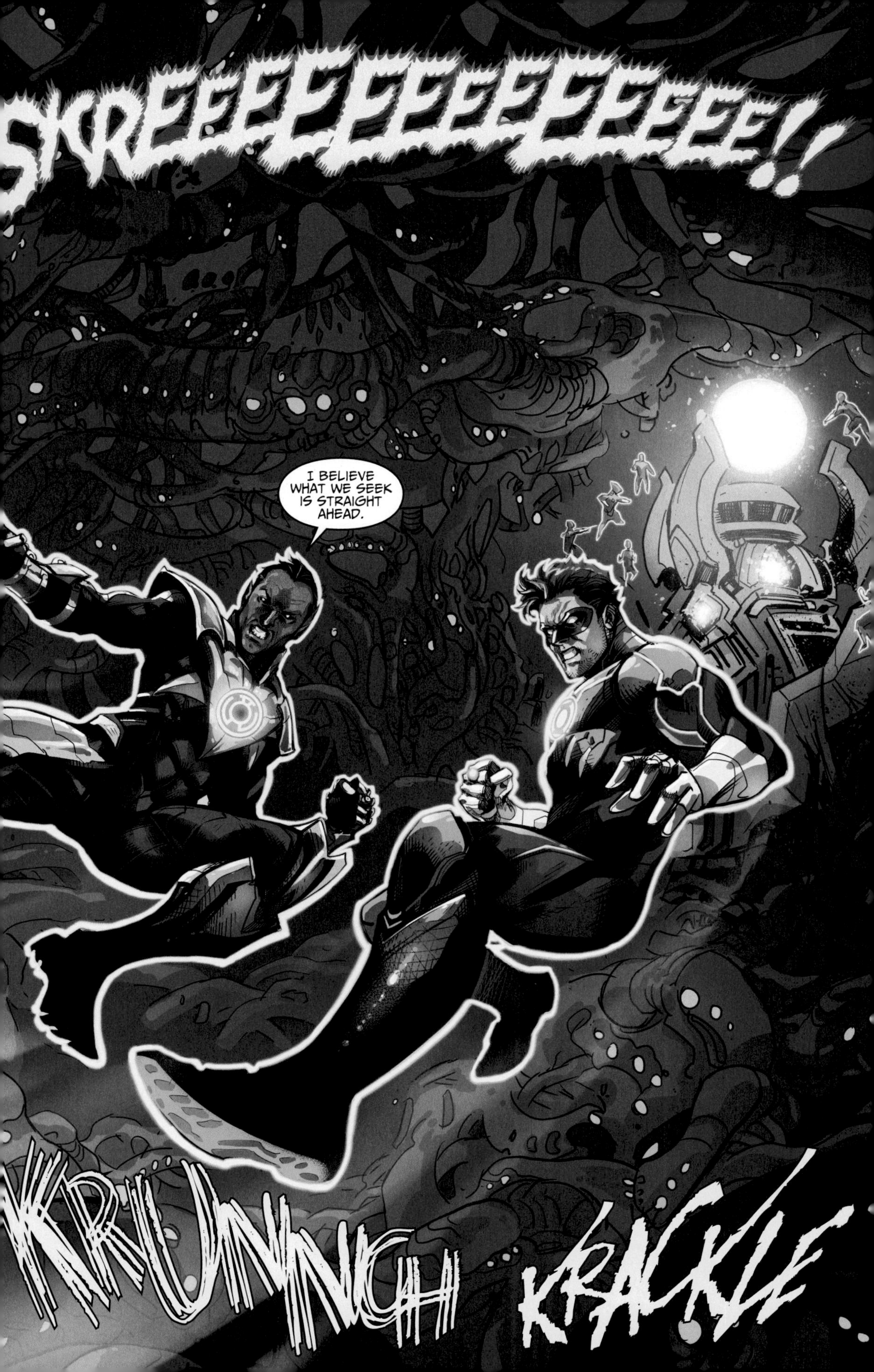
SKREEEEEEEEEEEEEEE!!
I BELIEVE WHAT WE SEEK IS STRAIGHT AHEAD.
KRUNNCH
KRACKLE

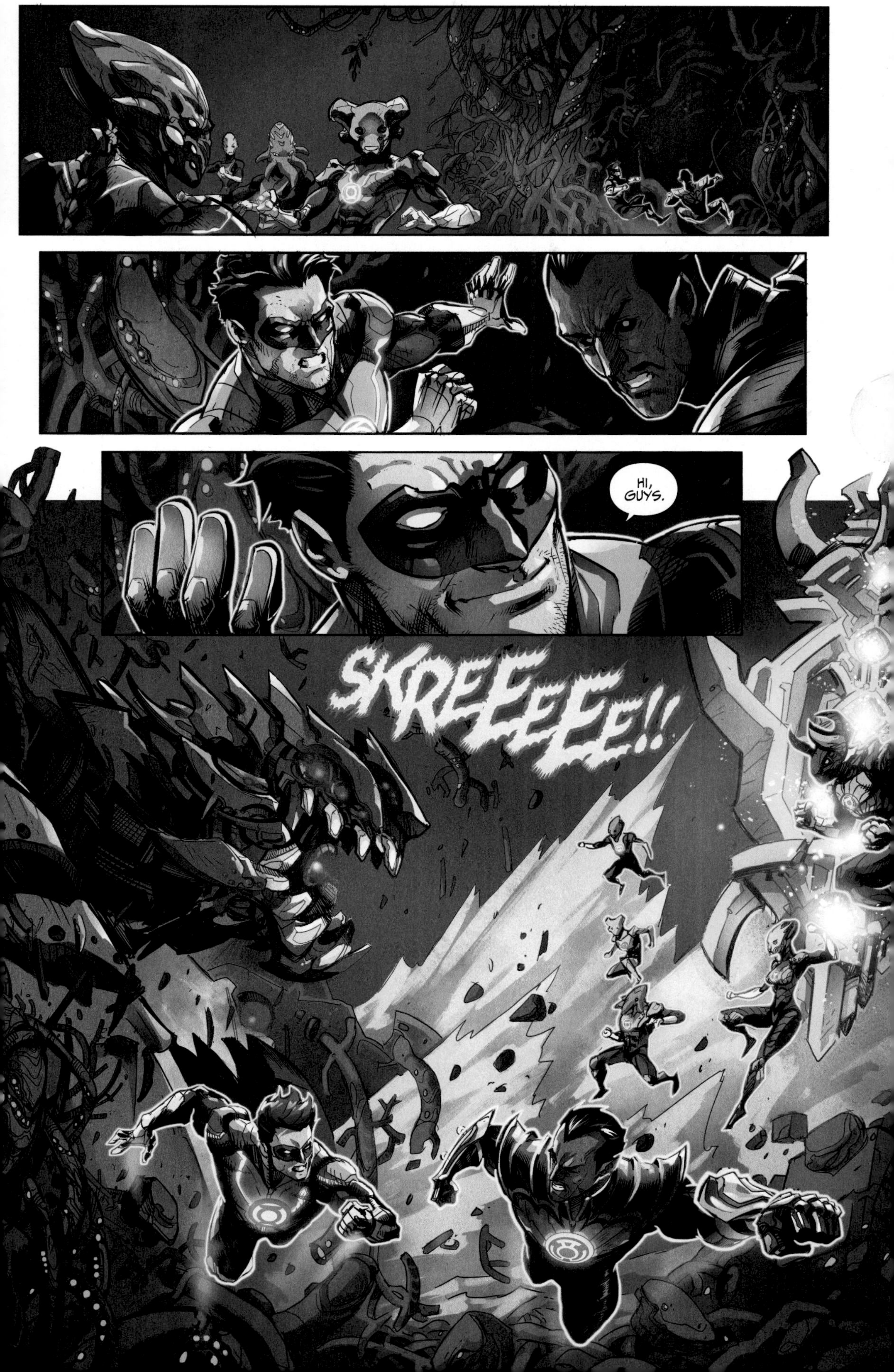
HI, GUYS.
SKREEEEEE!!

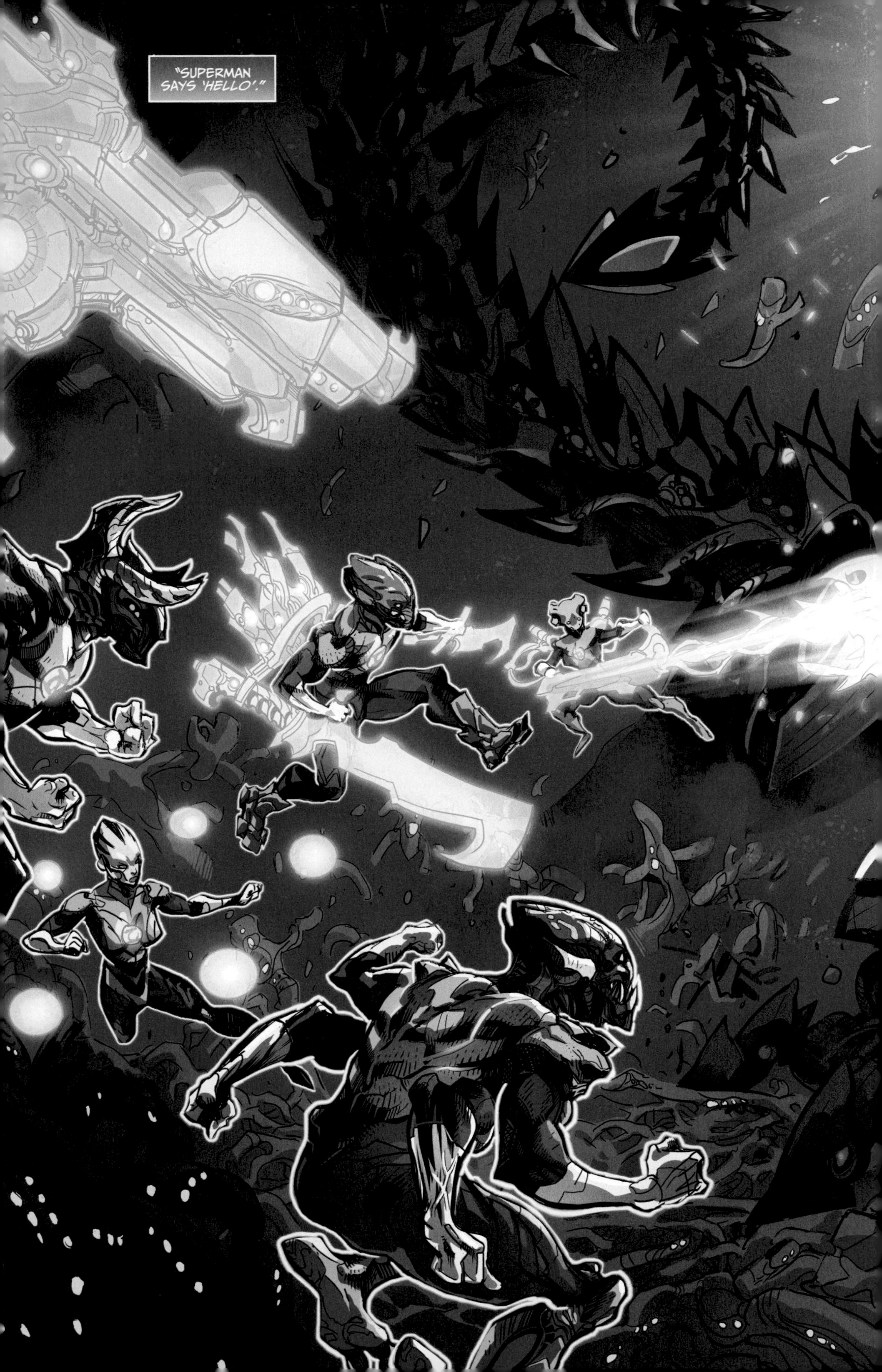
"SUPERMAN SAYS 'HELLO'."

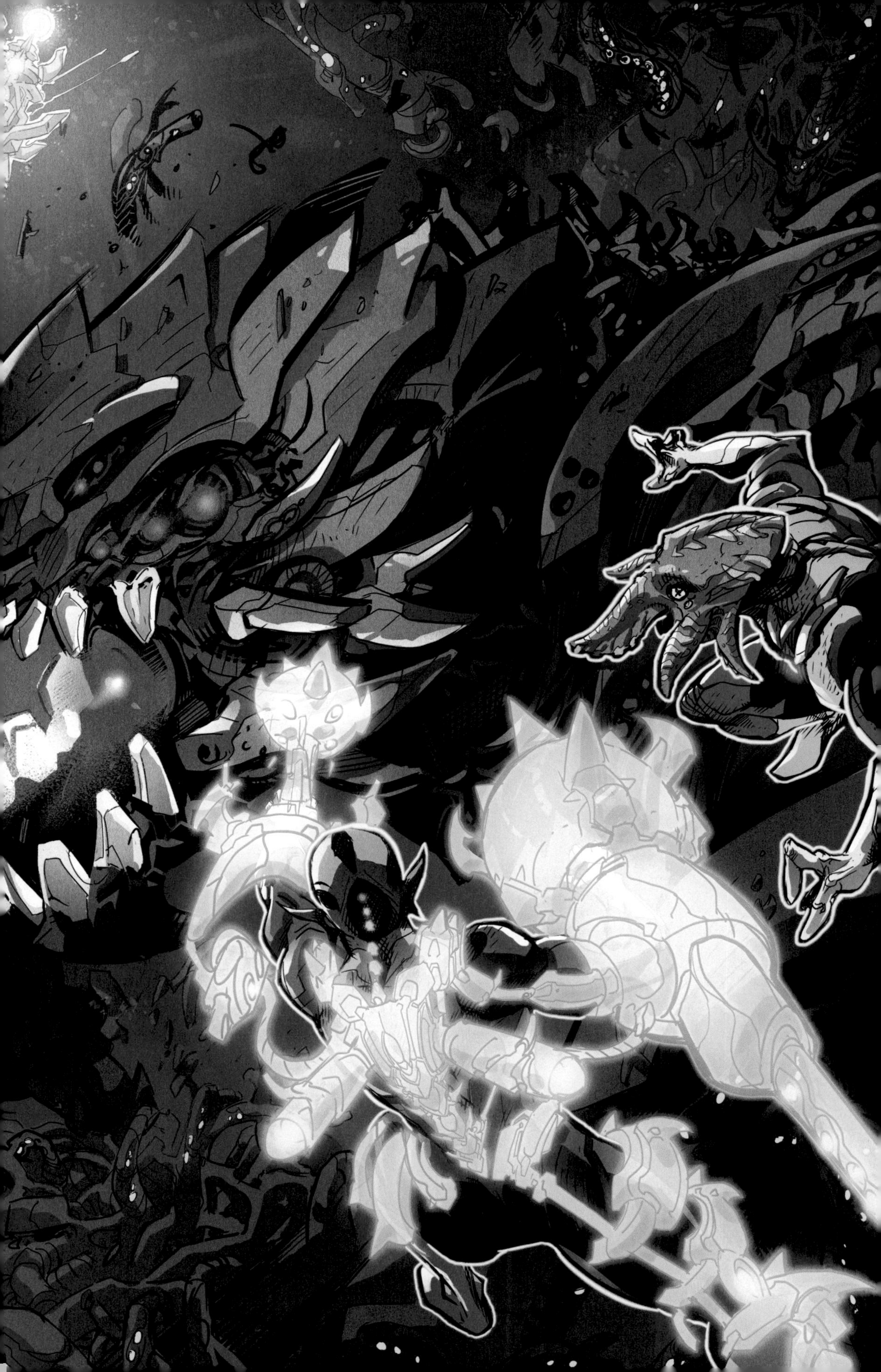

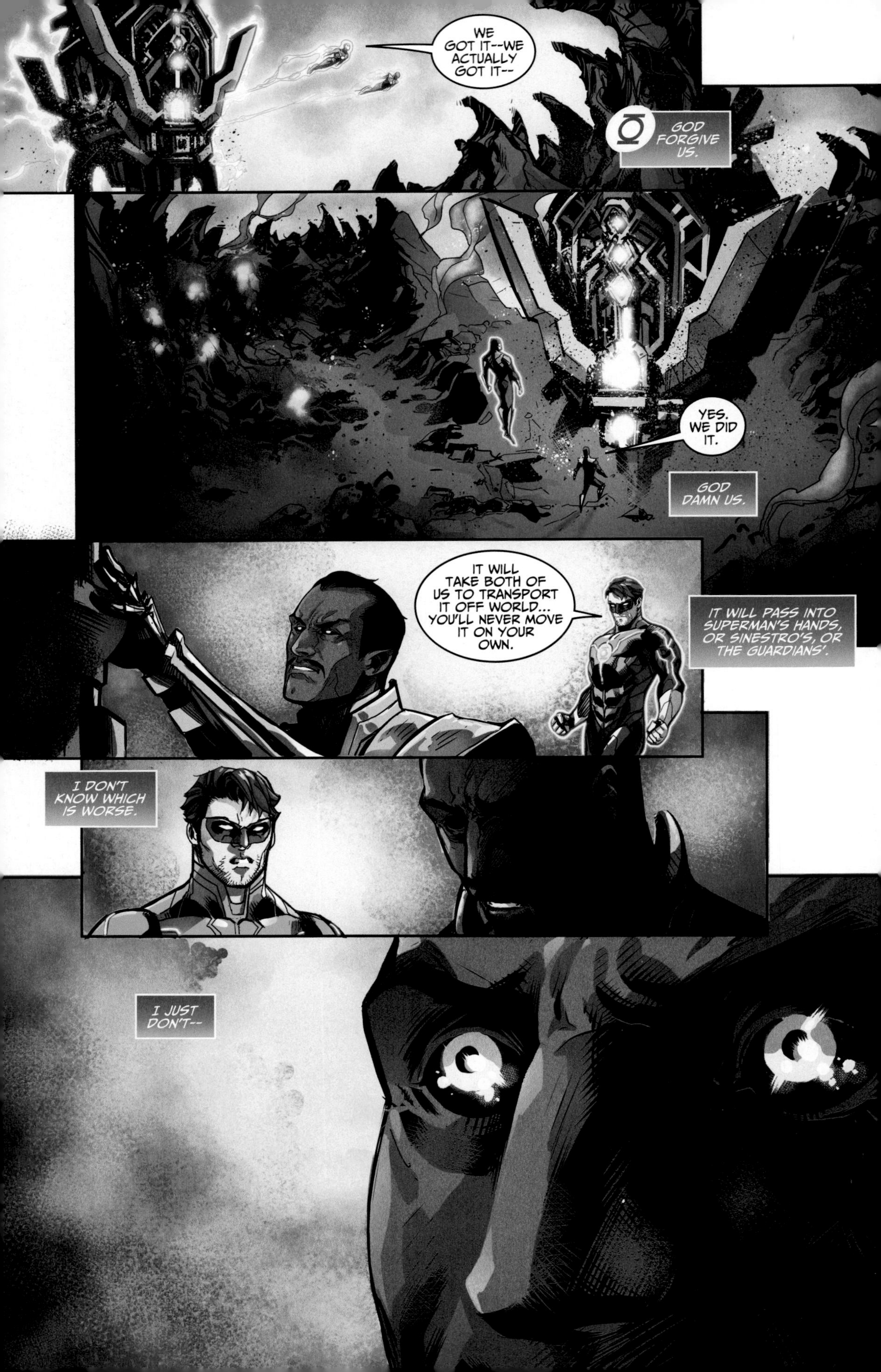
WE GOT IT--WE ACTUALLY GOT IT--
GOD FORGIVE US.
YES. WE DID IT.
GOD DAMN US.
IT WILL TAKE BOTH OF US TO TRANSPORT IT OFF WORLD... YOU'LL NEVER MOVE IT ON YOUR OWN.
IT WILL PASS INTO SUPERMAN'S HANDS, OR SINESTRO'S, OR THE GUARDIANS'.
I DON'T KNOW WHICH IS WORSE.
I JUST DON'T--

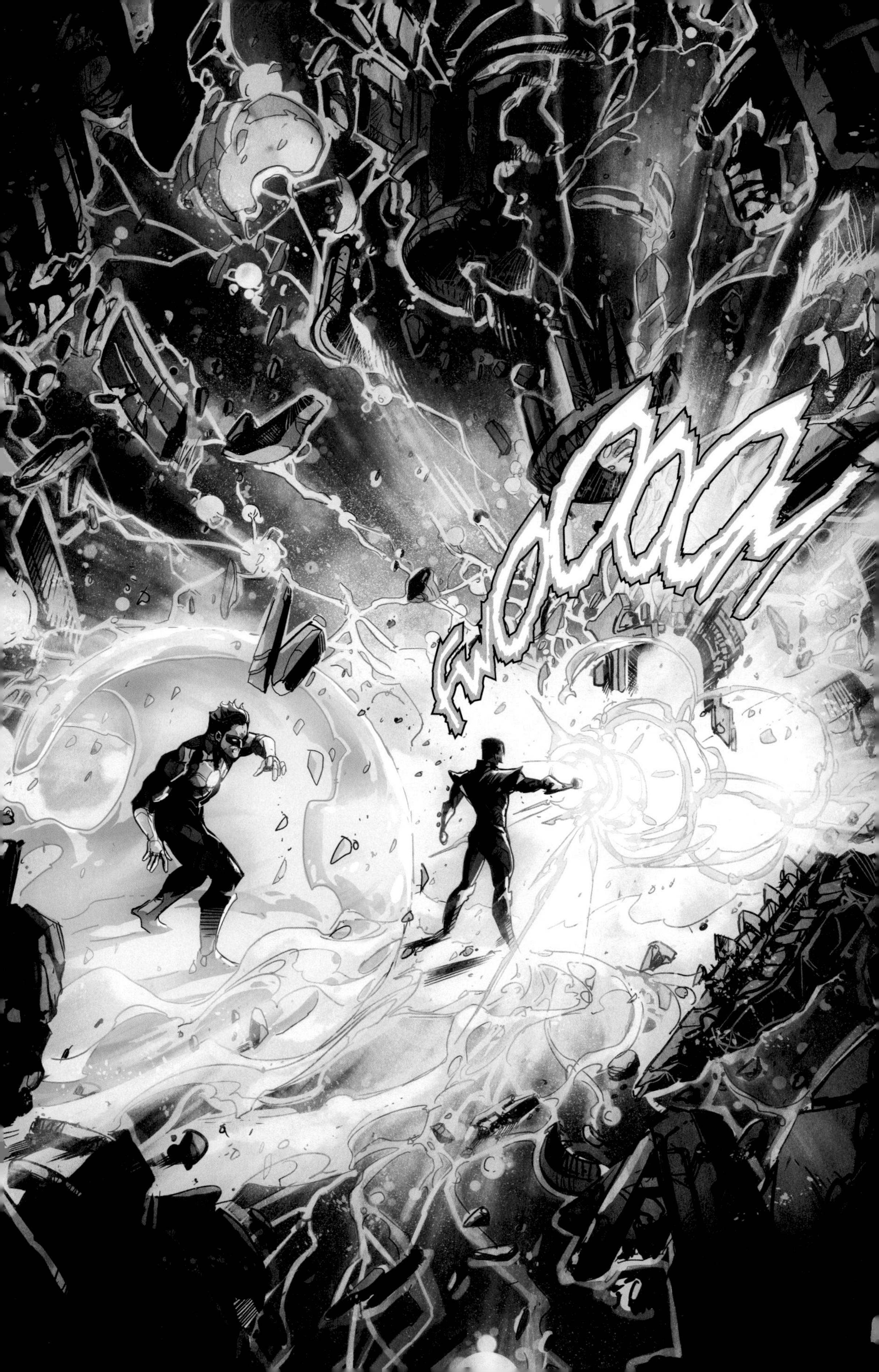

YOU... *YOU*, OF ALL PEOPLE...

NO ONE CAN USE IT NOW.

YOU WERE WORRIED, WEREN'T YOU? THAT LITTLE TANG OF NOT-*QUITE*-FEAR...

WERE YOU MORE AFRAID OF WHAT THE UR-FORGE WOULD DO IN THE GUARDIANS' HANDS, SUPERMAN'S... OR MINE?

HOW COULD I BE AFRAID...

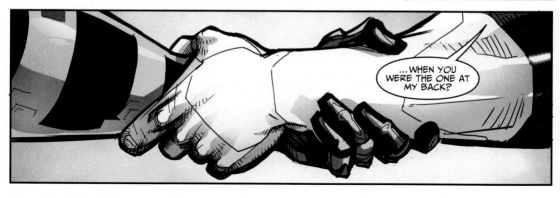

...WHEN YOU WERE THE ONE AT MY BACK?

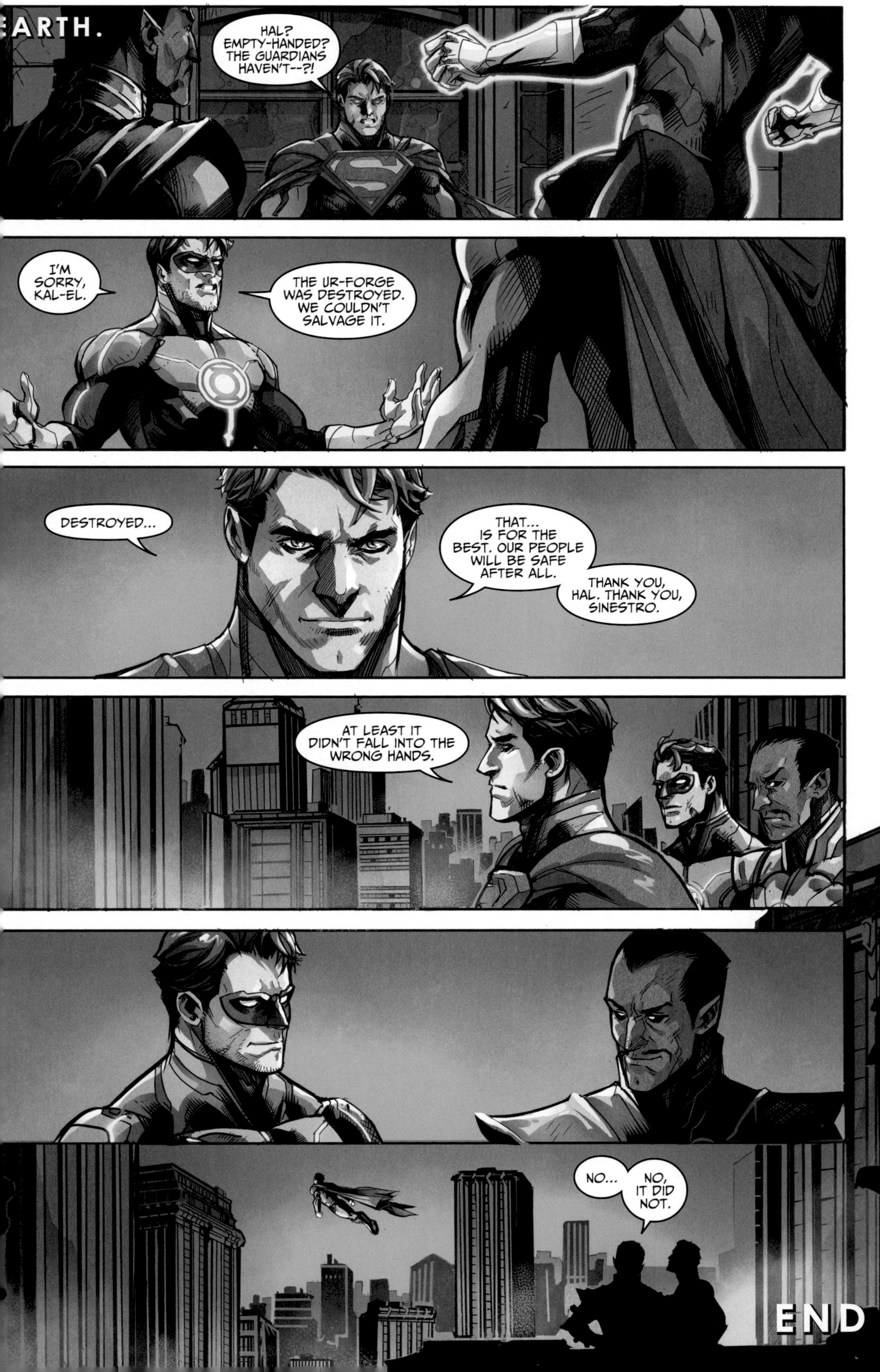
EARTH.
HAL? EMPTY-HANDED? THE GUARDIANS HAVEN'T--?!
I'M SORRY, KAL-EL.
THE UR-FORGE WAS DESTROYED. WE COULDN'T SALVAGE IT.
DESTROYED...
THAT... IS FOR THE BEST. OUR PEOPLE WILL BE SAFE AFTER ALL.
THANK YOU, HAL. THANK YOU, SINESTRO.
AT LEAST IT DIDN'T FALL INTO THE WRONG HANDS.
NO...
NO, IT DID NOT.
END

"War Is Coming" **Bruno Redondo** **Julien Hugonnard-Bert** Artists
"One Day More" **Xermanico** Artist
Rex Lokus Colorist Cover Art by **Jheremy Raapack & David Lopez** and **Santi Casas of Ikari Studio**

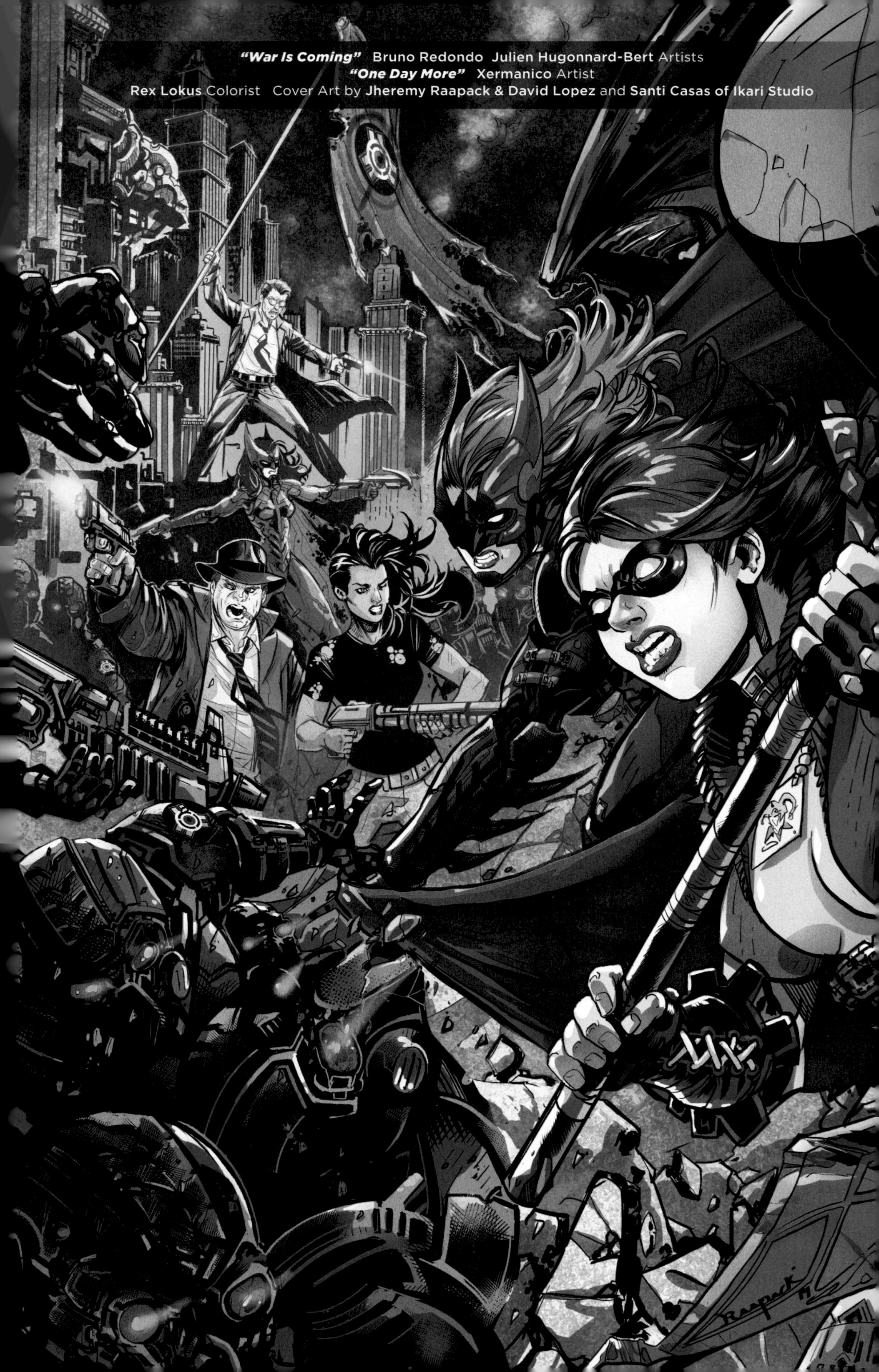

THIS SHOULD HURT. I KNOW IT SHOULD. BUT IT DOESN'T ANYMORE.

I'M TRYING TO SPEAK BUT THERE'S NOTHING TO SAY.

DINAH?

DINAH. IT'S A BOY.

CONNOR.

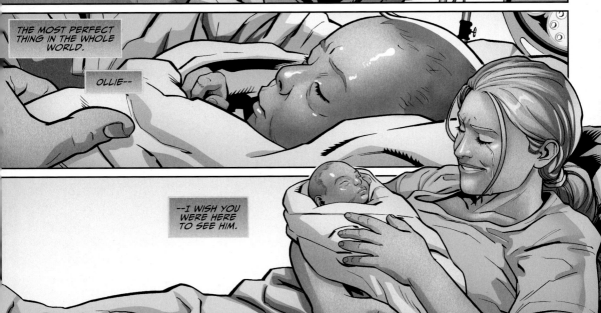

THE MOST PERFECT THING IN THE WHOLE WORLD.

OLLIE--

--I WISH YOU WERE HERE TO SEE HIM.

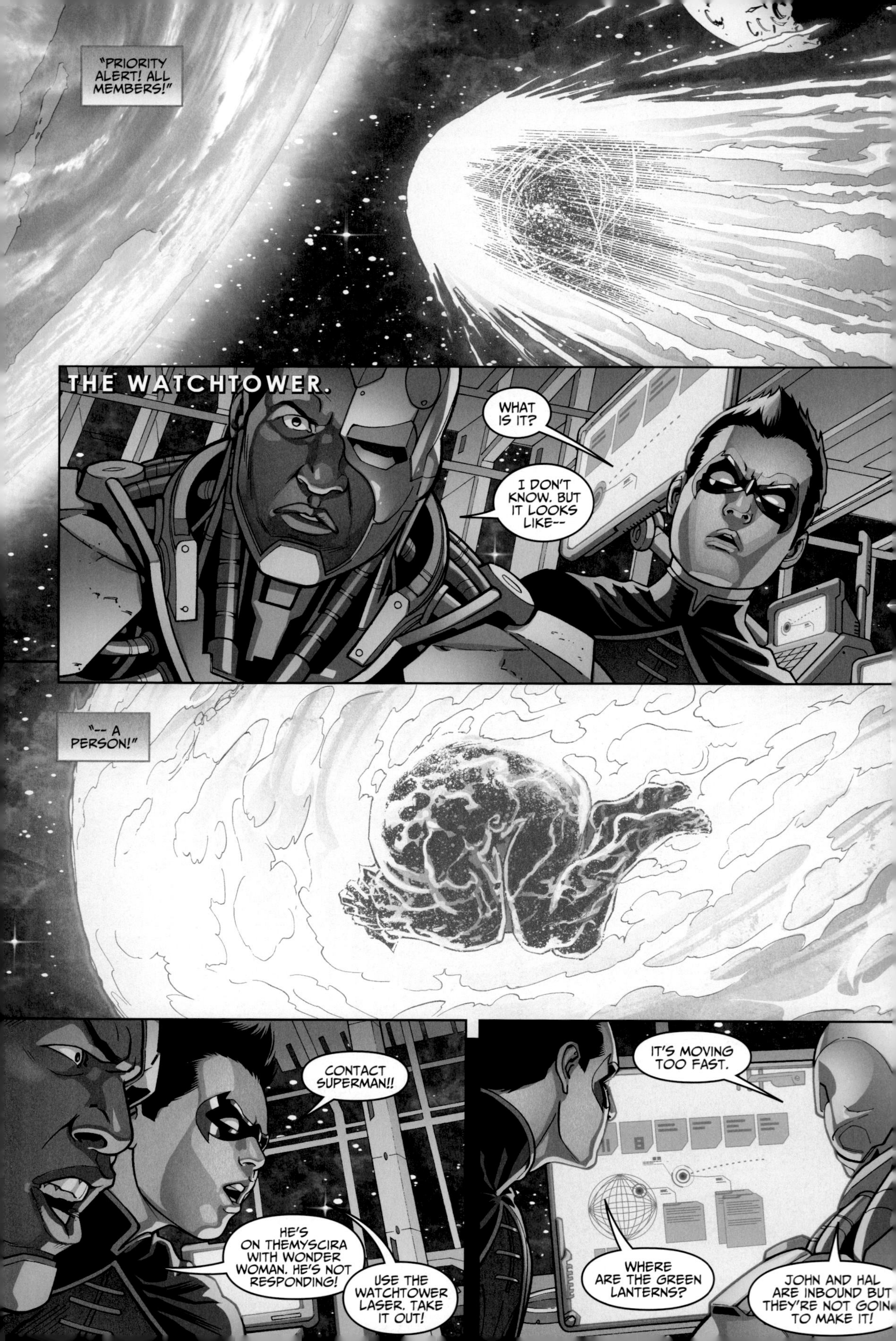
"PRIORITY ALERT! ALL MEMBERS!"
THE WATCHTOWER.
WHAT IS IT?
I DON'T KNOW. BUT IT LOOKS LIKE--
"-- A PERSON!"
CONTACT SUPERMAN!!
HE'S ON THEMYSCIRA WITH WONDER WOMAN. HE'S NOT RESPONDING!
USE THE WATCHTOWER LASER. TAKE IT OUT!
IT'S MOVING TOO FAST.
WHERE ARE THE GREEN LANTERNS?
JOHN AND HAL ARE INBOUND BUT THEY'RE NOT GOIN TO MAKE IT!

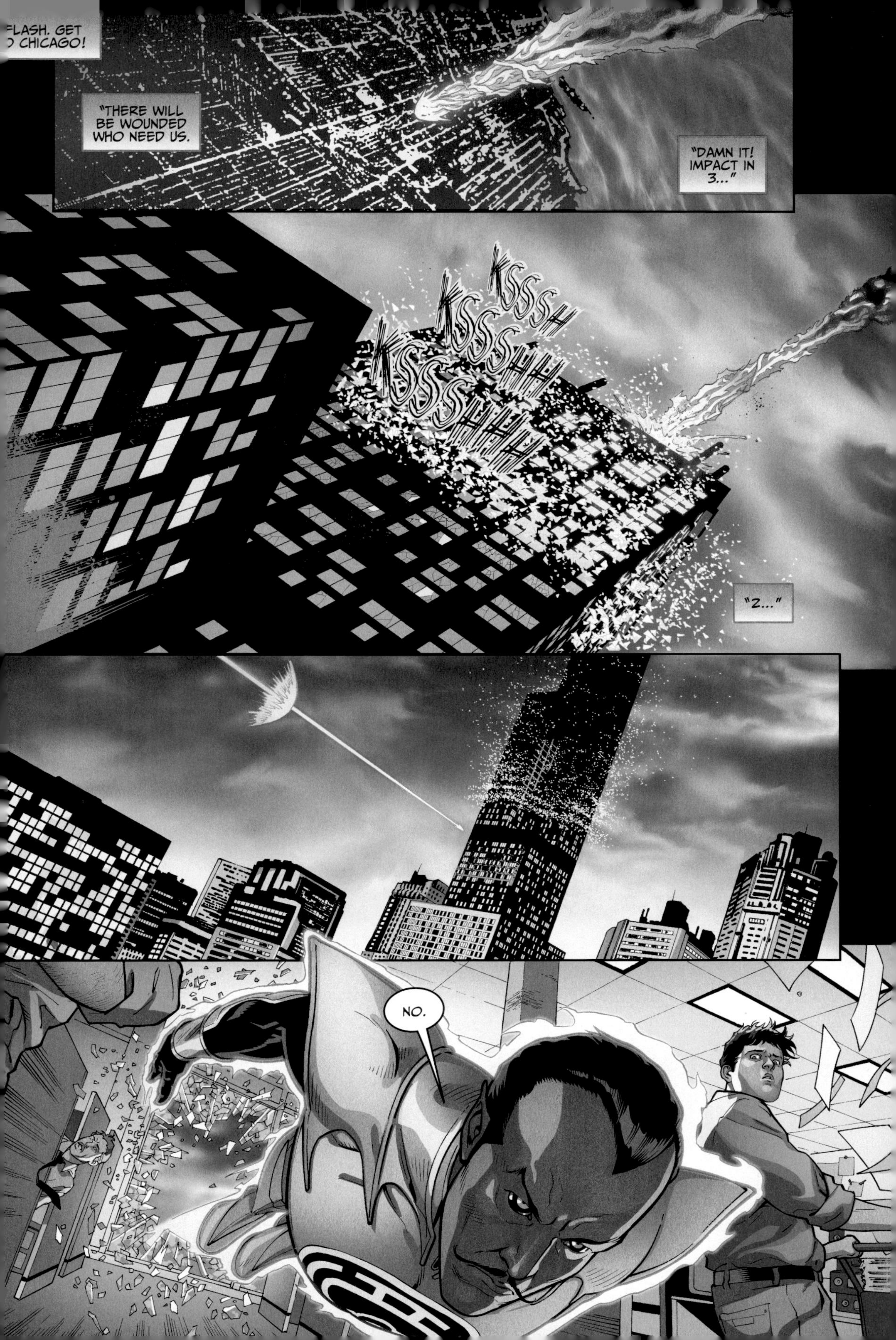
FLASH. GET
O CHICAGO!
"THERE WILL
BE WOUNDED
WHO NEED US.
"DAMN IT!
IMPACT IN
3..."
KSSSH
KSSSHH
KSSSHHH
"2..."
NO.

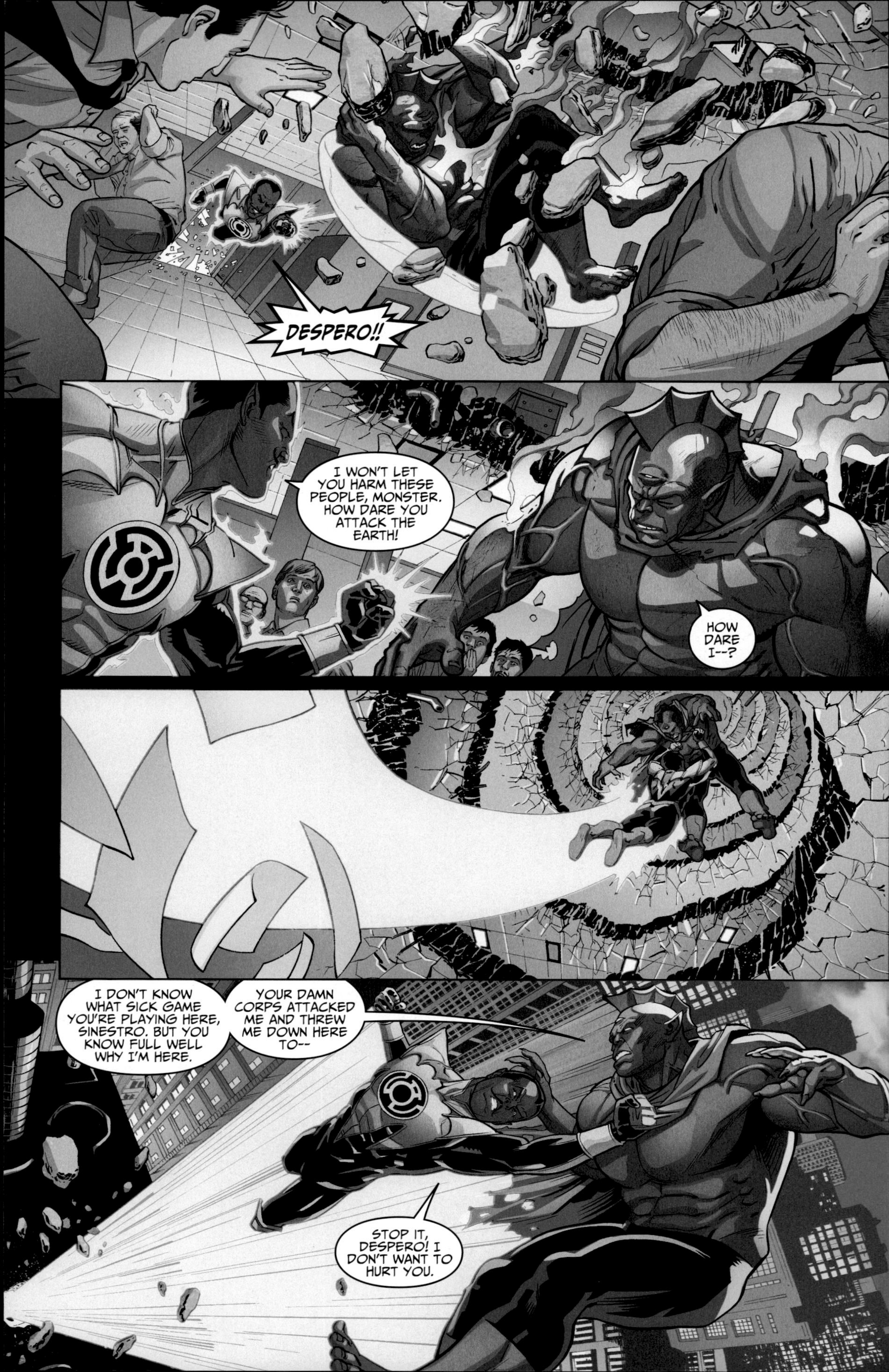
DESPERO!!
I WON'T LET YOU HARM THESE PEOPLE, MONSTER. HOW DARE YOU ATTACK THE EARTH!
HOW DARE I--?
I DON'T KNOW WHAT SICK GAME YOU'RE PLAYING HERE, SINESTRO. BUT YOU KNOW FULL WELL WHY I'M HERE.
YOUR DAMN CORPS ATTACKED ME AND THREW ME DOWN HERE TO--
STOP IT, DESPERO! I DON'T WANT TO HURT YOU.

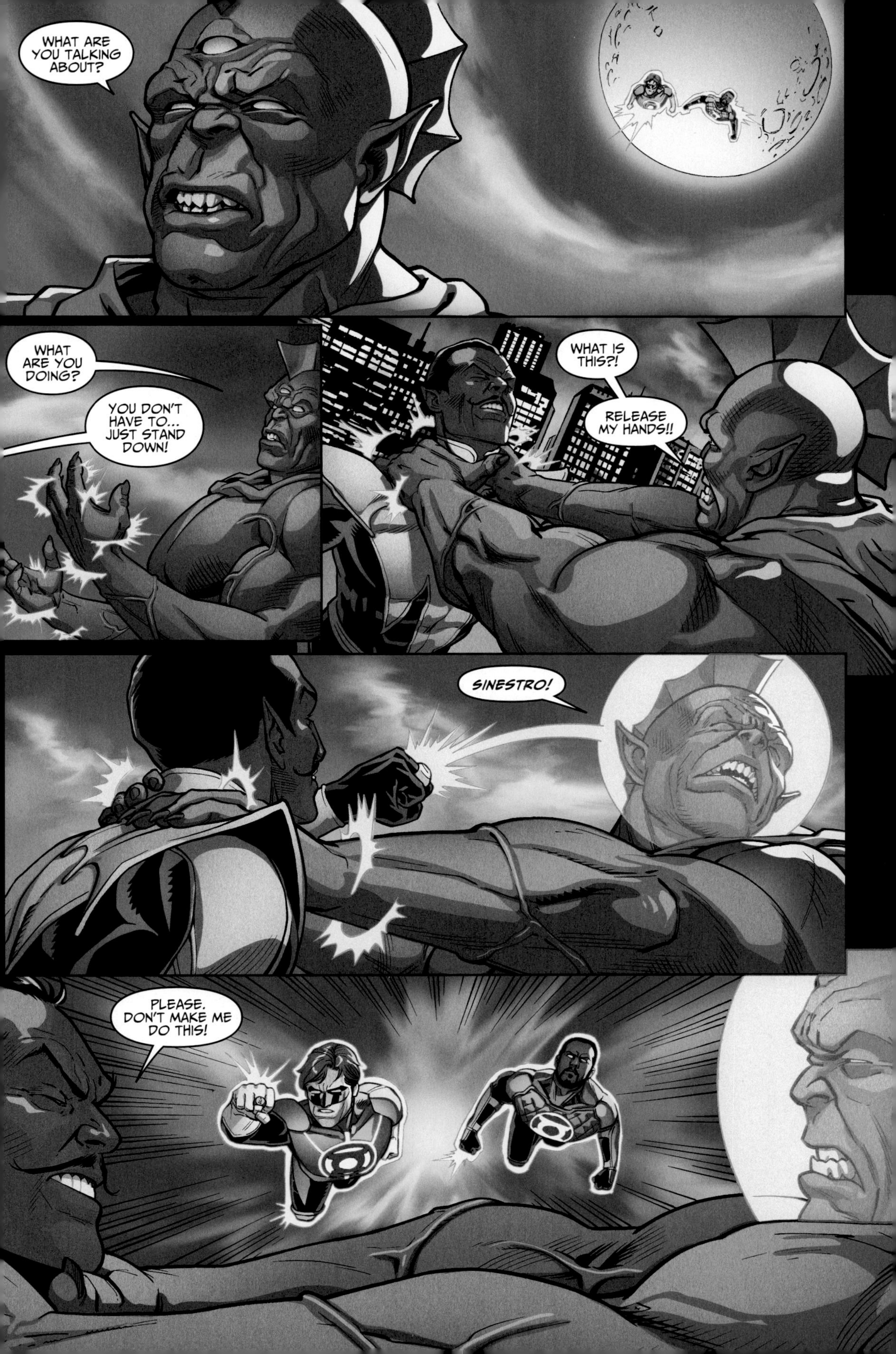
WHAT ARE YOU TALKING ABOUT?
WHAT ARE YOU DOING?
YOU DON'T HAVE TO... JUST STAND DOWN!
WHAT IS THIS?!
RELEASE MY HANDS!!
SINESTRO!
PLEASE. DON'T MAKE ME DO THIS!

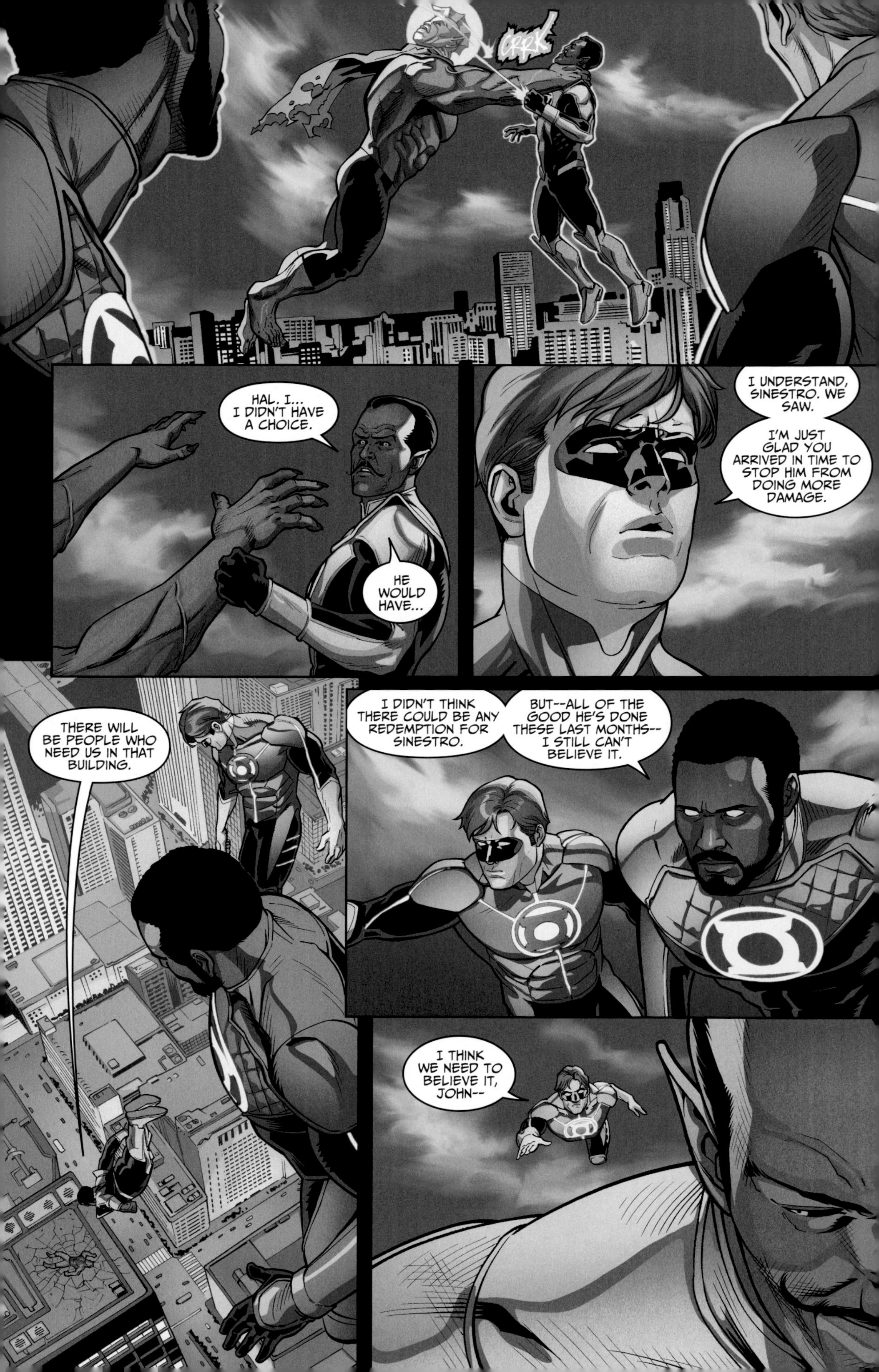
CRRK
HAL. I... I DIDN'T HAVE A CHOICE.
HE WOULD HAVE...
I UNDERSTAND, SINESTRO. WE SAW.
I'M JUST GLAD YOU ARRIVED IN TIME TO STOP HIM FROM DOING MORE DAMAGE.
THERE WILL BE PEOPLE WHO NEED US IN THAT BUILDING.
I DIDN'T THINK THERE COULD BE ANY REDEMPTION FOR SINESTRO.
BUT--ALL OF THE GOOD HE'S DONE THESE LAST MONTHS-- I STILL CAN'T BELIEVE IT.
I THINK WE NEED TO BELIEVE IT, JOHN--

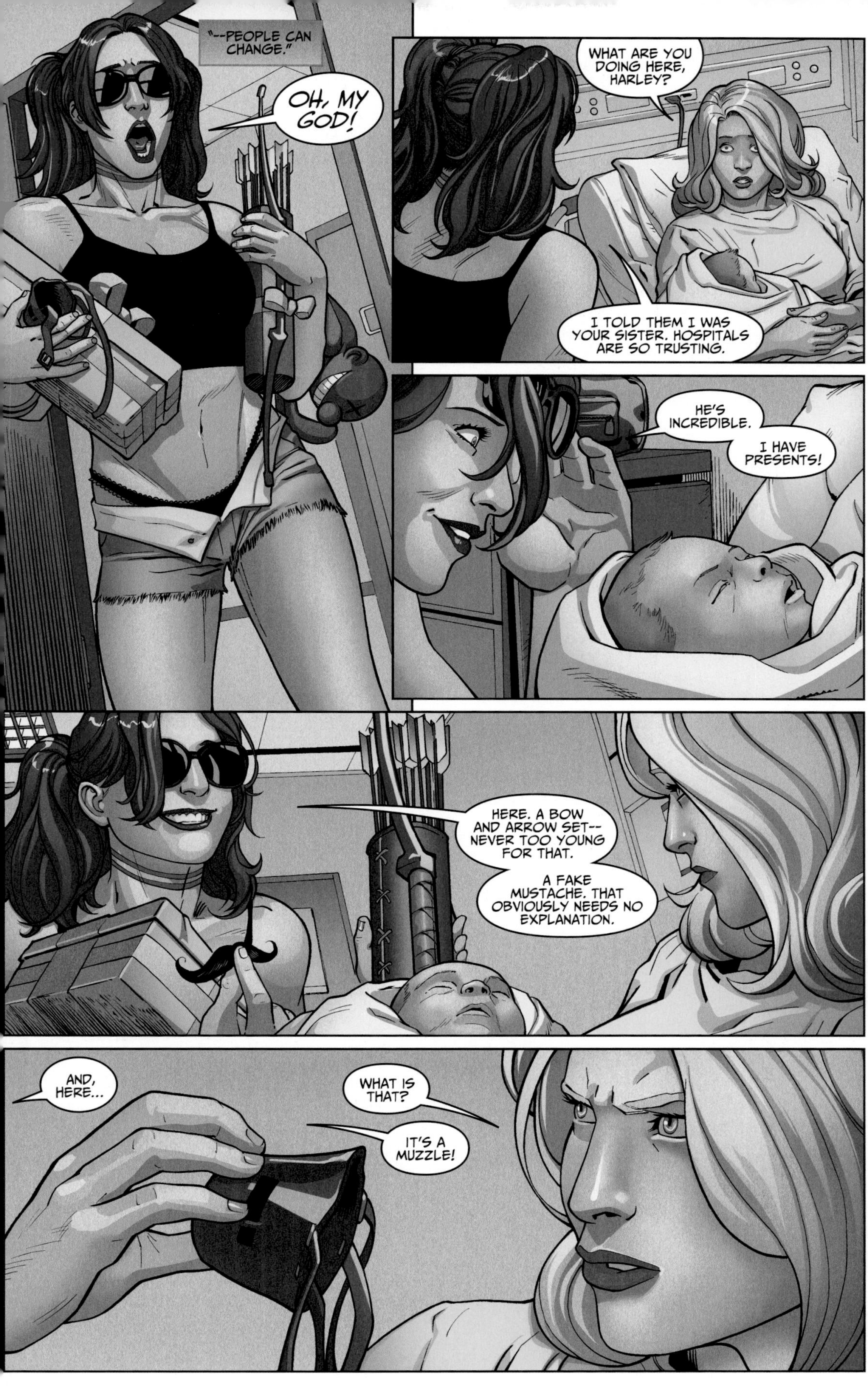
"--PEOPLE CAN CHANGE."
OH, MY GOD!
WHAT ARE YOU DOING HERE, HARLEY?
I TOLD THEM I WAS YOUR SISTER. HOSPITALS ARE SO TRUSTING.
HE'S INCREDIBLE.
I HAVE PRESENTS!
HERE. A BOW AND ARROW SET-- NEVER TOO YOUNG FOR THAT.
A FAKE MUSTACHE. THAT OBVIOUSLY NEEDS NO EXPLANATION.
AND, HERE...
WHAT IS THAT?
IT'S A MUZZLE!

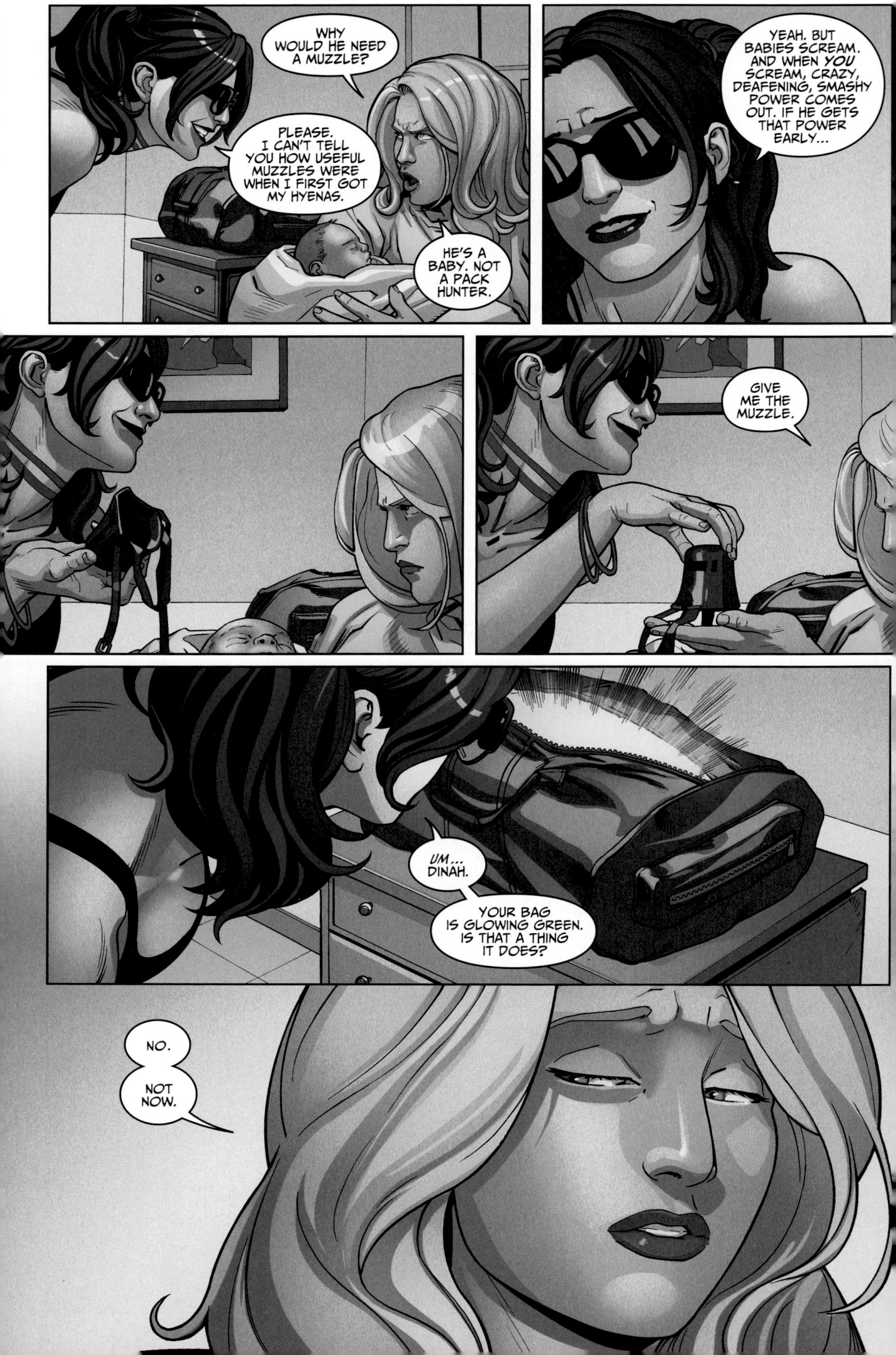

WHY WOULD HE NEED A MUZZLE?
PLEASE. I CAN'T TELL YOU HOW USEFUL MUZZLES WERE WHEN I FIRST GOT MY HYENAS.
HE'S A BABY. NOT A PACK HUNTER.
YEAH. BUT BABIES SCREAM. AND WHEN *YOU* SCREAM, CRAZY, DEAFENING, SMASHY POWER COMES OUT. IF HE GETS THAT POWER EARLY...
GIVE ME THE MUZZLE.
UM... DINAH.
YOUR BAG IS GLOWING GREEN. IS THAT A THING IT DOES?
NO.
NOT NOW.

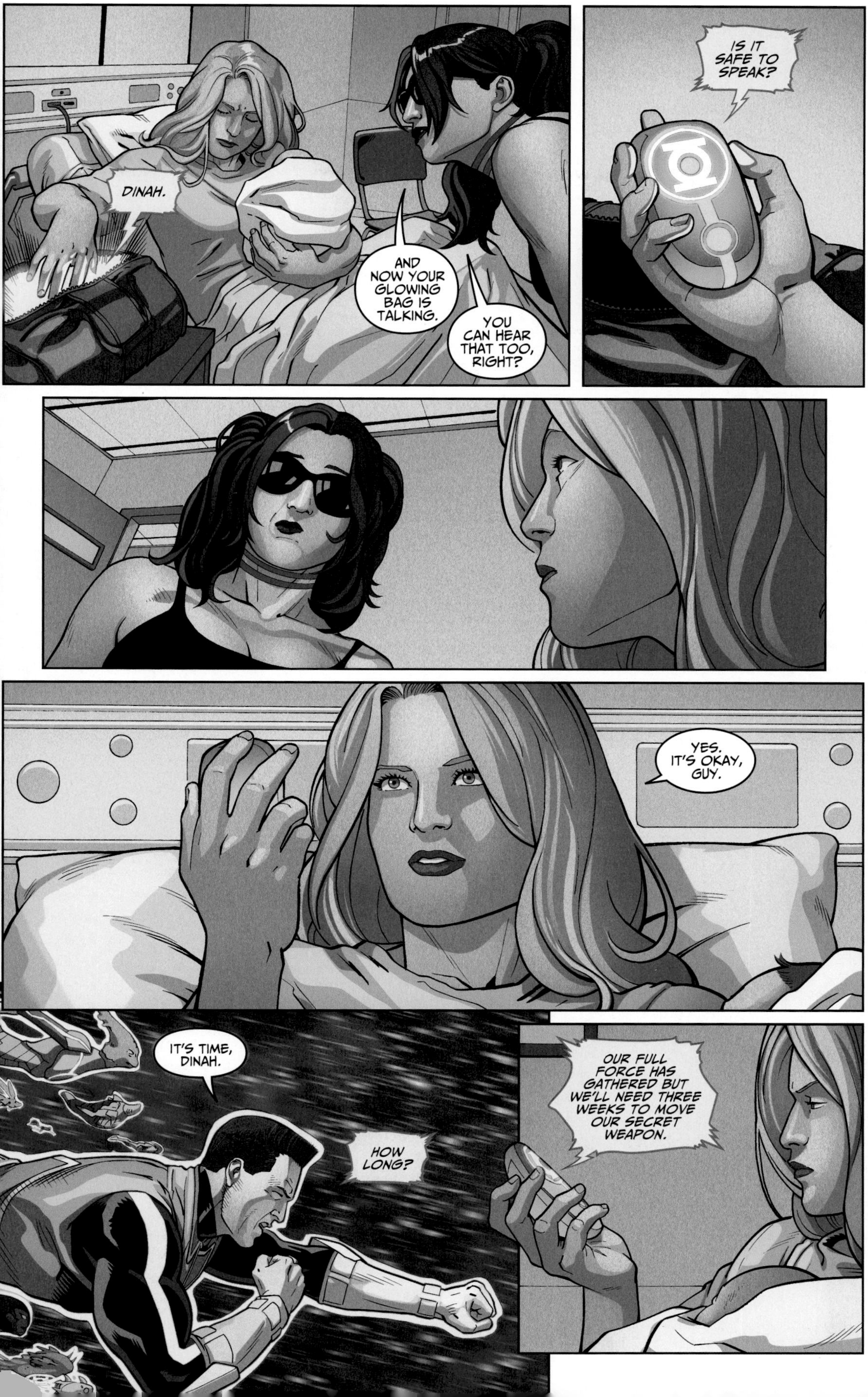
DINAH.
AND NOW YOUR GLOWING BAG IS TALKING.
YOU CAN HEAR THAT TOO, RIGHT?
IS IT SAFE TO SPEAK?
YES. IT'S OKAY, GUY.
IT'S TIME, DINAH.
HOW LONG?
OUR FULL FORCE HAS GATHERED BUT WE'LL NEED THREE WEEKS TO MOVE OUR SECRET WEAPON.

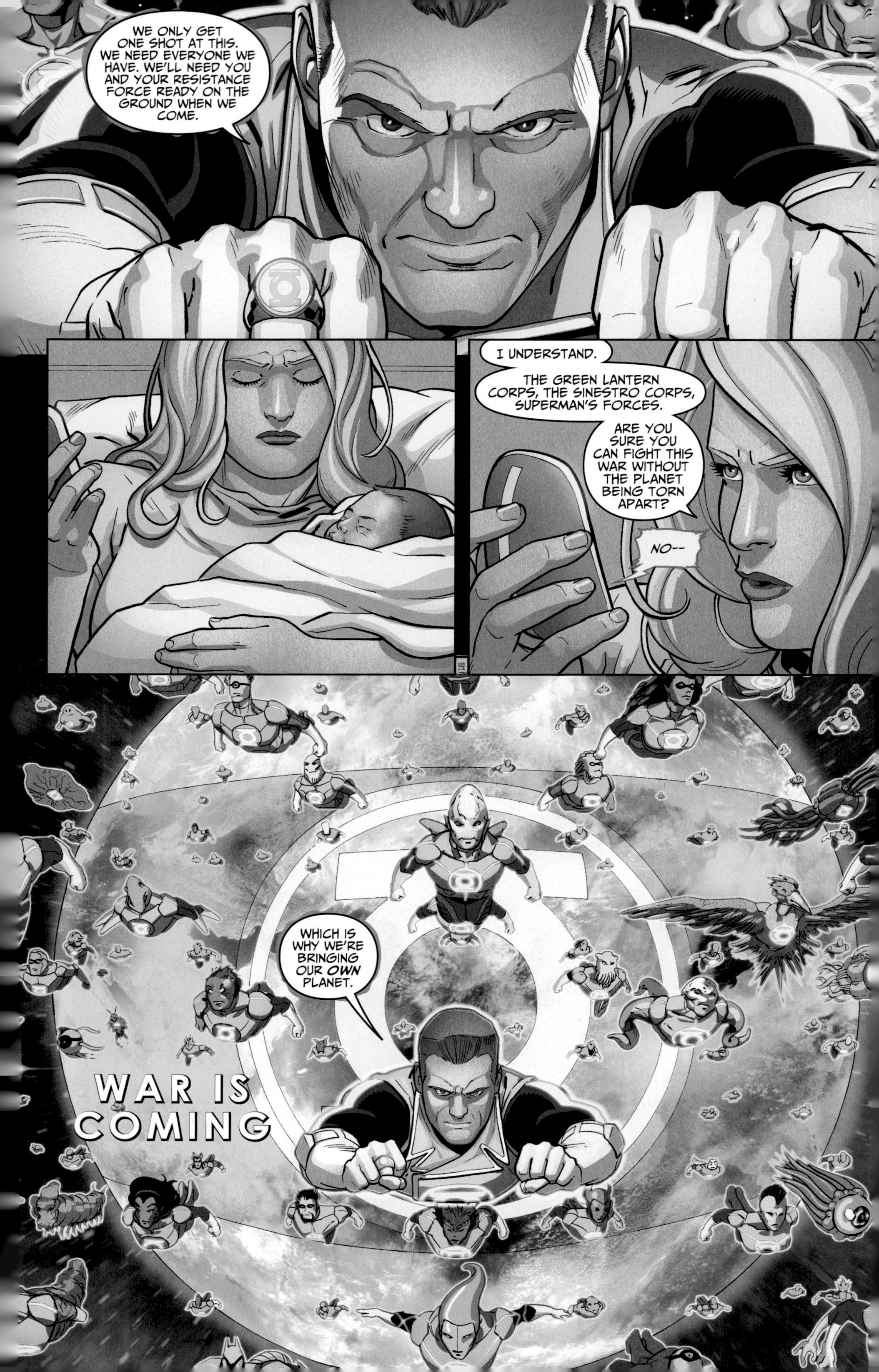
WE ONLY GET ONE SHOT AT THIS. WE NEED EVERYONE WE HAVE. WE'LL NEED YOU AND YOUR RESISTANCE FORCE READY ON THE GROUND WHEN WE COME.
I UNDERSTAND.
THE GREEN LANTERN CORPS, THE SINESTRO CORPS, SUPERMAN'S FORCES.
ARE YOU SURE YOU CAN FIGHT THIS WAR WITHOUT THE PLANET BEING TORN APART?
NO--
WHICH IS WHY WE'RE BRINGING OUR OWN PLANET.
WAR IS COMING

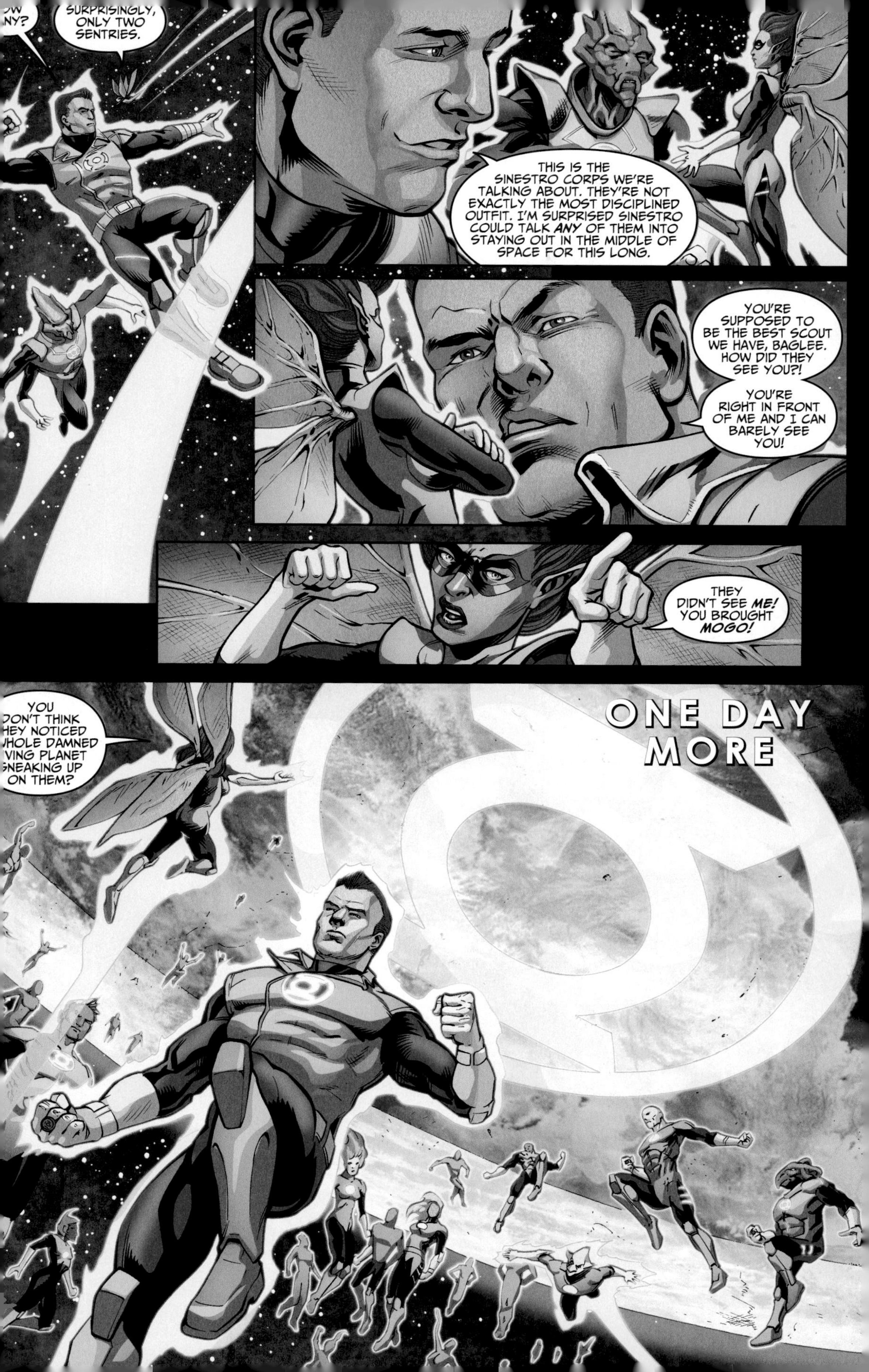
SURPRISINGLY, ONLY TWO SENTRIES.
THIS IS THE SINESTRO CORPS WE'RE TALKING ABOUT. THEY'RE NOT EXACTLY THE MOST DISCIPLINED OUTFIT. I'M SURPRISED SINESTRO COULD TALK ANY OF THEM INTO STAYING OUT IN THE MIDDLE OF SPACE FOR THIS LONG.
YOU'RE SUPPOSED TO BE THE BEST SCOUT WE HAVE, BAGLEE. HOW DID THEY SEE YOU?!
YOU'RE RIGHT IN FRONT OF ME AND I CAN BARELY SEE YOU!
THEY DIDN'T SEE ME! YOU BROUGHT MOGO!
ONE DAY MORE

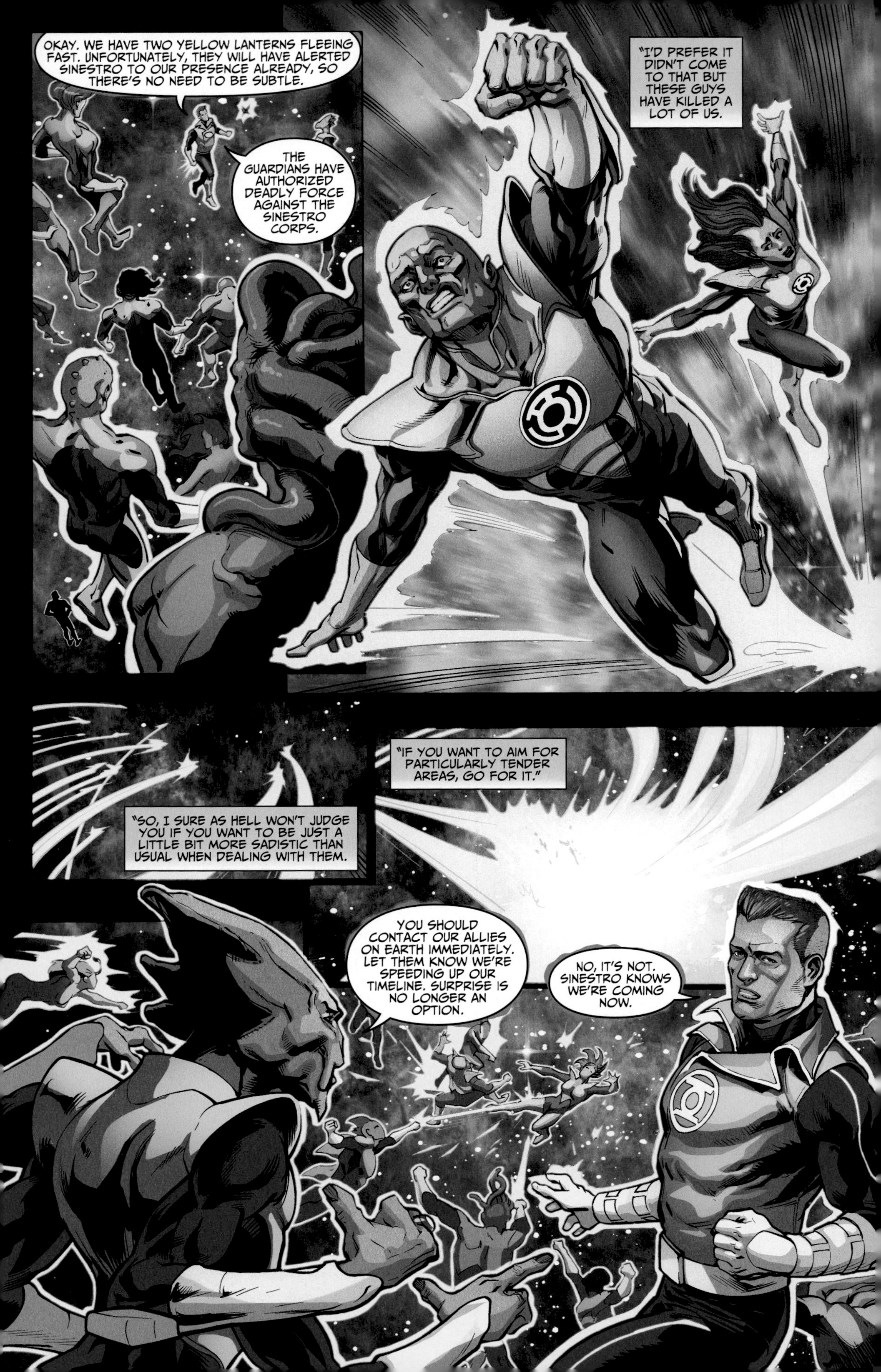
OKAY. WE HAVE TWO YELLOW LANTERNS FLEEING FAST. UNFORTUNATELY, THEY WILL HAVE ALERTED SINESTRO TO OUR PRESENCE ALREADY, SO THERE'S NO NEED TO BE SUBTLE.
THE GUARDIANS HAVE AUTHORIZED DEADLY FORCE AGAINST THE SINESTRO CORPS.
"I'D PREFER IT DIDN'T COME TO THAT BUT THESE GUYS HAVE KILLED A LOT OF US.
"SO, I SURE AS HELL WON'T JUDGE YOU IF YOU WANT TO BE JUST A LITTLE BIT MORE SADISTIC THAN USUAL WHEN DEALING WITH THEM.
"IF YOU WANT TO AIM FOR PARTICULARLY TENDER AREAS, GO FOR IT."
YOU SHOULD CONTACT OUR ALLIES ON EARTH IMMEDIATELY. LET THEM KNOW WE'RE SPEEDING UP OUR TIMELINE. SURPRISE IS NO LONGER AN OPTION.
NO, IT'S NOT. SINESTRO KNOWS WE'RE COMING NOW.

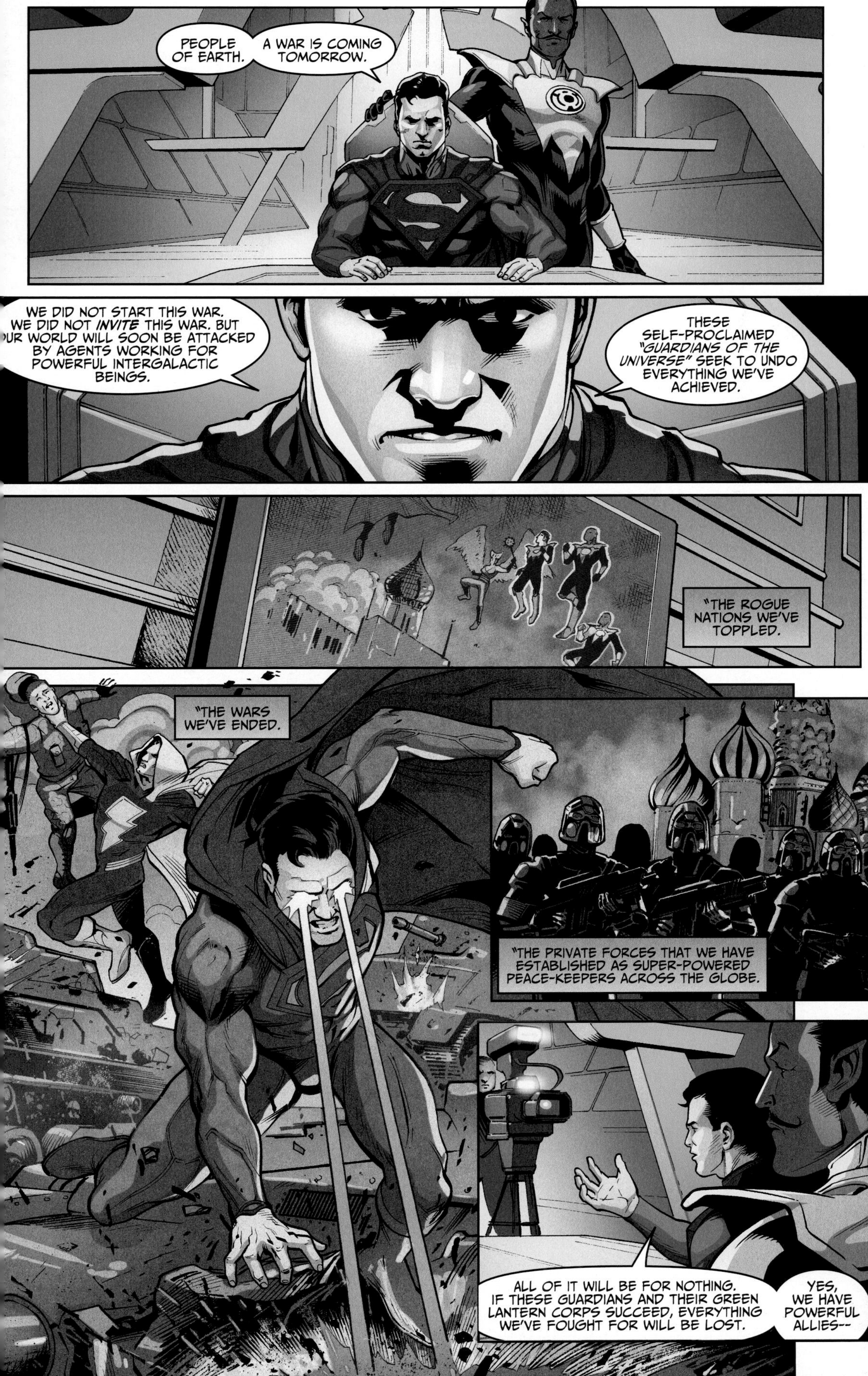

PEOPLE OF EARTH.
A WAR IS COMING TOMORROW.
WE DID NOT START THIS WAR. WE DID NOT *INVITE* THIS WAR. BUT OUR WORLD WILL SOON BE ATTACKED BY AGENTS WORKING FOR POWERFUL INTERGALACTIC BEINGS.
THESE SELF-PROCLAIMED *"GUARDIANS OF THE UNIVERSE"* SEEK TO UNDO EVERYTHING WE'VE ACHIEVED.
"THE ROGUE NATIONS WE'VE TOPPLED.
"THE WARS WE'VE ENDED.
"THE PRIVATE FORCES THAT WE HAVE ESTABLISHED AS SUPER-POWERED PEACE-KEEPERS ACROSS THE GLOBE.
ALL OF IT WILL BE FOR NOTHING. IF THESE GUARDIANS AND THEIR GREEN LANTERN CORPS SUCCEED, EVERYTHING WE'VE FOUGHT FOR WILL BE LOST.
YES, WE HAVE POWERFUL ALLIES--

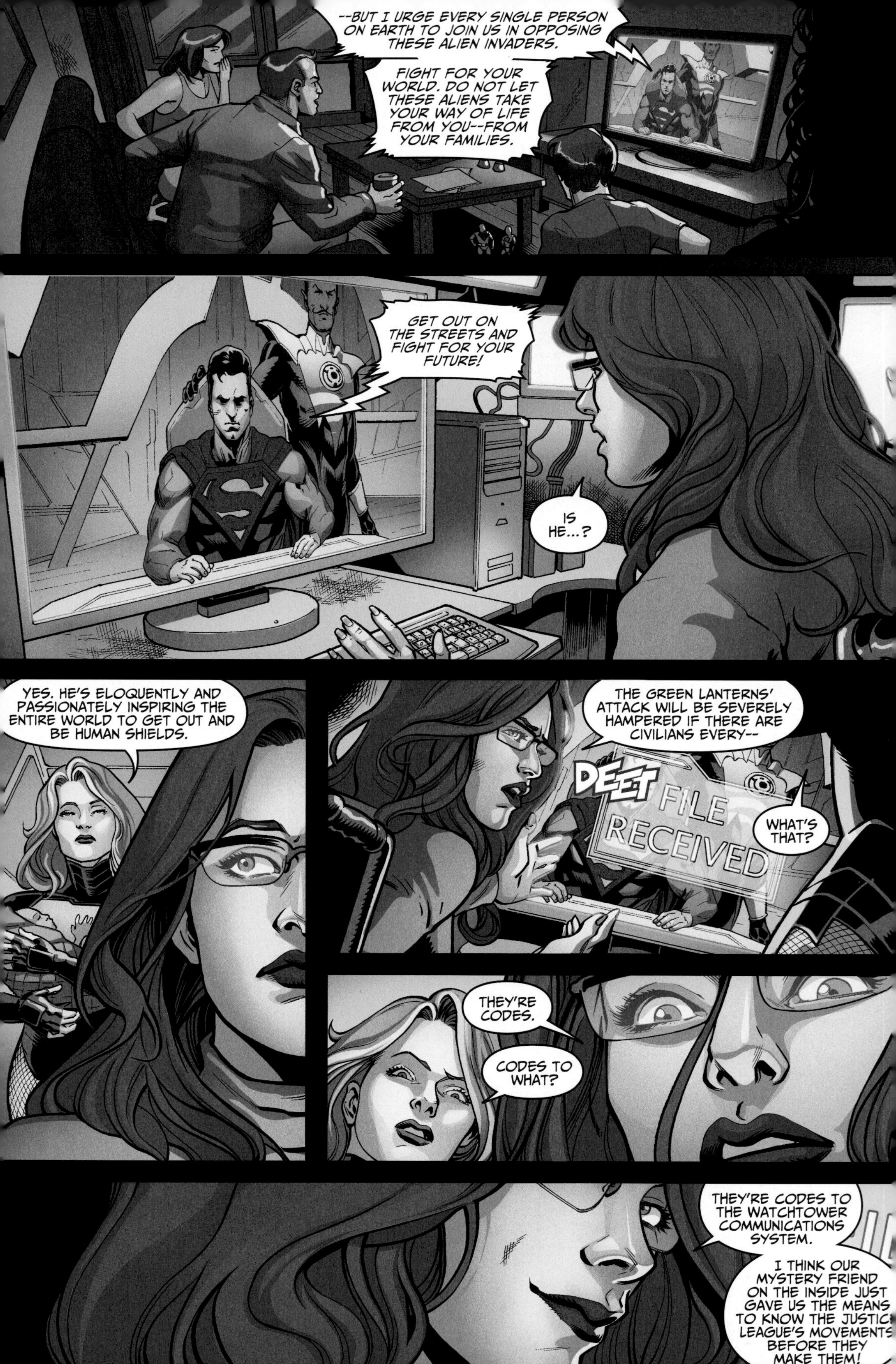
--BUT I URGE EVERY SINGLE PERSON ON EARTH TO JOIN US IN OPPOSING THESE ALIEN INVADERS.
FIGHT FOR YOUR WORLD. DO NOT LET THESE ALIENS TAKE YOUR WAY OF LIFE FROM YOU--FROM YOUR FAMILIES.
GET OUT ON THE STREETS AND FIGHT FOR YOUR FUTURE!
IS HE...?
YES. HE'S ELOQUENTLY AND PASSIONATELY INSPIRING THE ENTIRE WORLD TO GET OUT AND BE HUMAN SHIELDS.
THE GREEN LANTERNS' ATTACK WILL BE SEVERELY HAMPERED IF THERE ARE CIVILIANS EVERY--
DEET
FILE RECEIVED
WHAT'S THAT?
THEY'RE CODES.
CODES TO WHAT?
THEY'RE CODES TO THE WATCHTOWER COMMUNICATIONS SYSTEM.
I THINK OUR MYSTERY FRIEND ON THE INSIDE JUST GAVE US THE MEANS TO KNOW THE JUSTICE LEAGUE'S MOVEMENTS BEFORE THEY MAKE THEM!

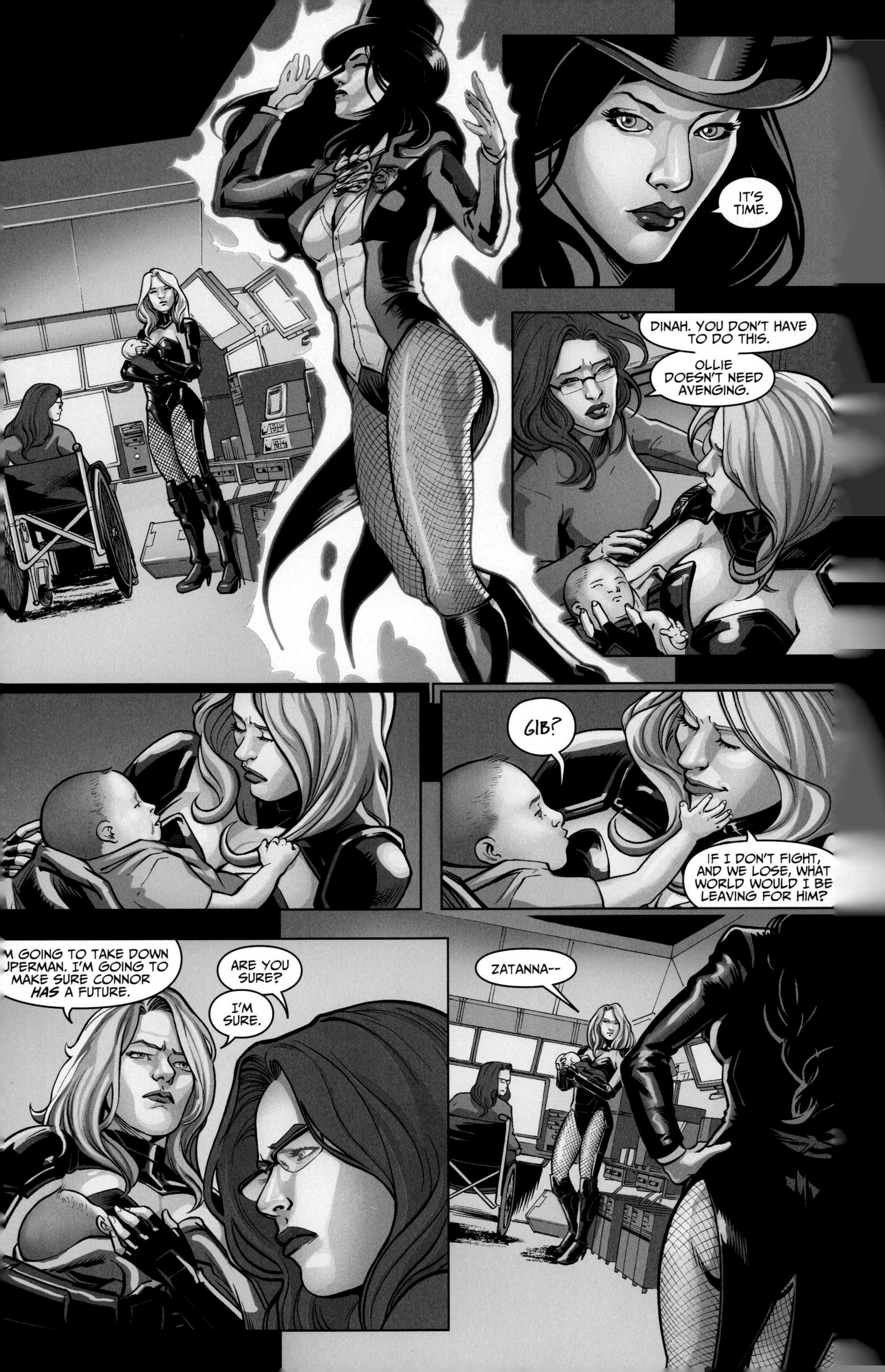
IT'S TIME.
DINAH. YOU DON'T HAVE TO DO THIS.
OLLIE DOESN'T NEED AVENGING.
GIB?
IF I DON'T FIGHT, AND WE LOSE, WHAT WORLD WOULD I BE LEAVING FOR HIM?
M GOING TO TAKE DOWN
UPERMAN. I'M GOING TO MAKE SURE CONNOR *HAS* A FUTURE.
ARE YOU SURE?
I'M SURE.
ZATANNA--

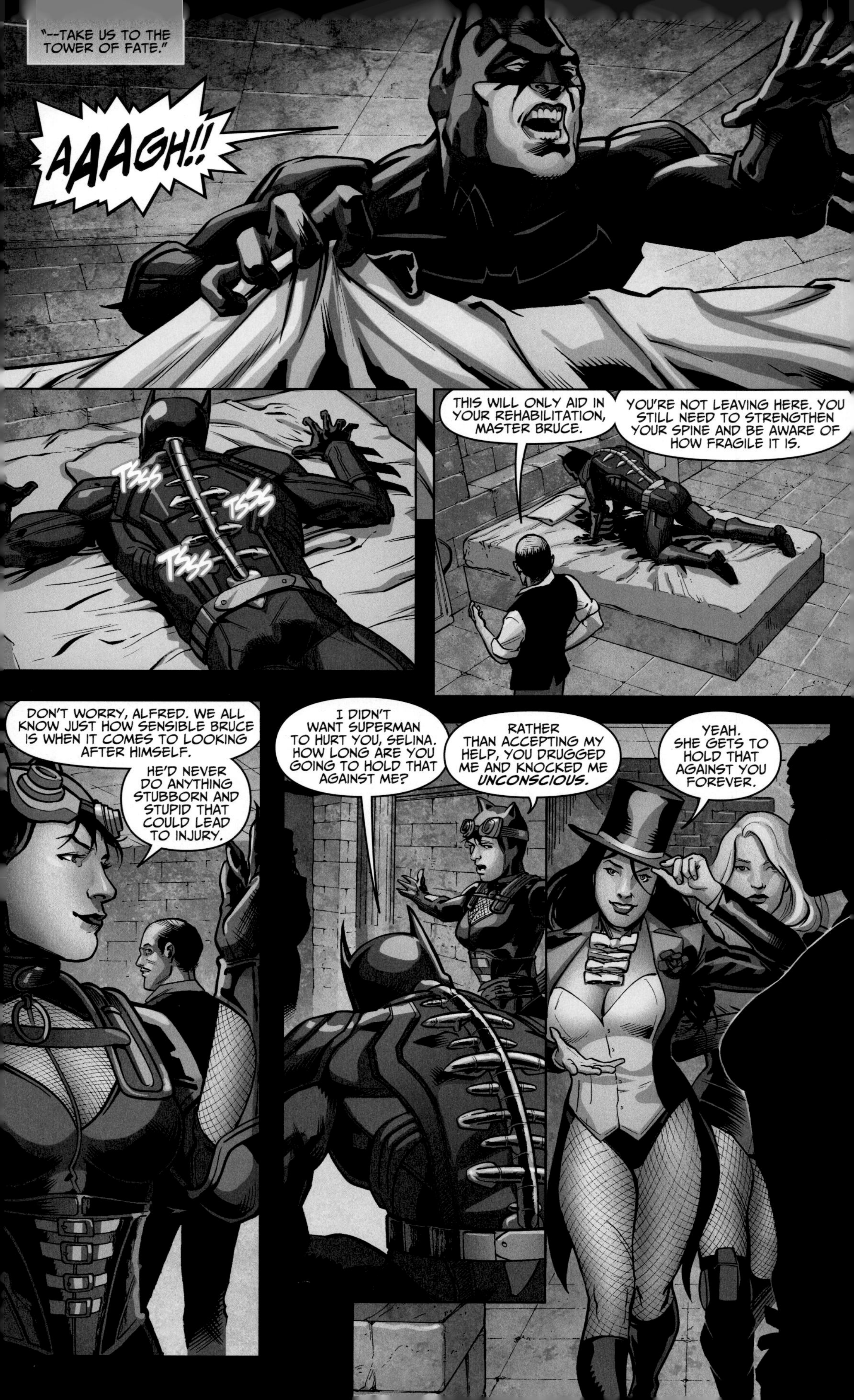
"--TAKE US TO THE TOWER OF FATE."
AAAGH!!
TSSS
TSSS
TSSS
THIS WILL ONLY AID IN YOUR REHABILITATION, MASTER BRUCE.
YOU'RE NOT LEAVING HERE. YOU STILL NEED TO STRENGTHEN YOUR SPINE AND BE AWARE OF HOW FRAGILE IT IS.
DON'T WORRY, ALFRED. WE ALL KNOW JUST HOW SENSIBLE BRUCE IS WHEN IT COMES TO LOOKING AFTER HIMSELF.
HE'D NEVER DO ANYTHING STUBBORN AND STUPID THAT COULD LEAD TO INJURY.
I DIDN'T WANT SUPERMAN TO HURT YOU, SELINA. HOW LONG ARE YOU GOING TO HOLD THAT AGAINST ME?
RATHER THAN ACCEPTING MY HELP, YOU DRUGGED ME AND KNOCKED ME *UNCONSCIOUS.*
YEAH. SHE GETS TO HOLD THAT AGAINST YOU FOREVER.

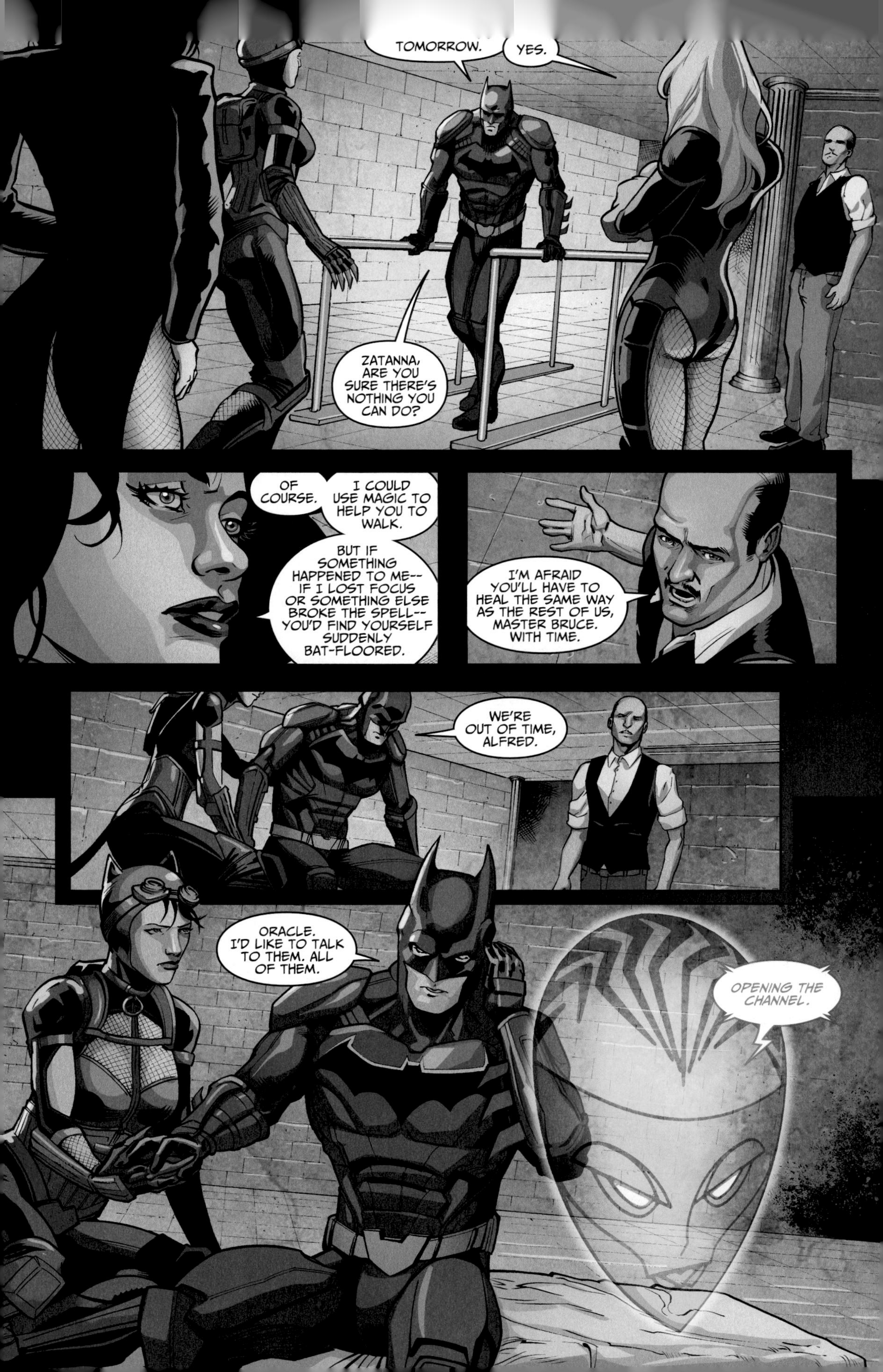
TOMORROW.
YES.
ZATANNA, ARE YOU SURE THERE'S NOTHING YOU CAN DO?
OF COURSE.
I COULD USE MAGIC TO HELP YOU TO WALK.
BUT IF SOMETHING HAPPENED TO ME-- IF I LOST FOCUS OR SOMETHING ELSE BROKE THE SPELL-- YOU'D FIND YOURSELF SUDDENLY BAT-FLOORED.
I'M AFRAID YOU'LL HAVE TO HEAL THE SAME WAY AS THE REST OF US, MASTER BRUCE. WITH TIME.
WE'RE OUT OF TIME, ALFRED.
ORACLE. I'D LIKE TO TALK TO THEM. ALL OF THEM.
OPENING THE CHANNEL.

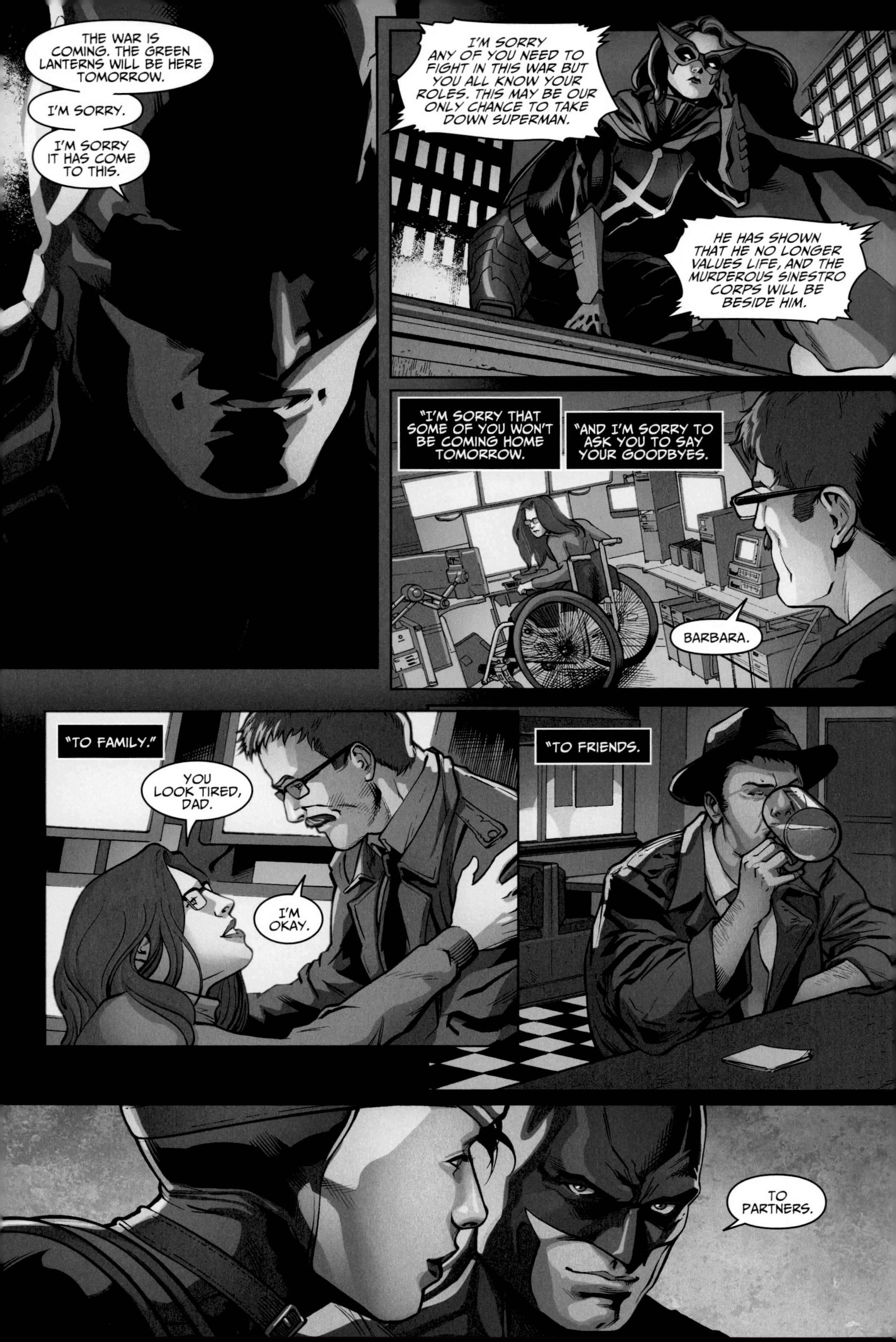
THE WAR IS COMING. THE GREEN LANTERNS WILL BE HERE TOMORROW.
I'M SORRY.
I'M SORRY IT HAS COME TO THIS.
I'M SORRY ANY OF YOU NEED TO FIGHT IN THIS WAR BUT YOU ALL KNOW YOUR ROLES. THIS MAY BE OUR ONLY CHANCE TO TAKE DOWN SUPERMAN.
HE HAS SHOWN THAT HE NO LONGER VALUES LIFE, AND THE MURDEROUS SINESTRO CORPS WILL BE BESIDE HIM.
"I'M SORRY THAT SOME OF YOU WON'T BE COMING HOME TOMORROW.
"AND I'M SORRY TO ASK YOU TO SAY YOUR GOODBYES.
BARBARA.
"TO FAMILY."
YOU LOOK TIRED, DAD.
I'M OKAY.
"TO FRIENDS.
TO PARTNERS.

"TO CHILDREN."

MOMMY WILL COME BACK FOR YOU, CONNOR.

BLP.

I PROMISE.

"TO HUSBANDS--"

"--AND WIVES."

RENEE, I...

IT'S OKAY, KATE. I'LL SEE YOU OUT THERE.

NO. DON'T LOOK AT ME LIKE THAT.

YOU NEED TO STAY BEHIND. I COULDN'T HANDLE IT IF ANYTHING WERE TO HAPPEN TO YOU, LITTLE MUSTACHE.

TOMORROW, THE TYRANNY OF SUPERMAN WILL BE ENDED BY ALL OF YOU.

AND I'M SORRY I CAN'T FIGHT ALONGSIDE YOU.

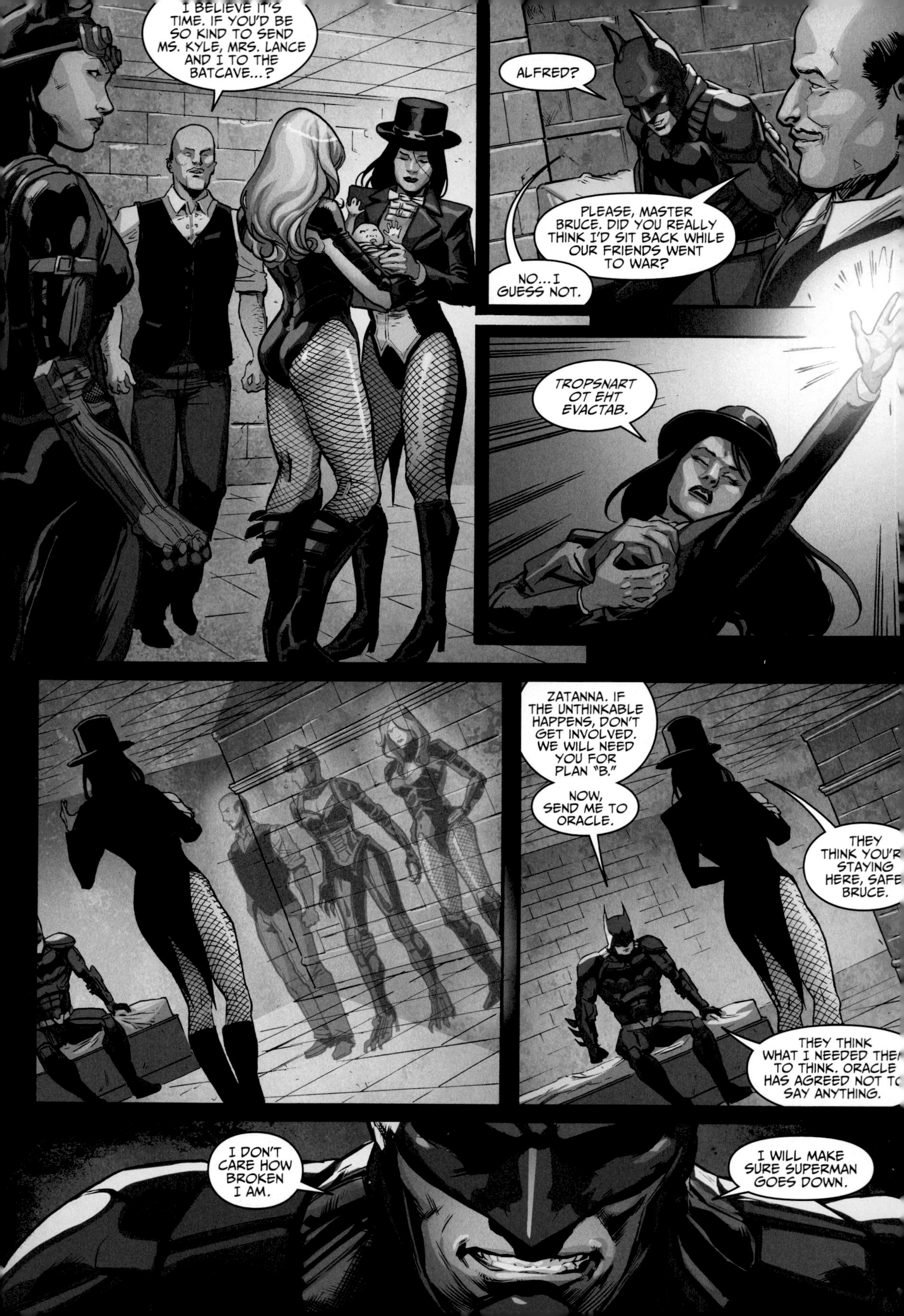
I BELIEVE IT'S TIME. IF YOU'D BE SO KIND TO SEND MS. KYLE, MRS. LANCE AND I TO THE BATCAVE...?
ALFRED?
PLEASE, MASTER BRUCE. DID YOU REALLY THINK I'D SIT BACK WHILE OUR FRIENDS WENT TO WAR?
NO... I GUESS NOT.
TROPSNART OT EHT EVACTAB.
ZATANNA. IF THE UNTHINKABLE HAPPENS, DON'T GET INVOLVED. WE WILL NEED YOU FOR PLAN "B."
NOW, SEND ME TO ORACLE.
THEY THINK YOU'R STAYING HERE, SAFE BRUCE.
THEY THINK WHAT I NEEDED THE TO THINK. ORACLE HAS AGREED NOT TO SAY ANYTHING.
I DON'T CARE HOW BROKEN I AM.
I WILL MAKE SURE SUPERMAN GOES DOWN.

"Absolute Freaking Carnage" Mike S. Miller Artist
"Ground Assault" **Bruno Redondo** **Julien Hugonnard-Bert** Artists
Rex Lokus Colorist Cover Art by **Stephane Roux**

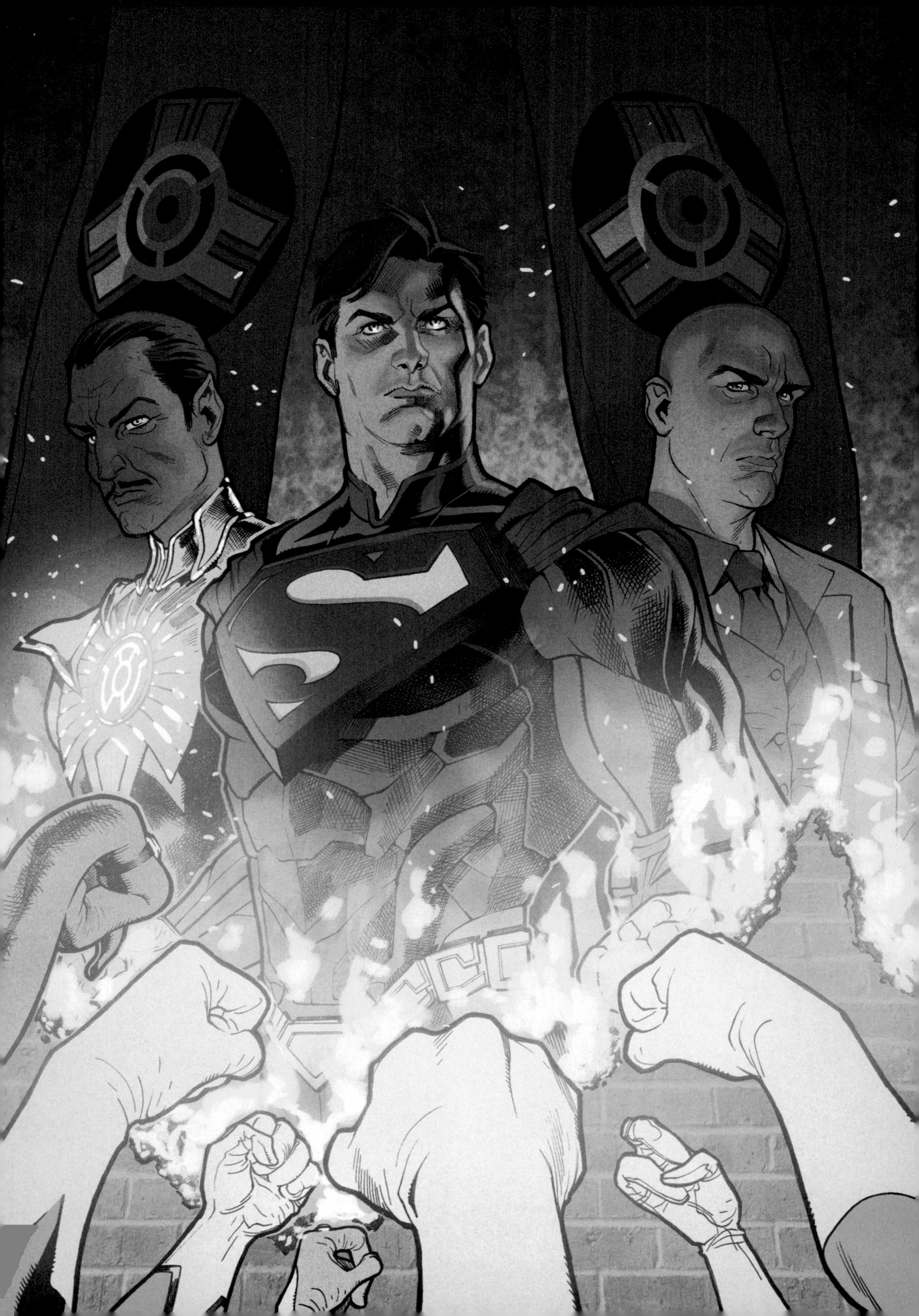

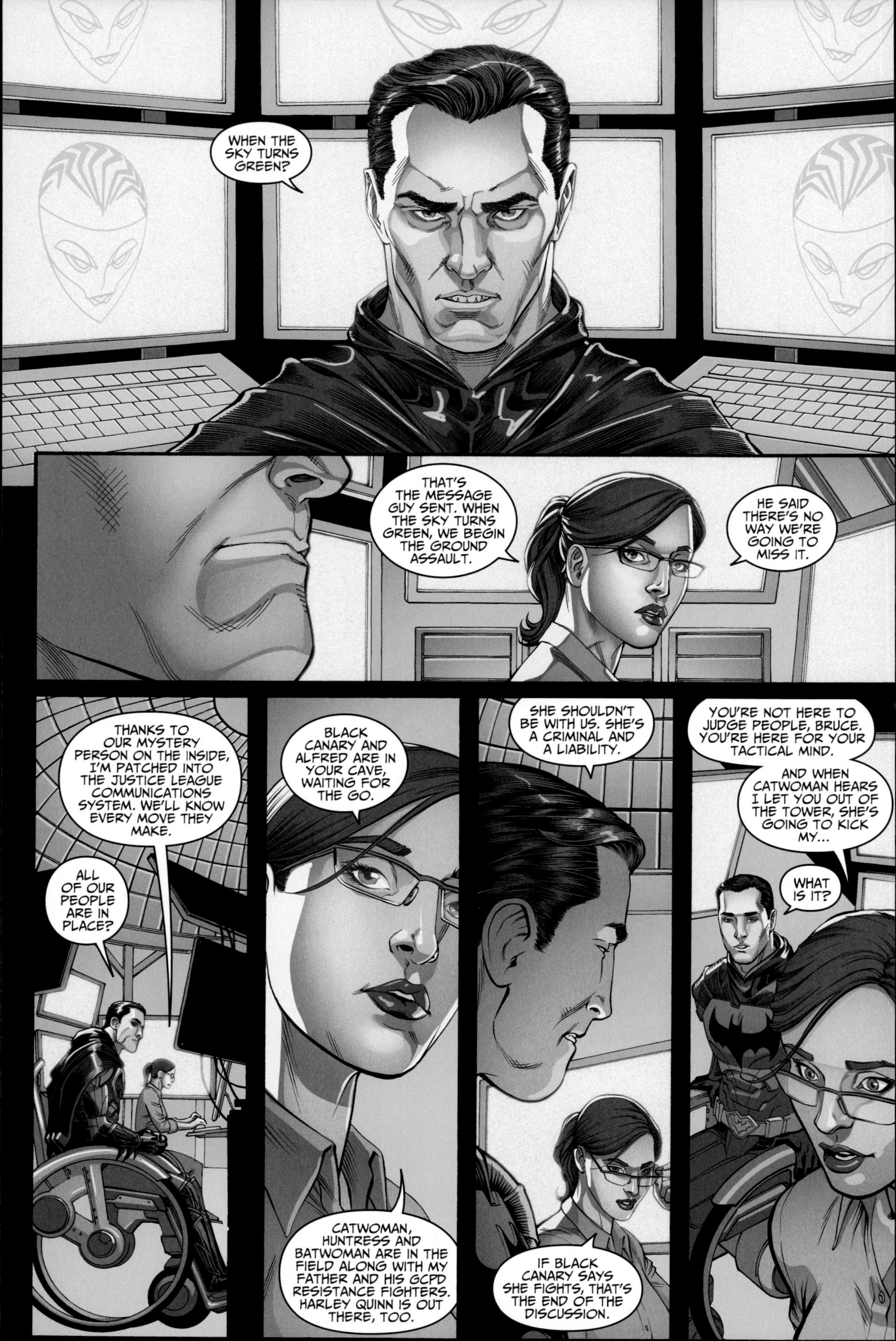
WHEN THE SKY TURNS GREEN?
THAT'S THE MESSAGE GUY SENT. WHEN THE SKY TURNS GREEN, WE BEGIN THE GROUND ASSAULT.
HE SAID THERE'S NO WAY WE'RE GOING TO MISS IT.
THANKS TO OUR MYSTERY PERSON ON THE INSIDE, I'M PATCHED INTO THE JUSTICE LEAGUE COMMUNICATIONS SYSTEM. WE'LL KNOW EVERY MOVE THEY MAKE.
ALL OF OUR PEOPLE ARE IN PLACE?
BLACK CANARY AND ALFRED ARE IN YOUR CAVE, WAITING FOR THE GO.
CATWOMAN, HUNTRESS AND BATWOMAN ARE IN THE FIELD ALONG WITH MY FATHER AND HIS GCPD RESISTANCE FIGHTERS. HARLEY QUINN IS OUT THERE, TOO.
SHE SHOULDN'T BE WITH US. SHE'S A CRIMINAL AND A LIABILITY.
IF BLACK CANARY SAYS SHE FIGHTS, THAT'S THE END OF THE DISCUSSION.
YOU'RE NOT HERE TO JUDGE PEOPLE, BRUCE. YOU'RE HERE FOR YOUR TACTICAL MIND.
AND WHEN CATWOMAN HEARS I LET YOU OUT OF THE TOWER, SHE'S GOING TO KICK MY...
WHAT IS IT?

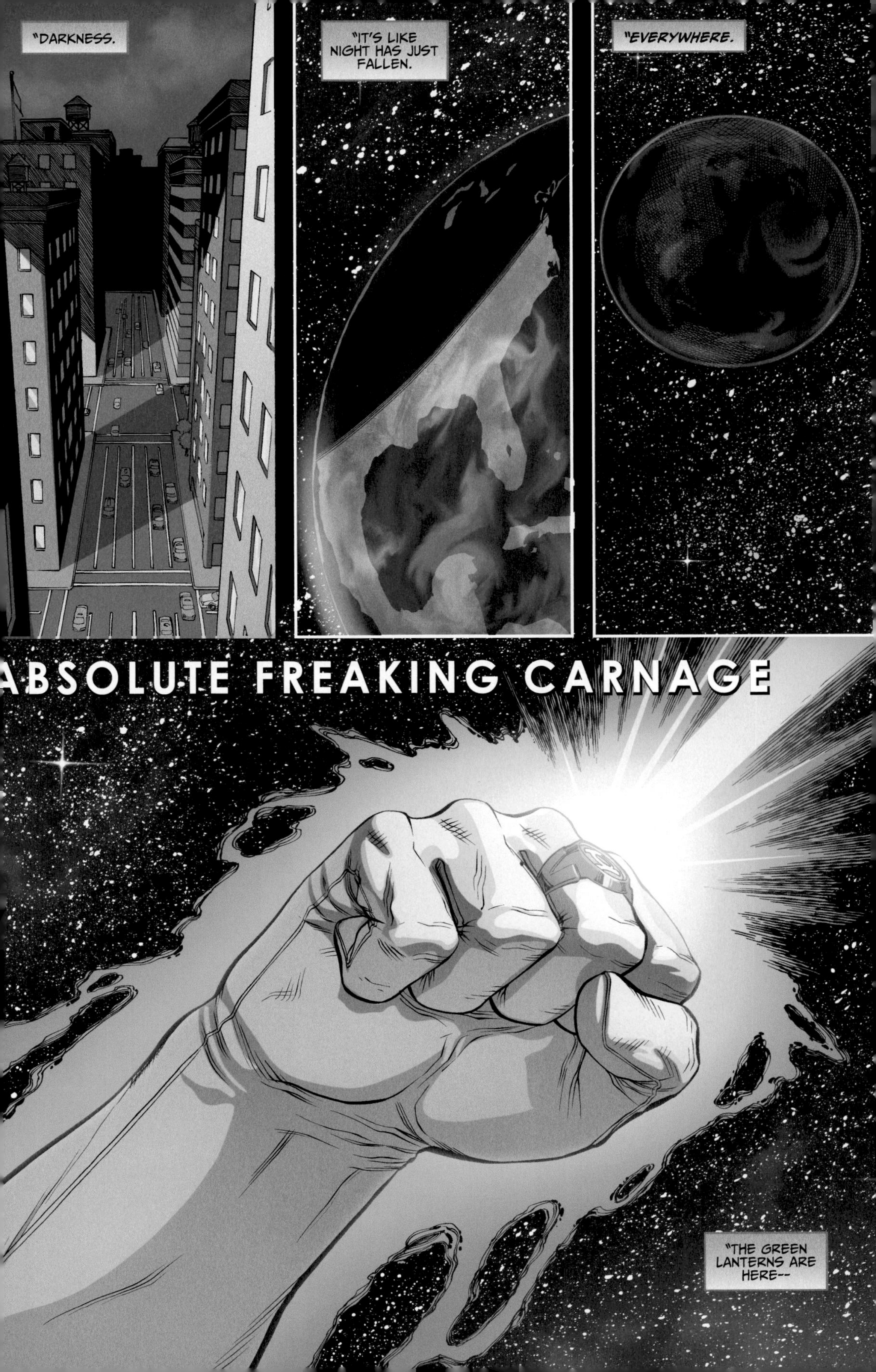

"DARKNESS.
"IT'S LIKE NIGHT HAS JUST FALLEN.
"EVERYWHERE.
ABSOLUTE FREAKING CARNAGE
"THE GREEN LANTERNS ARE HERE--

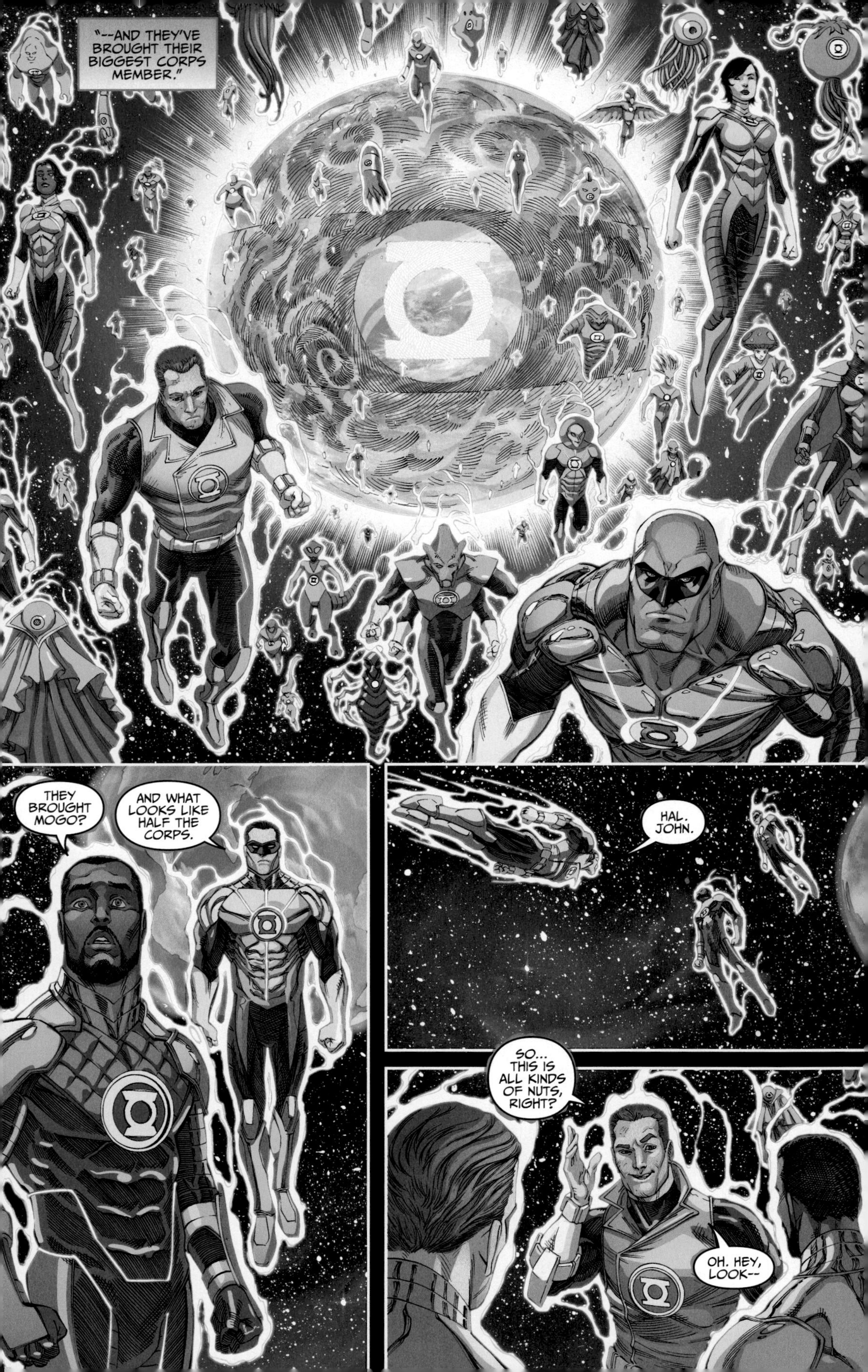
"--AND THEY'VE BROUGHT THEIR BIGGEST CORPS MEMBER."
THEY BROUGHT MOGO?
AND WHAT LOOKS LIKE HALF THE CORPS.
HAL. JOHN.
SO... THIS IS ALL KINDS OF NUTS, RIGHT?
OH. HEY, LOOK--

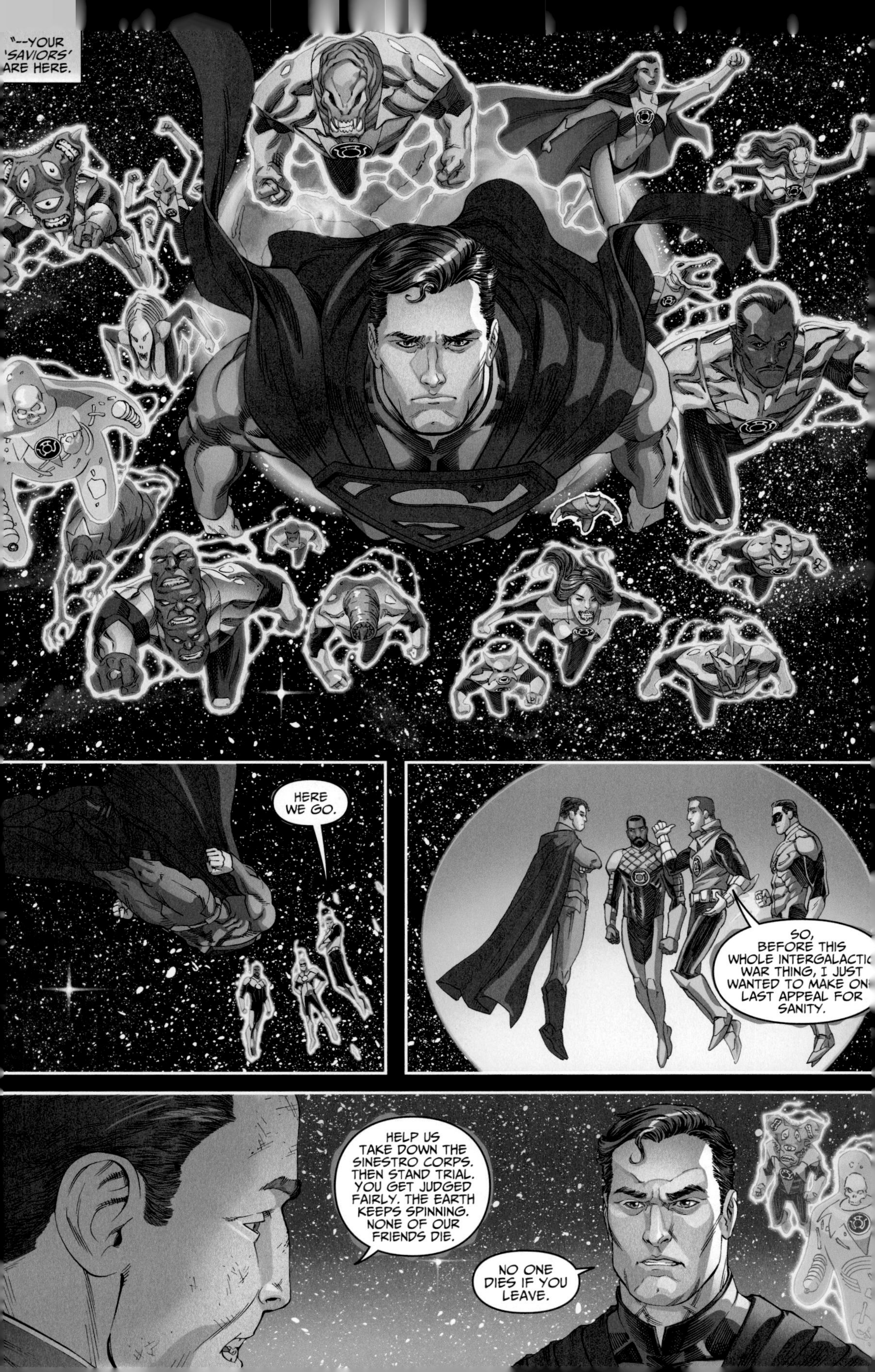
"--YOUR 'SAVIORS' ARE HERE.
HERE WE GO.
SO, BEFORE THIS WHOLE INTERGALACTIC WAR THING, I JUST WANTED TO MAKE ONE LAST APPEAL FOR SANITY.
HELP US TAKE DOWN THE SINESTRO CORPS. THEN STAND TRIAL. YOU GET JUDGED FAIRLY. THE EARTH KEEPS SPINNING. NONE OF OUR FRIENDS DIE.
NO ONE DIES IF YOU LEAVE.

MAN. HAVE SOME PERSPECTIVE. YOU HAVE SUPER-VISION OR WHATEVER. TAKE A GOOD LOOK AT YOUR 'ALLIES.'

SINESTRO CORPS. CHOSEN BECAUSE THEY CAN INSTILL FEAR. THEY'RE THE VERY DEFINITION OF BAD GUY. HALF OF THEM ARE JUST SPIKES AND SHARP TEETH.

THAT GUY'S NAME IS ARKILLO.

HE LITERALLY HAS 'KILL' IN HIS NAME.

FOR NOW, THEY ARE USEFUL. THE ENEMY OF MY ENEMY--

IS SOMETIMES JUST A MUCH WORSE ENEMY.

YOU'RE NOT GOING TO WIN THIS. I DON'T WANT TO HURT YOU--ANY OF YOU. I'M TRYING TO *PROTECT* YOU, AND OUR FRIENDS.

WE DON'T NEED YOUR 'PROTECTION.' WE KNOW HOW YOUR 'GUARDIANS' HAVE GUARDED WORLDS IN THE PAST.

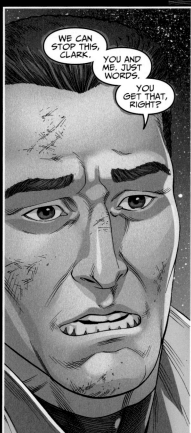

WE CAN STOP THIS, CLARK.

YOU AND ME. JUST WORDS.

YOU GET THAT, RIGHT?

GUY...

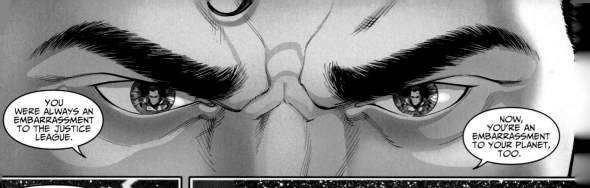

YOU WERE ALWAYS AN EMBARRASSMENT TO THE JUSTICE LEAGUE.

NOW, YOU'RE AN EMBARRASSMENT TO YOUR PLANET, TOO.

OH, SCREW YOU, YOU SANCTIMONIOUS PIECE OF--

CRK

HNGG!

I DON'T WANT YOU IN THIS FIGHT.

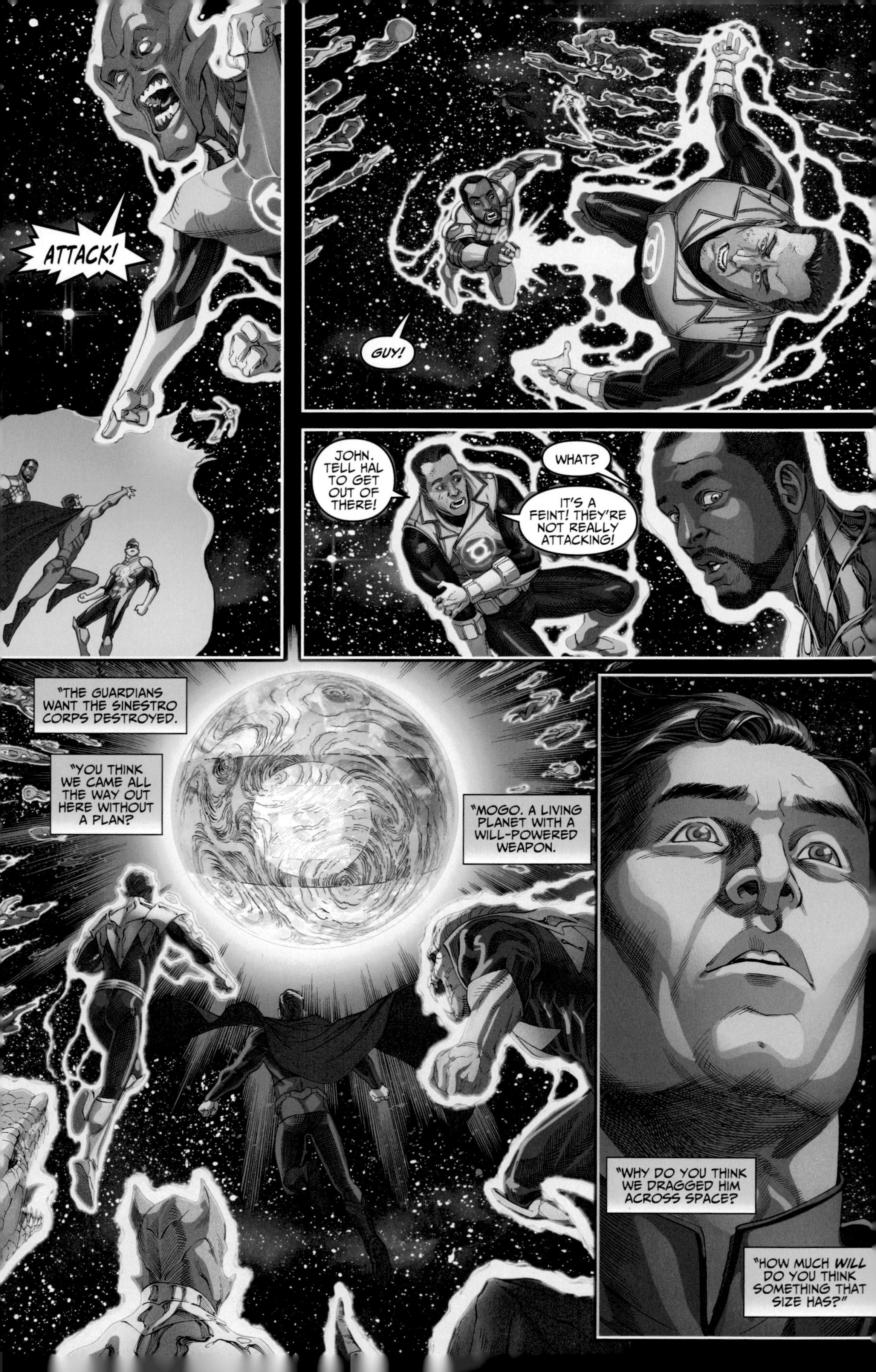
ATTACK!
GUY!
JOHN. TELL HAL TO GET OUT OF THERE!
WHAT?
IT'S A FEINT! THEY'RE NOT REALLY ATTACKING!
"THE GUARDIANS WANT THE SINESTRO CORPS DESTROYED.
"YOU THINK WE CAME ALL THE WAY OUT HERE WITHOUT A PLAN?
"MOGO. A LIVING PLANET WITH A WILL-POWERED WEAPON.
"WHY DO YOU THINK WE DRAGGED HIM ACROSS SPACE?
"HOW MUCH WILL DO YOU THINK SOMETHING THAT SIZE HAS?"

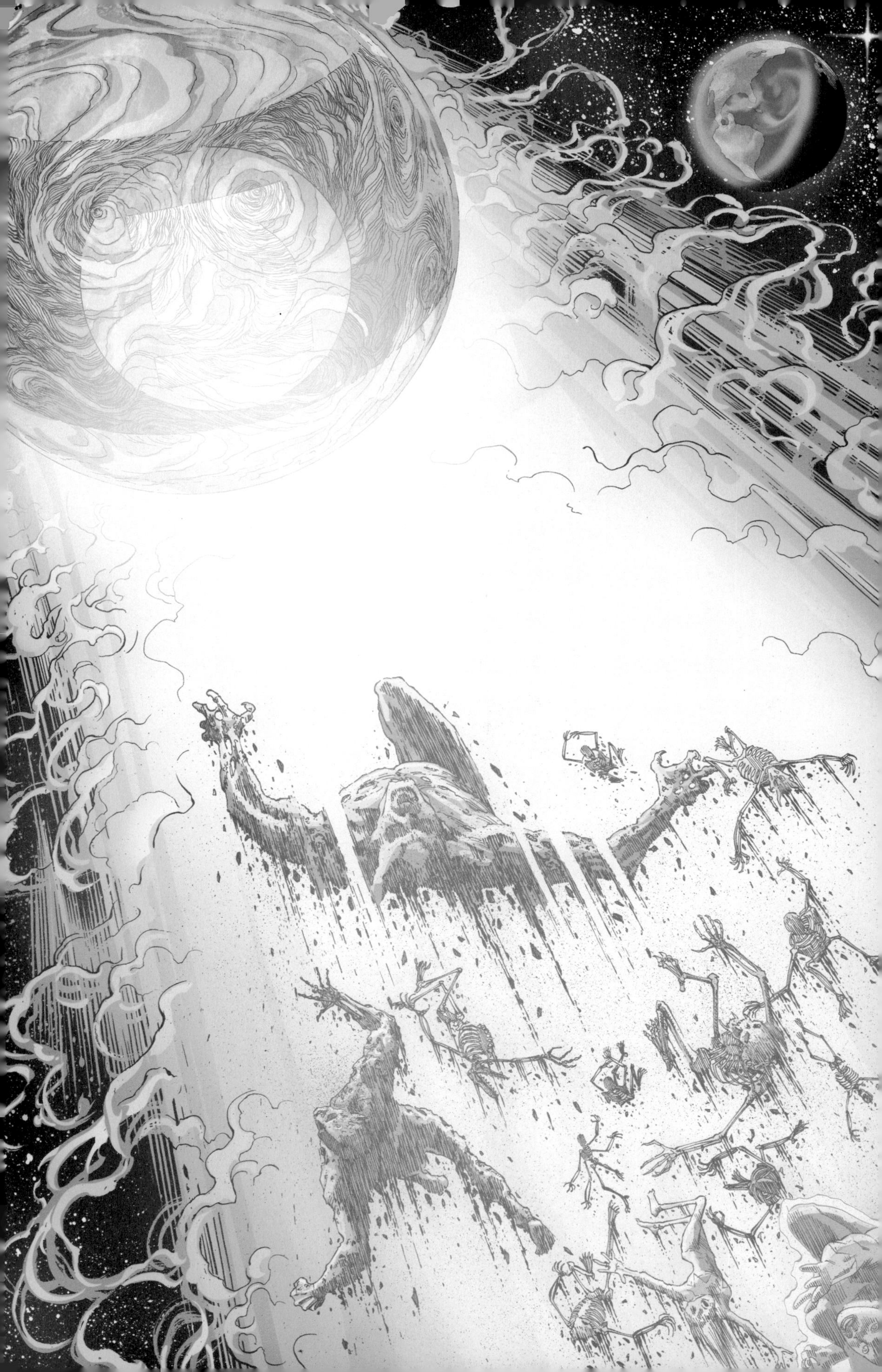

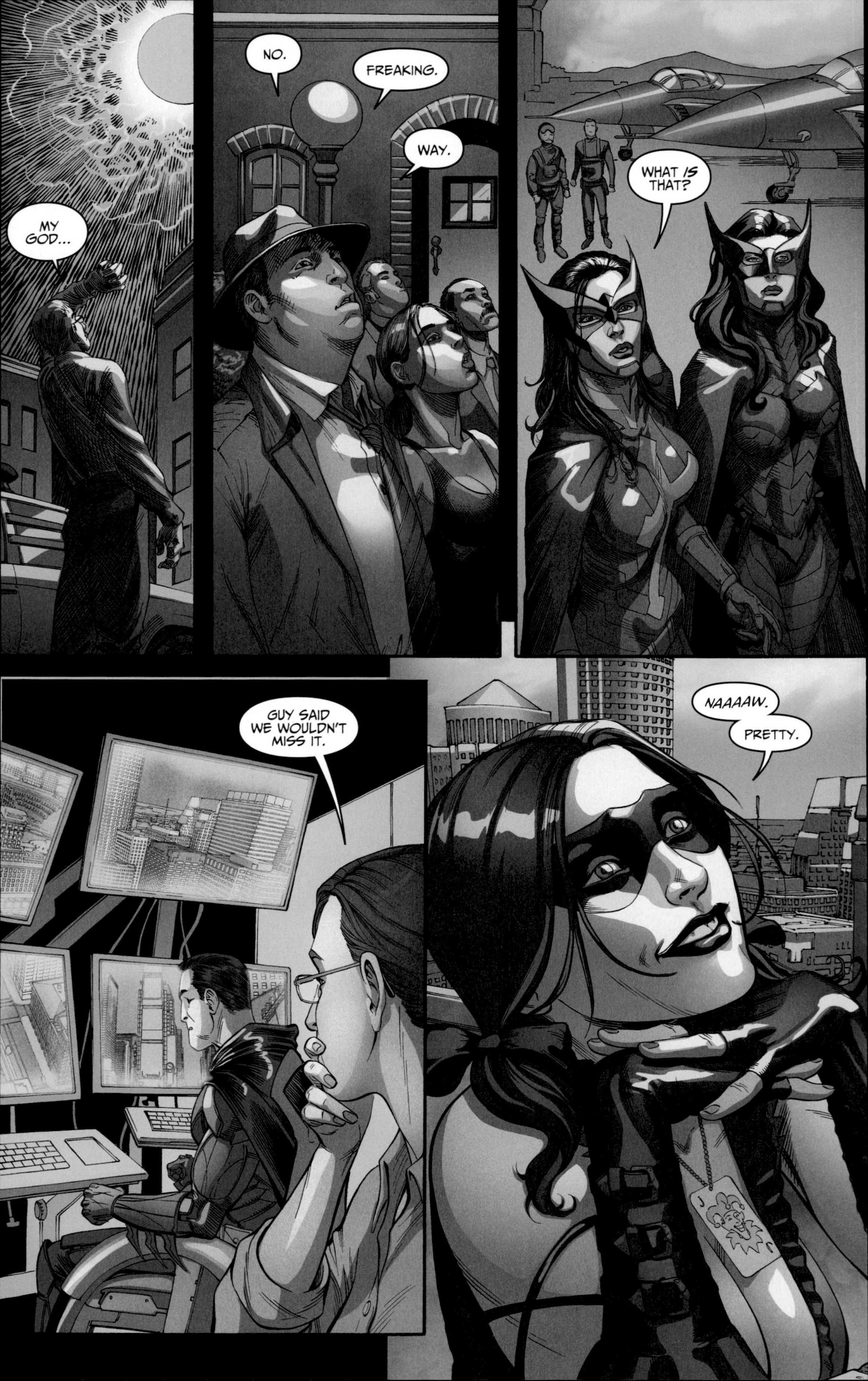
MY GOD...
NO.
FREAKING.
WAY.
WHAT *IS* THAT?
GUY SAID WE WOULDN'T MISS IT.
NAAAAW.
PRETTY.

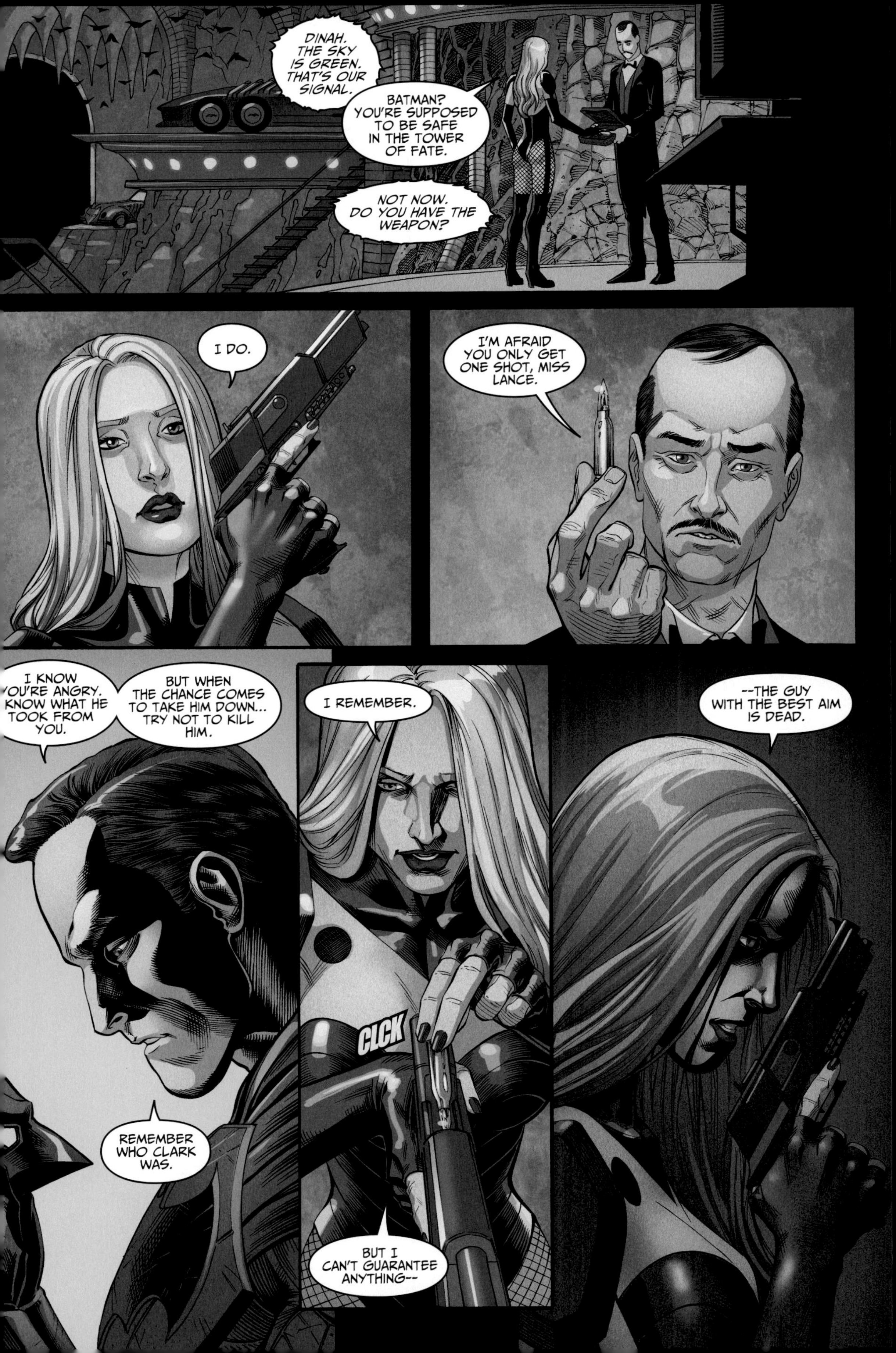

DINAH. THE SKY IS GREEN. THAT'S OUR SIGNAL.
BATMAN? YOU'RE SUPPOSED TO BE SAFE IN THE TOWER OF FATE.
NOT NOW. DO YOU HAVE THE WEAPON?
I DO.
I'M AFRAID YOU ONLY GET ONE SHOT, MISS LANCE.
I KNOW YOU'RE ANGRY. KNOW WHAT HE TOOK FROM YOU.
BUT WHEN THE CHANCE COMES TO TAKE HIM DOWN... TRY NOT TO KILL HIM.
REMEMBER WHO CLARK WAS.
I REMEMBER.
CLCK
BUT I CAN'T GUARANTEE ANYTHING--
--THE GUY WITH THE BEST AIM IS DEAD.

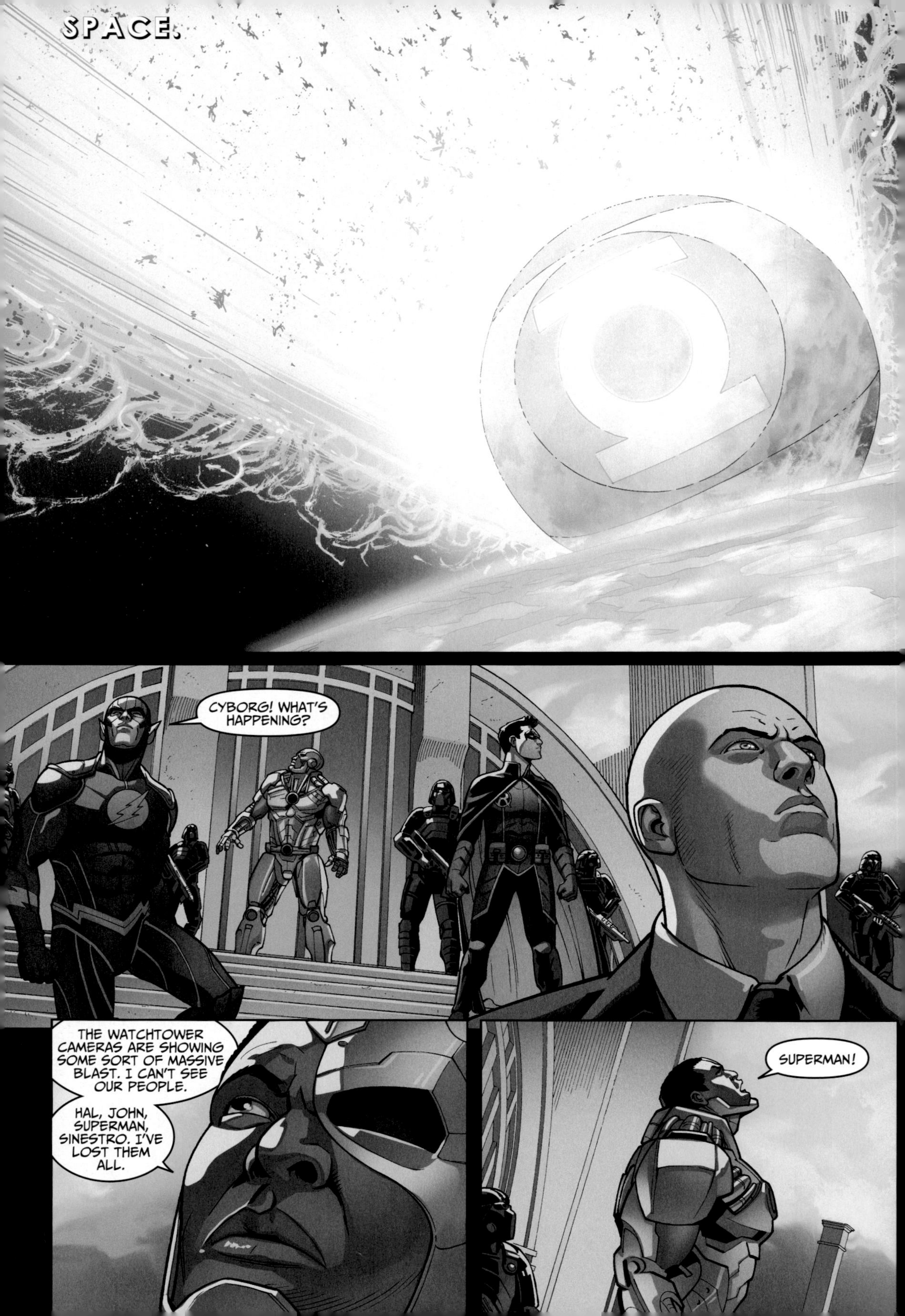
SPACE.
CYBORG! WHAT'S HAPPENING?
THE WATCHTOWER CAMERAS ARE SHOWING SOME SORT OF MASSIVE BLAST. I CAN'T SEE OUR PEOPLE.
HAL, JOHN, SUPERMAN, SINESTRO. I'VE LOST THEM ALL.
SUPERMAN!

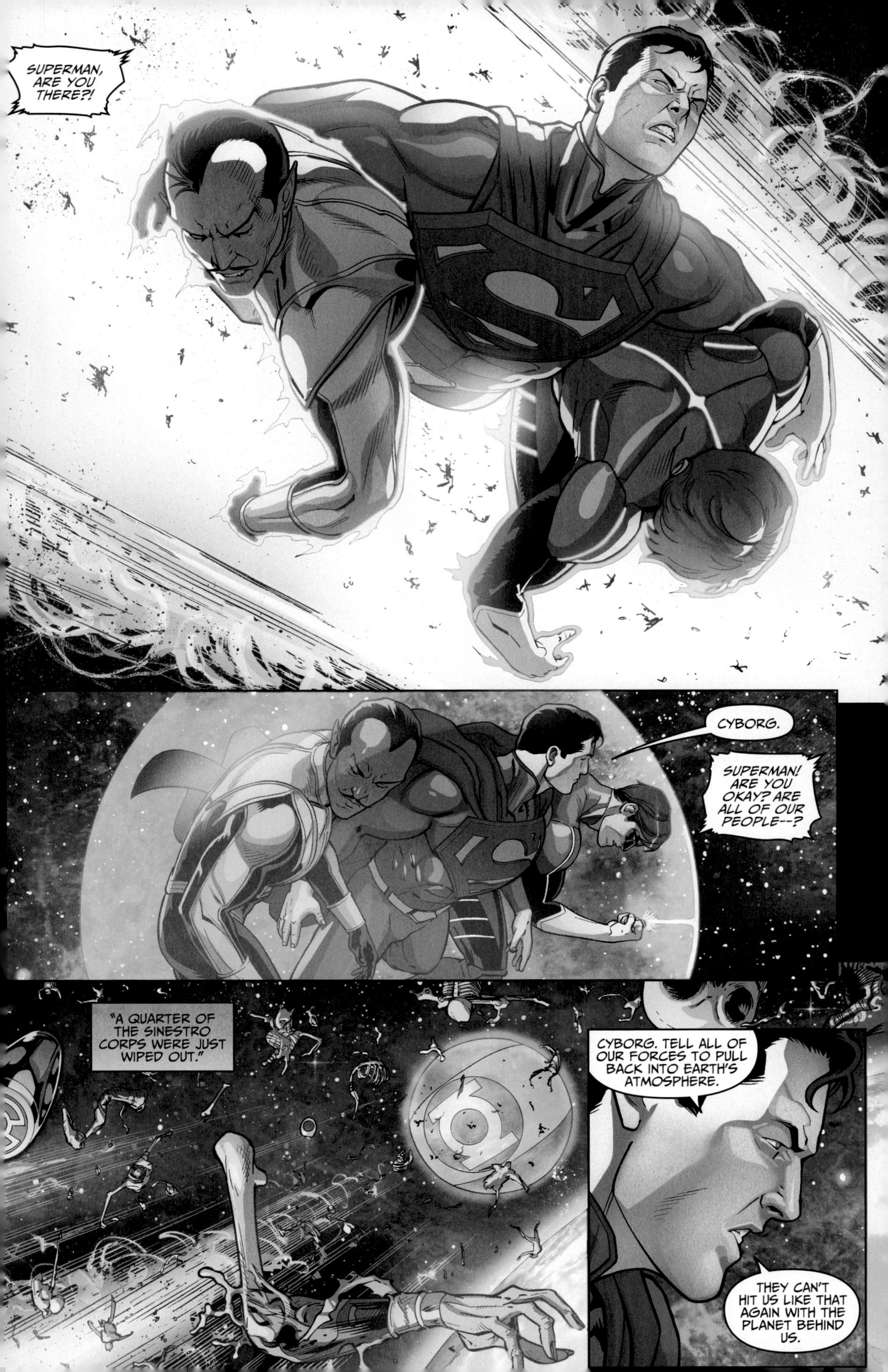
SUPERMAN, ARE YOU THERE?!
CYBORG.
SUPERMAN! ARE YOU OKAY? ARE ALL OF OUR PEOPLE--?
"A QUARTER OF THE SINESTRO CORPS WERE JUST WIPED OUT."
CYBORG. TELL ALL OF OUR FORCES TO PULL BACK INTO EARTH'S ATMOSPHERE.
THEY CAN'T HIT US LIKE THAT AGAIN WITH THE PLANET BEHIND US.

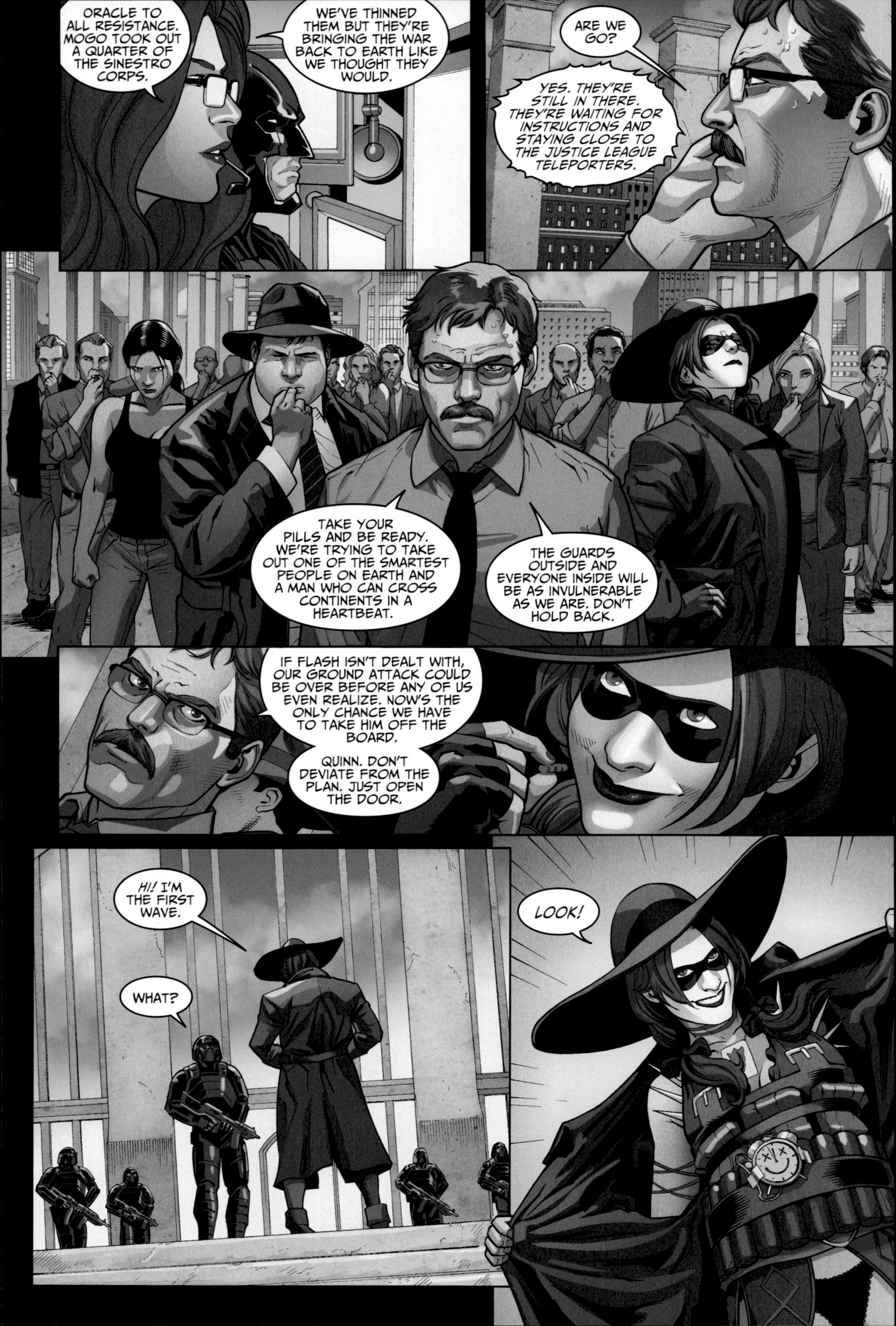
ORACLE TO ALL RESISTANCE. MOGO TOOK OUT A QUARTER OF THE SINESTRO CORPS.
WE'VE THINNED THEM BUT THEY'RE BRINGING THE WAR BACK TO EARTH LIKE WE THOUGHT THEY WOULD.
ARE WE GO?
YES. THEY'RE STILL IN THERE. THEY'RE WAITING FOR INSTRUCTIONS AND STAYING CLOSE TO THE JUSTICE LEAGUE TELEPORTERS.
TAKE YOUR PILLS AND BE READY. WE'RE TRYING TO TAKE OUT ONE OF THE SMARTEST PEOPLE ON EARTH AND A MAN WHO CAN CROSS CONTINENTS IN A HEARTBEAT.
THE GUARDS OUTSIDE AND EVERYONE INSIDE WILL BE AS INVULNERABLE AS WE ARE. DON'T HOLD BACK.
IF FLASH ISN'T DEALT WITH, OUR GROUND ATTACK COULD BE OVER BEFORE ANY OF US EVEN REALIZE. NOW'S THE ONLY CHANCE WE HAVE TO TAKE HIM OFF THE BOARD.
QUINN. DON'T DEVIATE FROM THE PLAN. JUST OPEN THE DOOR.
HI! I'M THE FIRST WAVE.
WHAT?
LOOK!

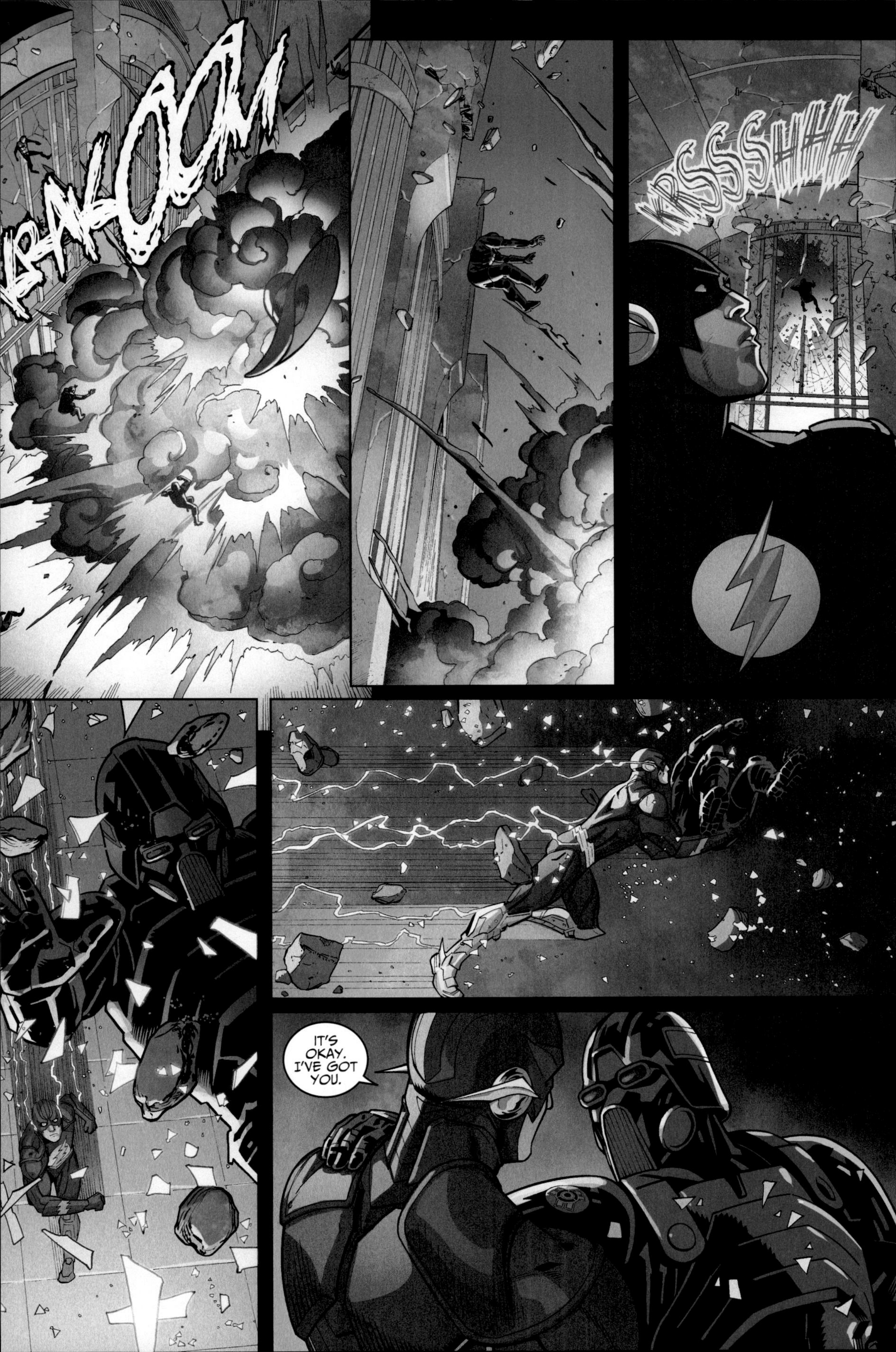
KRAKOOM
KRSSSHHH
IT'S OKAY. I'VE GOT YOU.

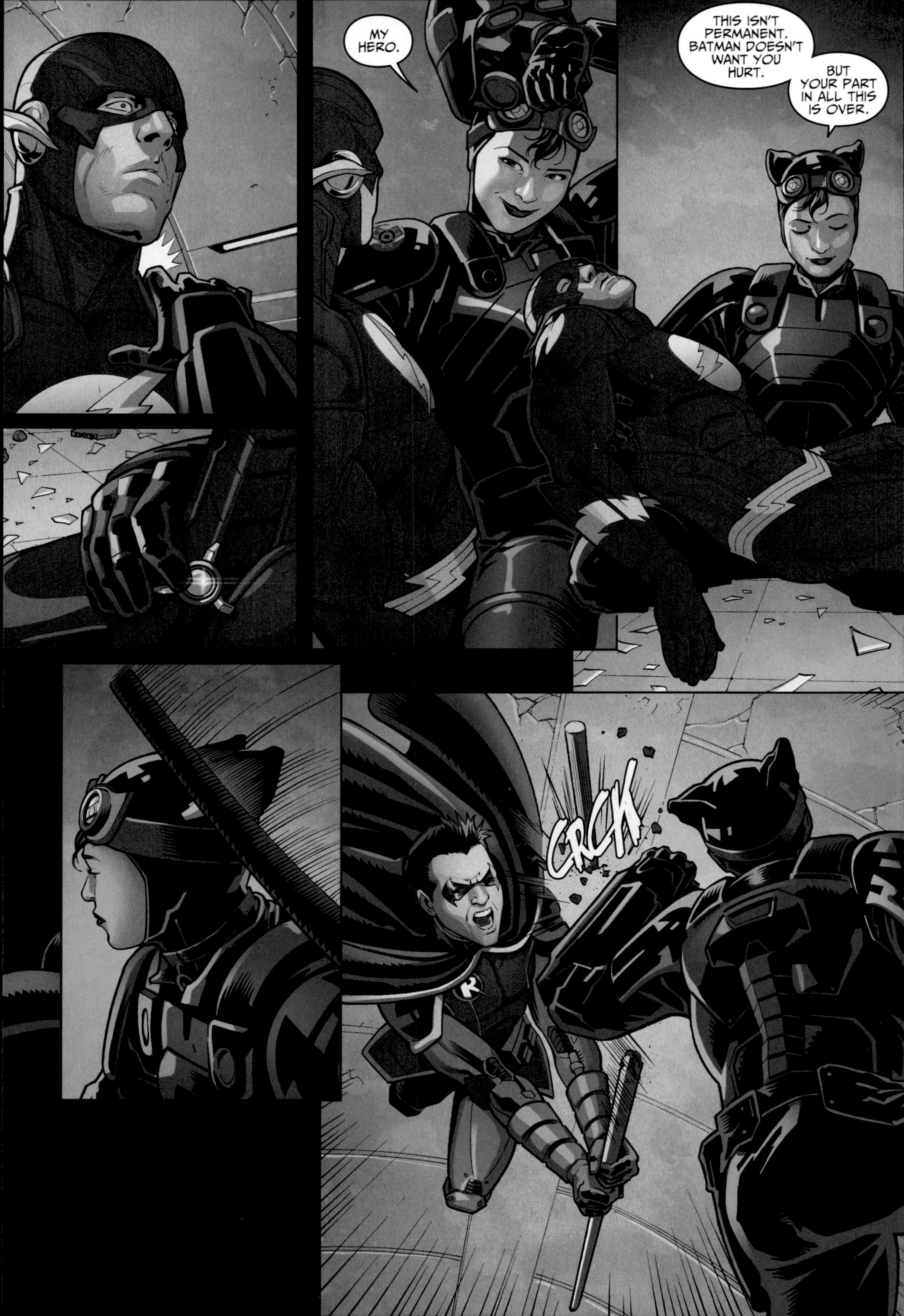
MY HERO.
THIS ISN'T PERMANENT. BATMAN DOESN'T WANT YOU HURT.
BUT YOUR PART IN ALL THIS IS OVER.
CRCK

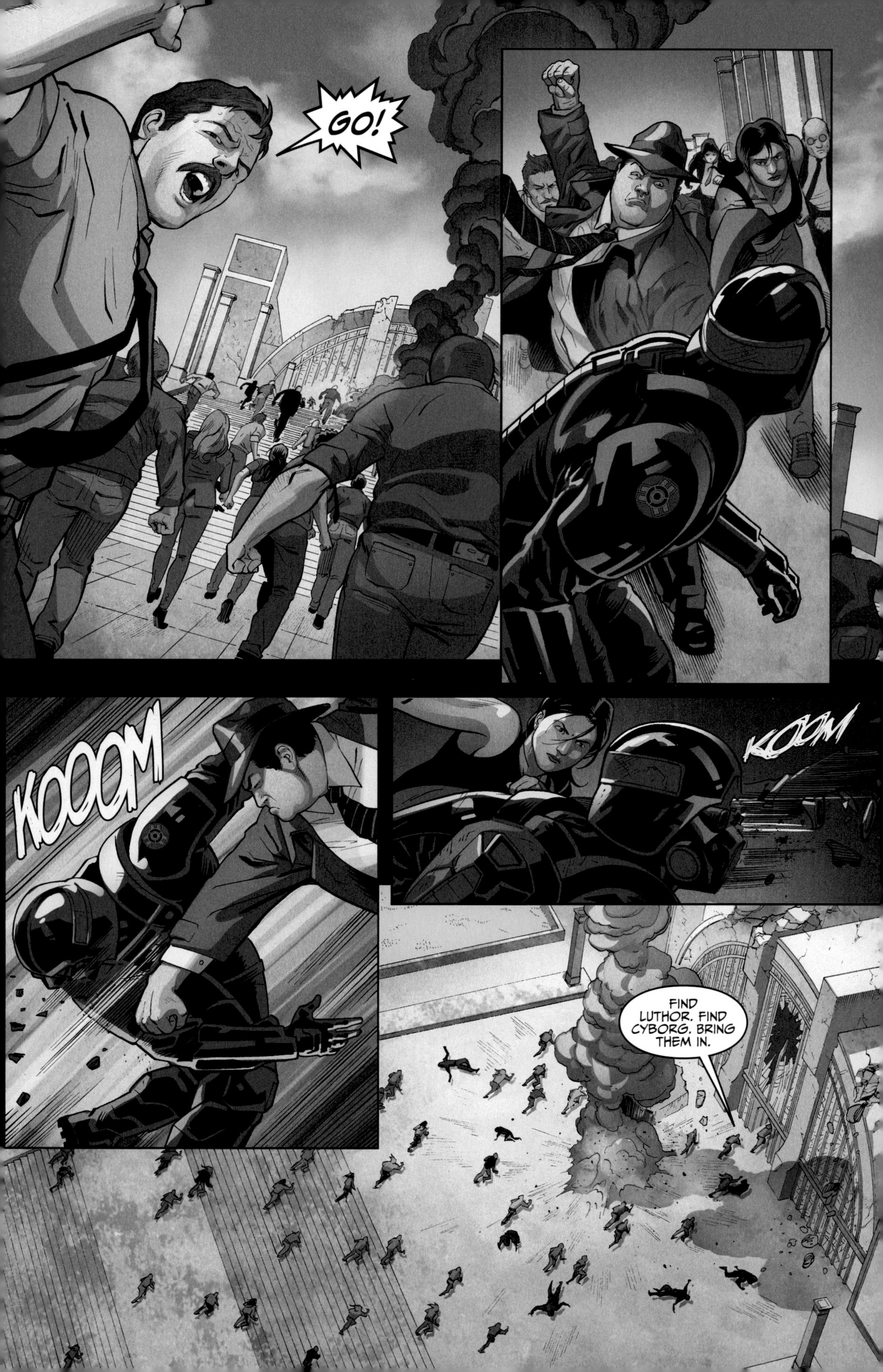
GO!
KOOOM
KOOM
FIND LUTHOR. FIND CYBORG. BRING THEM IN.

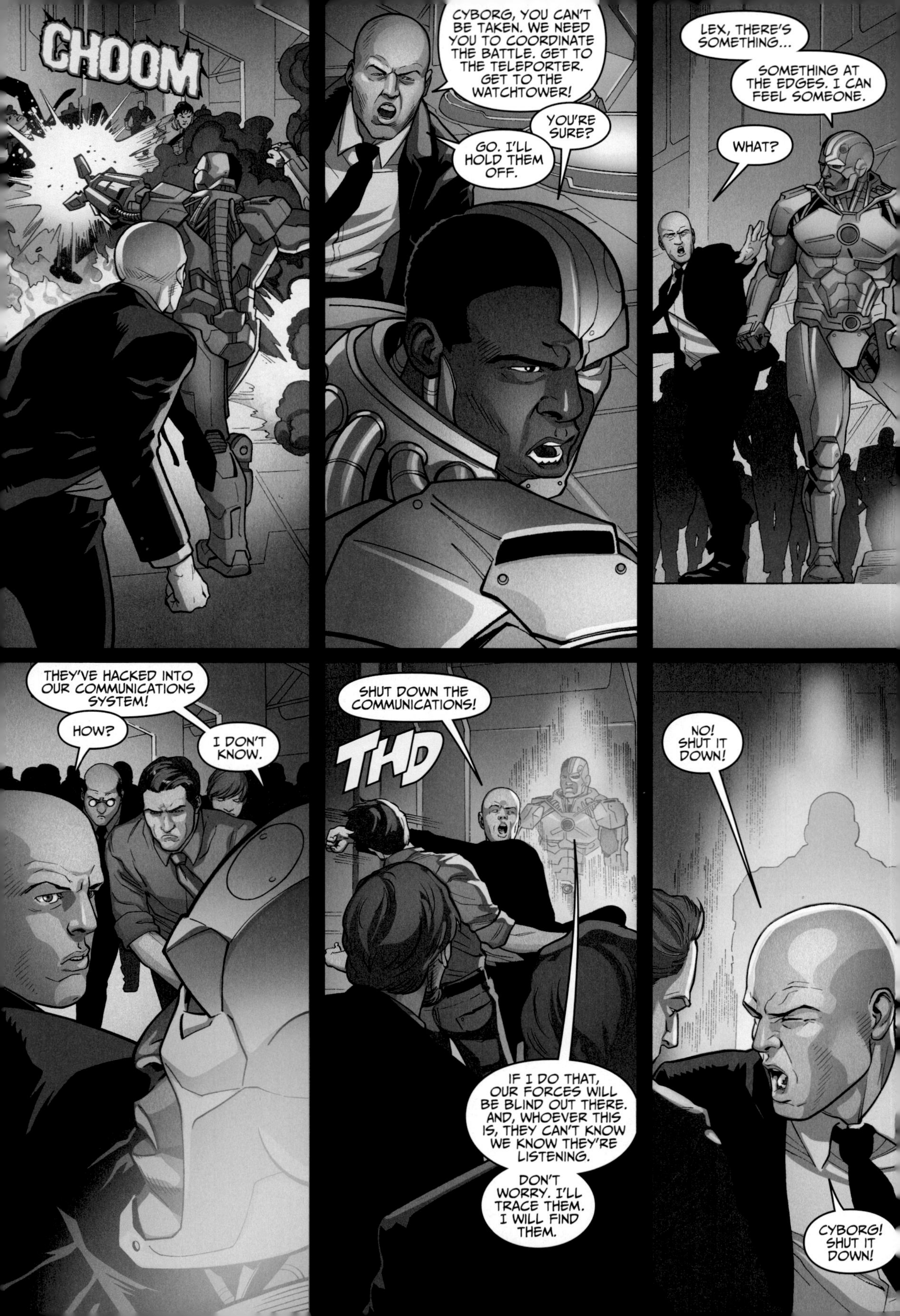
CHOOM
CYBORG, YOU CAN'T BE TAKEN. WE NEED YOU TO COORDINATE THE BATTLE. GET TO THE TELEPORTER. GET TO THE WATCHTOWER!
YOU'RE SURE?
GO. I'LL HOLD THEM OFF.
LEX, THERE'S SOMETHING...
SOMETHING AT THE EDGES. I CAN FEEL SOMEONE.
WHAT?
THEY'VE HACKED INTO OUR COMMUNICATIONS SYSTEM!
HOW?
I DON'T KNOW.
SHUT DOWN THE COMMUNICATIONS!
THD
IF I DO THAT, OUR FORCES WILL BE BLIND OUT THERE. AND, WHOEVER THIS IS, THEY CAN'T KNOW WE KNOW THEY'RE LISTENING.
DON'T WORRY. I'LL TRACE THEM. I WILL FIND THEM.
NO! SHUT IT DOWN!
CYBORG! SHUT IT DOWN!

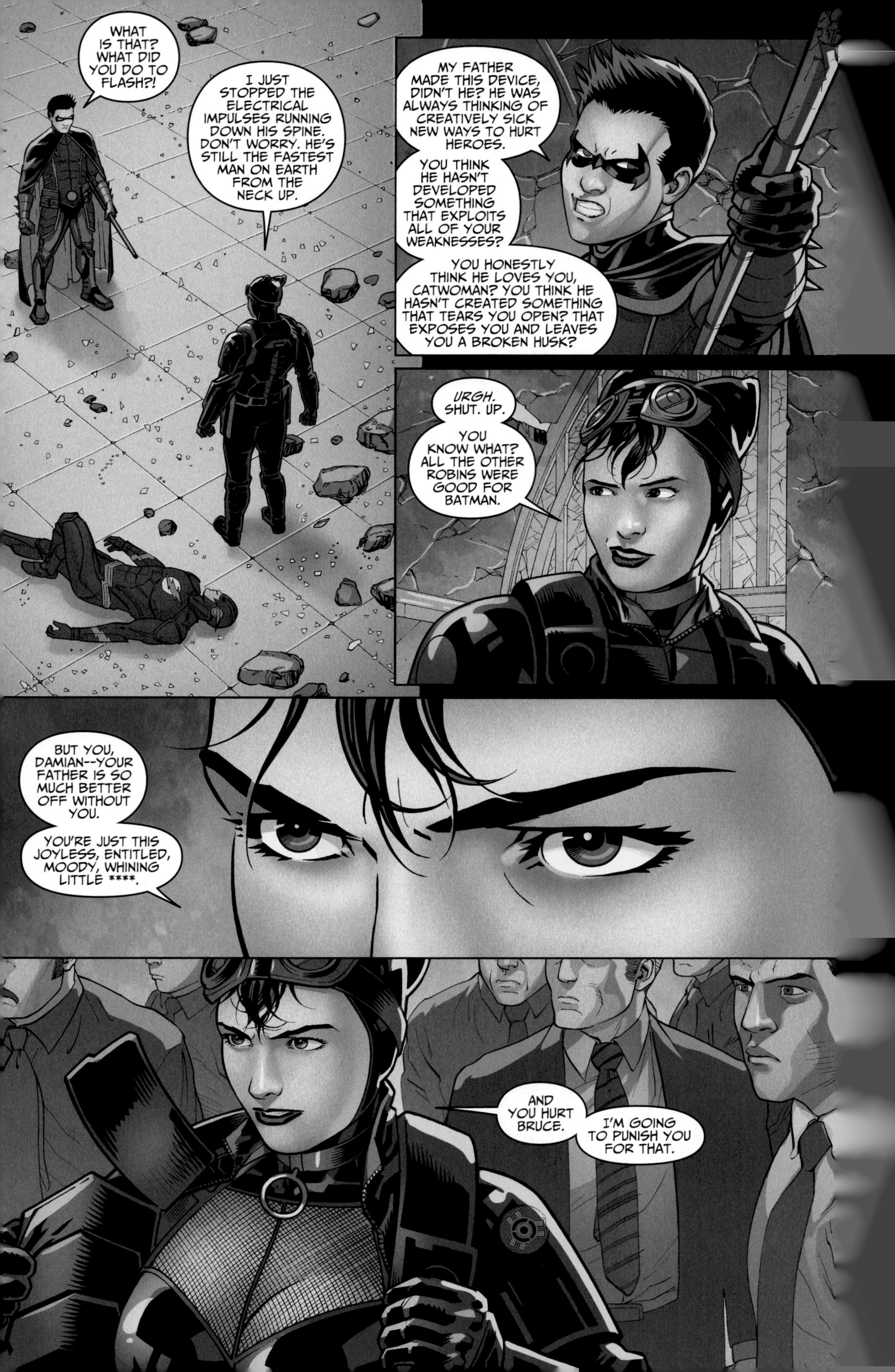
WHAT IS THAT? WHAT DID YOU DO TO FLASH?!
I JUST STOPPED THE ELECTRICAL IMPULSES RUNNING DOWN HIS SPINE. DON'T WORRY. HE'S STILL THE FASTEST MAN ON EARTH FROM THE NECK UP.
MY FATHER MADE THIS DEVICE, DIDN'T HE? HE WAS ALWAYS THINKING OF CREATIVELY SICK NEW WAYS TO HURT HEROES.
YOU THINK HE HASN'T DEVELOPED SOMETHING THAT EXPLOITS ALL OF YOUR WEAKNESSES?
YOU HONESTLY THINK HE LOVES YOU, CATWOMAN? YOU THINK HE HASN'T CREATED SOMETHING THAT TEARS YOU OPEN? THAT EXPOSES YOU AND LEAVES YOU A BROKEN HUSK?
URGH. SHUT. UP.
YOU KNOW WHAT? ALL THE OTHER ROBINS WERE GOOD FOR BATMAN.
BUT YOU, DAMIAN--YOUR FATHER IS SO MUCH BETTER OFF WITHOUT YOU.
YOU'RE JUST THIS JOYLESS, ENTITLED, MOODY, WHINING LITTLE ****.
AND YOU HURT BRUCE.
I'M GOING TO PUNISH YOU FOR THAT.

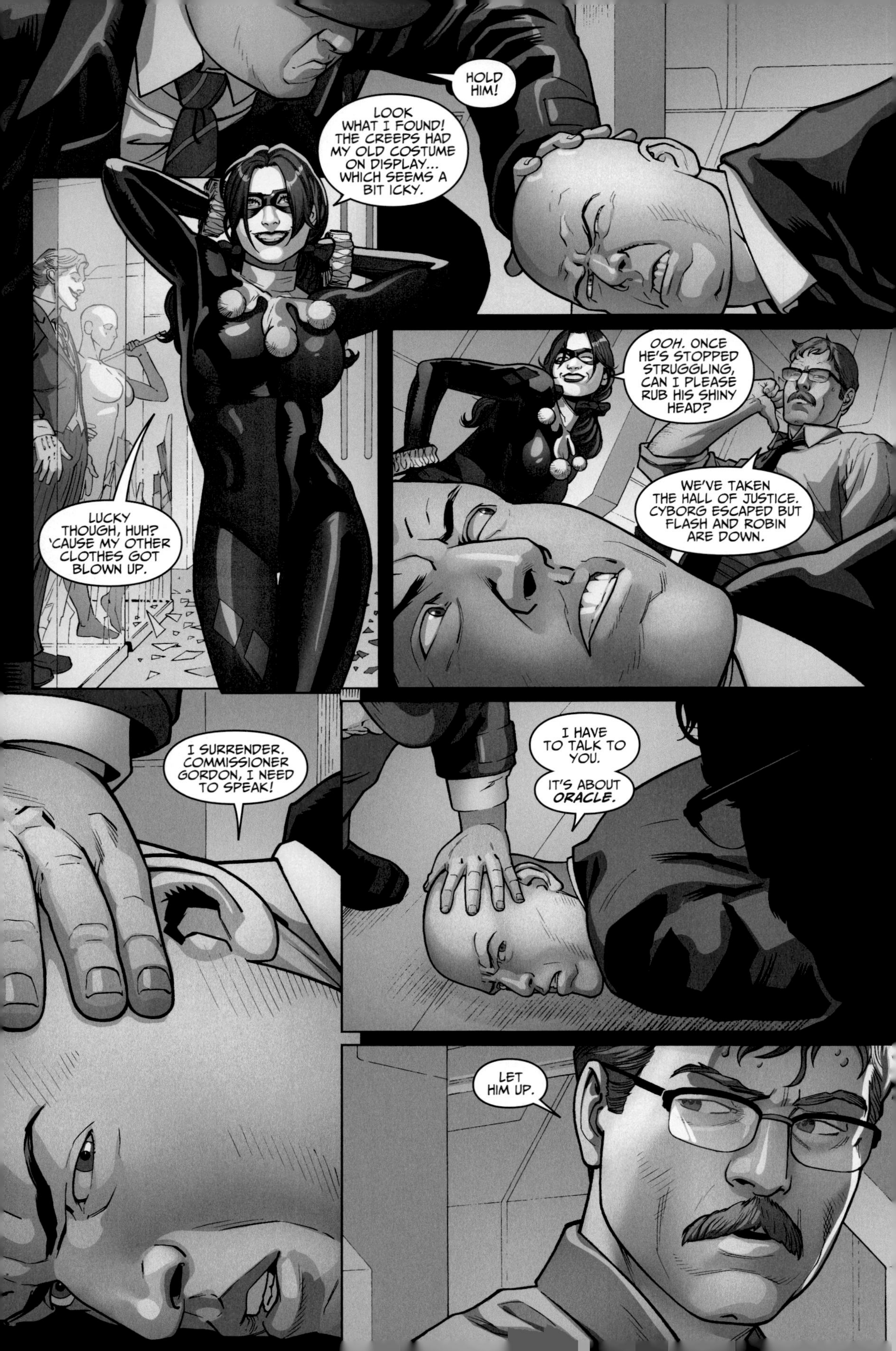
HOLD HIM!
LOOK WHAT I FOUND! THE CREEPS HAD MY OLD COSTUME ON DISPLAY... WHICH SEEMS A BIT ICKY.
LUCKY THOUGH, HUH? 'CAUSE MY OTHER CLOTHES GOT BLOWN UP.
OOH. ONCE HE'S STOPPED STRUGGLING, CAN I PLEASE RUB HIS SHINY HEAD?
WE'VE TAKEN THE HALL OF JUSTICE. CYBORG ESCAPED BUT FLASH AND ROBIN ARE DOWN.
I SURRENDER. COMMISSIONER GORDON, I NEED TO SPEAK!
I HAVE TO TALK TO YOU.
IT'S ABOUT ORACLE.
LET HIM UP.

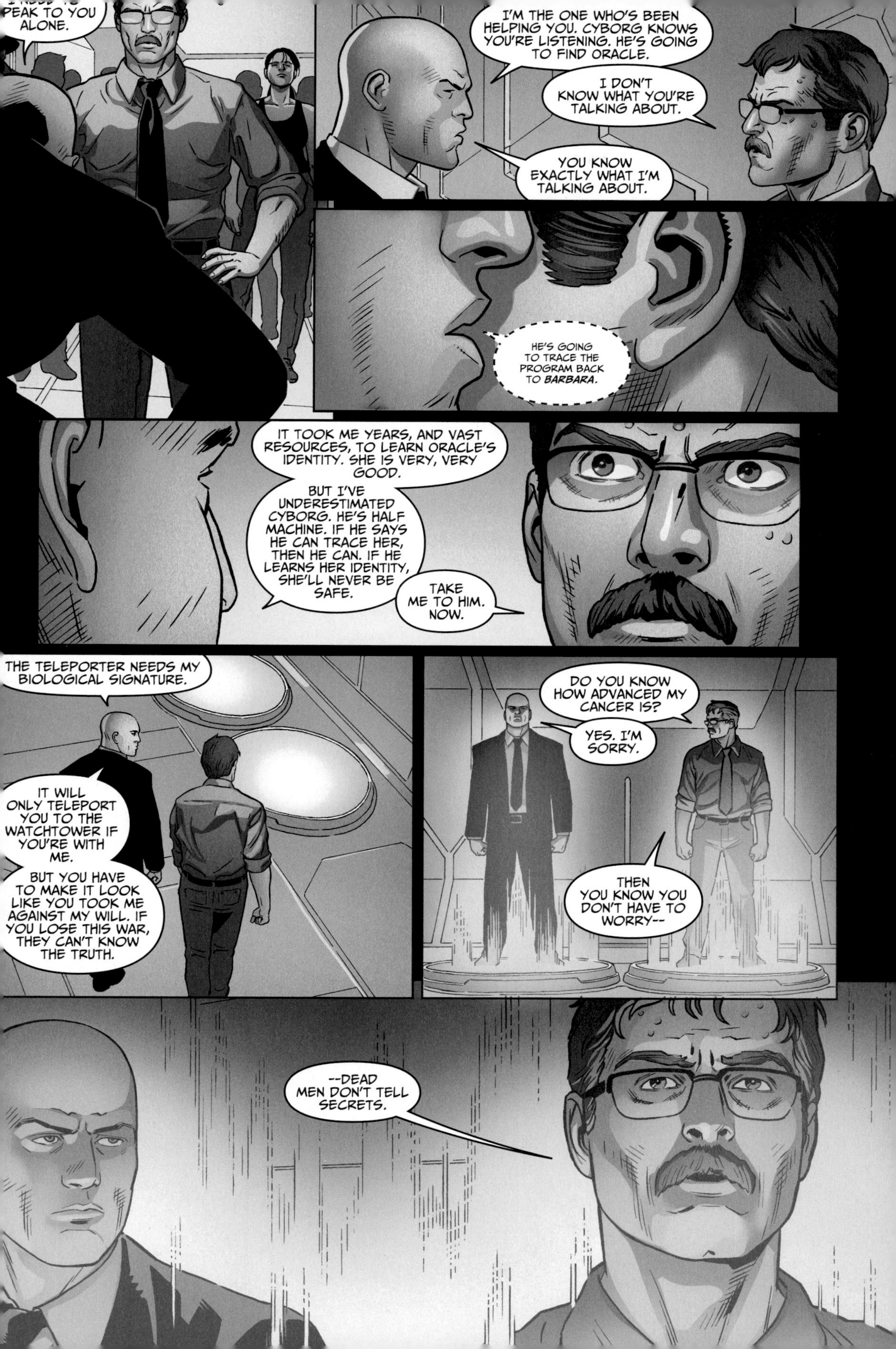
PEAK TO YOU ALONE.
I'M THE ONE WHO'S BEEN HELPING YOU. CYBORG KNOWS YOU'RE LISTENING. HE'S GOING TO FIND ORACLE.
I DON'T KNOW WHAT YOU'RE TALKING ABOUT.
YOU KNOW EXACTLY WHAT I'M TALKING ABOUT.
HE'S GOING TO TRACE THE PROGRAM BACK TO BARBARA.
IT TOOK ME YEARS, AND VAST RESOURCES, TO LEARN ORACLE'S IDENTITY. SHE IS VERY, VERY GOOD.
BUT I'VE UNDERESTIMATED CYBORG. HE'S HALF MACHINE. IF HE SAYS HE CAN TRACE HER, THEN HE CAN. IF HE LEARNS HER IDENTITY, SHE'LL NEVER BE SAFE.
TAKE ME TO HIM. NOW.
THE TELEPORTER NEEDS MY BIOLOGICAL SIGNATURE.
IT WILL ONLY TELEPORT YOU TO THE WATCHTOWER IF YOU'RE WITH ME.
BUT YOU HAVE TO MAKE IT LOOK LIKE YOU TOOK ME AGAINST MY WILL. IF YOU LOSE THIS WAR, THEY CAN'T KNOW THE TRUTH.
DO YOU KNOW HOW ADVANCED MY CANCER IS?
YES. I'M SORRY.
THEN YOU KNOW YOU DON'T HAVE TO WORRY--
--DEAD MEN DON'T TELL SECRETS.

"Air Assault" **Mike S. Miller** Artist
"Gordon" **Bruno Redondo** **Julien Hugonnard-Bert** Artists
Rex Lokus Colorist Cover Art by **Jheremy Raapack & David Lopez** and **Santi Casas of Ikari Studio**

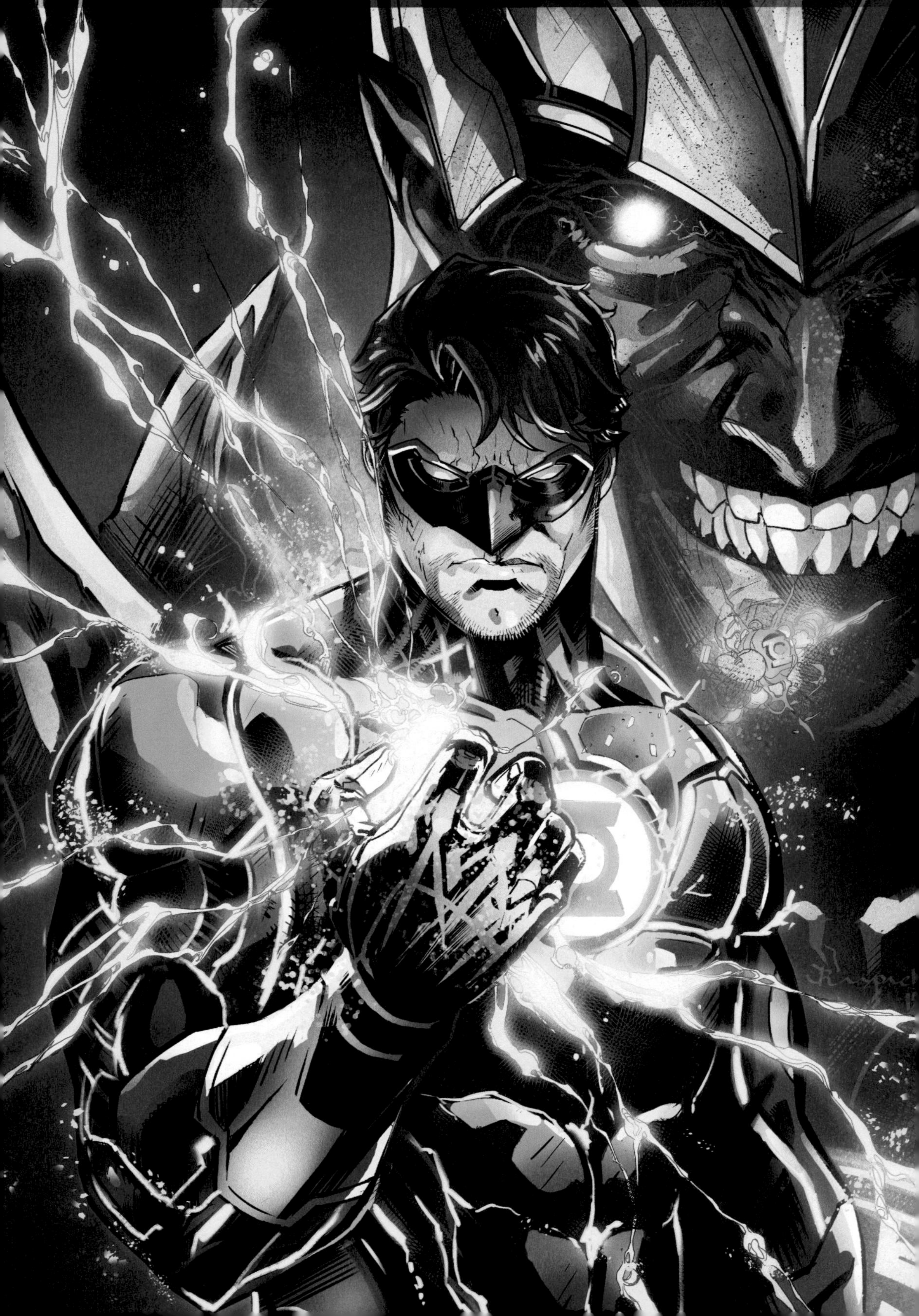

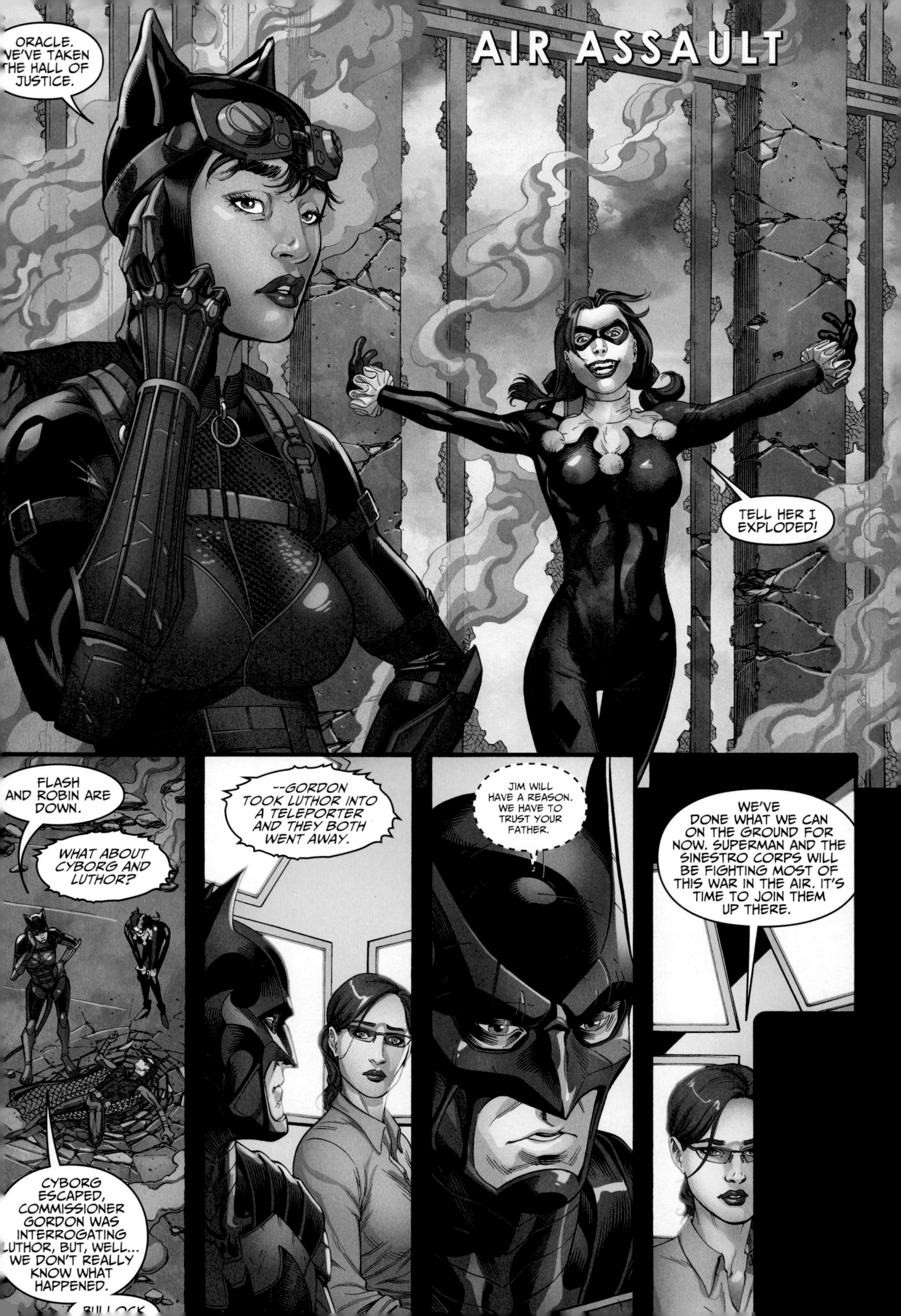
AIR ASSAULT
ORACLE. WE'VE TAKEN THE HALL OF JUSTICE.
TELL HER I EXPLODED!
FLASH AND ROBIN ARE DOWN.
WHAT ABOUT CYBORG AND LUTHOR?
CYBORG ESCAPED, COMMISSIONER GORDON WAS INTERROGATING LUTHOR, BUT, WELL... WE DON'T REALLY KNOW WHAT HAPPENED.
--GORDON TOOK LUTHOR INTO A TELEPORTER AND THEY BOTH WENT AWAY.
JIM WILL HAVE A REASON. WE HAVE TO TRUST YOUR FATHER.
WE'VE DONE WHAT WE CAN ON THE GROUND FOR NOW. SUPERMAN AND THE SINESTRO CORPS WILL BE FIGHTING MOST OF THIS WAR IN THE AIR. IT'S TIME TO JOIN THEM UP THERE.

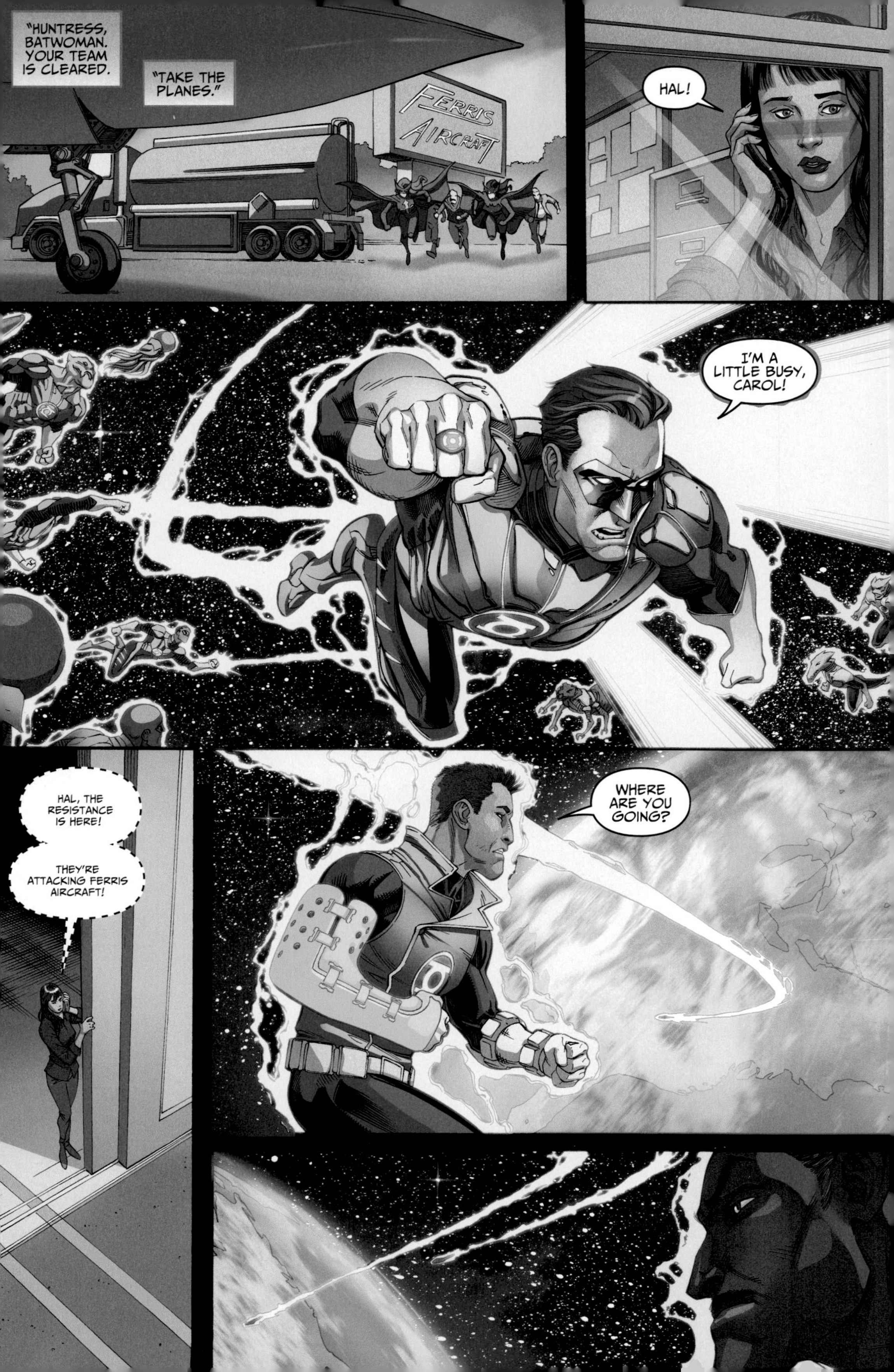
"HUNTRESS, BATWOMAN. YOUR TEAM IS CLEARED.
"TAKE THE PLANES."
FERRIS AIRCRAFT
HAL!
I'M A LITTLE BUSY, CAROL!
HAL, THE RESISTANCE IS HERE!
THEY'RE ATTACKING FERRIS AIRCRAFT!
WHERE ARE YOU GOING?

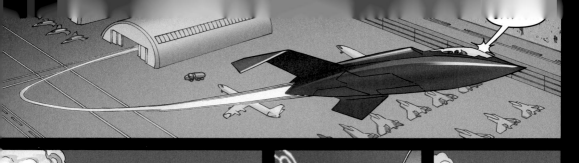

CAROL, ARE YOU OKAY?

I'M FINE. WHAT ARE THEY DOING HERE?

THEY'RE TRYING TO HELP.

LET THE PLANE GO.

THAT'S NOT GOING TO HAPPEN, GUY.

ARE WE REALLY GOING TO DO THIS?

NO. YOU'RE ABSOLUTELY NOT.

I CAN ACCEPT A CERTAIN AMOUNT OF MACHO CRAP FROM YOU TWO BUT I'M NOT GOING TO WATCH YOU BEAT EACH OTHER--

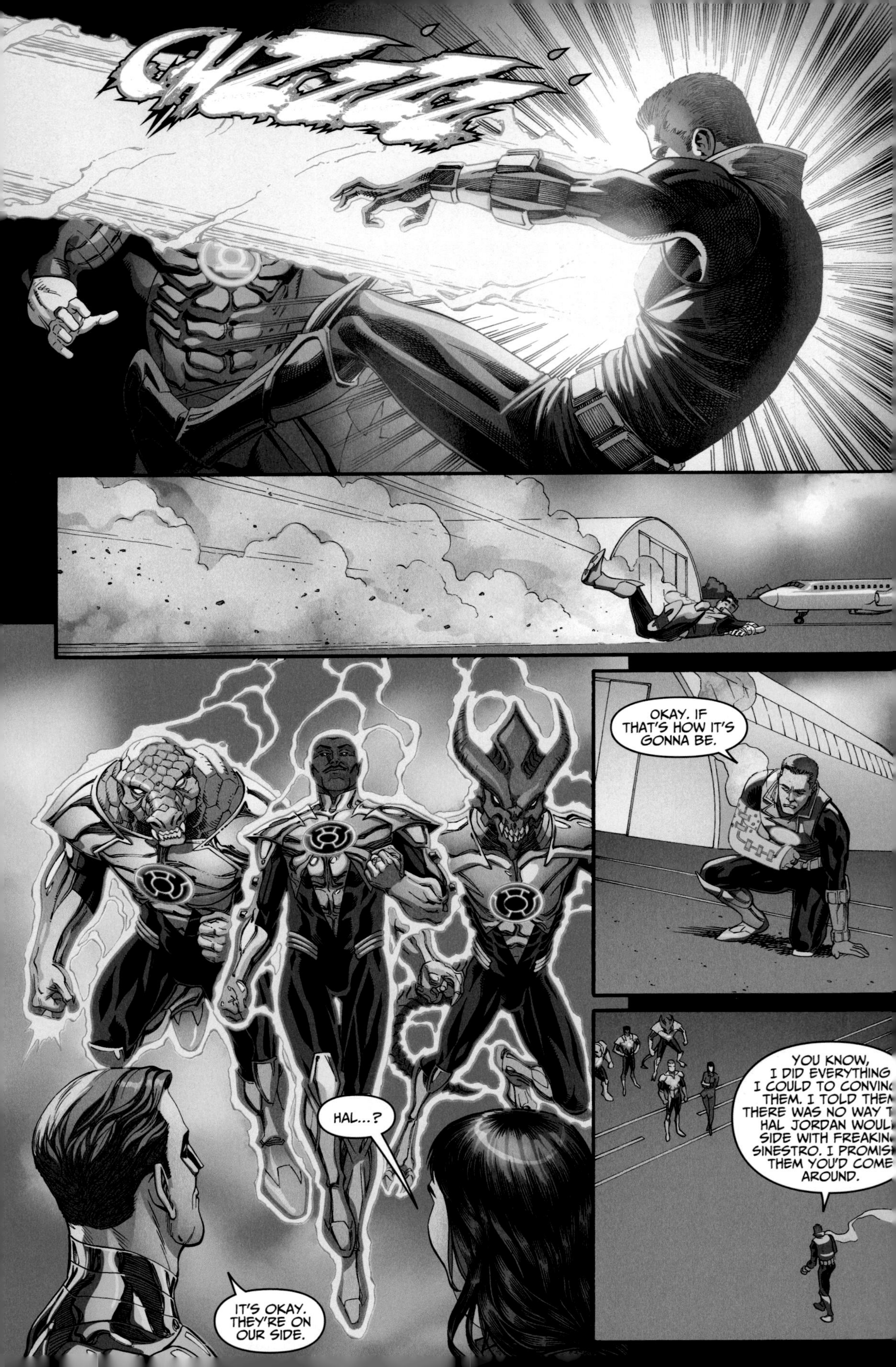
CHZZT
OKAY. IF THAT'S HOW IT'S GONNA BE.
HAL...?
IT'S OKAY. THEY'RE ON OUR SIDE.
YOU KNOW, I DID EVERYTHING I COULD TO CONVINC THEM. I TOLD THEM THERE WAS NO WAY T HAL JORDAN WOUL SIDE WITH FREAKIN SINESTRO. I PROMIS THEM YOU'D COME AROUND.

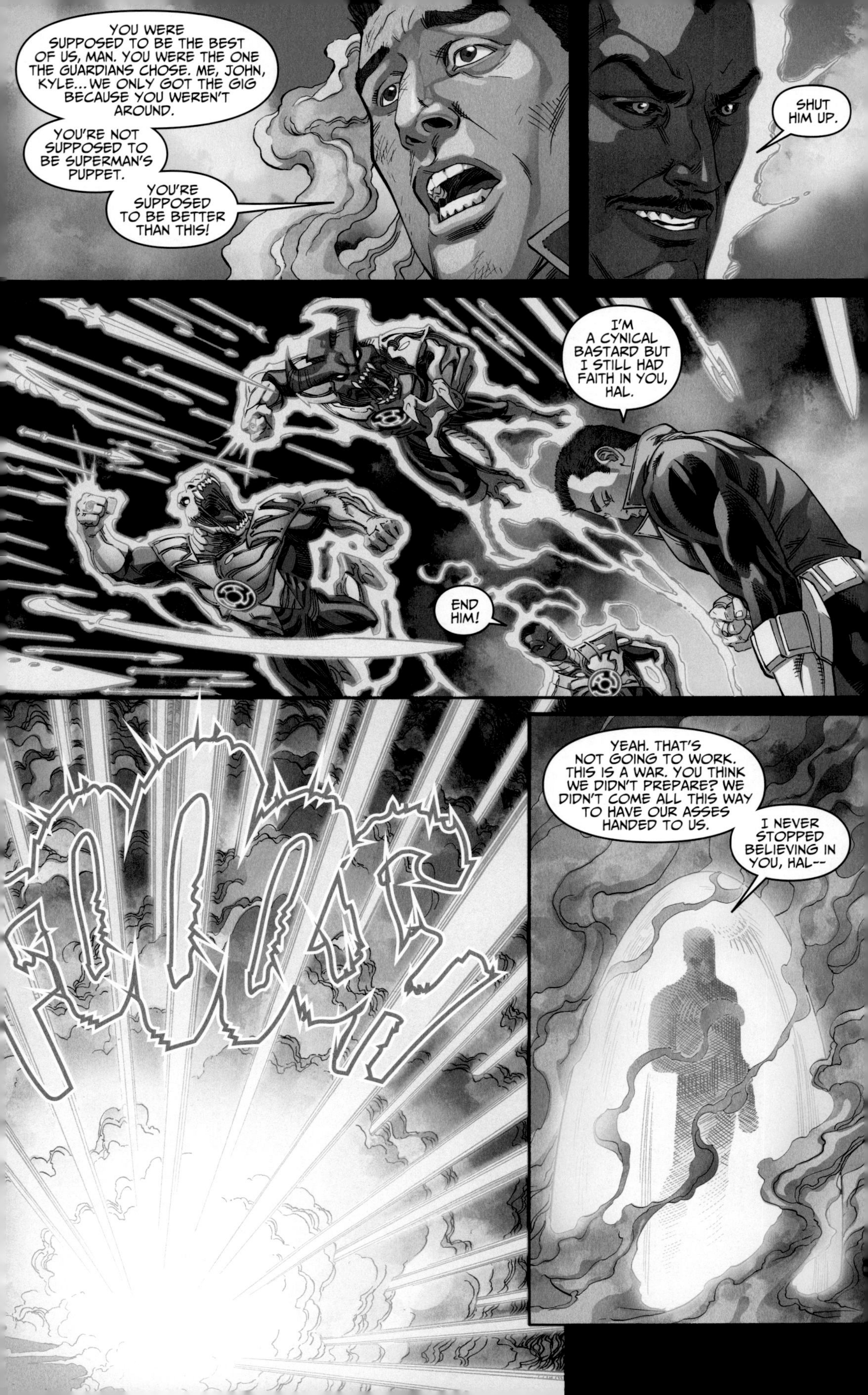
YOU WERE SUPPOSED TO BE THE BEST OF US, MAN. YOU WERE THE ONE THE GUARDIANS CHOSE. ME, JOHN, KYLE...WE ONLY GOT THE GIG BECAUSE YOU WEREN'T AROUND.
YOU'RE NOT SUPPOSED TO BE SUPERMAN'S PUPPET.
YOU'RE SUPPOSED TO BE BETTER THAN THIS!
SHUT HIM UP.
I'M A CYNICAL BASTARD BUT I STILL HAD FAITH IN YOU, HAL.
END HIM!
YEAH. THAT'S NOT GOING TO WORK. THIS IS A WAR. YOU THINK WE DIDN'T PREPARE? WE DIDN'T COME ALL THIS WAY TO HAVE OUR ASSES HANDED TO US.
I NEVER STOPPED BELIEVING IN YOU, HAL--

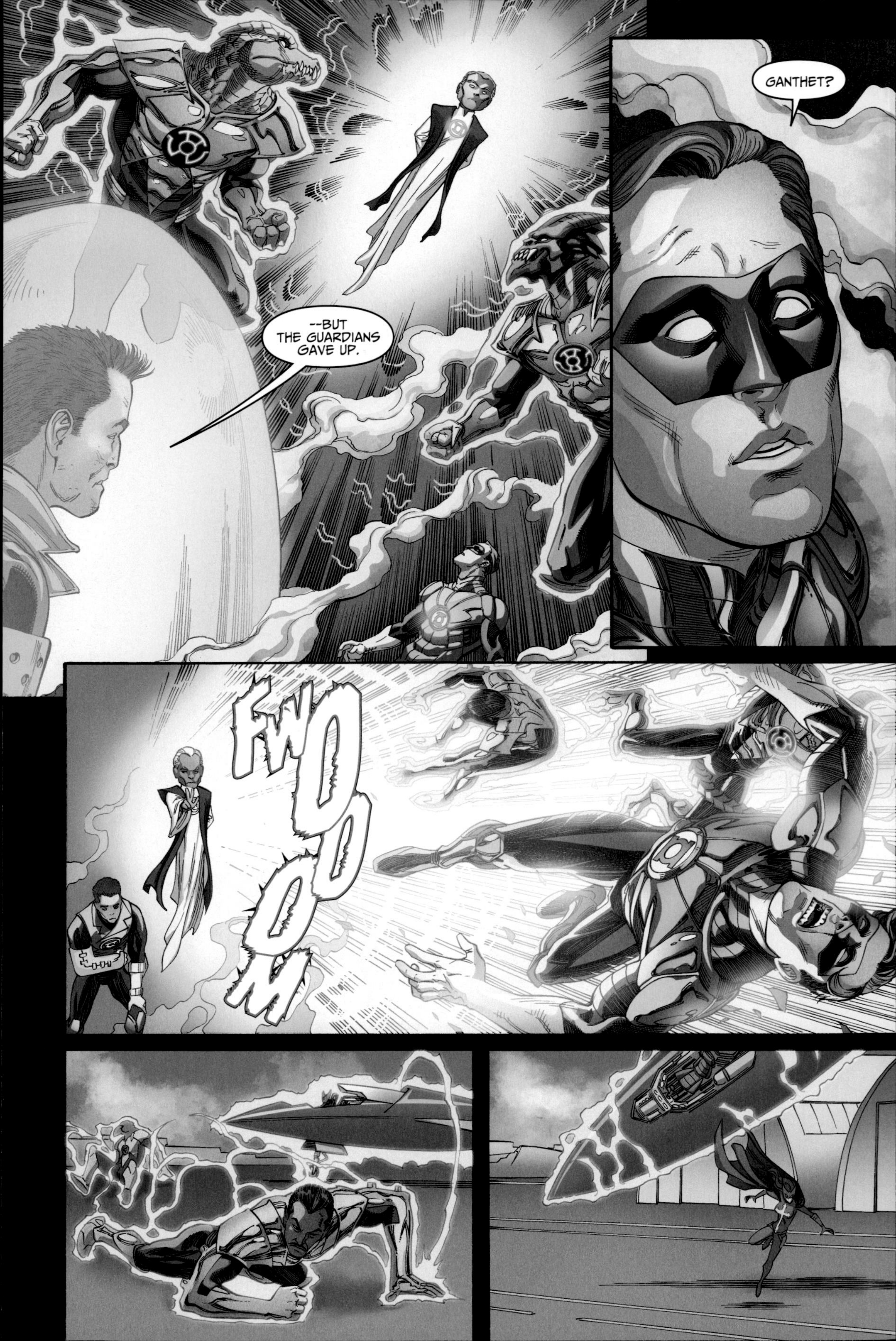
--BUT THE GUARDIANS GAVE UP.
GANTHET?
FWOOOOM

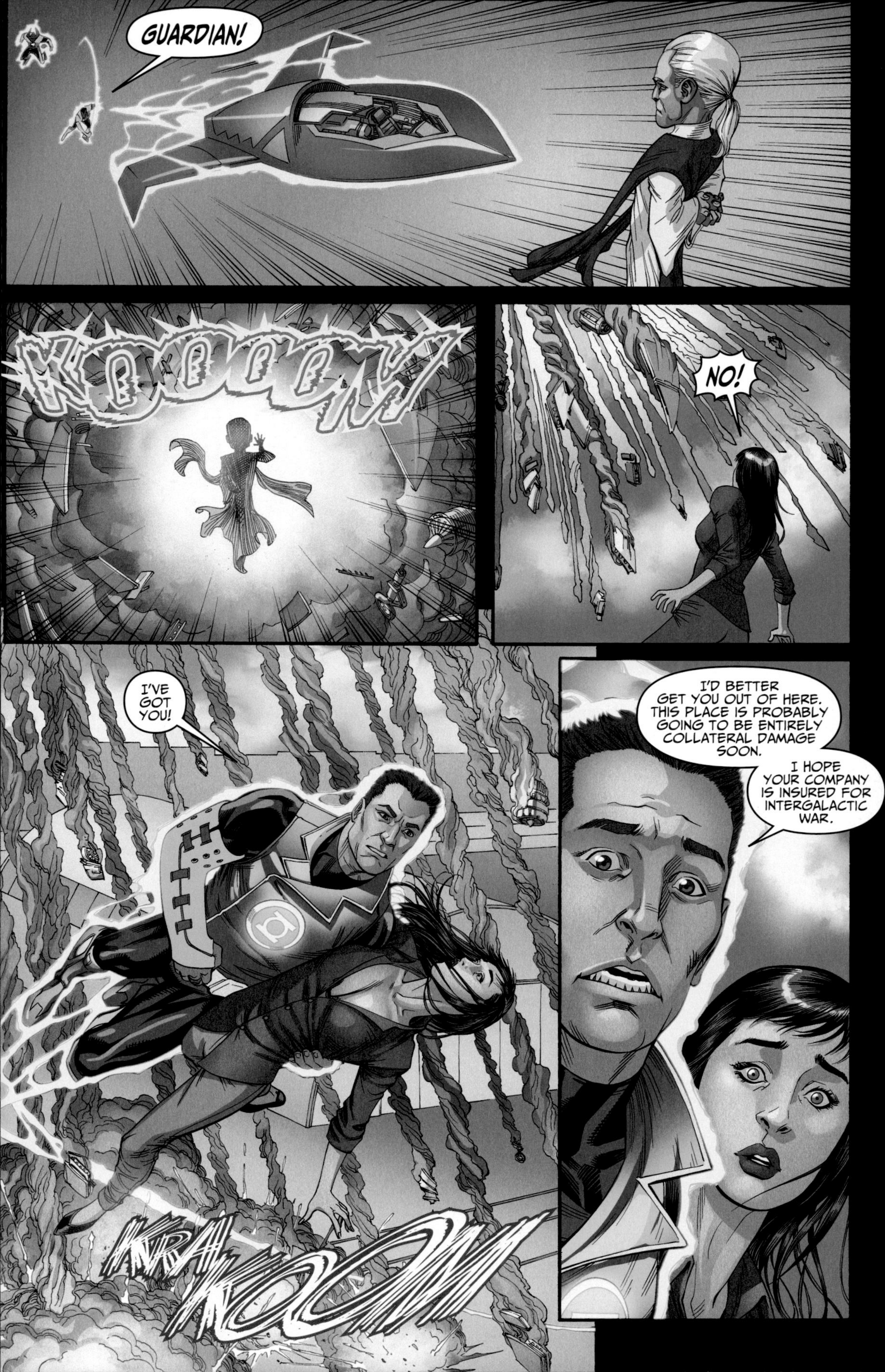

GUARDIAN!
KRAAAAM
NO!
I'VE GOT YOU!
KRAKOOM
I'D BETTER GET YOU OUT OF HERE. THIS PLACE IS PROBABLY GOING TO BE ENTIRELY COLLATERAL DAMAGE SOON.
I HOPE YOUR COMPANY IS INSURED FOR INTERGALACTIC WAR.

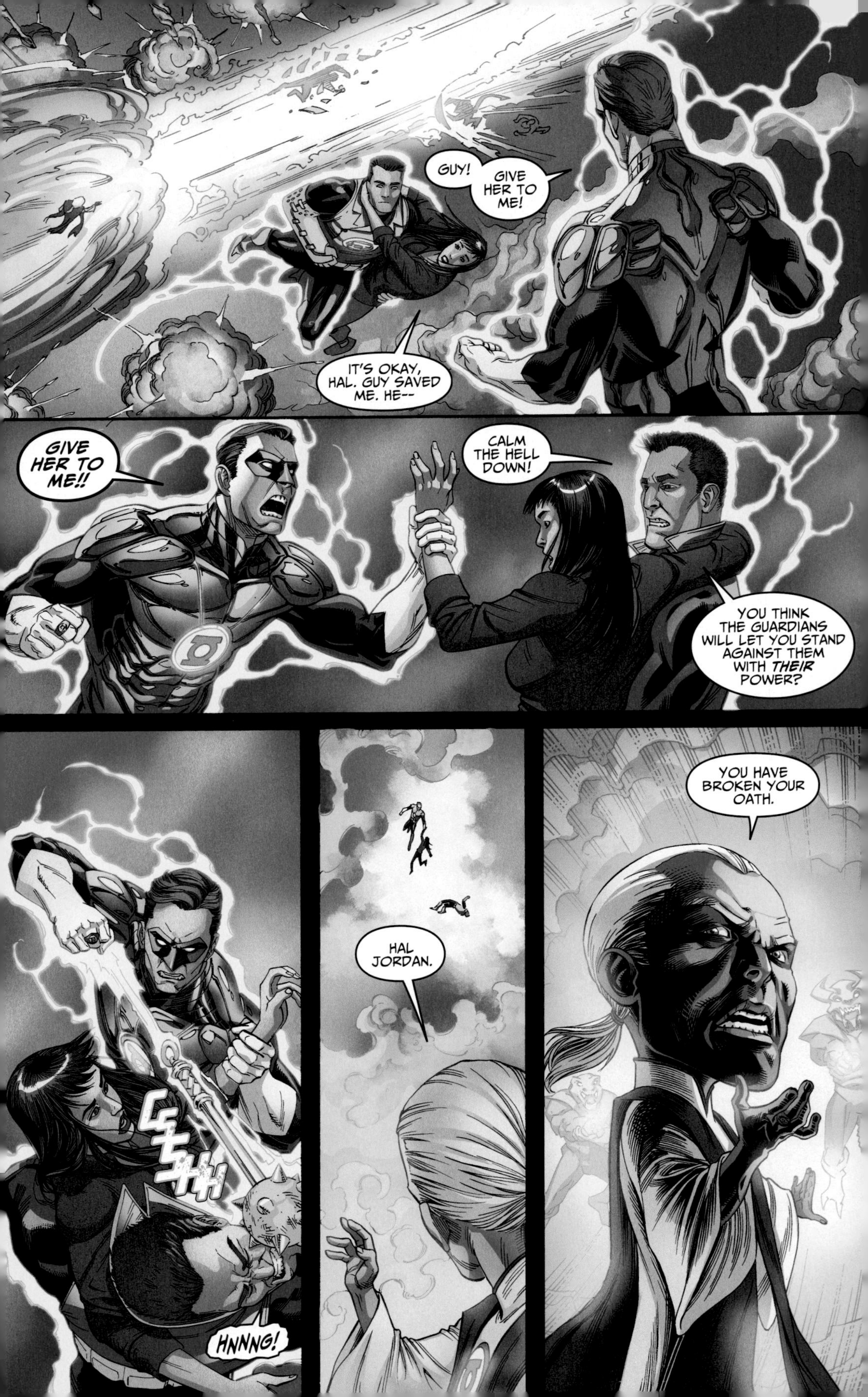
GUY!
GIVE HER TO ME!
IT'S OKAY, HAL. GUY SAVED ME. HE--
GIVE HER TO ME!!
CALM THE HELL DOWN!
YOU THINK THE GUARDIANS WILL LET YOU STAND AGAINST THEM WITH THEIR POWER?
CSSHH
HNNNG!
HAL JORDAN.
YOU HAVE BROKEN YOUR OATH.

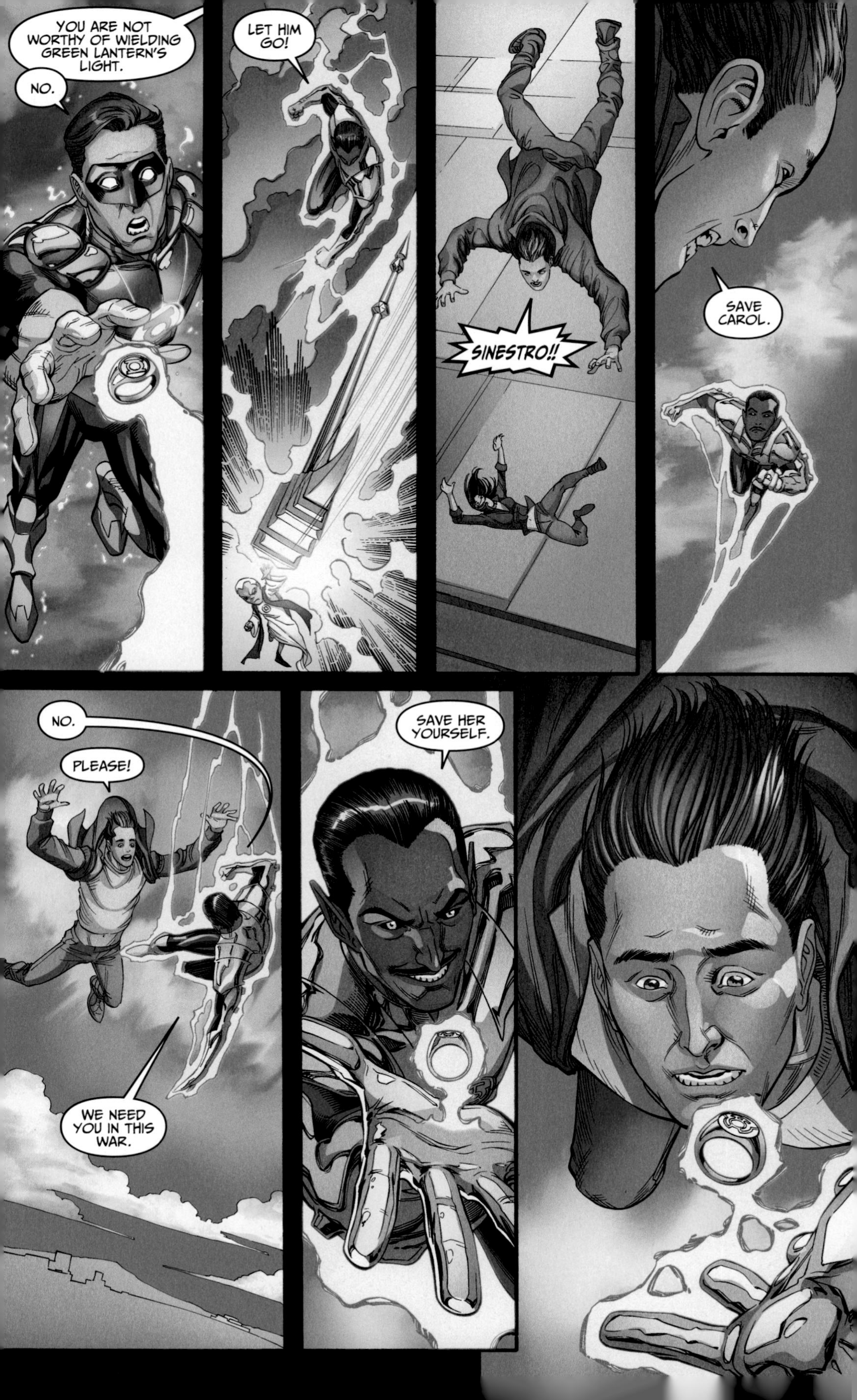
YOU ARE NOT WORTHY OF WIELDING GREEN LANTERN'S LIGHT.
NO.
LET HIM GO!
SINESTRO!!
SAVE CAROL.
NO.
PLEASE!
WE NEED YOU IN THIS WAR.
SAVE HER YOURSELF.

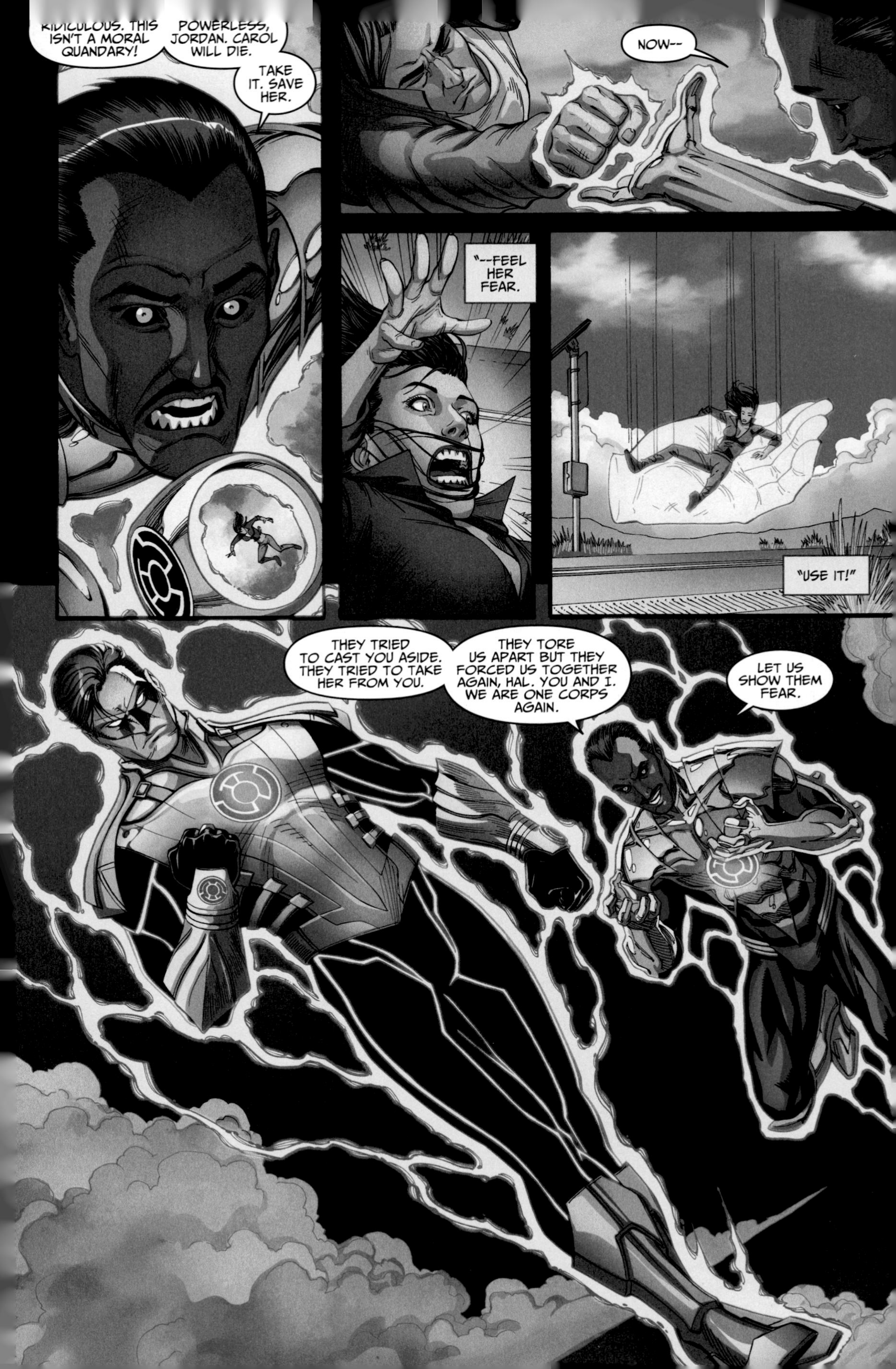
RIDICULOUS. THIS ISN'T A MORAL QUANDARY!
POWERLESS, JORDAN. CAROL WILL DIE.
TAKE IT. SAVE HER.
NOW--
"--FEEL HER FEAR.
"USE IT!"
THEY TRIED TO CAST YOU ASIDE. THEY TRIED TO TAKE HER FROM YOU.
THEY TORE US APART BUT THEY FORCED US TOGETHER AGAIN, HAL. YOU AND I. WE ARE ONE CORPS AGAIN.
LET US SHOW THEM FEAR.

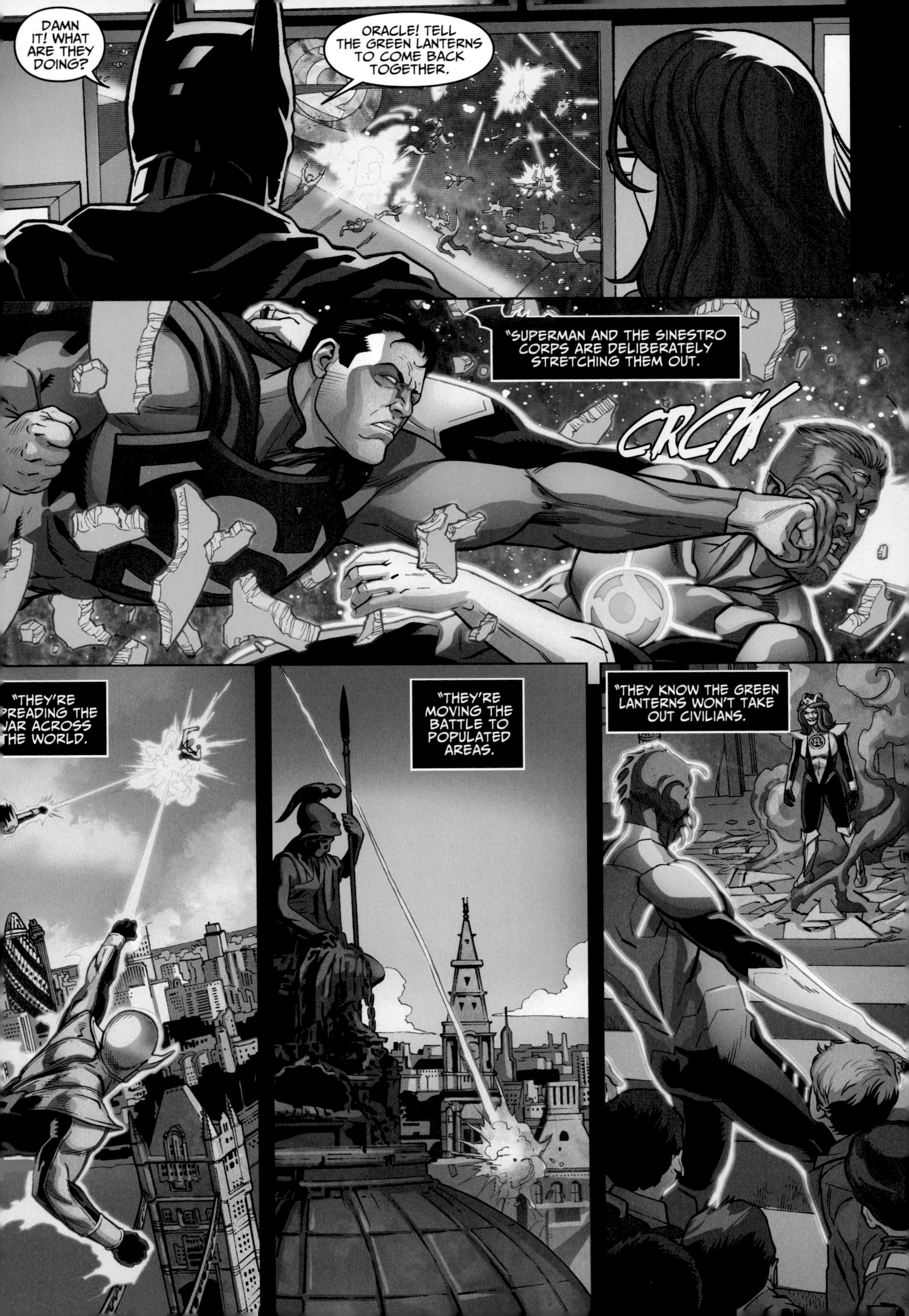
DAMN IT! WHAT ARE THEY DOING?
ORACLE! TELL THE GREEN LANTERNS TO COME BACK TOGETHER.
"SUPERMAN AND THE SINESTRO CORPS ARE DELIBERATELY STRETCHING THEM OUT.
CRCK
"THEY'RE PREADING THE WAR ACROSS THE WORLD.
"THEY'RE MOVING THE BATTLE TO POPULATED AREAS.
"THEY KNOW THE GREEN LANTERNS WON'T TAKE OUT CIVILIANS.

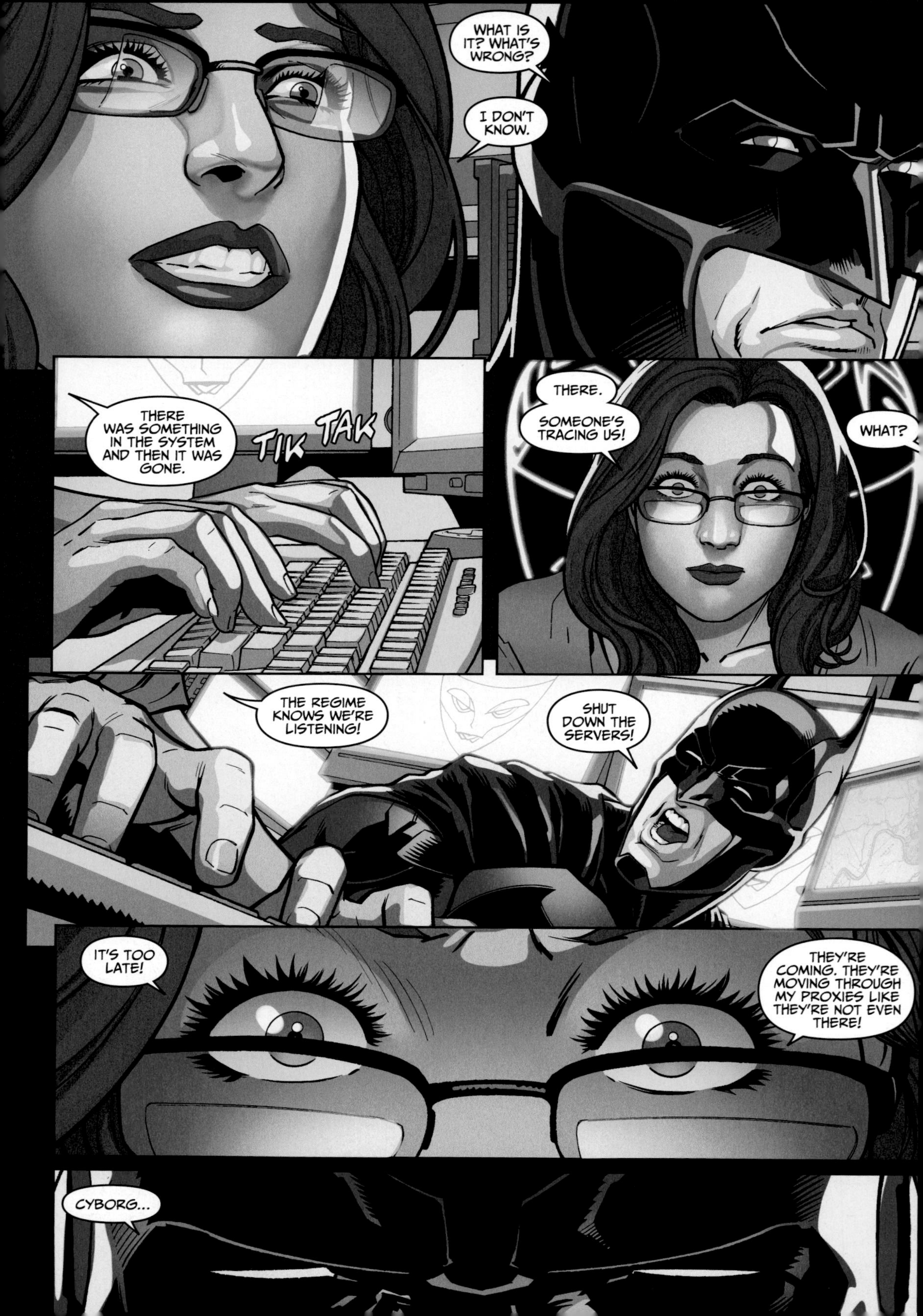
WHAT IS IT? WHAT'S WRONG?
I DON'T KNOW.
THERE WAS SOMETHING IN THE SYSTEM AND THEN IT WAS GONE.
TIK TAK
THERE.
SOMEONE'S TRACING US!
WHAT?
THE REGIME KNOWS WE'RE LISTENING!
SHUT DOWN THE SERVERS!
IT'S TOO LATE!
THEY'RE COMING. THEY'RE MOVING THROUGH MY PROXIES LIKE THEY'RE NOT EVEN THERE!
CYBORG...

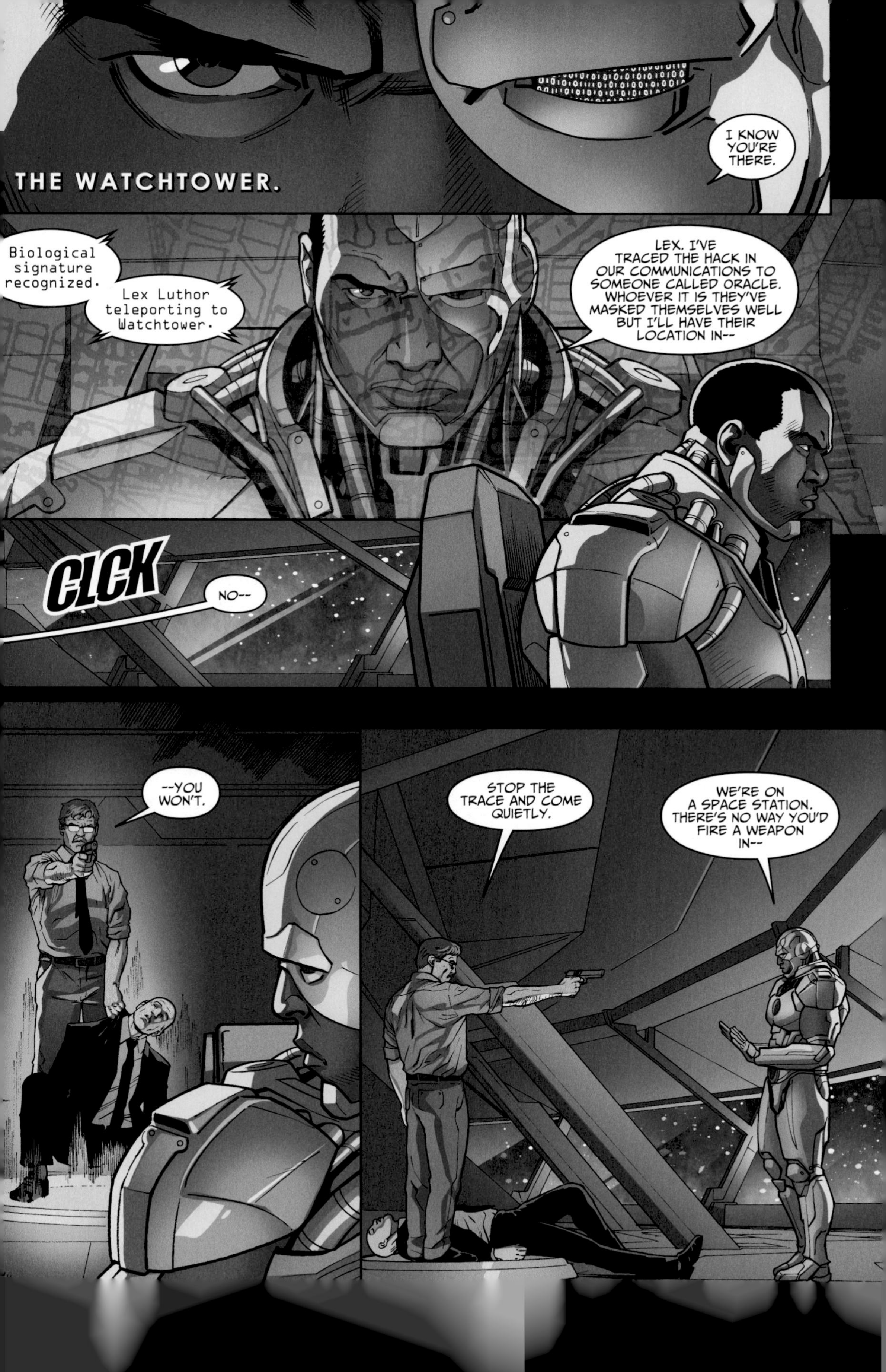
THE WATCHTOWER.
I KNOW YOU'RE THERE.
Biological signature recognized.
Lex Luthor teleporting to Watchtower.
LEX. I'VE TRACED THE HACK IN OUR COMMUNICATIONS TO SOMEONE CALLED ORACLE. WHOEVER IT IS THEY'VE MASKED THEMSELVES WELL BUT I'LL HAVE THEIR LOCATION IN--
CLCK
NO--
--YOU WON'T.
STOP THE TRACE AND COME QUIETLY.
WE'RE ON A SPACE STATION. THERE'S NO WAY YOU'D FIRE A WEAPON IN--

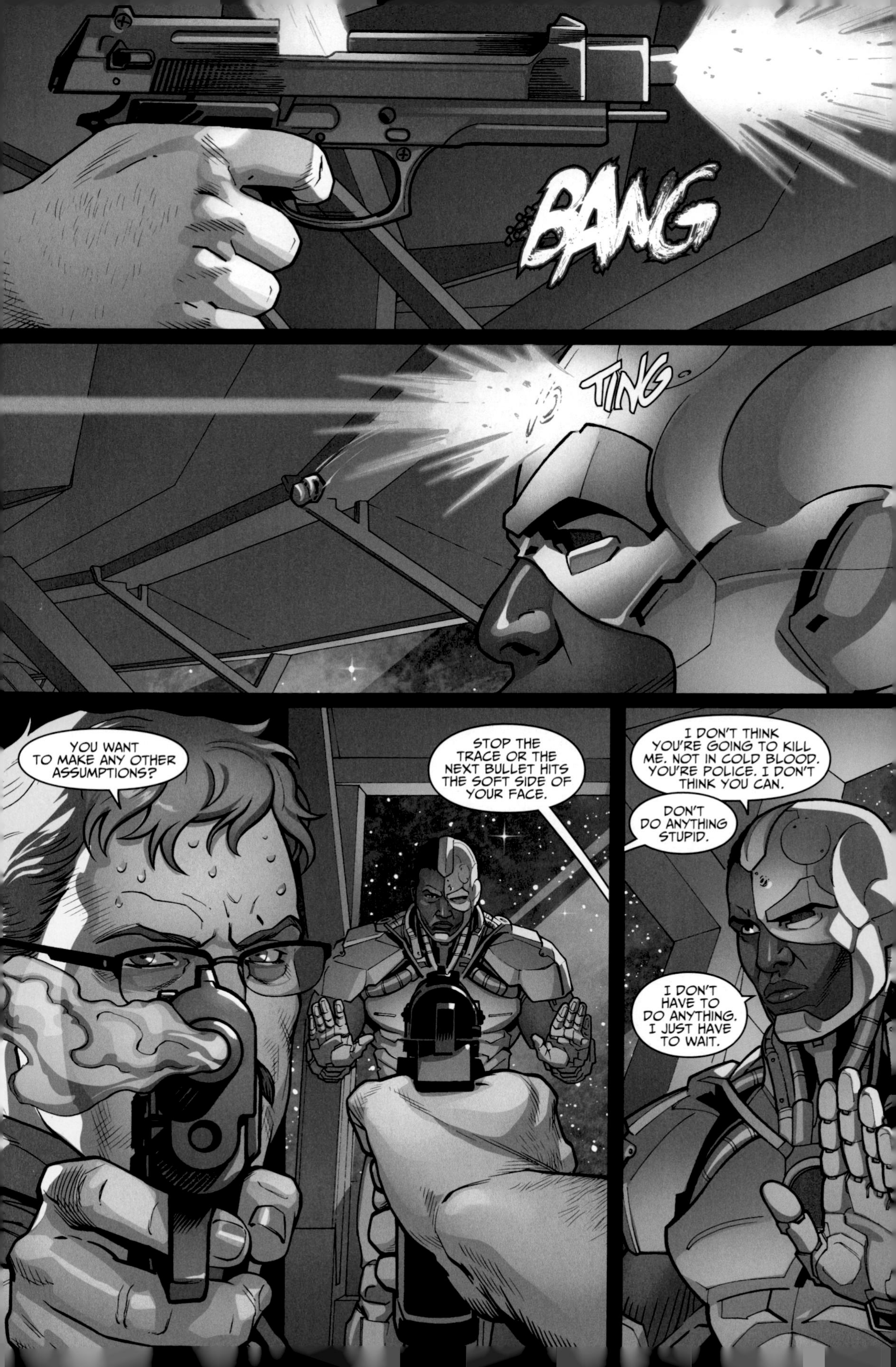
BANG
TING
YOU WANT TO MAKE ANY OTHER ASSUMPTIONS?
STOP THE TRACE OR THE NEXT BULLET HITS THE SOFT SIDE OF YOUR FACE.
I DON'T THINK YOU'RE GOING TO KILL ME. NOT IN COLD BLOOD. YOU'RE POLICE. I DON'T THINK YOU CAN.
DON'T DO ANYTHING STUPID.
I DON'T HAVE TO DO ANYTHING. I JUST HAVE TO WAIT.

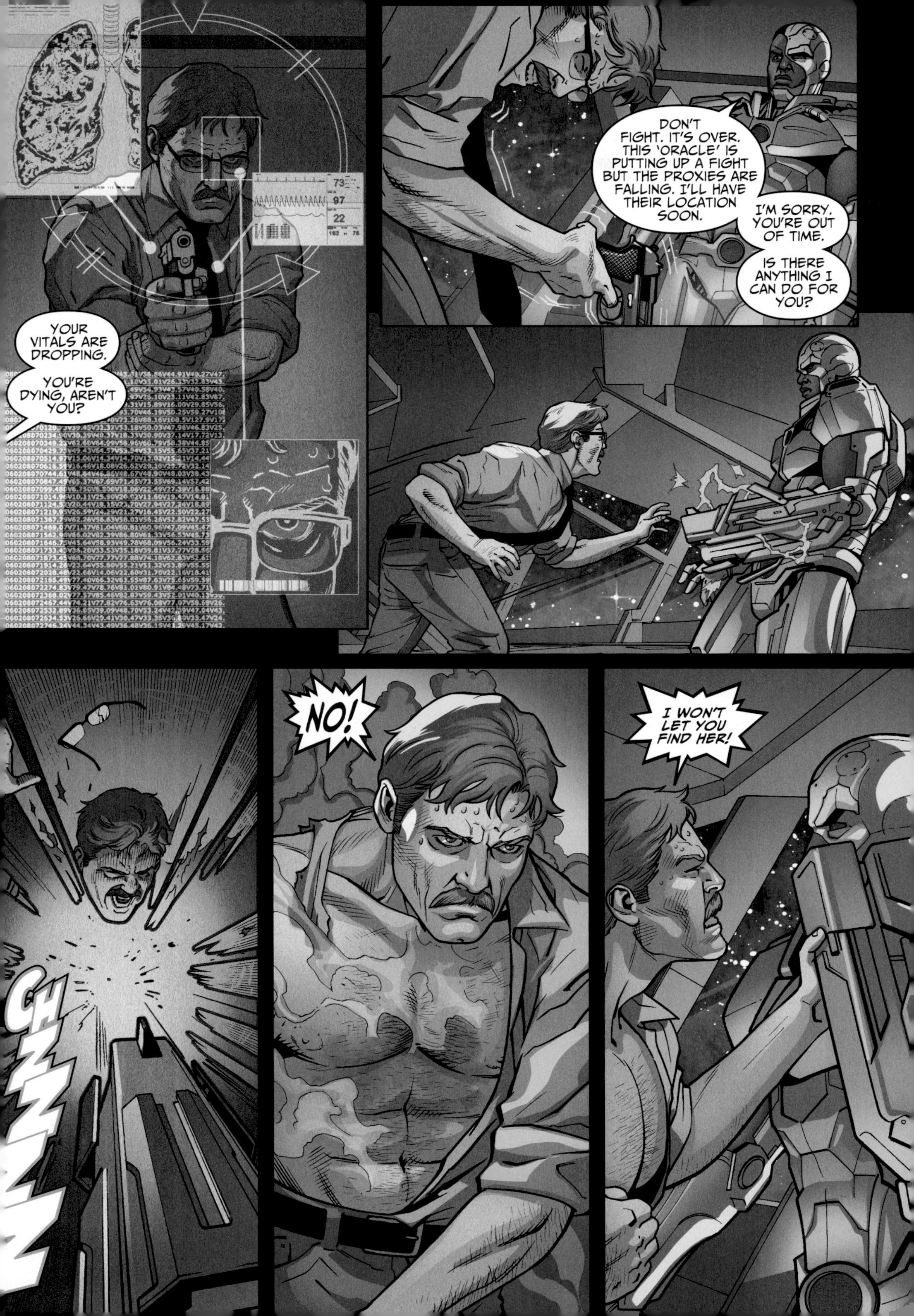
YOUR VITALS ARE DROPPING.
YOU'RE DYING, AREN'T YOU?
DON'T FIGHT. IT'S OVER. THIS 'ORACLE' IS PUTTING UP A FIGHT BUT THE PROXIES ARE FALLING. I'LL HAVE THEIR LOCATION SOON.
I'M SORRY. YOU'RE OUT OF TIME.
IS THERE ANYTHING I CAN DO FOR YOU?
CHNNNNN
NO!
I WON'T LET YOU FIND HER!

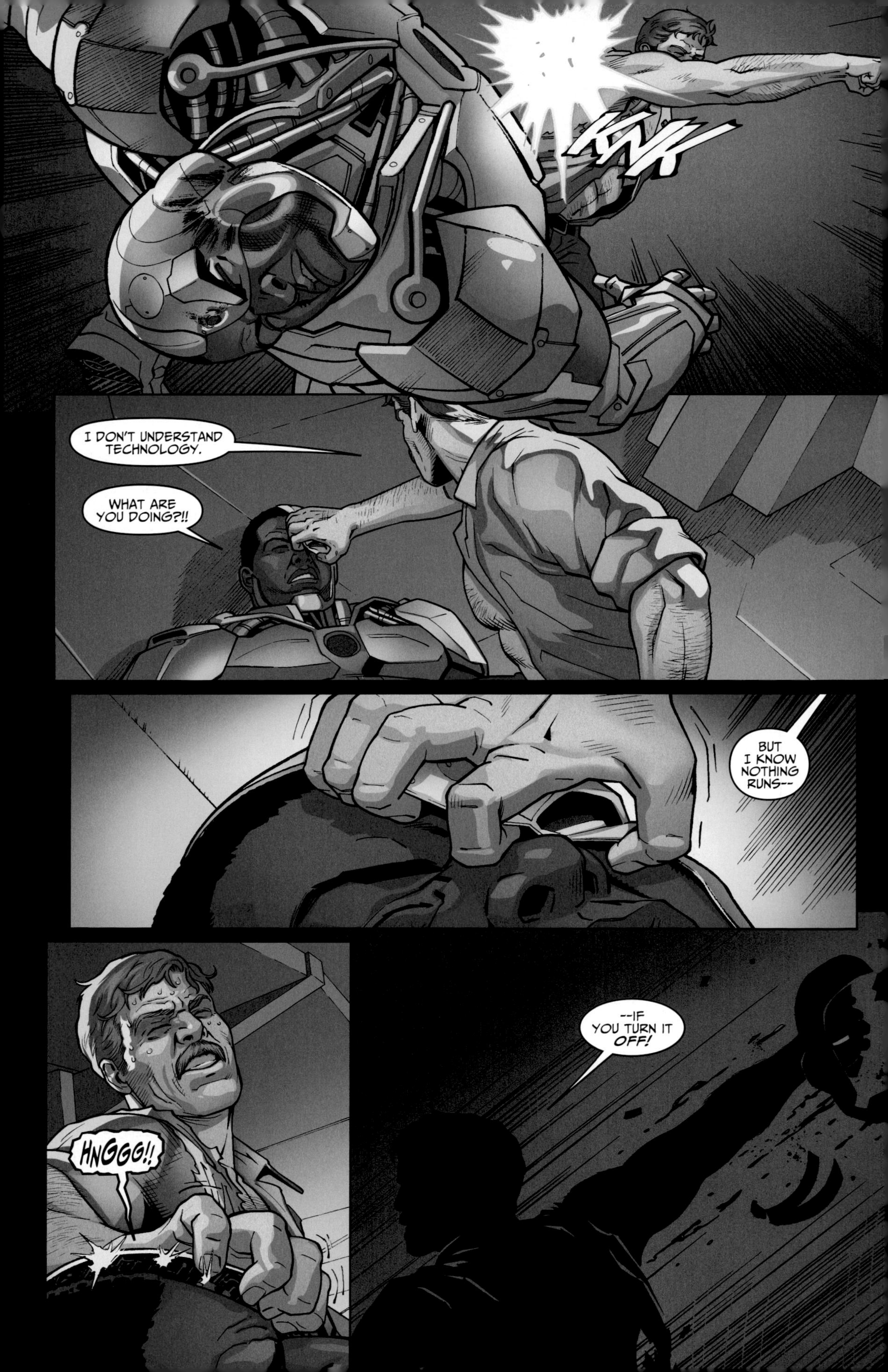
KNK
I DON'T UNDERSTAND TECHNOLOGY.
WHAT ARE YOU DOING?!!
BUT I KNOW NOTHING RUNS--
HNGGG!!
--IF YOU TURN IT OFF!

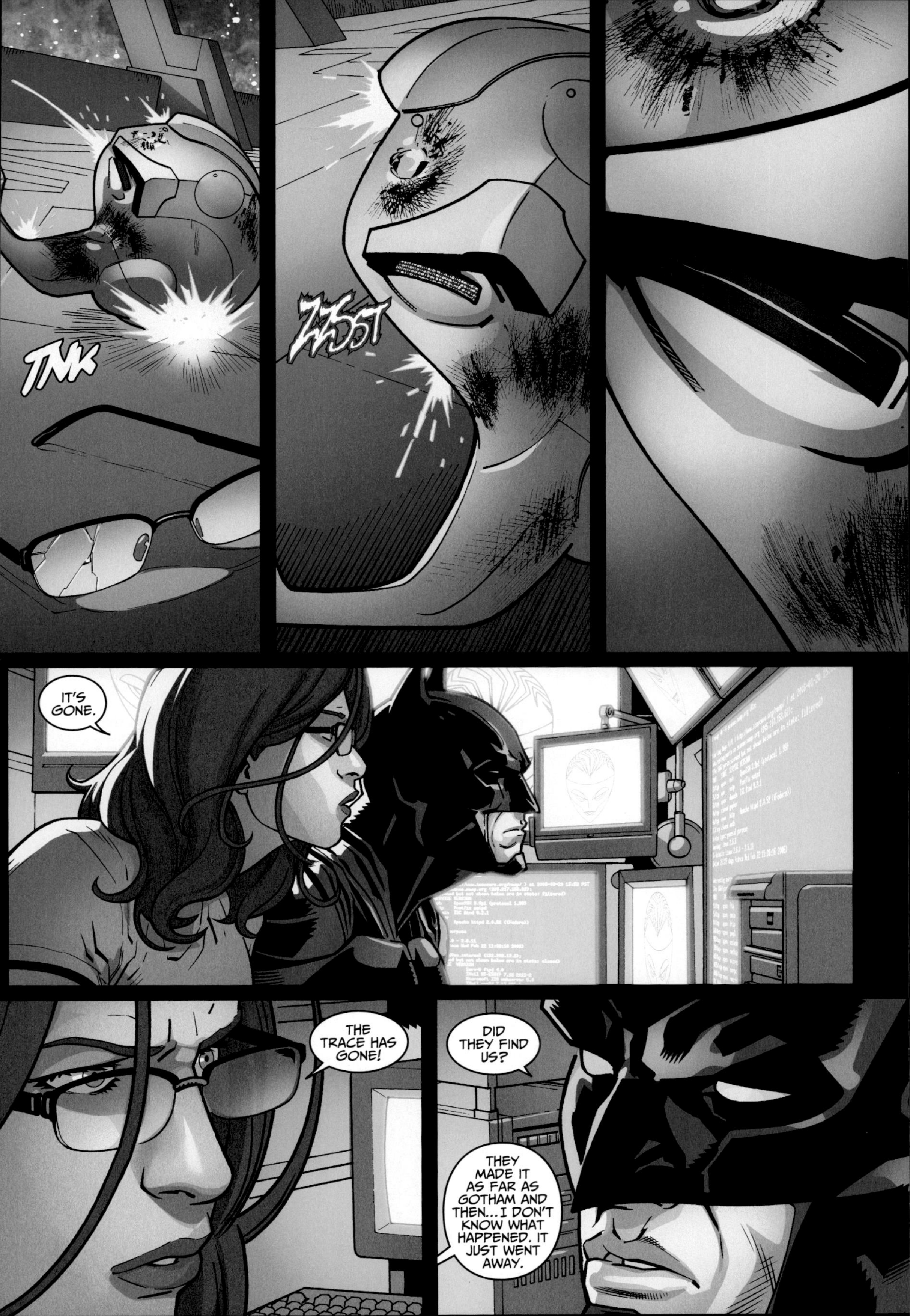
TNK
ZZSST
IT'S GONE.
THE TRACE HAS GONE!
DID THEY FIND US?
THEY MADE IT AS FAR AS GOTHAM AND THEN...I DON'T KNOW WHAT HAPPENED. IT JUST WENT AWAY.

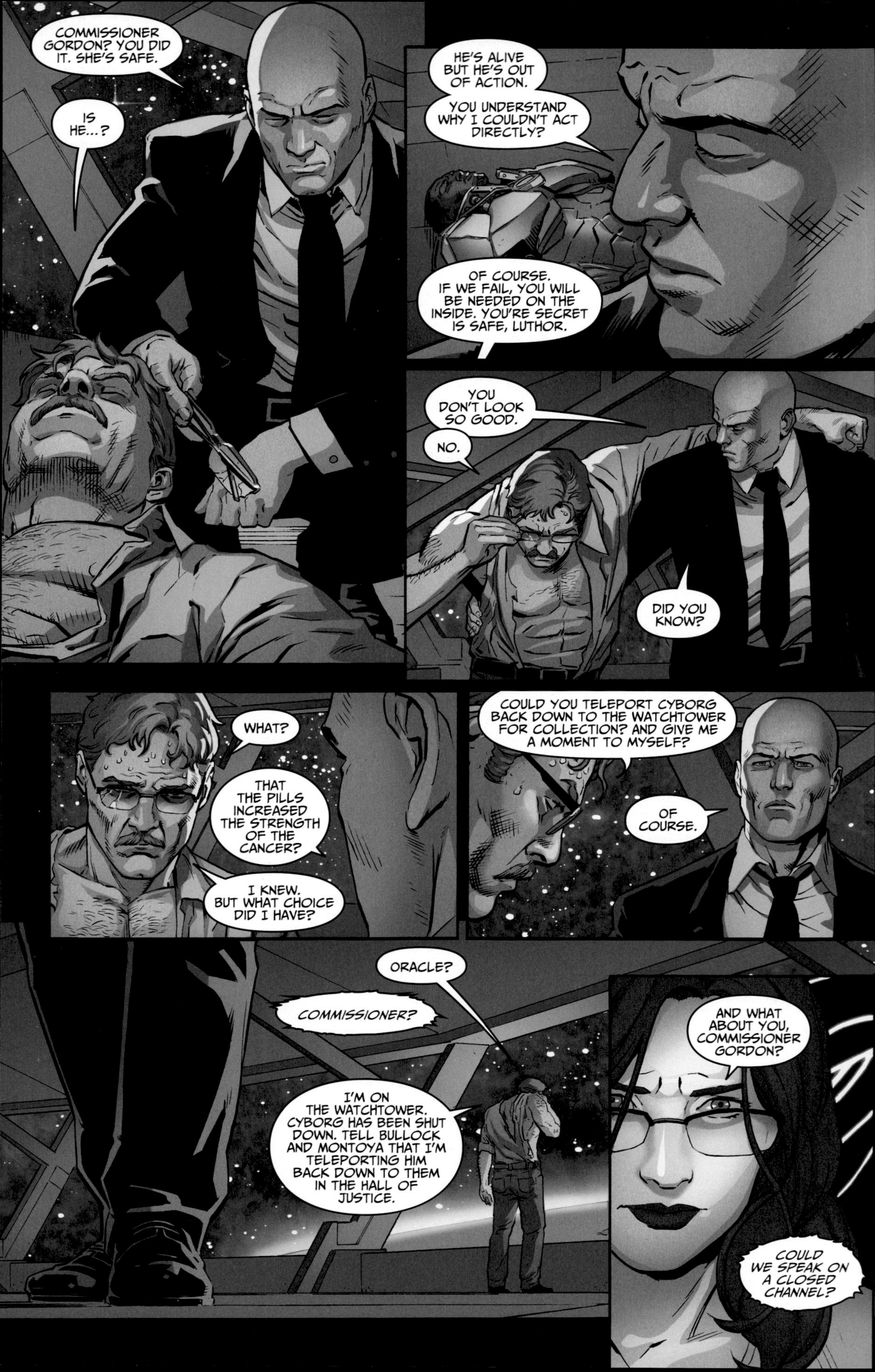
COMMISSIONER GORDON? YOU DID IT. SHE'S SAFE.
IS HE...?
HE'S ALIVE BUT HE'S OUT OF ACTION.
YOU UNDERSTAND WHY I COULDN'T ACT DIRECTLY?
OF COURSE. IF WE FAIL, YOU WILL BE NEEDED ON THE INSIDE. YOU'RE SECRET IS SAFE, LUTHOR.
YOU DON'T LOOK SO GOOD.
NO.
DID YOU KNOW?
WHAT?
THAT THE PILLS INCREASED THE STRENGTH OF THE CANCER?
I KNEW. BUT WHAT CHOICE DID I HAVE?
COULD YOU TELEPORT CYBORG BACK DOWN TO THE WATCHTOWER FOR COLLECTION? AND GIVE ME A MOMENT TO MYSELF?
OF COURSE.
ORACLE?
COMMISSIONER?
I'M ON THE WATCHTOWER. CYBORG HAS BEEN SHUT DOWN. TELL BULLOCK AND MONTOYA THAT I'M TELEPORTING HIM BACK DOWN TO THEM IN THE HALL OF JUSTICE.
AND WHAT ABOUT YOU, COMMISSIONER GORDON?
COULD WE SPEAK ON A CLOSED CHANNEL?

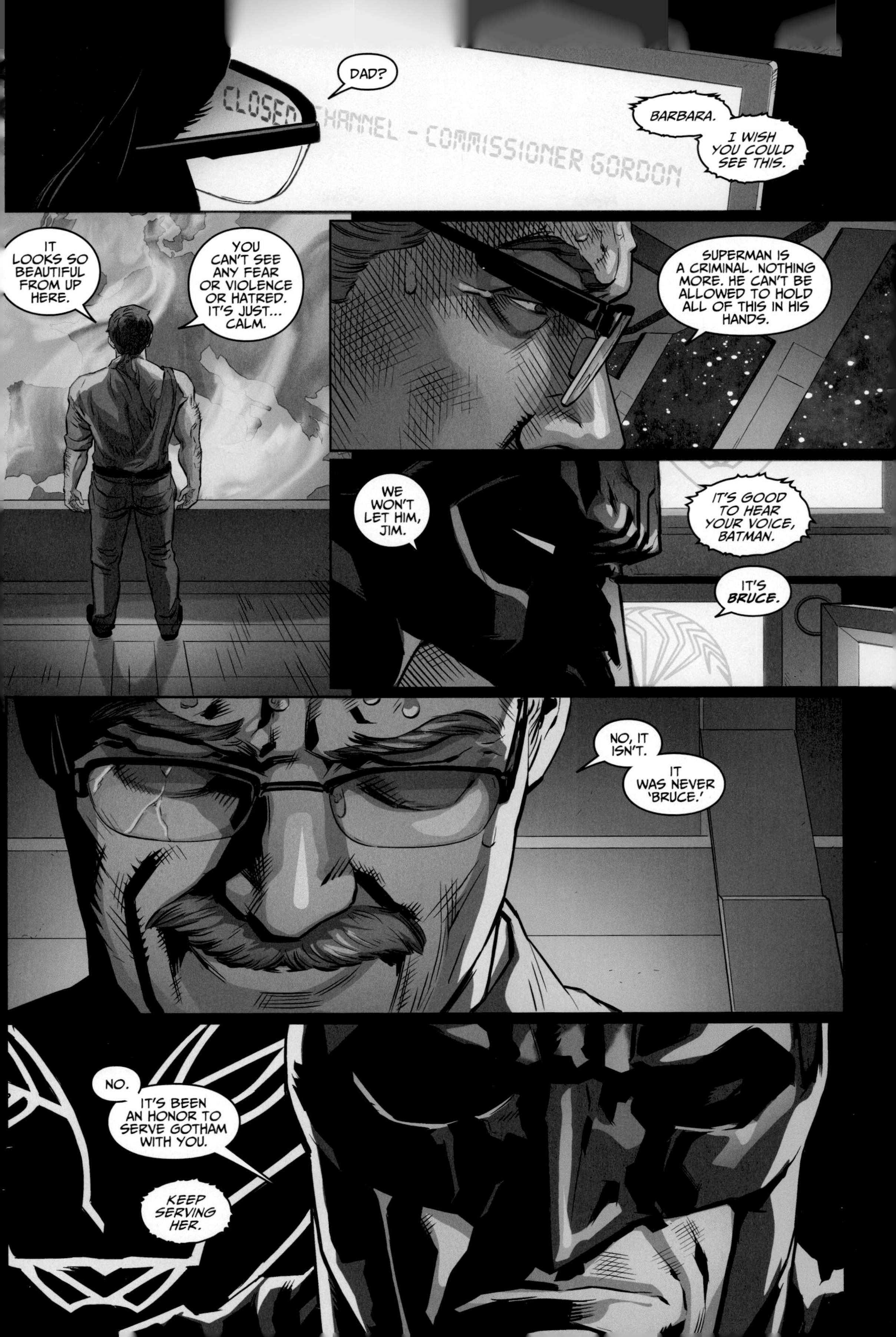
DAD?
CLOSED CHANNEL - COMMISSIONER GORDON
BARBARA.
I WISH YOU COULD SEE THIS.
IT LOOKS SO BEAUTIFUL FROM UP HERE.
YOU CAN'T SEE ANY FEAR OR VIOLENCE OR HATRED. IT'S JUST... CALM.
SUPERMAN IS A CRIMINAL. NOTHING MORE. HE CAN'T BE ALLOWED TO HOLD ALL OF THIS IN HIS HANDS.
WE WON'T LET HIM, JIM.
IT'S GOOD TO HEAR YOUR VOICE, BATMAN.
IT'S BRUCE.
NO, IT ISN'T.
IT WAS NEVER 'BRUCE.'
NO.
IT'S BEEN AN HONOR TO SERVE GOTHAM WITH YOU.
KEEP SERVING HER.

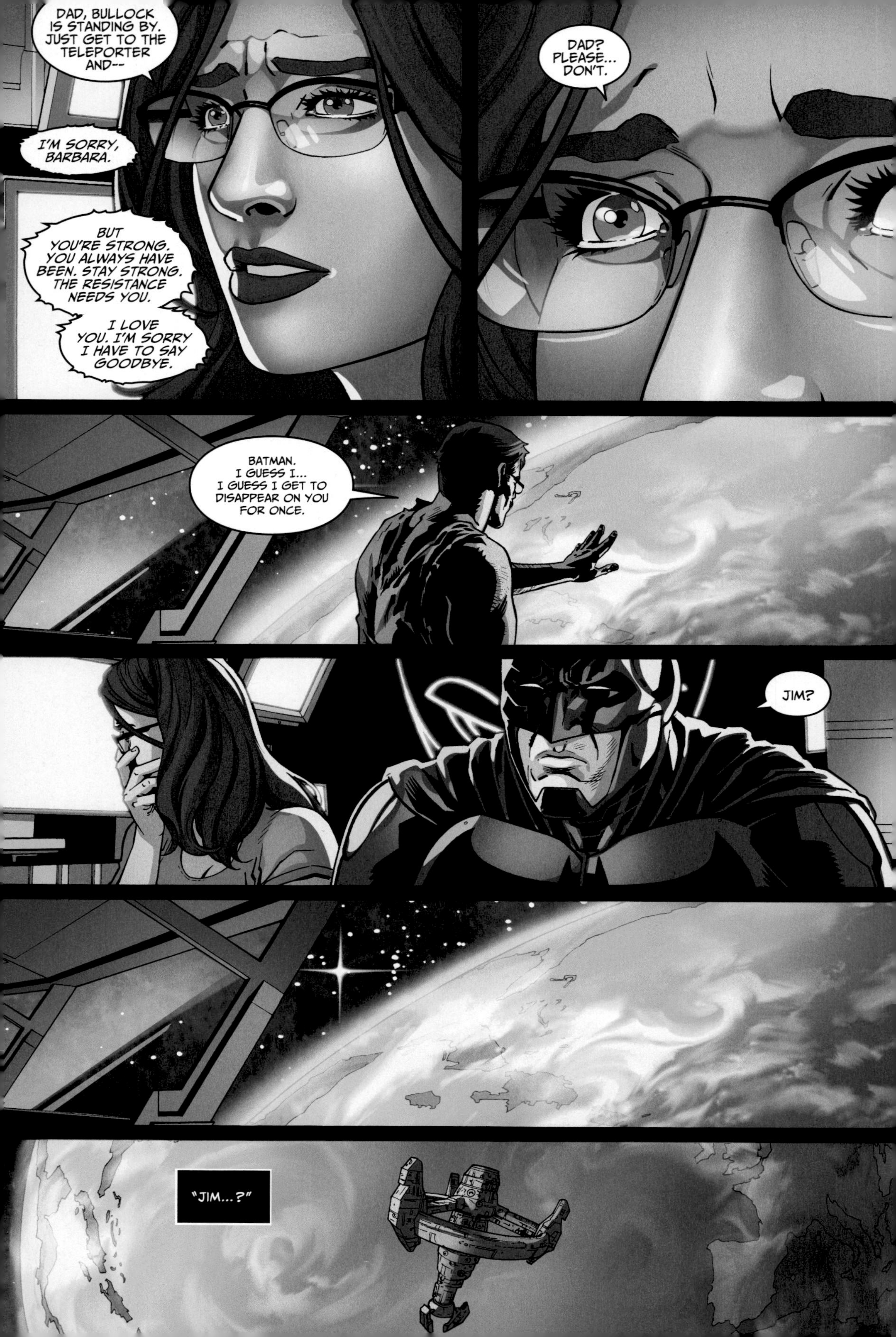
DAD, BULLOCK IS STANDING BY. JUST GET TO THE TELEPORTER AND--
I'M SORRY, BARBARA.
BUT YOU'RE STRONG. YOU ALWAYS HAVE BEEN. STAY STRONG. THE RESISTANCE NEEDS YOU.
I LOVE YOU. I'M SORRY I HAVE TO SAY GOODBYE.
DAD? PLEASE... DON'T.
BATMAN. I GUESS I... I GUESS I GET TO DISAPPEAR ON YOU FOR ONCE.
JIM?
"JIM...?"

"Crashing to Earth" **Mike S. Miller** Artist **J. Nanjan (NS Studios)** Colorist
"Canary's Revenge" **Tom Derenick** Artist **Rex Lokus** Colorist
Cover Art by **Jheremy Raapack & David Lopez** and **Santi Casas of Ikari Studio**

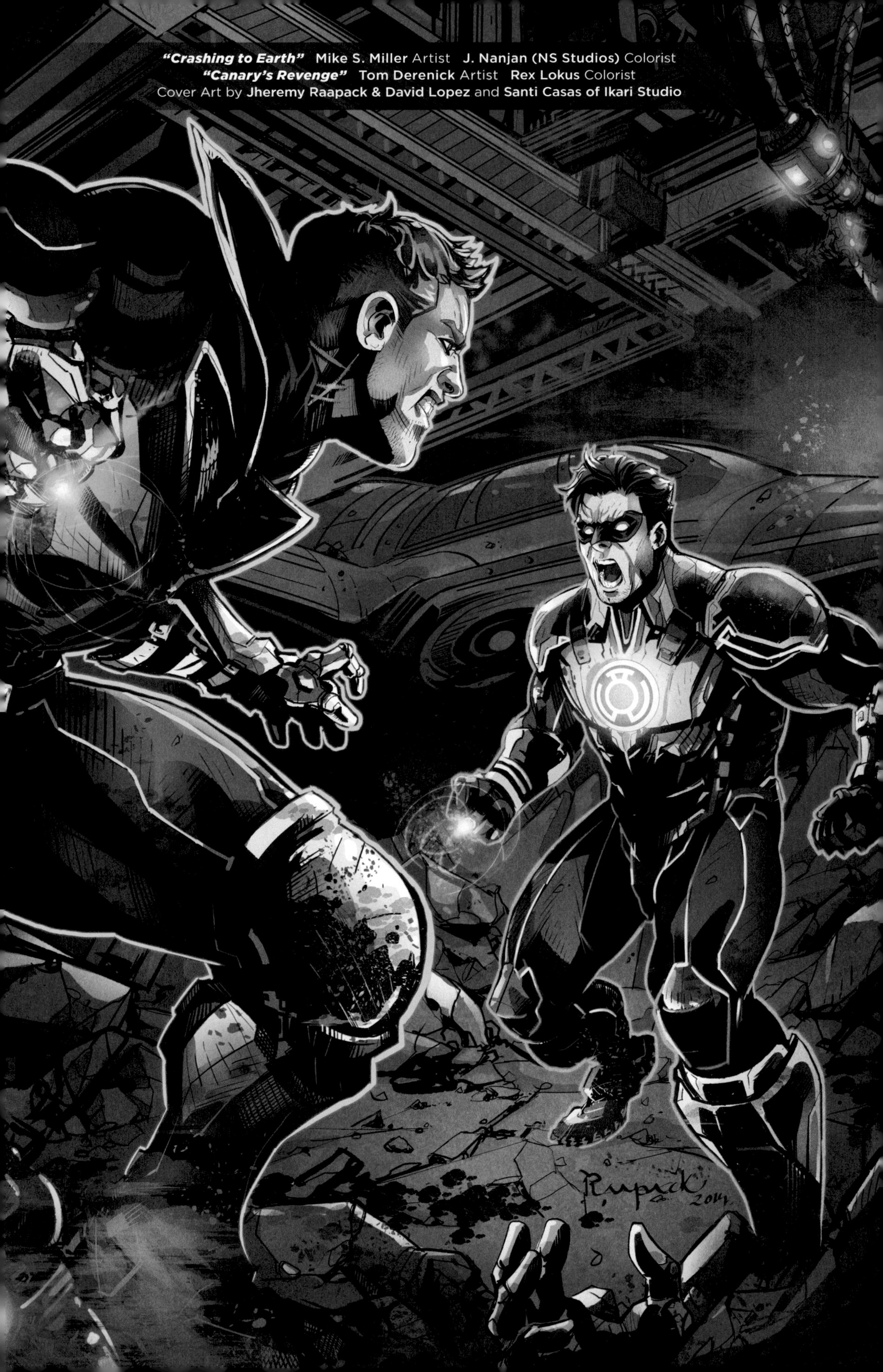

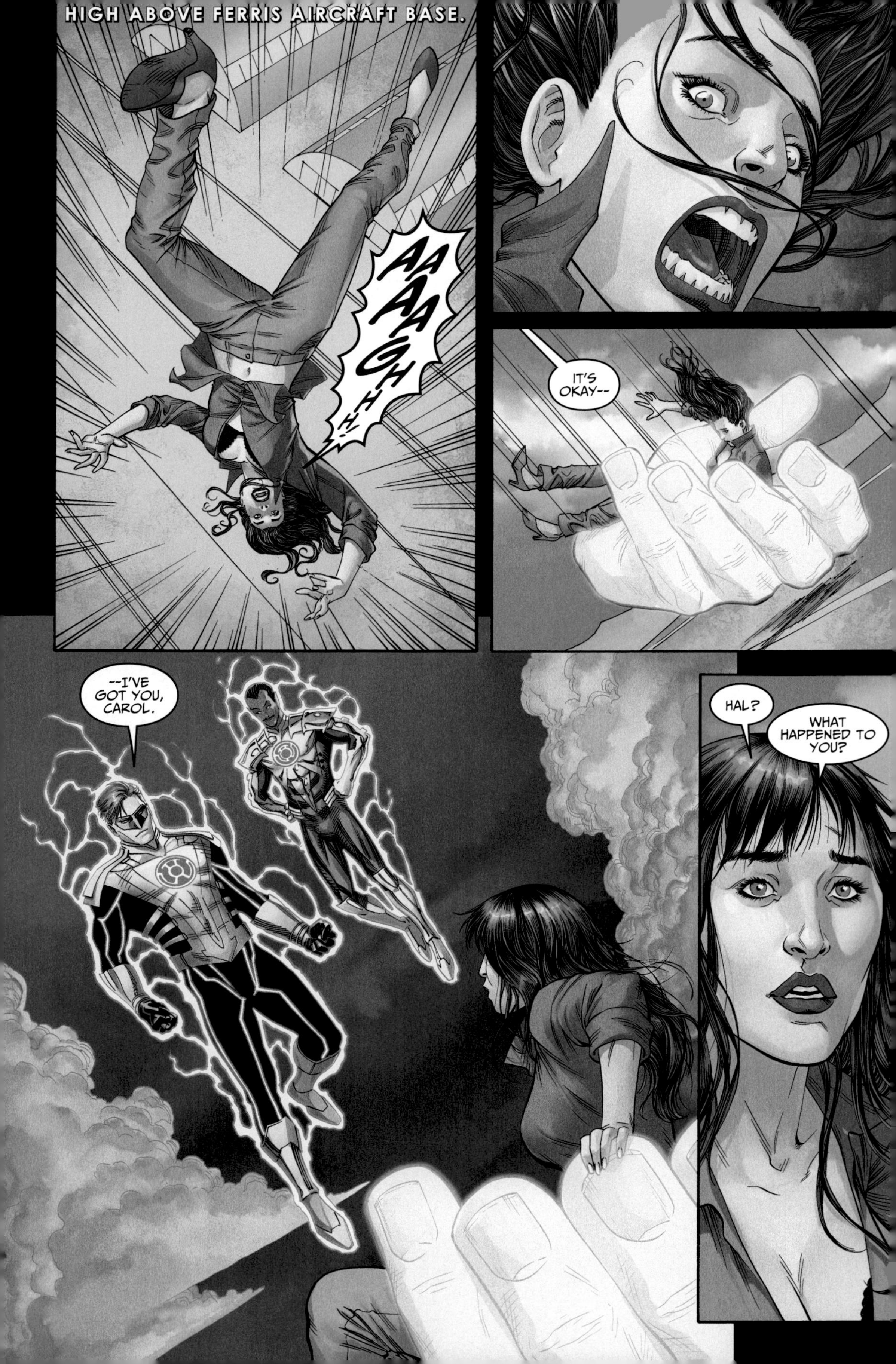
HIGH ABOVE FERRIS AIRCRAFT BASE.
AAAAGHH!
IT'S OKAY--
--I'VE GOT YOU, CAROL.
HAL?
WHAT HAPPENED TO YOU?

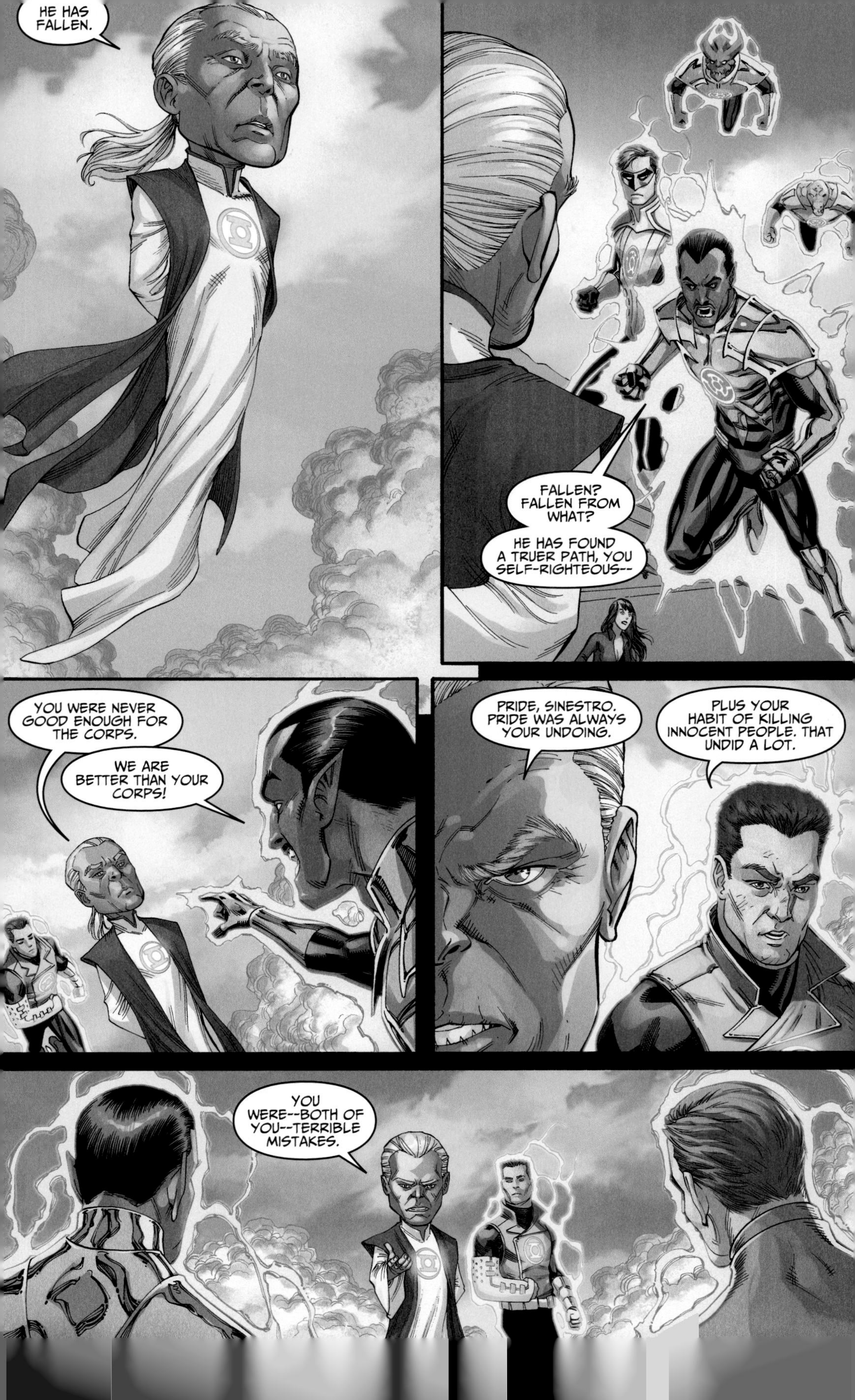
HE HAS FALLEN.
FALLEN? FALLEN FROM WHAT?
HE HAS FOUND A TRUER PATH, YOU SELF-RIGHTEOUS--
YOU WERE NEVER GOOD ENOUGH FOR THE CORPS.
WE ARE BETTER THAN YOUR CORPS!
PRIDE, SINESTRO. PRIDE WAS ALWAYS YOUR UNDOING.
PLUS YOUR HABIT OF KILLING INNOCENT PEOPLE. THAT UNDID A LOT.
YOU WERE--BOTH OF YOU--TERRIBLE MISTAKES.

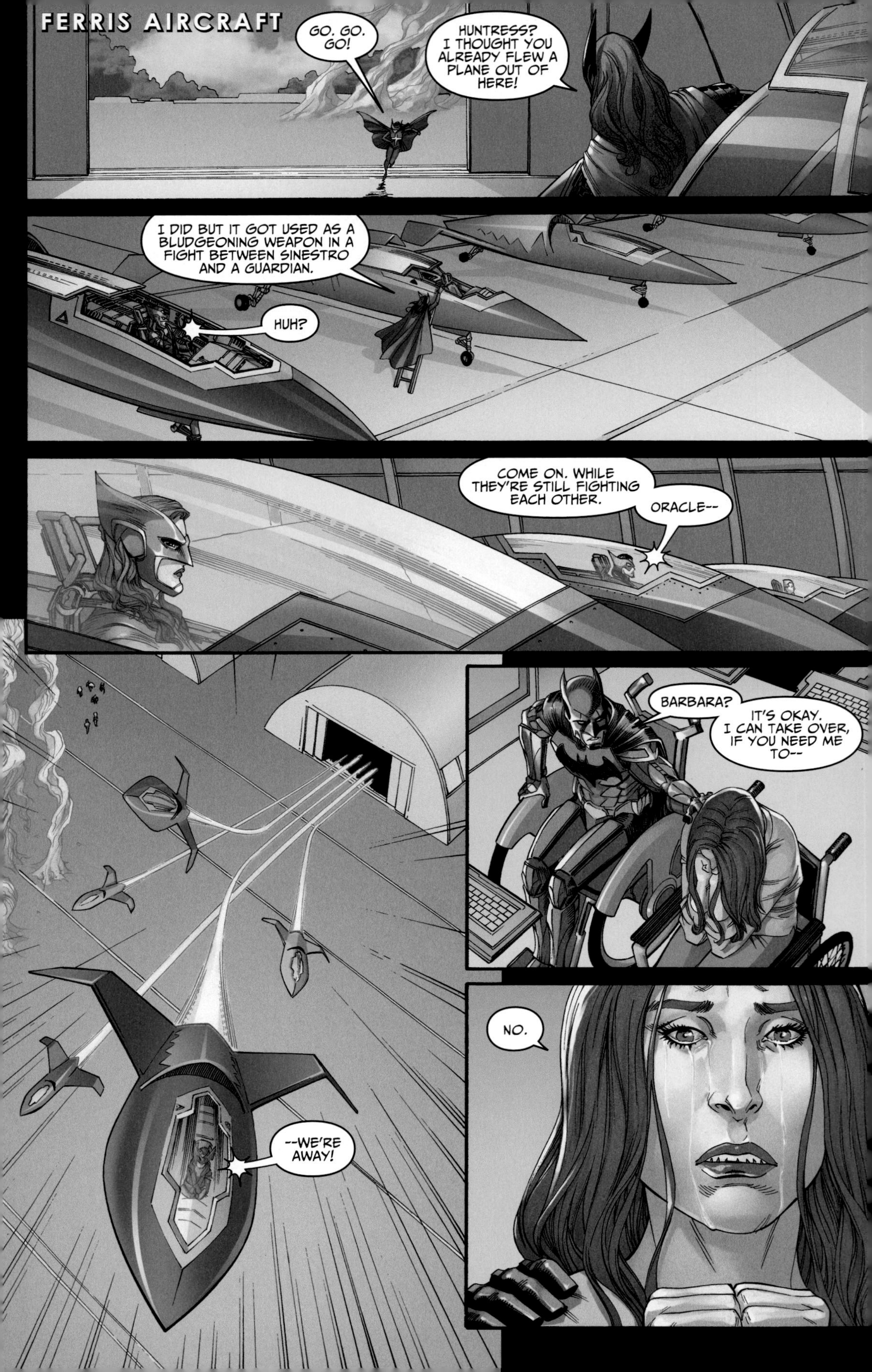
FERRIS AIRCRAFT
GO. GO. GO!
HUNTRESS? I THOUGHT YOU ALREADY FLEW A PLANE OUT OF HERE!
I DID BUT IT GOT USED AS A BLUDGEONING WEAPON IN A FIGHT BETWEEN SINESTRO AND A GUARDIAN.
HUH?
COME ON. WHILE THEY'RE STILL FIGHTING EACH OTHER.
ORACLE--
--WE'RE AWAY!
BARBARA?
IT'S OKAY. I CAN TAKE OVER, IF YOU NEED ME TO--
NO.

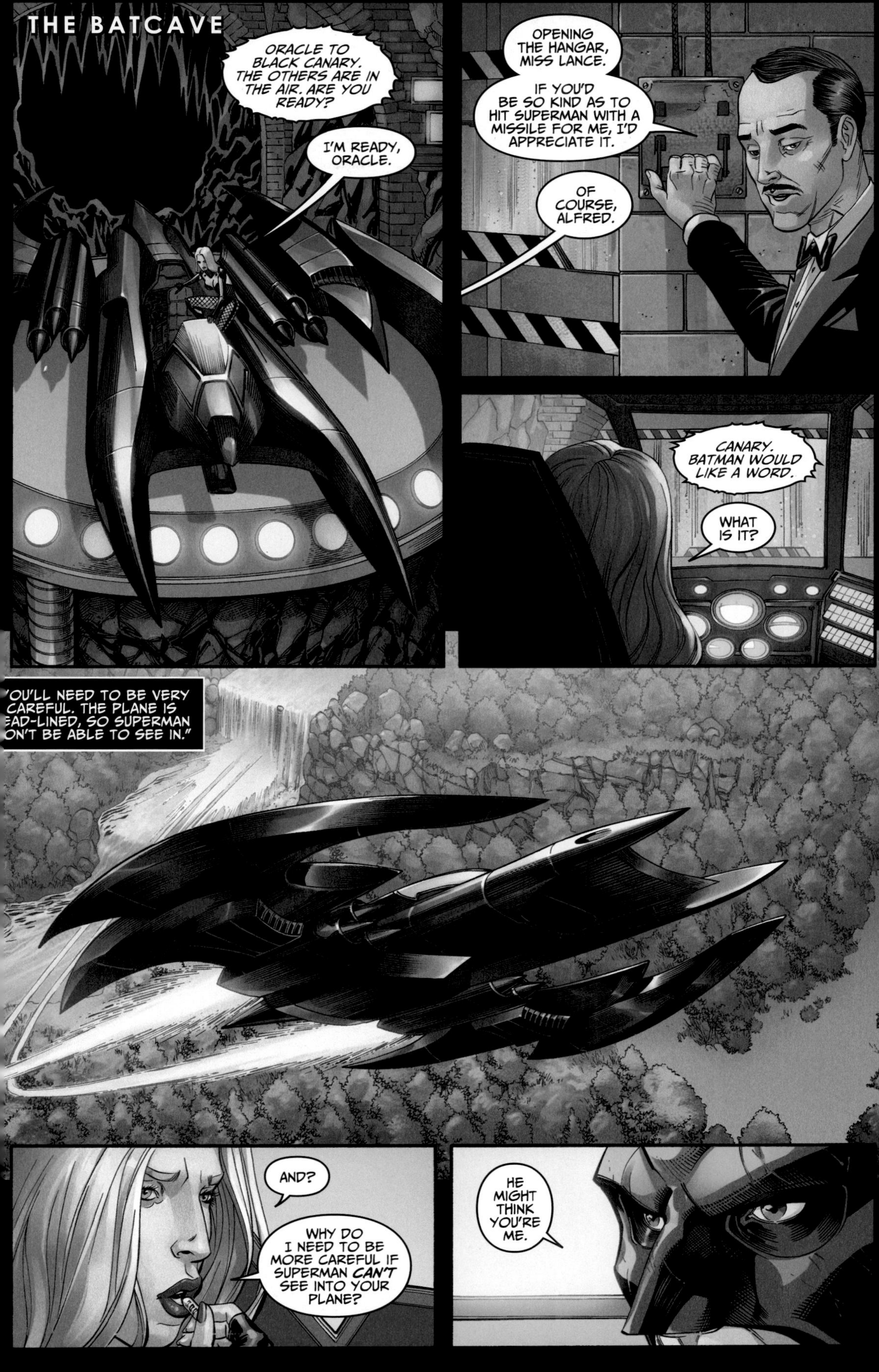
THE BATCAVE
ORACLE TO BLACK CANARY. THE OTHERS ARE IN THE AIR. ARE YOU READY?
I'M READY, ORACLE.
OPENING THE HANGAR, MISS LANCE.
IF YOU'D BE SO KIND AS TO HIT SUPERMAN WITH A MISSILE FOR ME, I'D APPRECIATE IT.
OF COURSE, ALFRED.
CANARY. BATMAN WOULD LIKE A WORD.
WHAT IS IT?
OU'LL NEED TO BE VERY CAREFUL. THE PLANE IS EAD-LINED, SO SUPERMAN ON'T BE ABLE TO SEE IN."
AND?
WHY DO I NEED TO BE MORE CAREFUL IF SUPERMAN CAN'T SEE INTO YOUR PLANE?
HE MIGHT THINK YOU'RE ME.

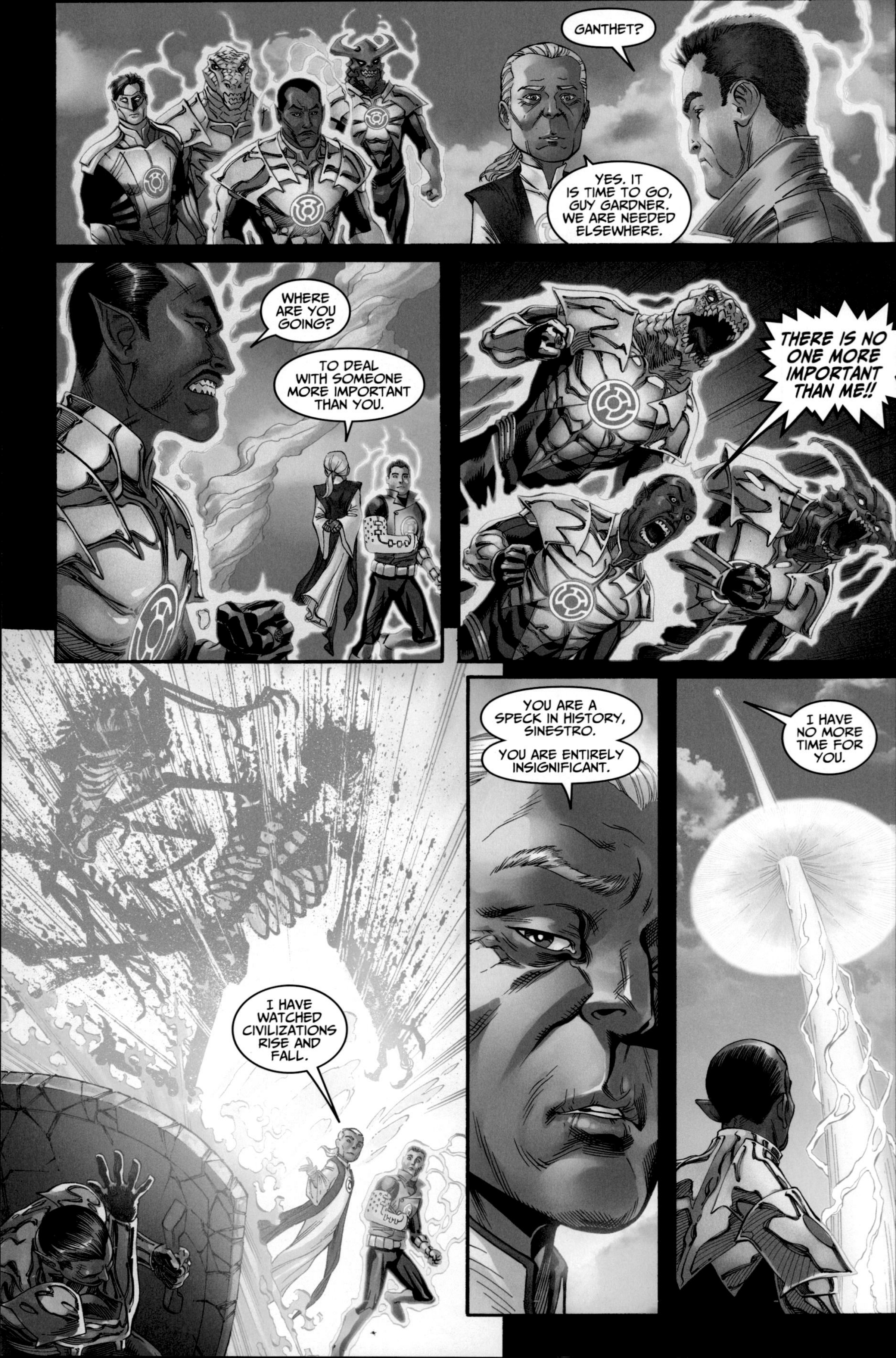
GANTHET?
YES. IT IS TIME TO GO, GUY GARDNER. WE ARE NEEDED ELSEWHERE.
WHERE ARE YOU GOING?
TO DEAL WITH SOMEONE MORE IMPORTANT THAN YOU.
THERE IS NO ONE MORE IMPORTANT THAN ME!!
I HAVE WATCHED CIVILIZATIONS RISE AND FALL.
YOU ARE A SPECK IN HISTORY, SINESTRO.
YOU ARE ENTIRELY INSIGNIFICANT.
I HAVE NO MORE TIME FOR YOU.

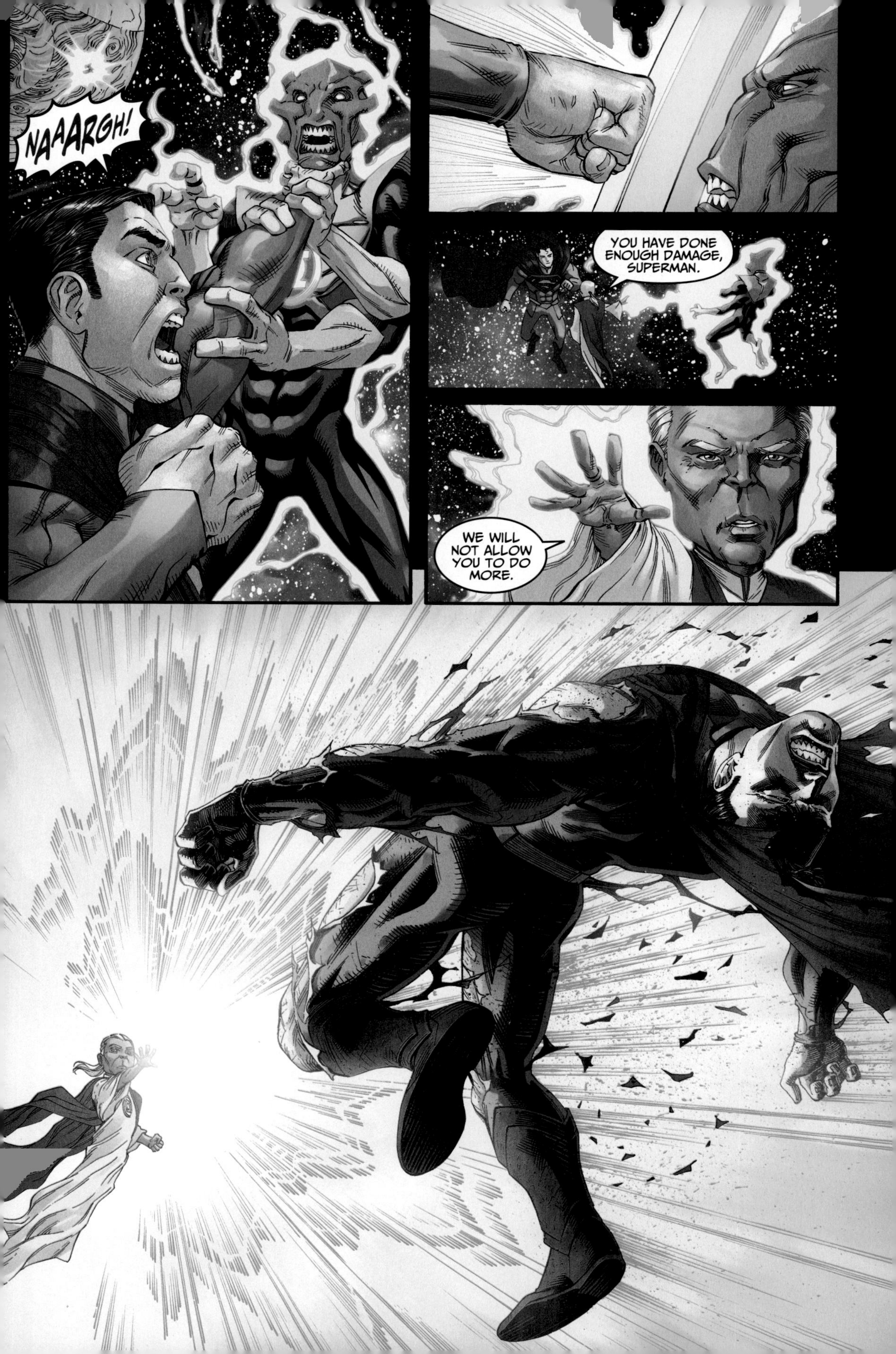

NAAARGH!
YOU HAVE DONE ENOUGH DAMAGE, SUPERMAN.
WE WILL NOT ALLOW YOU TO DO MORE.

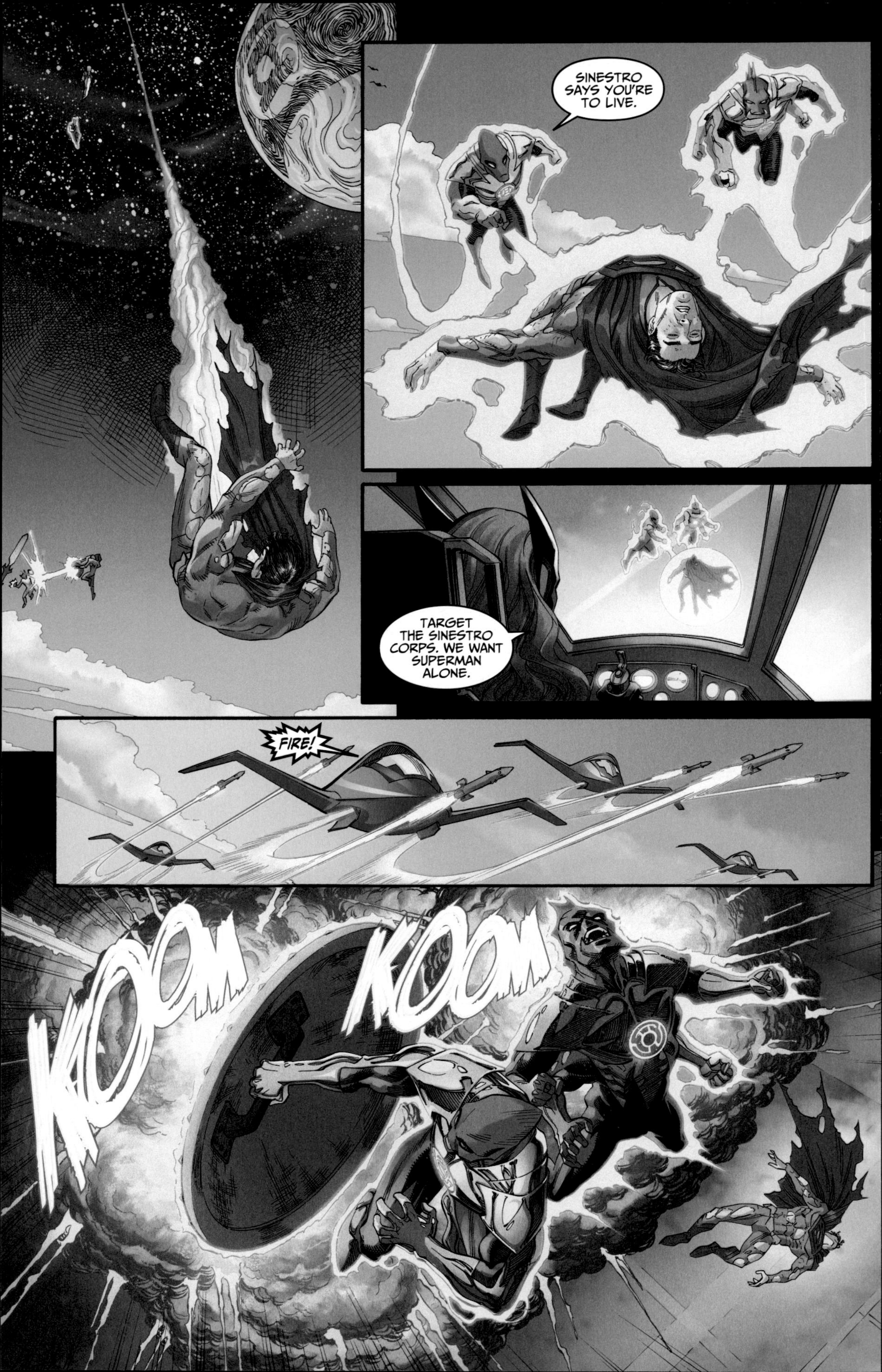
SINESTRO SAYS YOU'RE TO LIVE.
TARGET THE SINESTRO CORPS. WE WANT SUPERMAN ALONE.
FIRE!
KAOOM
KOOM

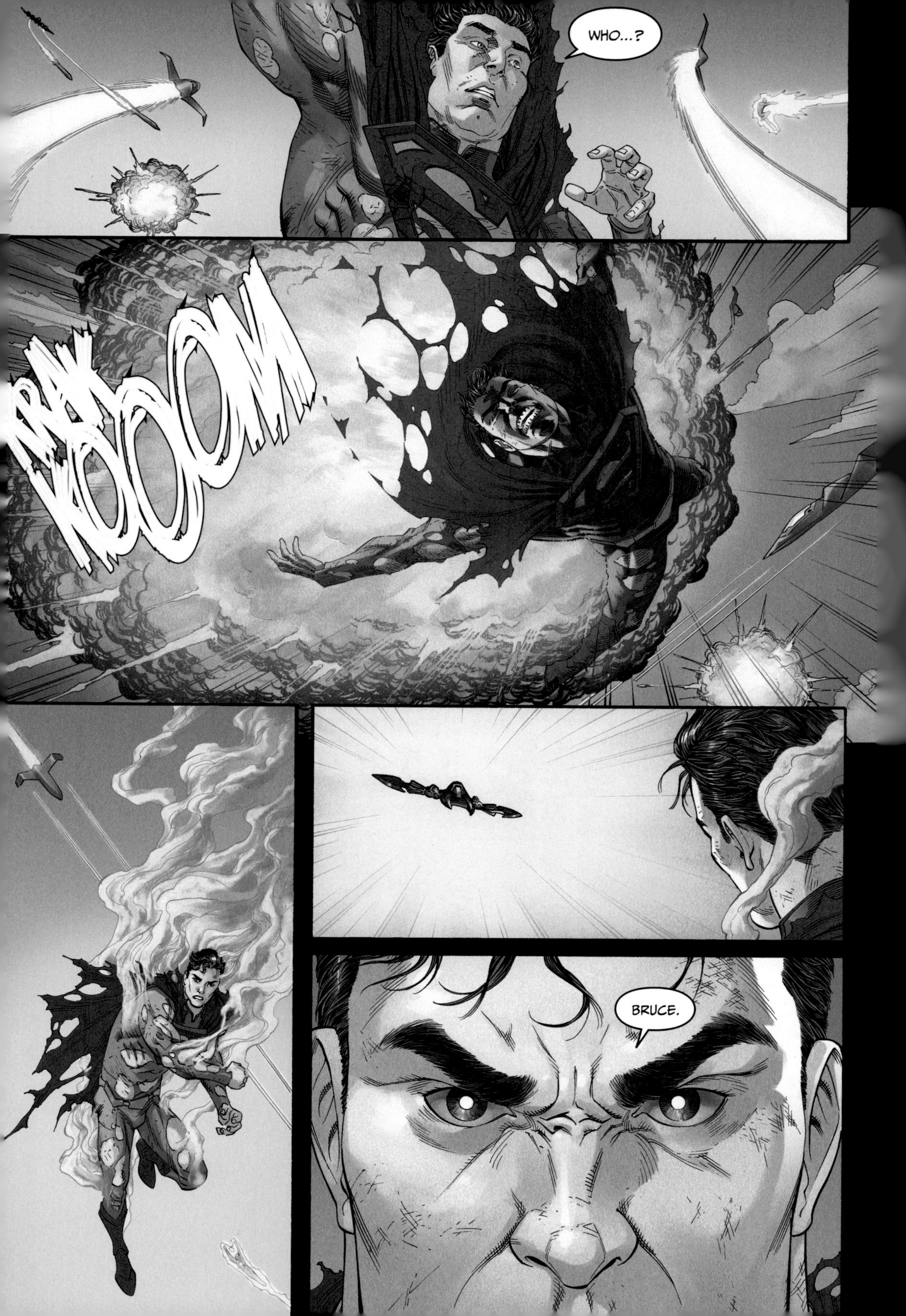
WHO...?
KRAKKOOOM
BRUCE.

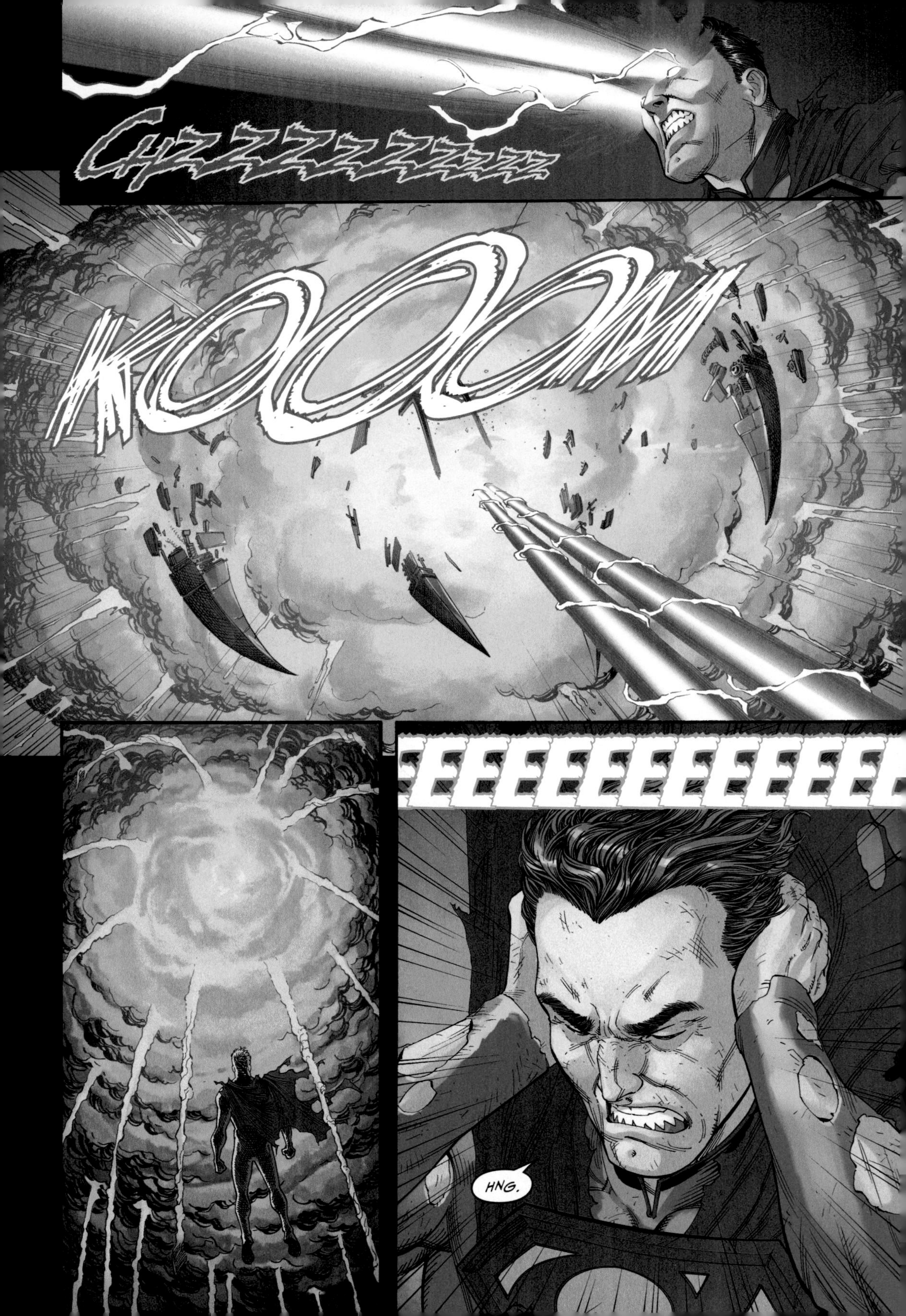
CHZZZZZZZZZZ
KOOOOM
EEEEEEEEEEEEEE
HNG.

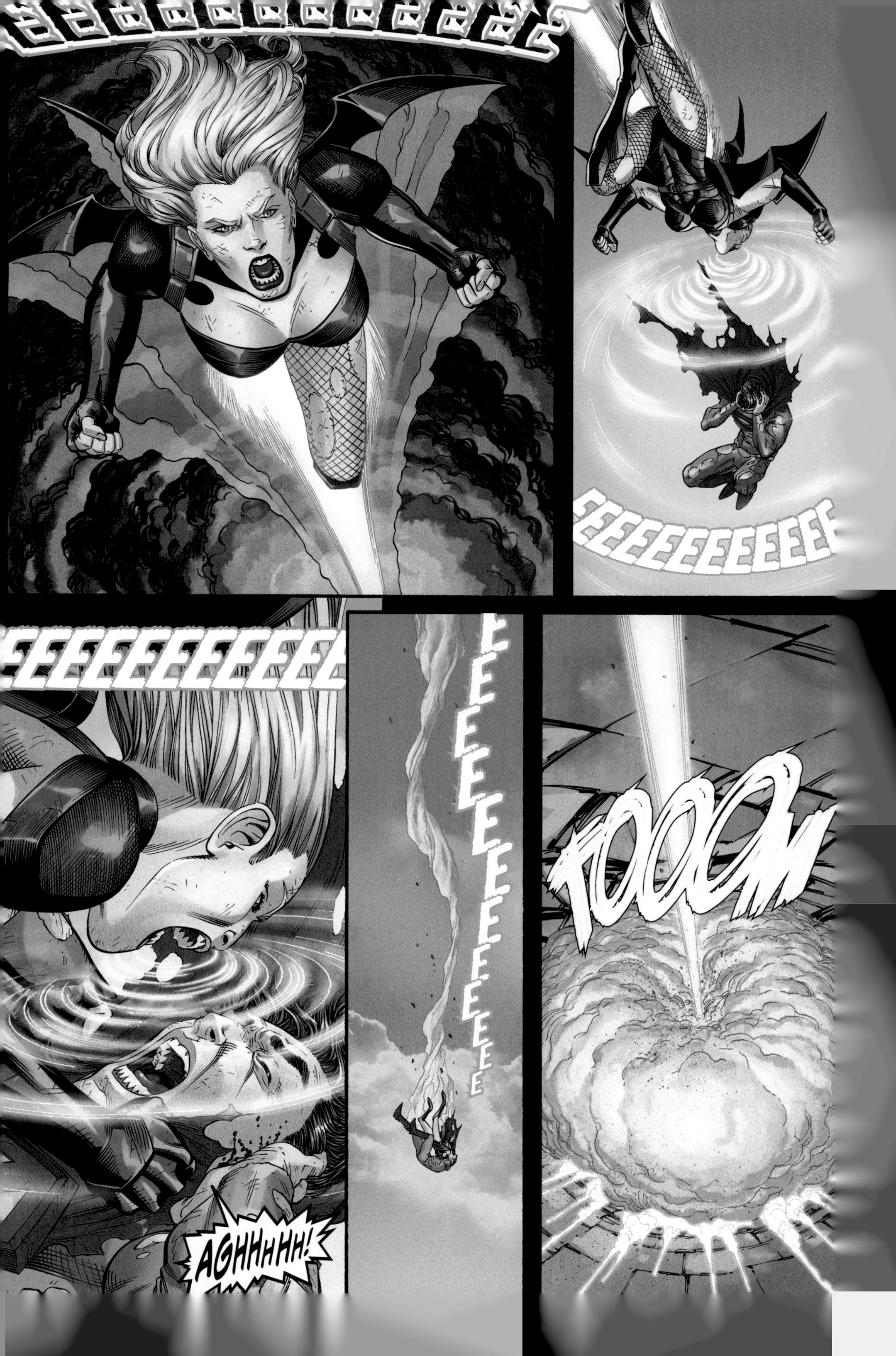
EEEEEEEEEEEE
EEEEEEEEEEEEE
EEEEEEEEEEEEEE
AGHHHHH!
FOOOM

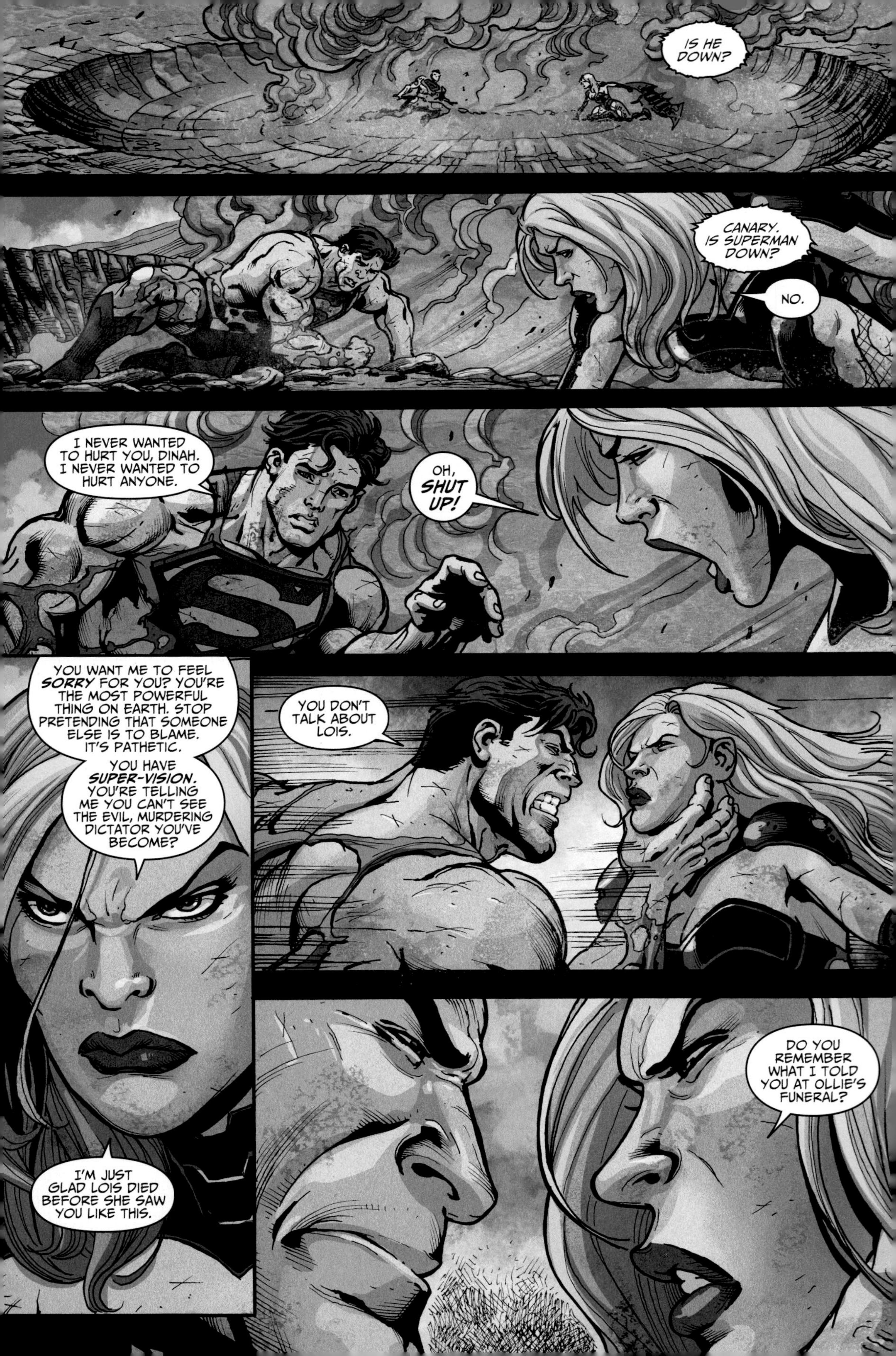
IS HE DOWN?
CANARY. IS SUPERMAN DOWN?
NO.
I NEVER WANTED TO HURT YOU, DINAH. I NEVER WANTED TO HURT ANYONE.
OH, SHUT UP!
YOU WANT ME TO FEEL SORRY FOR YOU? YOU'RE THE MOST POWERFUL THING ON EARTH. STOP PRETENDING THAT SOMEONE ELSE IS TO BLAME. IT'S PATHETIC.
YOU HAVE SUPER-VISION. YOU'RE TELLING ME YOU CAN'T SEE THE EVIL, MURDERING DICTATOR YOU'VE BECOME?
I'M JUST GLAD LOIS DIED BEFORE SHE SAW YOU LIKE THIS.
YOU DON'T TALK ABOUT LOIS.
DO YOU REMEMBER WHAT I TOLD YOU AT OLLIE'S FUNERAL?

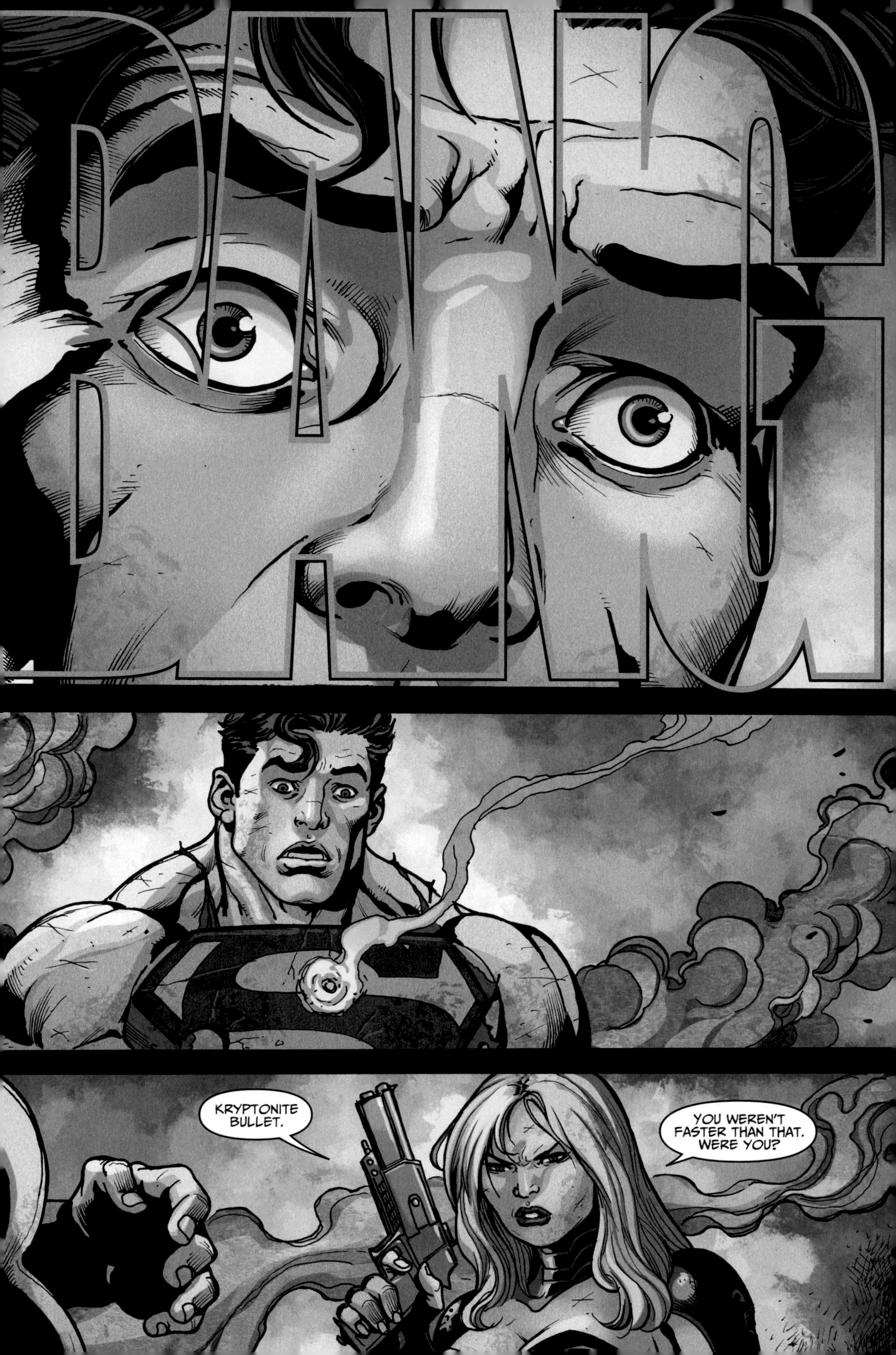
KRYPTONITE BULLET.
YOU WEREN'T FASTER THAN THAT. WERE YOU?

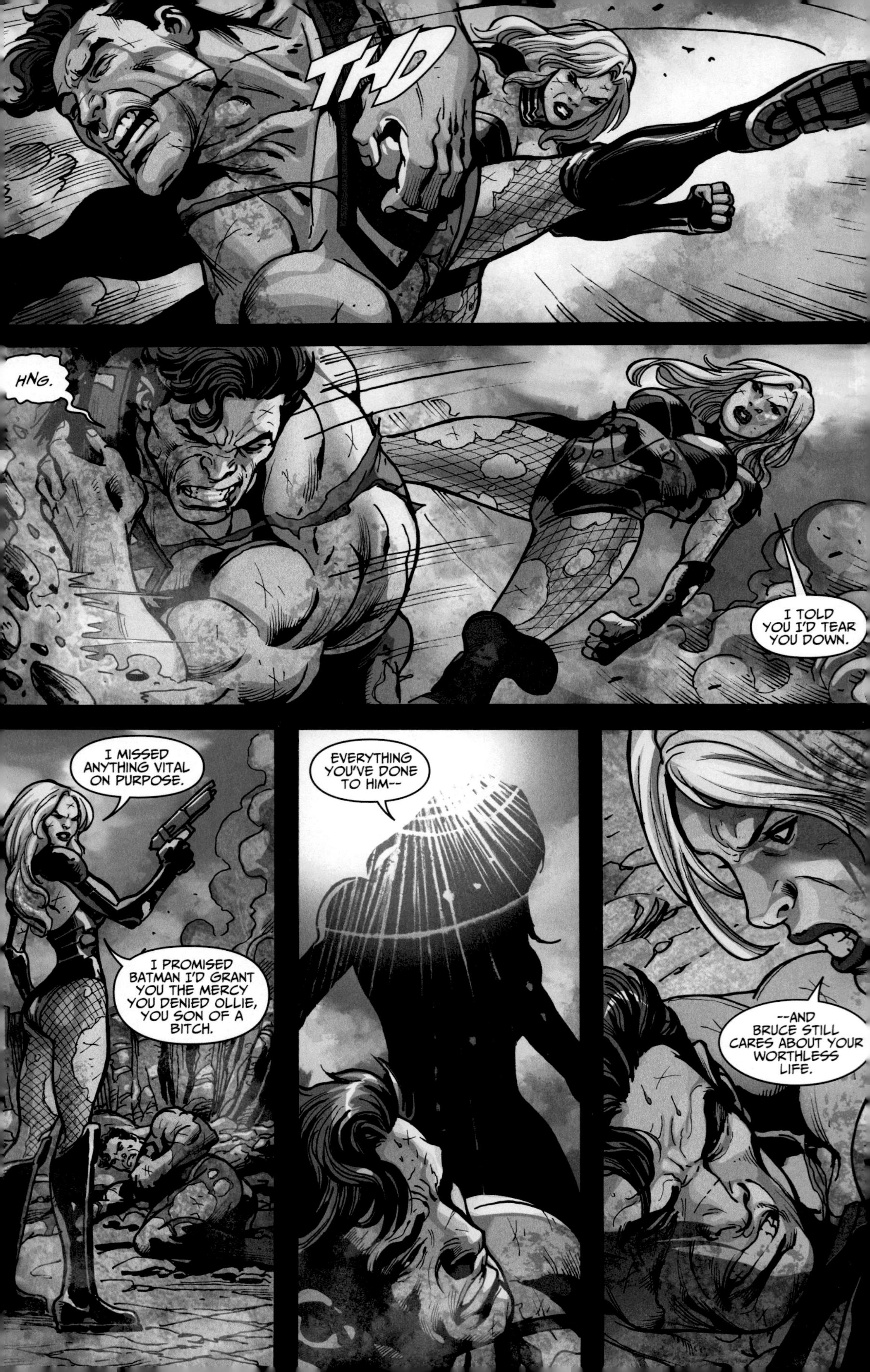
THD
HNG.
I TOLD YOU I'D TEAR YOU DOWN.
I MISSED ANYTHING VITAL ON PURPOSE.
I PROMISED BATMAN I'D GRANT YOU THE MERCY YOU DENIED OLLIE, YOU SON OF A BITCH.
EVERYTHING YOU'VE DONE TO HIM--
--AND BRUCE STILL CARES ABOUT YOUR WORTHLESS LIFE.

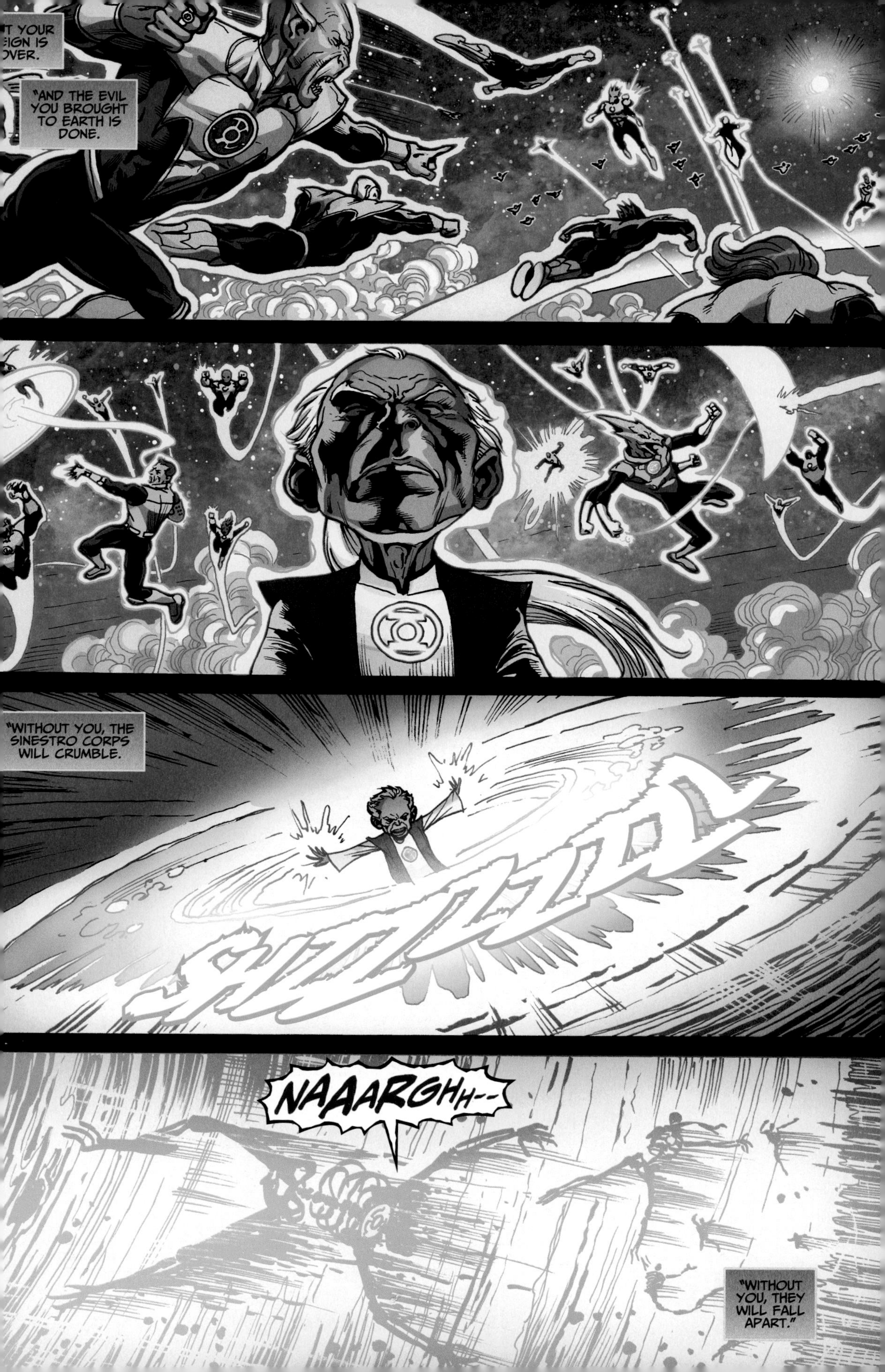

...T YOUR
...EIGN IS
...OVER.
"AND THE EVIL YOU BROUGHT TO EARTH IS DONE.
"WITHOUT YOU, THE SINESTRO CORPS WILL CRUMBLE.
NAAARGHH--
"WITHOUT YOU, THEY WILL FALL APART."

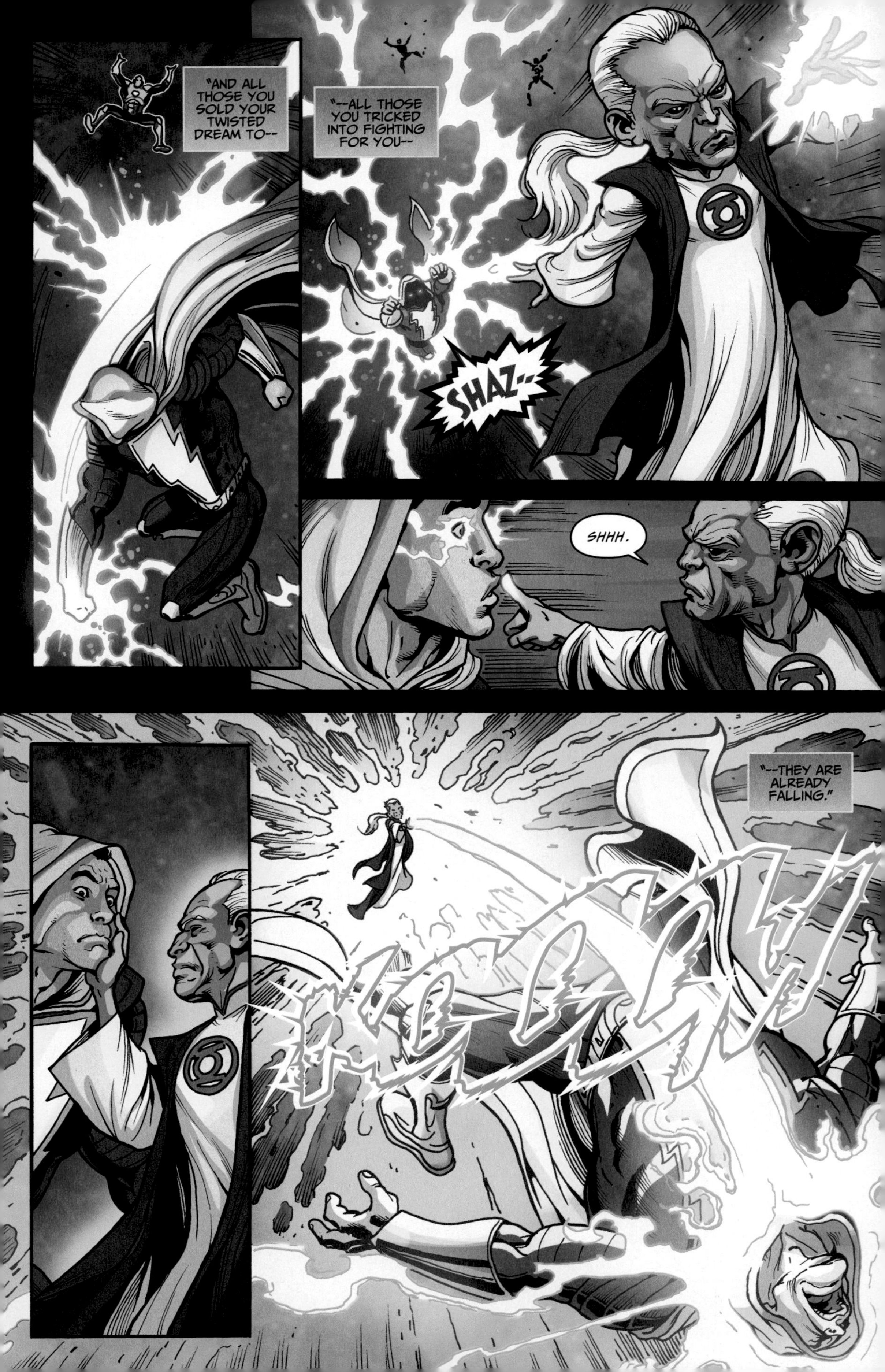
"AND ALL THOSE YOU SOLD YOUR TWISTED DREAM TO--
"--ALL THOSE YOU TRICKED INTO FIGHTING FOR YOU--
SHAZ--
SHHH.
"--THEY ARE ALREADY FALLING."

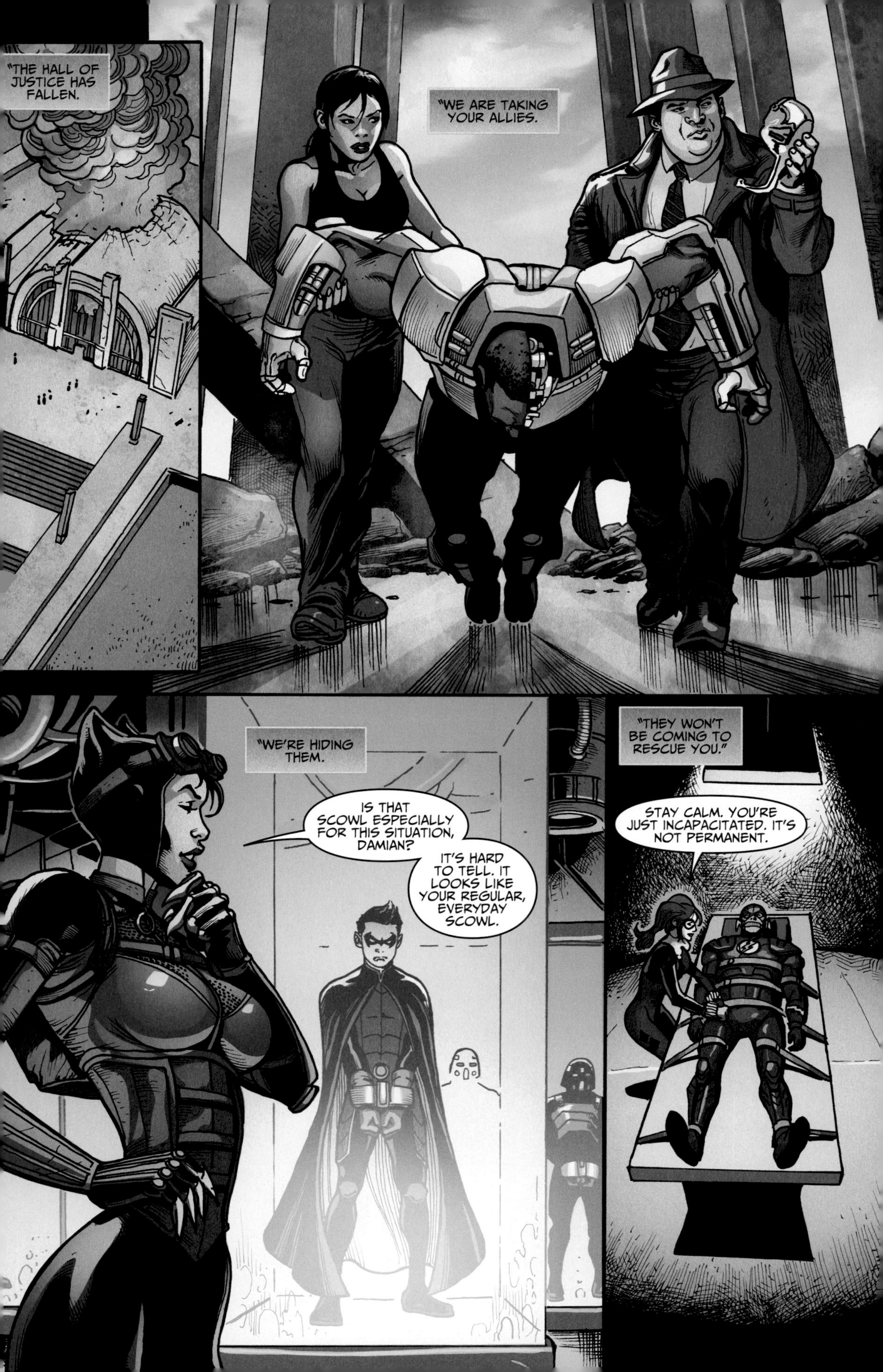
"THE HALL OF JUSTICE HAS FALLEN.
"WE ARE TAKING YOUR ALLIES.
"WE'RE HIDING THEM.
IS THAT SCOWL ESPECIALLY FOR THIS SITUATION, DAMIAN?
IT'S HARD TO TELL. IT LOOKS LIKE YOUR REGULAR, EVERYDAY SCOWL.
"THEY WON'T BE COMING TO RESCUE YOU."
STAY CALM. YOU'RE JUST INCAPACITATED. IT'S NOT PERMANENT.

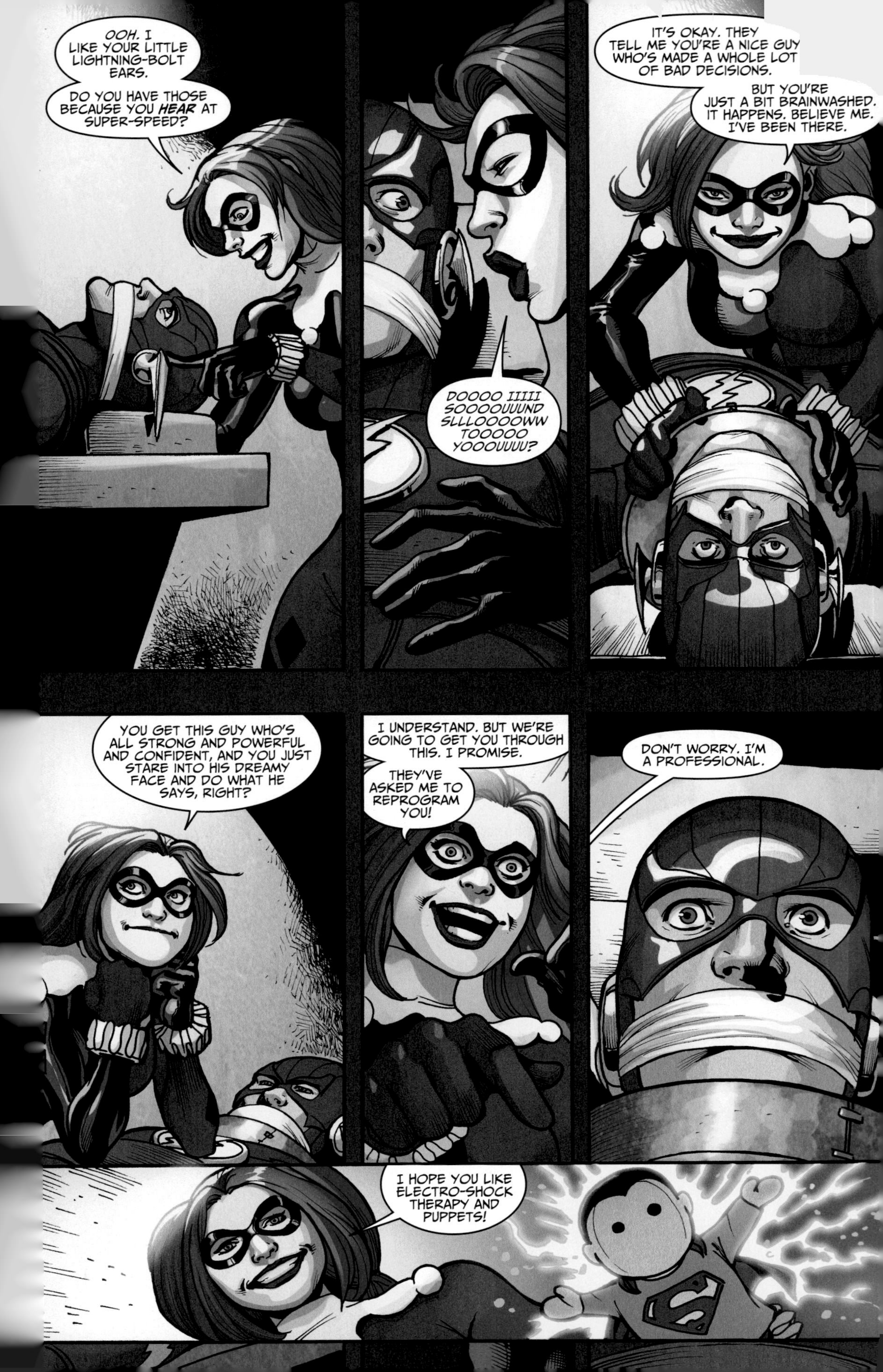
OOH. I LIKE YOUR LITTLE LIGHTNING-BOLT EARS.
DO YOU HAVE THOSE BECAUSE YOU *HEAR* AT SUPER-SPEED?
DOOOO IIIII SOOOOUUUND SLLLOOOOWW TOOOOO YOOOUUUU?
IT'S OKAY. THEY TELL ME YOU'RE A NICE GUY WHO'S MADE A WHOLE LOT OF BAD DECISIONS.
BUT YOU'RE JUST A BIT BRAINWASHED. IT HAPPENS. BELIEVE ME. I'VE BEEN THERE.
YOU GET THIS GUY WHO'S ALL STRONG AND POWERFUL AND CONFIDENT, AND YOU JUST STARE INTO HIS DREAMY FACE AND DO WHAT HE SAYS, RIGHT?
I UNDERSTAND. BUT WE'RE GOING TO GET YOU THROUGH THIS. I PROMISE.
THEY'VE ASKED ME TO REPROGRAM YOU!
DON'T WORRY. I'M A PROFESSIONAL.
I HOPE YOU LIKE ELECTRO-SHOCK THERAPY AND PUPPETS!

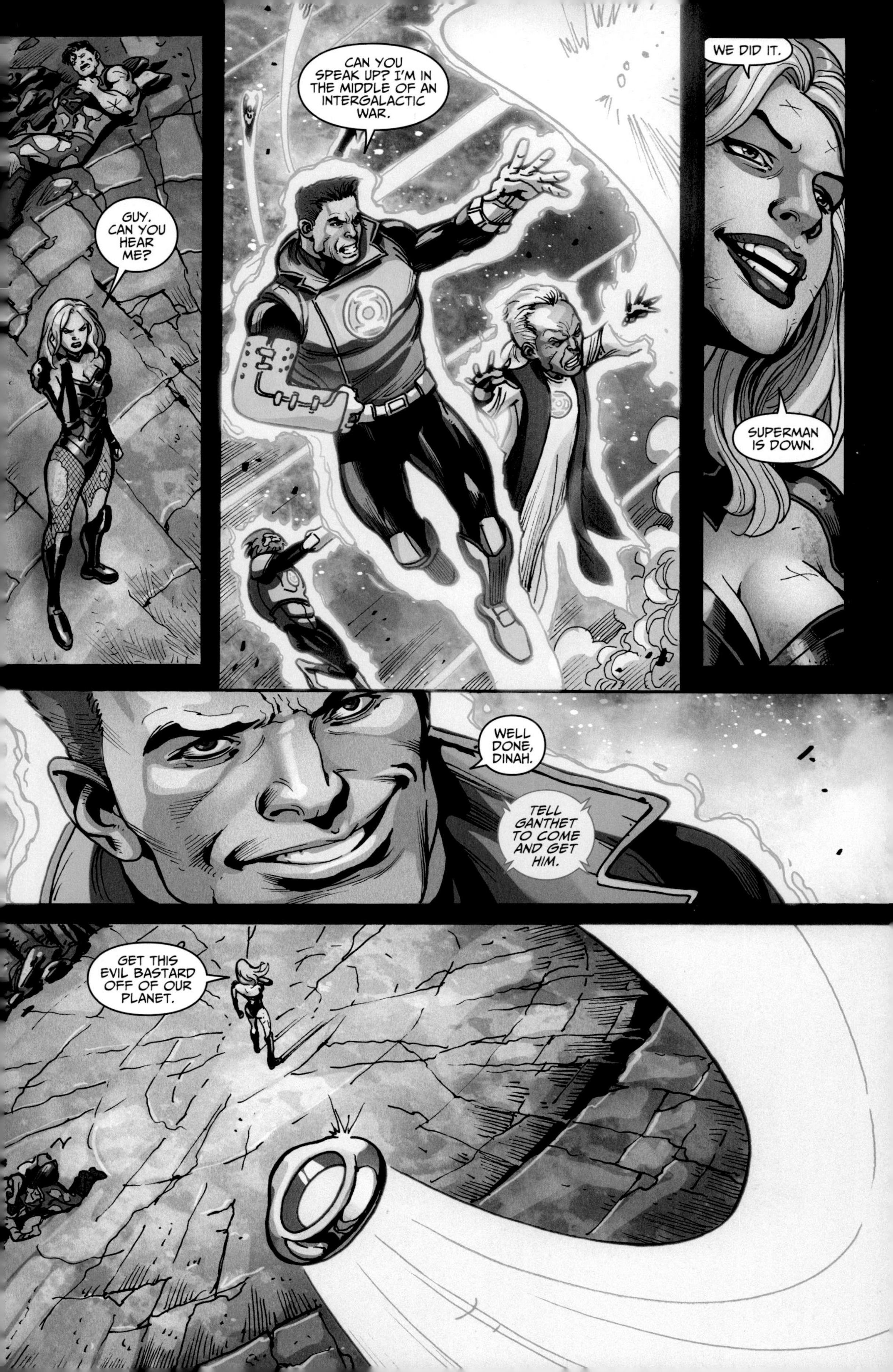
GUY. CAN YOU HEAR ME?
CAN YOU SPEAK UP? I'M IN THE MIDDLE OF AN INTERGALACTIC WAR.
WE DID IT.
SUPERMAN IS DOWN.
WELL DONE, DINAH.
TELL GANTHET TO COME AND GET HIM.
GET THIS EVIL BASTARD OFF OF OUR PLANET.

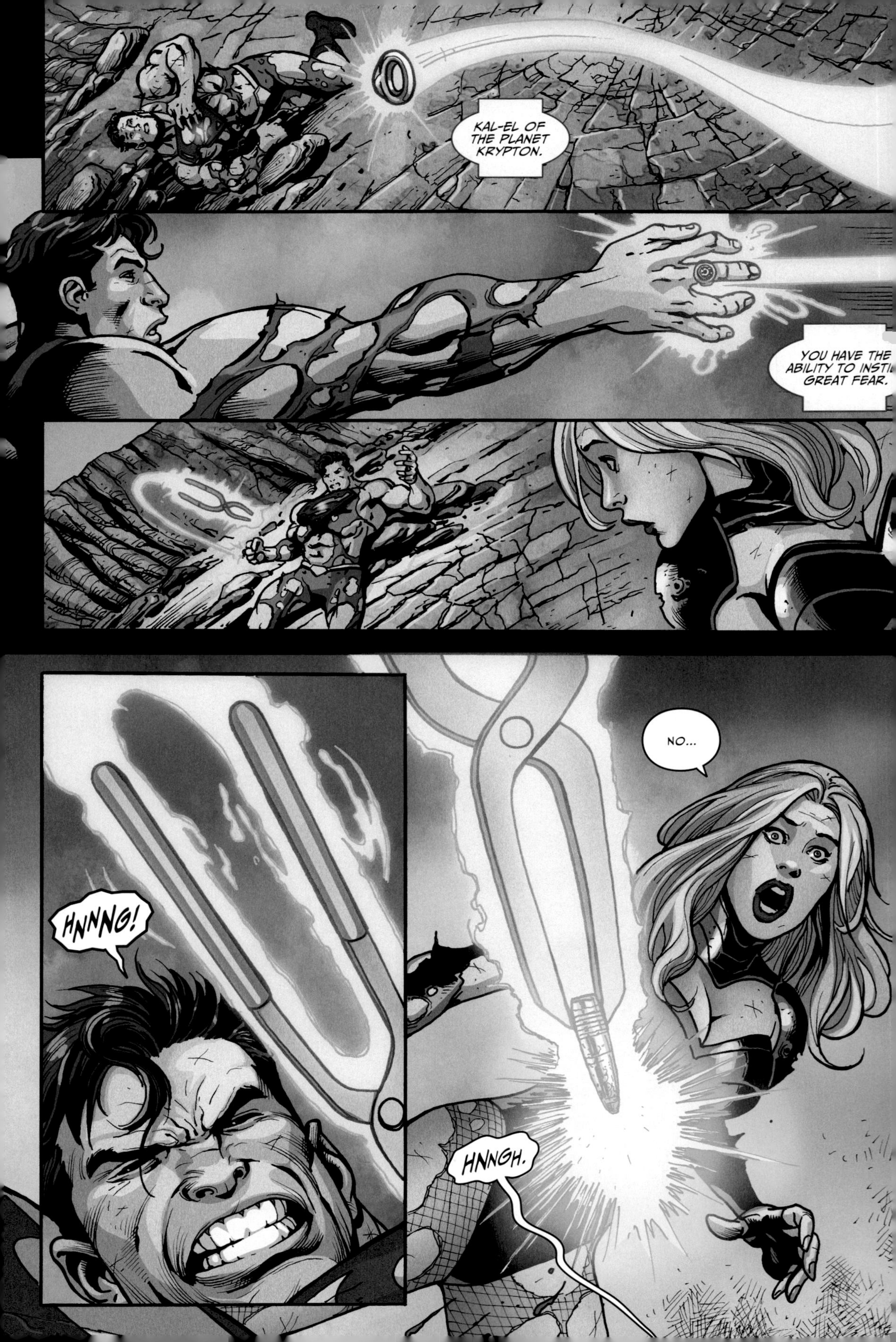
KAL-EL OF THE PLANET KRYPTON.
YOU HAVE THE ABILITY TO INSTI GREAT FEAR.
NO...
HNNNG!
HNNGH.

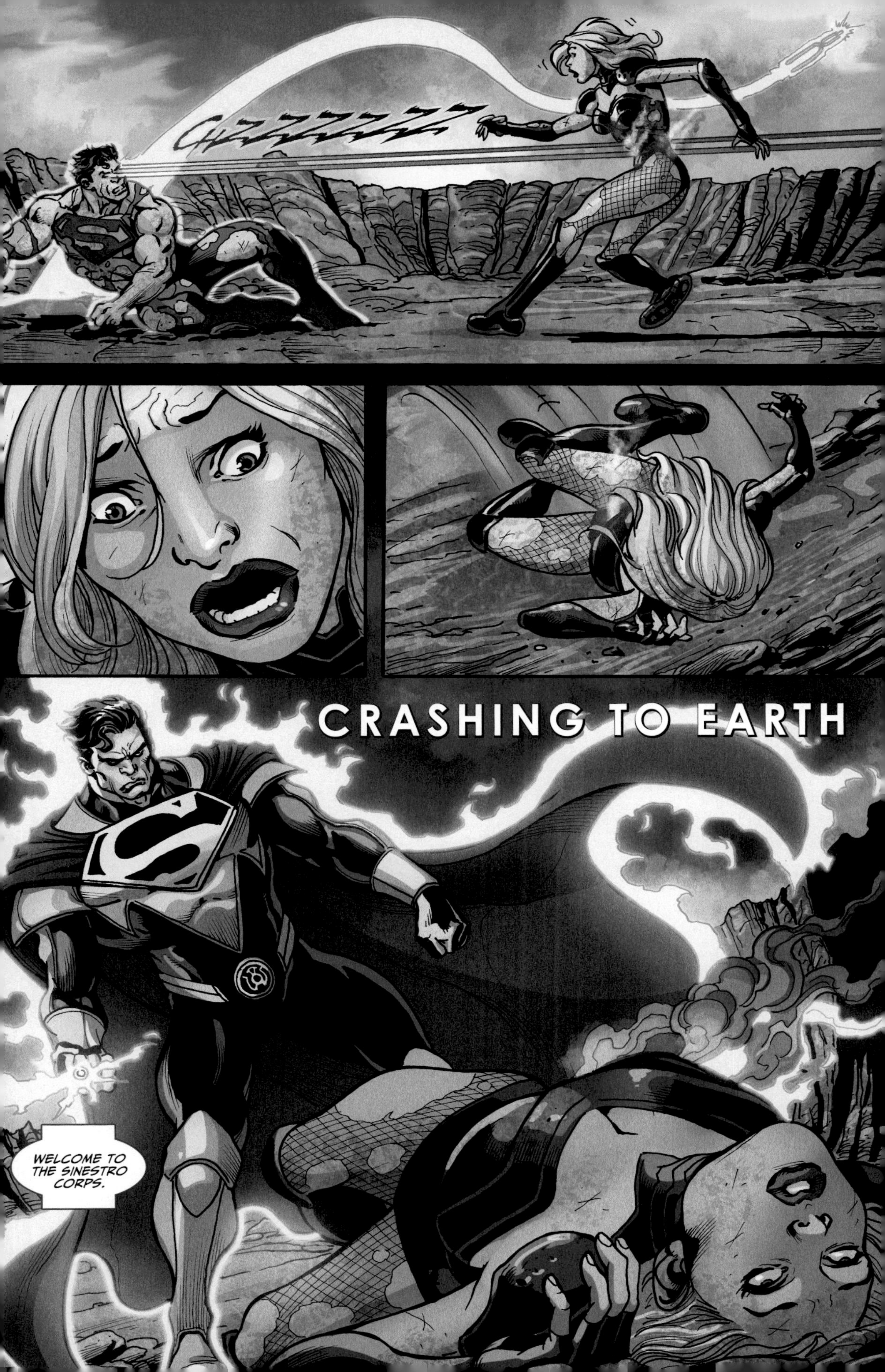
CHZZZZZZ
CRASHING TO EARTH
WELCOME TO THE SINESTRO CORPS.

"Fall of the Gods" **Bruno Redondo** **Xermanico** **Julien Hugonnard-Bert** Artists **Rex Lokus** Colorist
"World's End" **Bruno Redondo** **Xermanico** **Julien Hugonnard-Bert** **Juan Albarran** Artists
J. Nanjan (NS Studios) Colorist Cover Art by **Jheremy Raapack & David Lopez** and **Santi Casas of Ikari Studio**

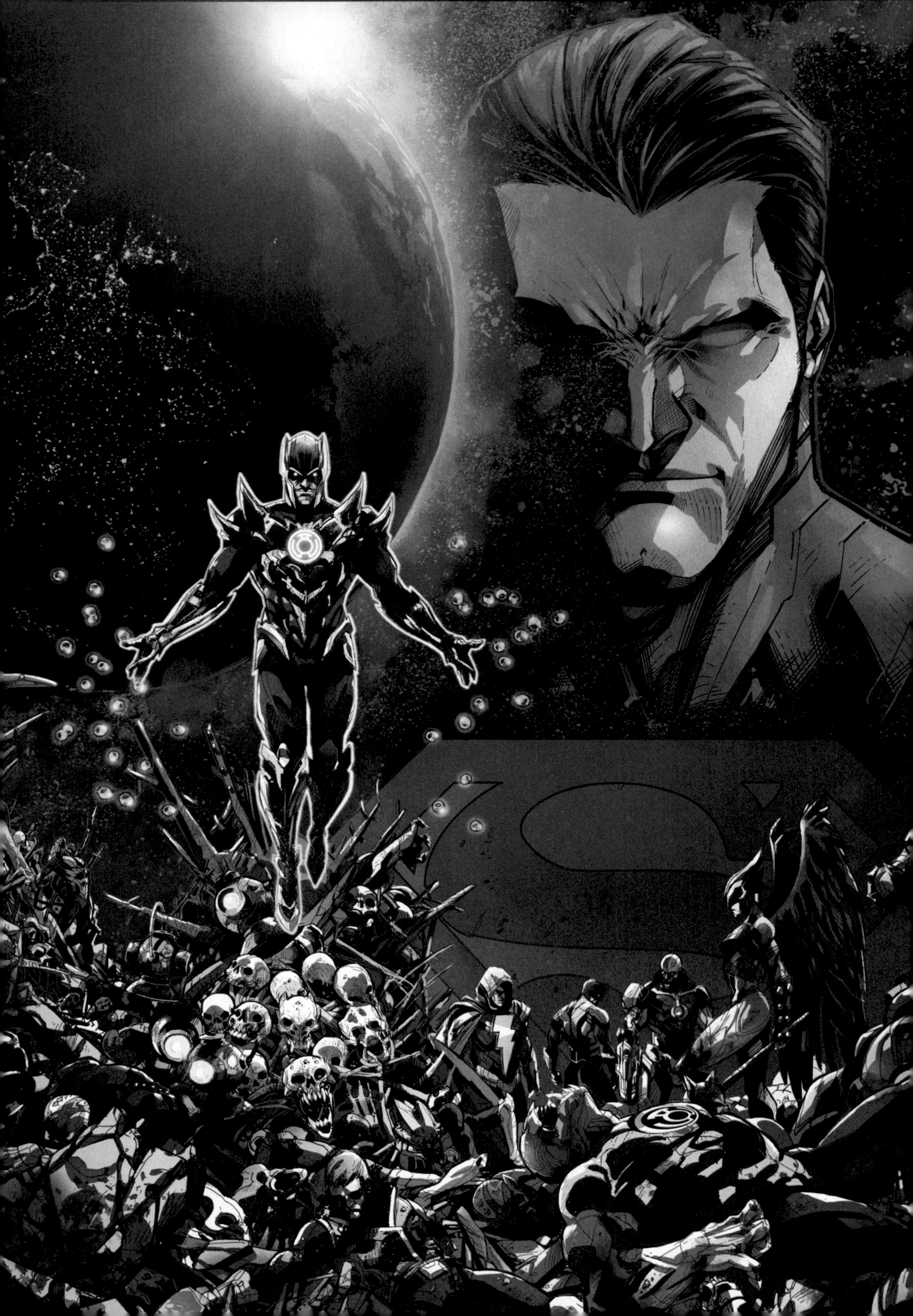

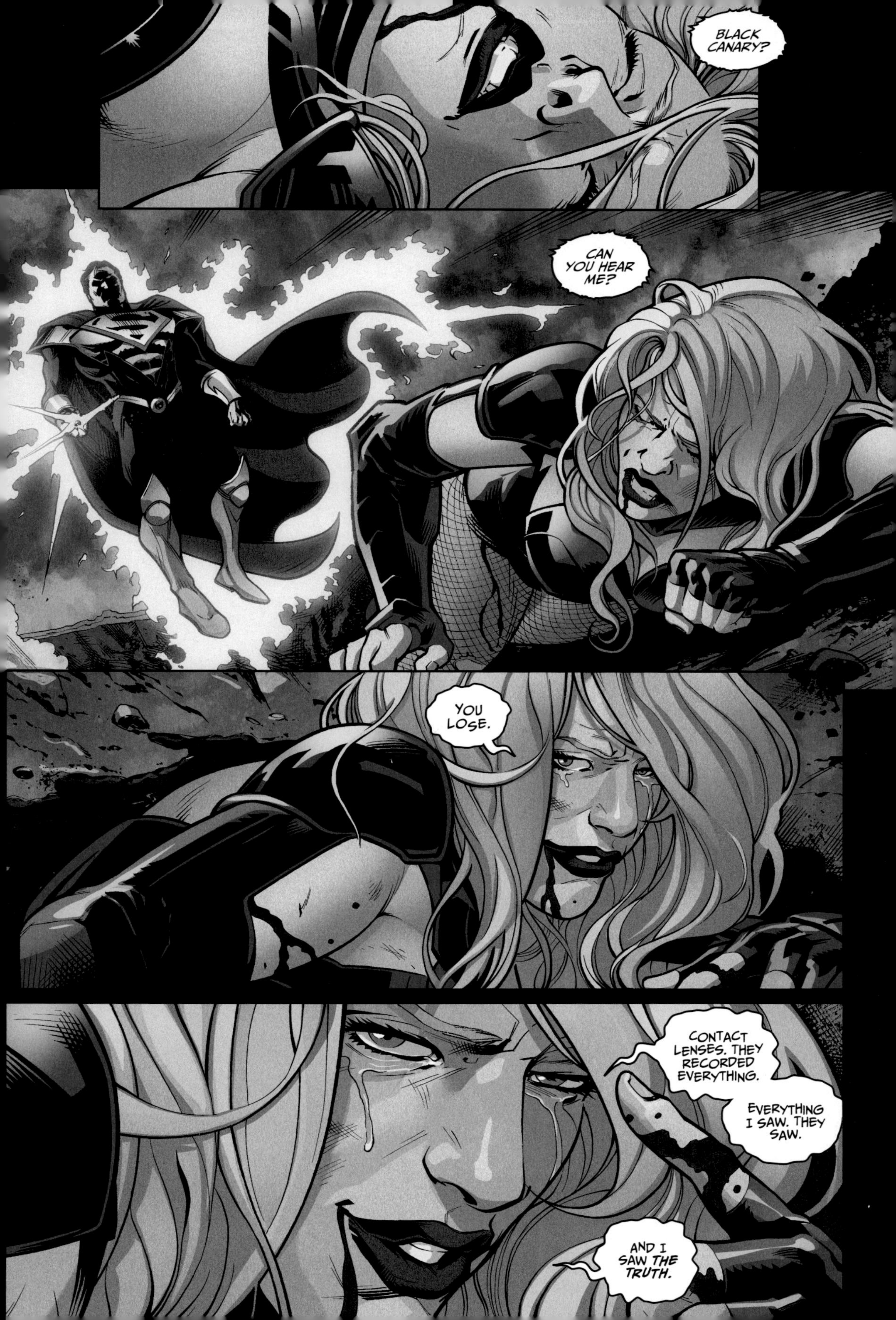
BLACK CANARY?
CAN YOU HEAR ME?
YOU LOSE.
CONTACT LENSES. THEY RECORDED EVERYTHING.
EVERYTHING I SAW. THEY SAW.
AND I SAW THE TRUTH.

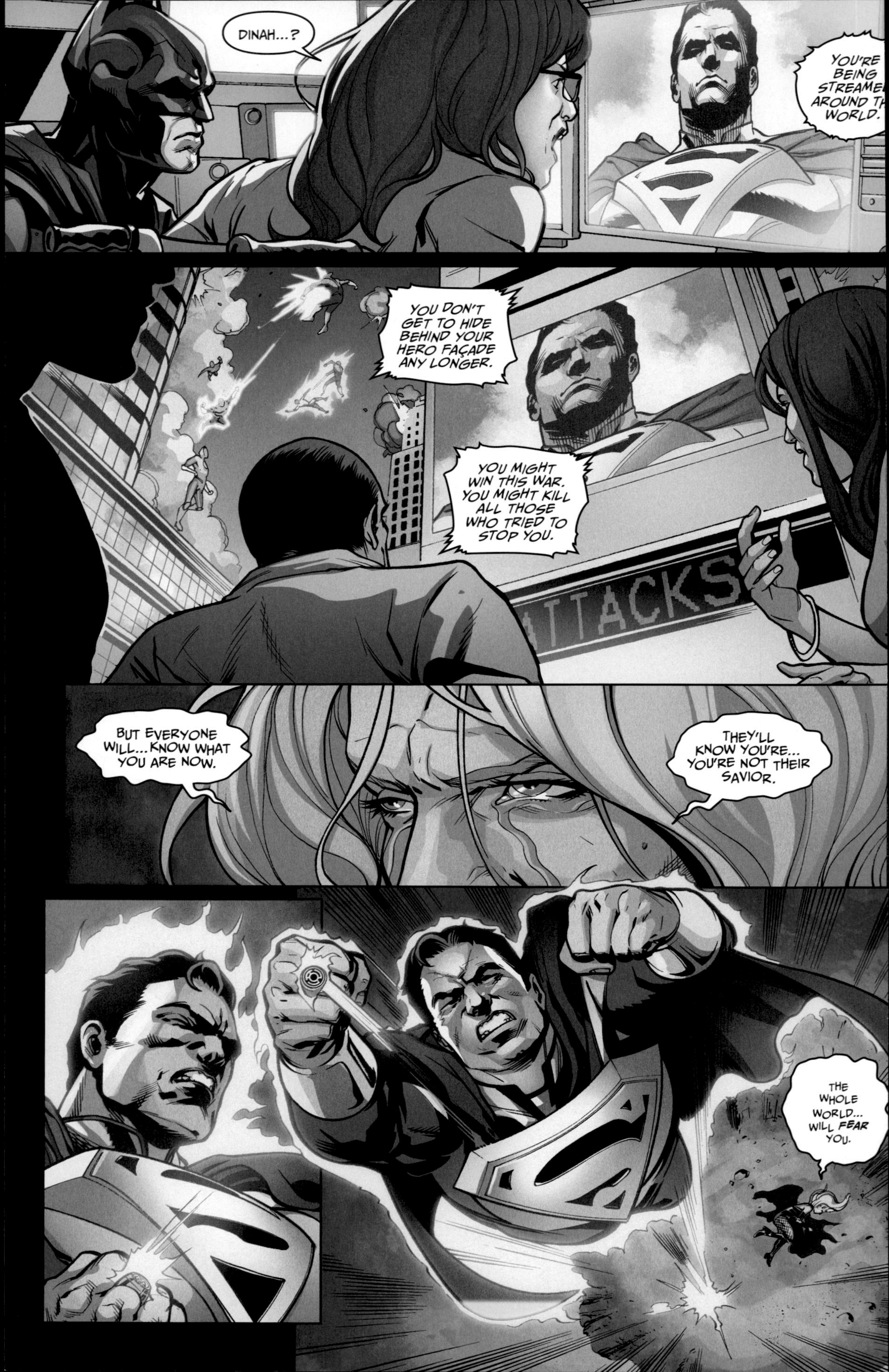
DINAH...?
YOU'RE BEING STREAMED AROUND THE WORLD.
YOU DON'T GET TO HIDE BEHIND YOUR HERO FAÇADE ANY LONGER.
YOU MIGHT WIN THIS WAR. YOU MIGHT KILL ALL THOSE WHO TRIED TO STOP YOU.
ATTACKS
BUT EVERYONE WILL... KNOW WHAT YOU ARE NOW.
THEY'LL KNOW YOU'RE... YOU'RE NOT THEIR SAVIOR.
THE WHOLE WORLD... WILL FEAR YOU.

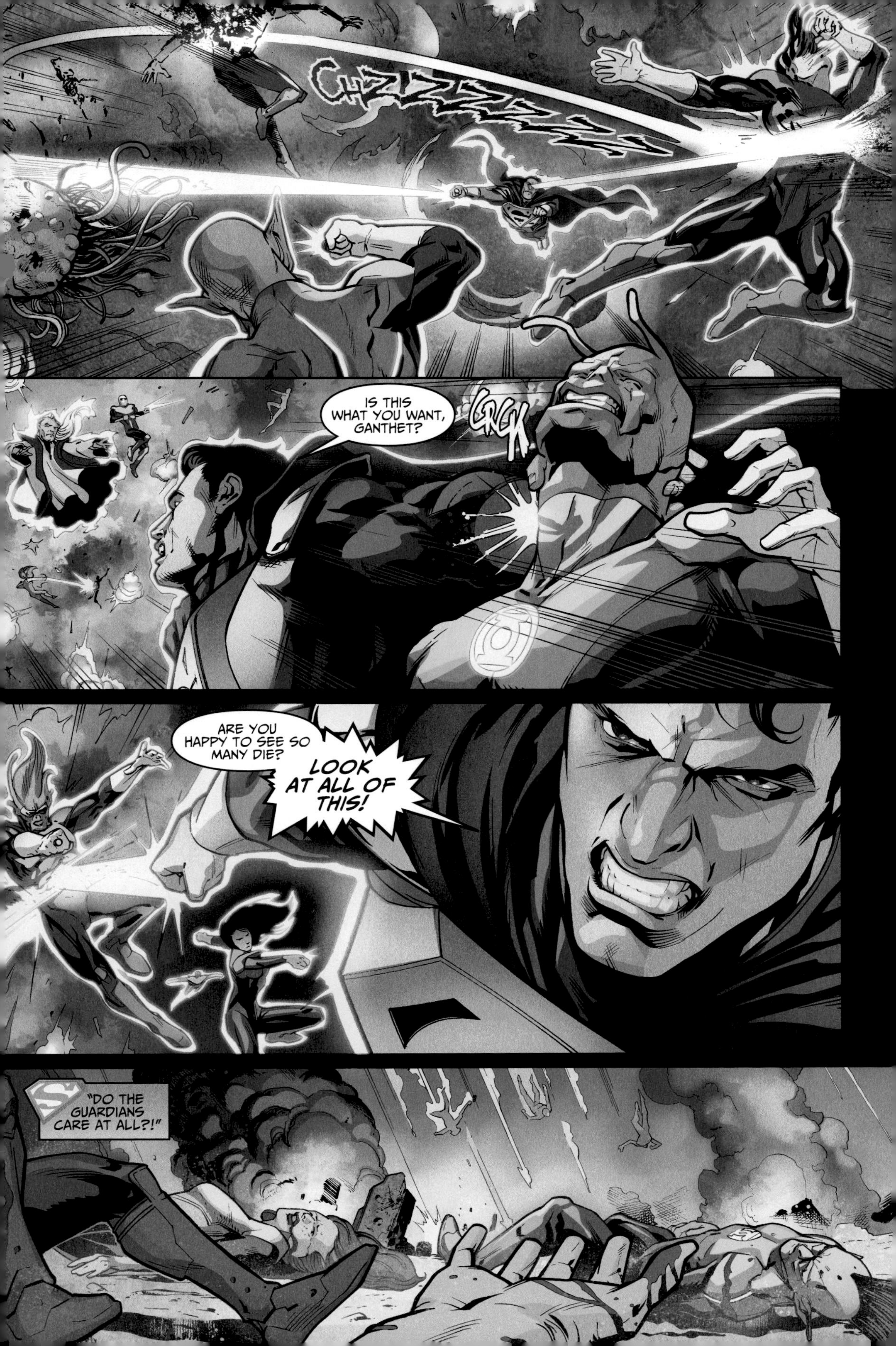
CHZZZZZZ
IS THIS WHAT YOU WANT, GANTHET?
GRCK
ARE YOU HAPPY TO SEE SO MANY DIE?
LOOK AT ALL OF THIS!
"DO THE GUARDIANS CARE AT ALL?!"

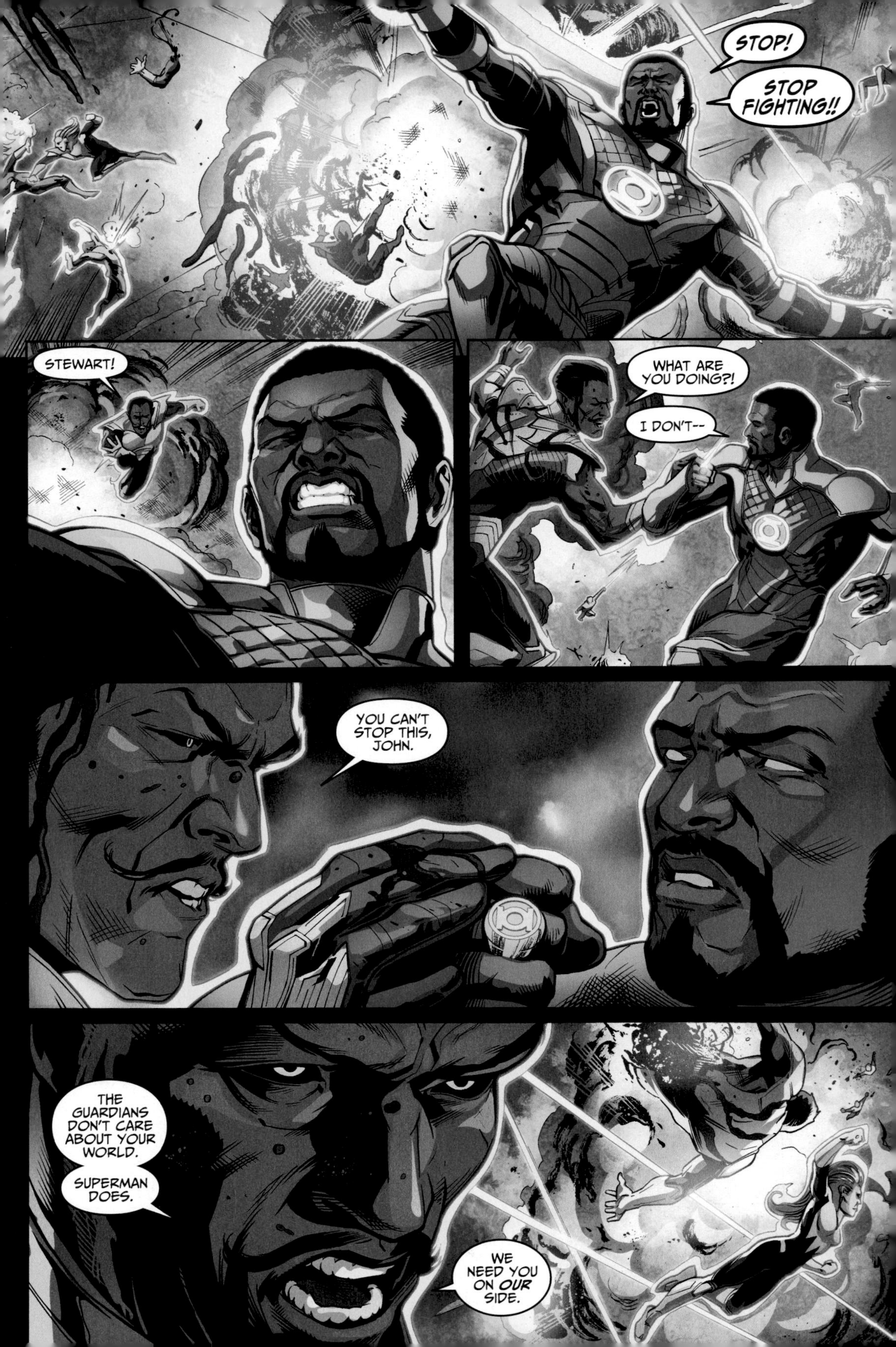
STOP!
STOP FIGHTING!!
STEWART!
WHAT ARE YOU DOING?!
I DON'T--
YOU CAN'T STOP THIS, JOHN.
THE GUARDIANS DON'T CARE ABOUT YOUR WORLD.
SUPERMAN DOES.
WE NEED YOU ON *OUR* SIDE.

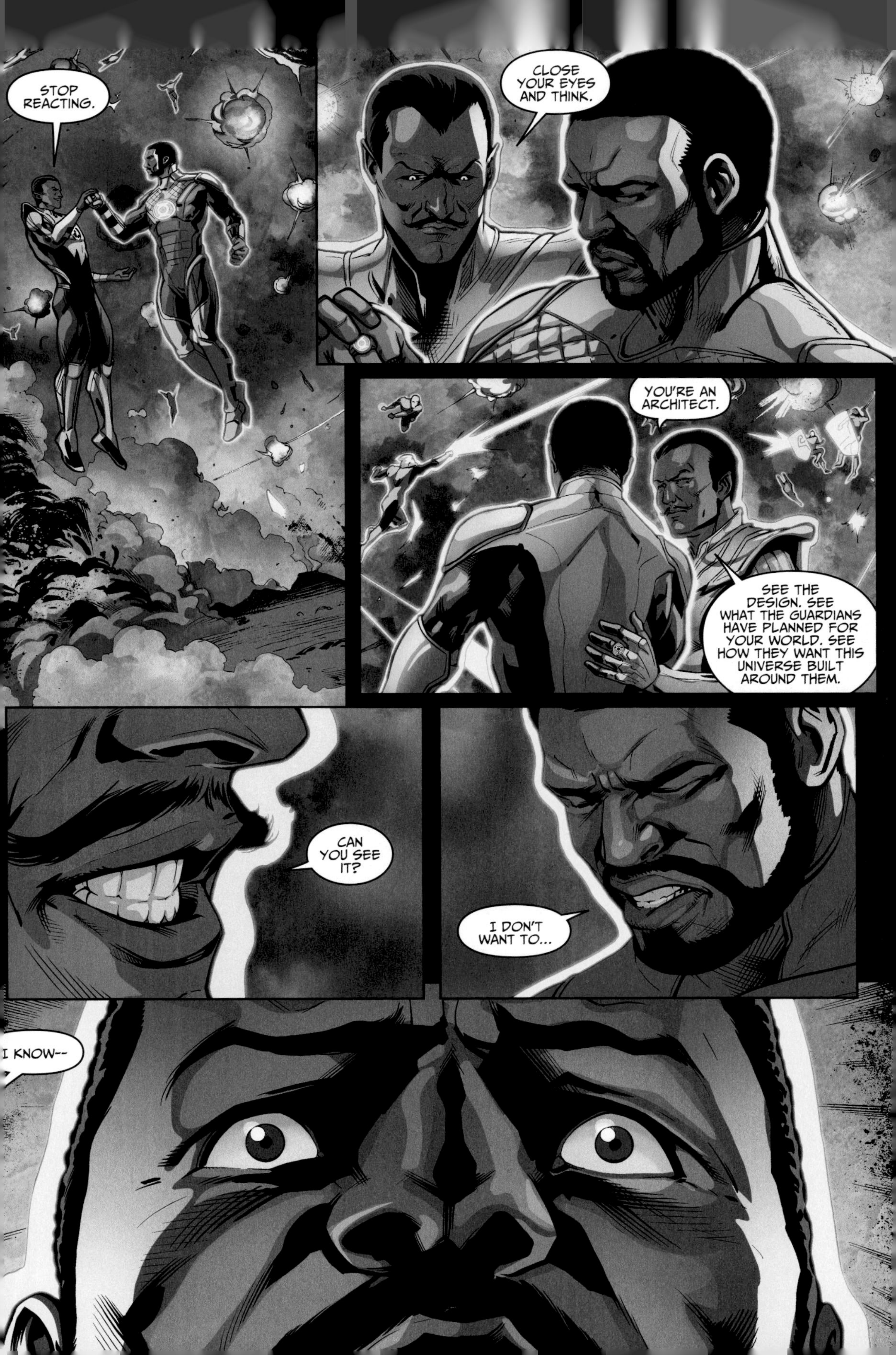
STOP REACTING.
CLOSE YOUR EYES AND THINK.
YOU'RE AN ARCHITECT.
SEE THE DESIGN. SEE WHAT THE GUARDIANS HAVE PLANNED FOR YOUR WORLD. SEE HOW THEY WANT THIS UNIVERSE BUILT AROUND THEM.
CAN YOU SEE IT?
I DON'T WANT TO...
I KNOW--

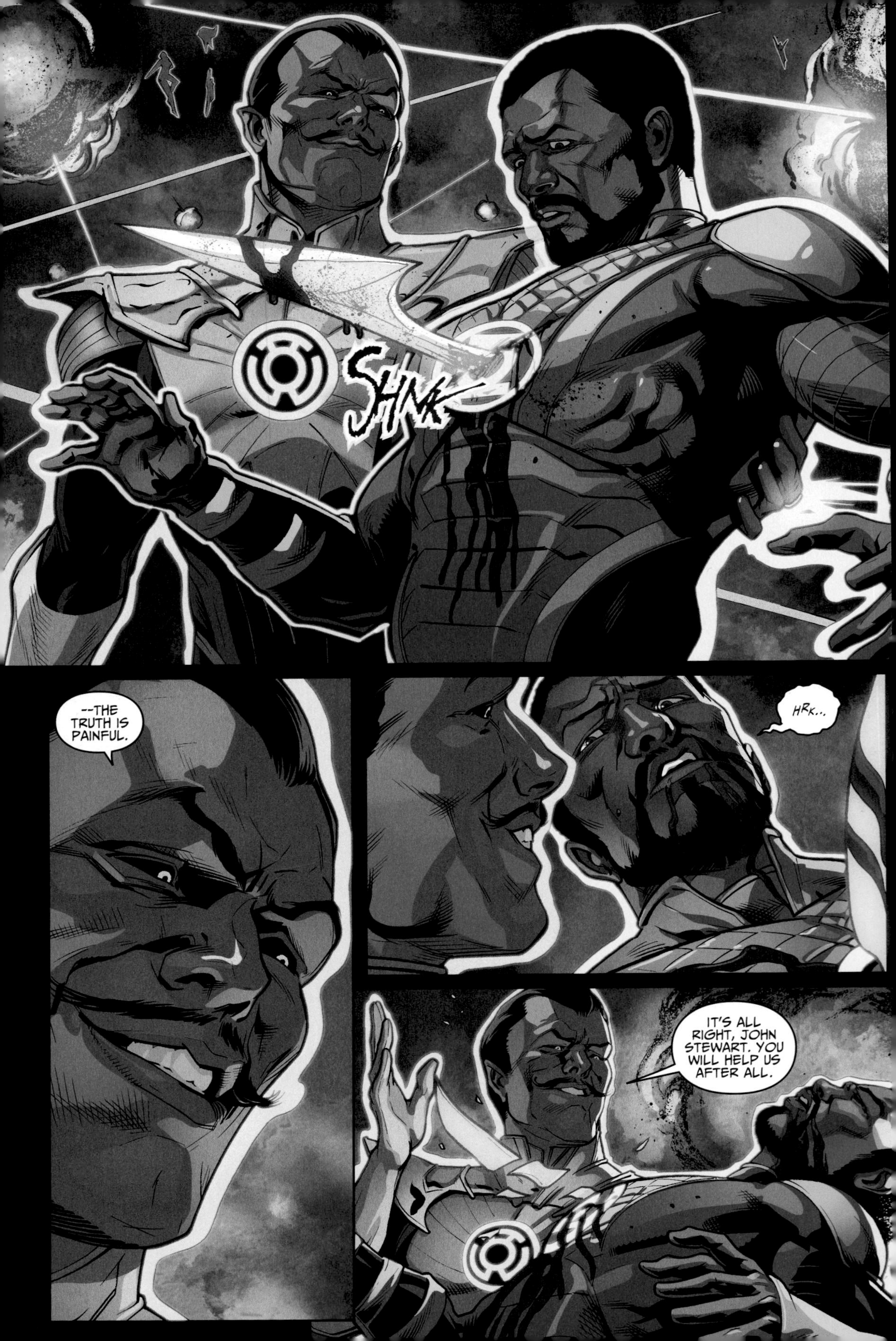
SHNK
--THE TRUTH IS PAINFUL.
HRK...
IT'S ALL RIGHT, JOHN STEWART. YOU WILL HELP US AFTER ALL.

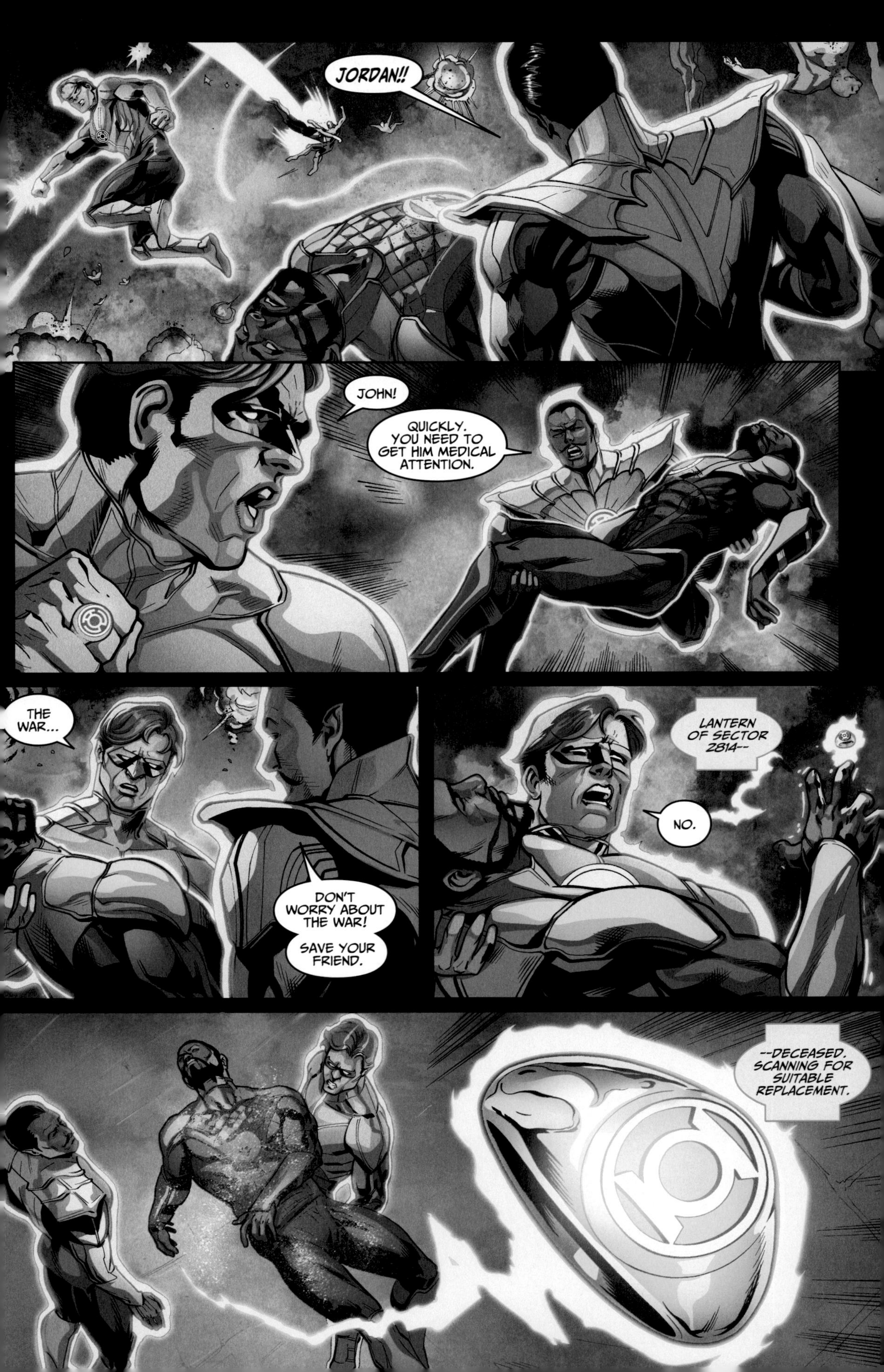
JORDAN!!
JOHN!
QUICKLY. YOU NEED TO GET HIM MEDICAL ATTENTION.
THE WAR...
DON'T WORRY ABOUT THE WAR!
SAVE YOUR FRIEND.
LANTERN OF SECTOR 2814--
NO.
--DECEASED. SCANNING FOR SUITABLE REPLACEMENT.

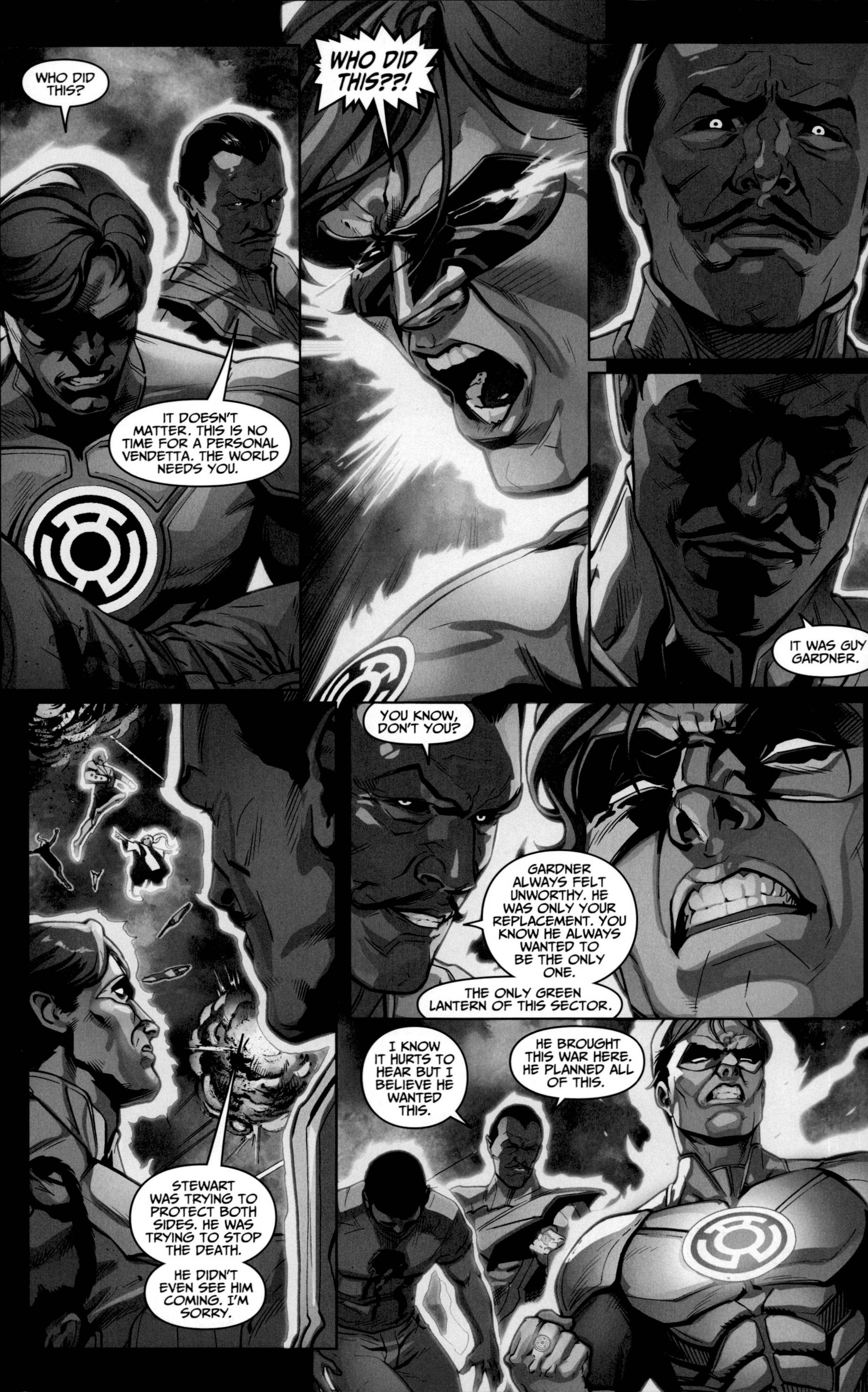
WHO DID THIS?
IT DOESN'T MATTER. THIS IS NO TIME FOR A PERSONAL VENDETTA. THE WORLD NEEDS YOU.
WHO DID THIS??!
IT WAS GUY GARDNER.
STEWART WAS TRYING TO PROTECT BOTH SIDES. HE WAS TRYING TO STOP THE DEATH.
HE DIDN'T EVEN SEE HIM COMING. I'M SORRY.
YOU KNOW, DON'T YOU?
GARDNER ALWAYS FELT UNWORTHY. HE WAS ONLY YOUR REPLACEMENT. YOU KNOW HE ALWAYS WANTED TO BE THE ONLY ONE.
THE ONLY GREEN LANTERN OF THIS SECTOR.
I KNOW IT HURTS TO HEAR BUT I BELIEVE HE WANTED THIS.
HE BROUGHT THIS WAR HERE. HE PLANNED ALL OF THIS.

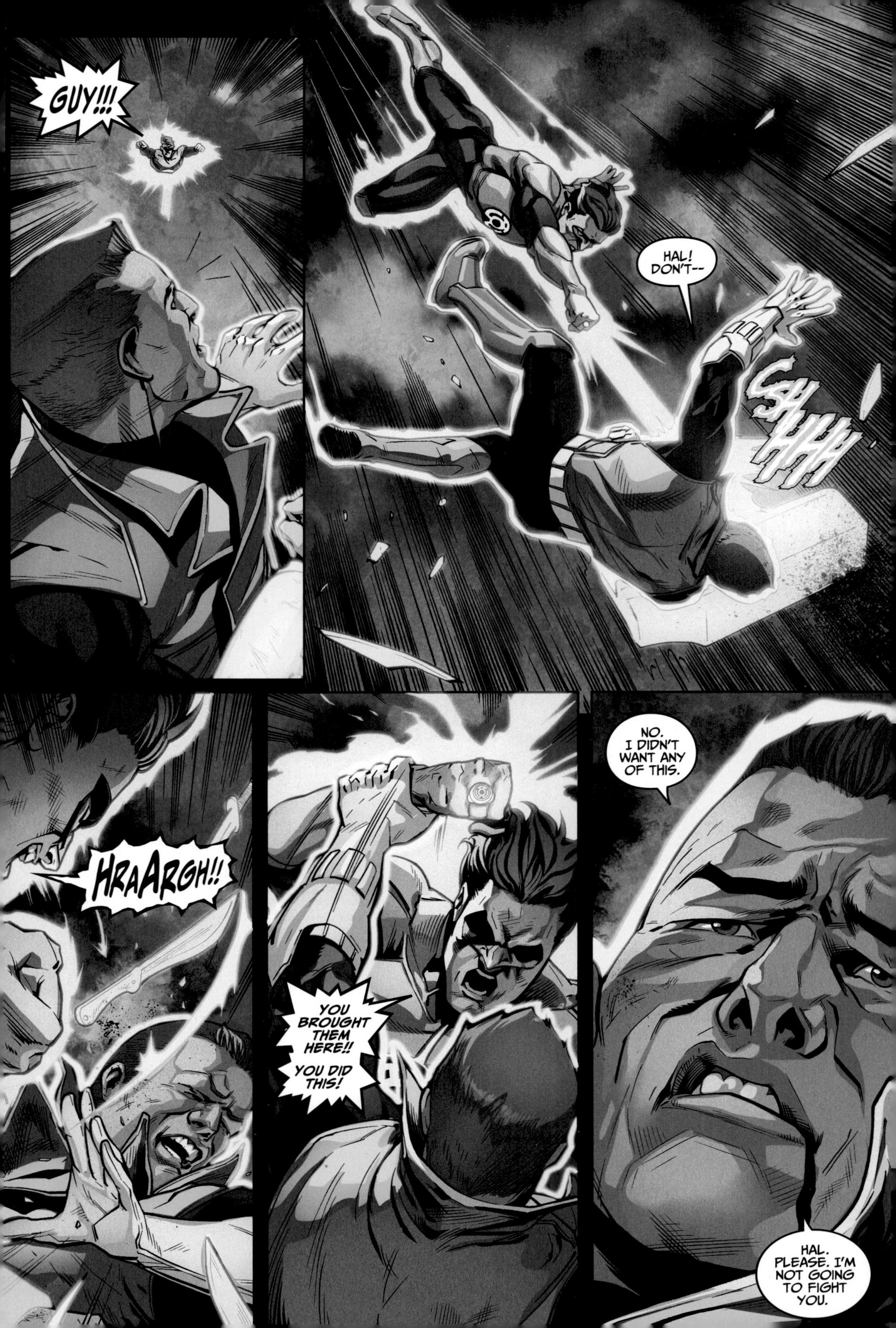
GUY!!!
HAL! DON'T--
SSHHHH
HRAARGH!!
YOU BROUGHT THEM HERE!! YOU DID THIS!
NO. I DIDN'T WANT ANY OF THIS.
HAL. PLEASE. I'M NOT GOING TO FIGHT YOU.

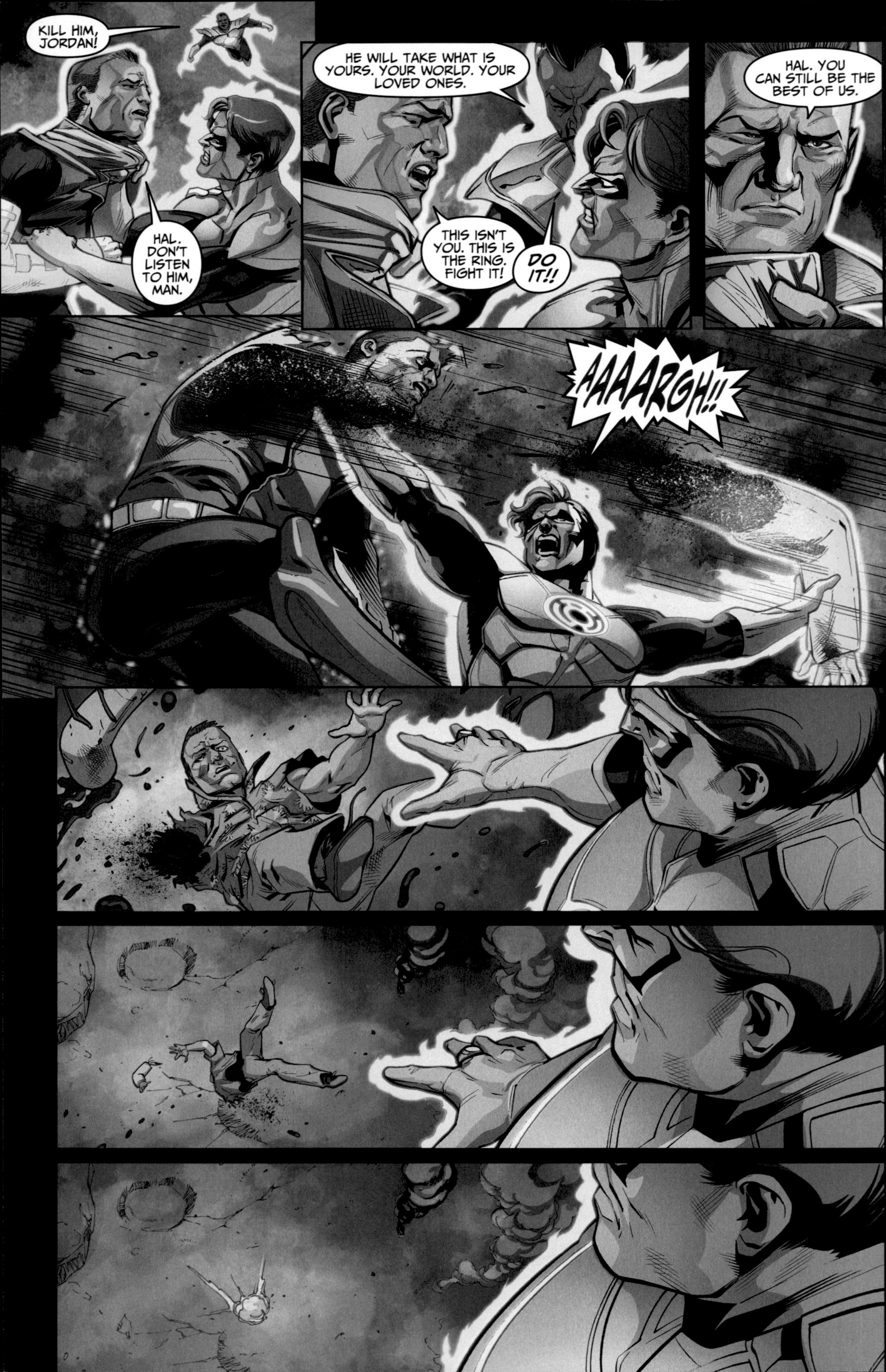
KILL HIM, JORDAN!
HAL. DON'T LISTEN TO HIM, MAN.
HE WILL TAKE WHAT IS YOURS. YOUR WORLD. YOUR LOVED ONES.
THIS ISN'T YOU. THIS IS THE RING. FIGHT IT!
DO IT!!
HAL. YOU CAN STILL BE THE BEST OF US.
AAAARGH!!

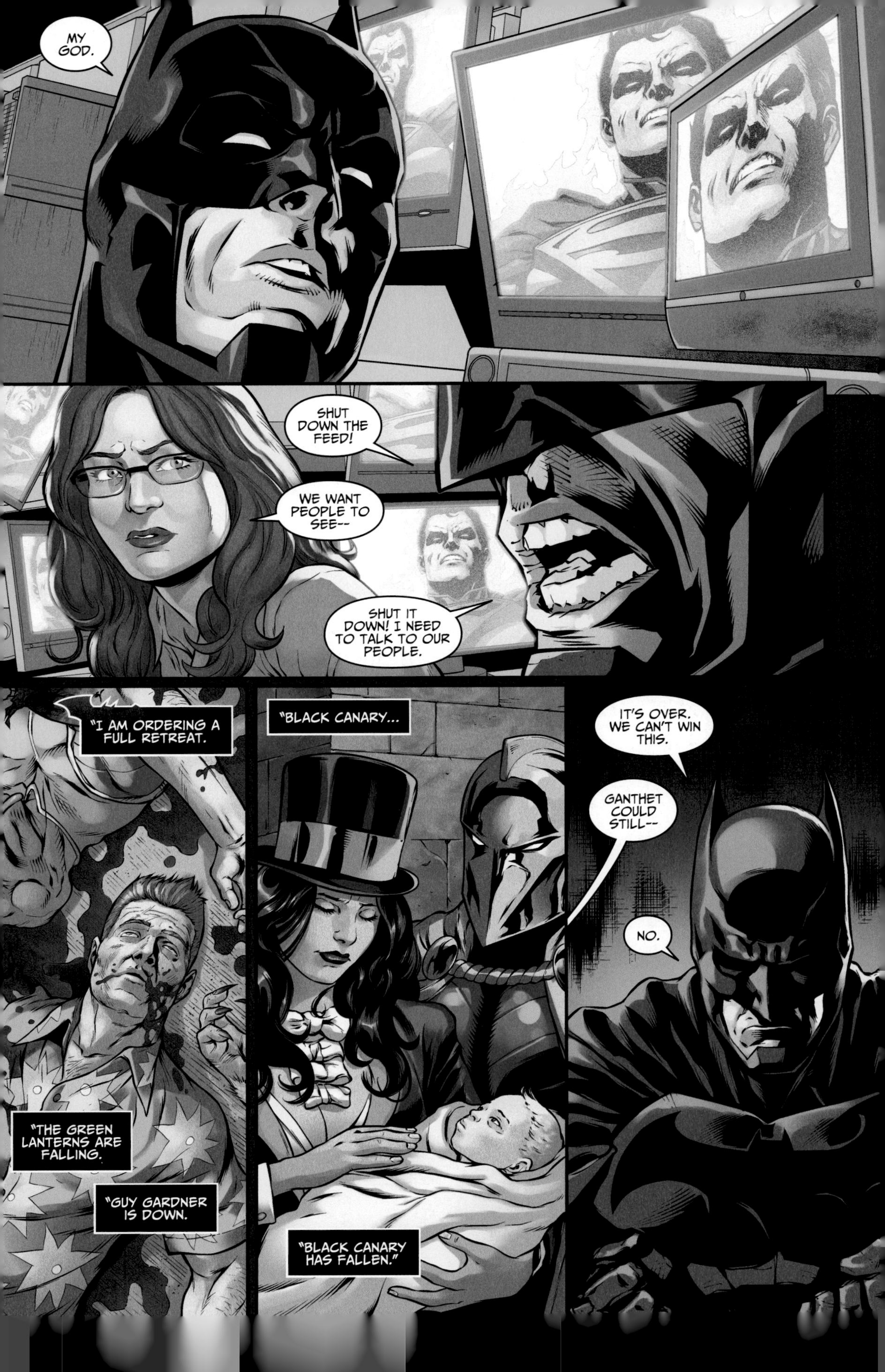
MY GOD.
SHUT DOWN THE FEED!
WE WANT PEOPLE TO SEE--
SHUT IT DOWN! I NEED TO TALK TO OUR PEOPLE.
"I AM ORDERING A FULL RETREAT.
"THE GREEN LANTERNS ARE FALLING.
"GUY GARDNER IS DOWN.
"BLACK CANARY...
"BLACK CANARY HAS FALLEN."
IT'S OVER. WE CAN'T WIN THIS.
GANTHET COULD STILL--
NO.

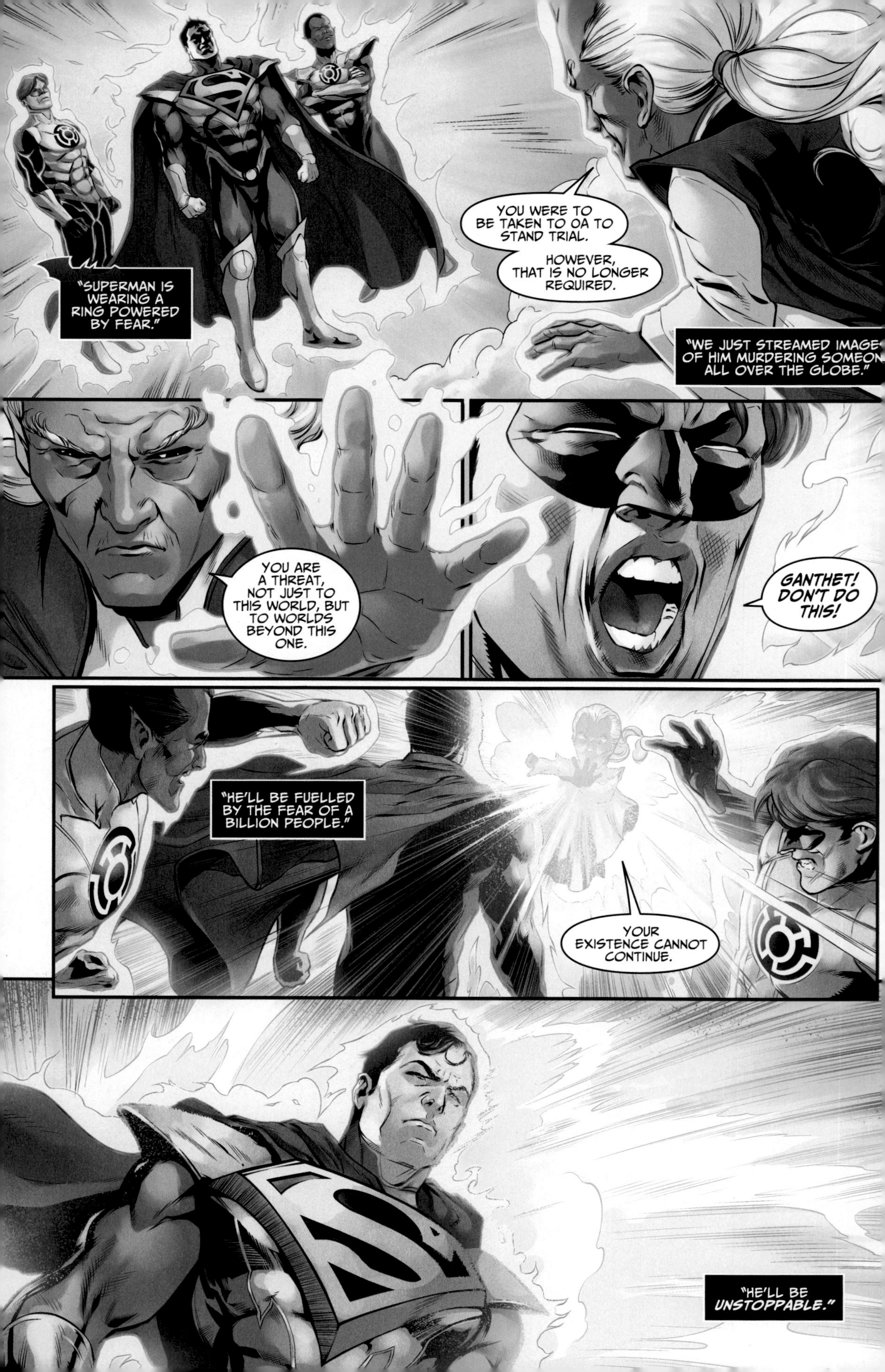
"SUPERMAN IS WEARING A RING POWERED BY FEAR."
YOU WERE TO BE TAKEN TO OA TO STAND TRIAL.
HOWEVER, THAT IS NO LONGER REQUIRED.
"WE JUST STREAMED IMAGE OF HIM MURDERING SOMEON ALL OVER THE GLOBE."
YOU ARE A THREAT, NOT JUST TO THIS WORLD, BUT TO WORLDS BEYOND THIS ONE.
GANTHET! DON'T DO THIS!
"HE'LL BE FUELLED BY THE FEAR OF A BILLION PEOPLE."
YOUR EXISTENCE CANNOT CONTINUE.
"HE'LL BE UNSTOPPABLE."

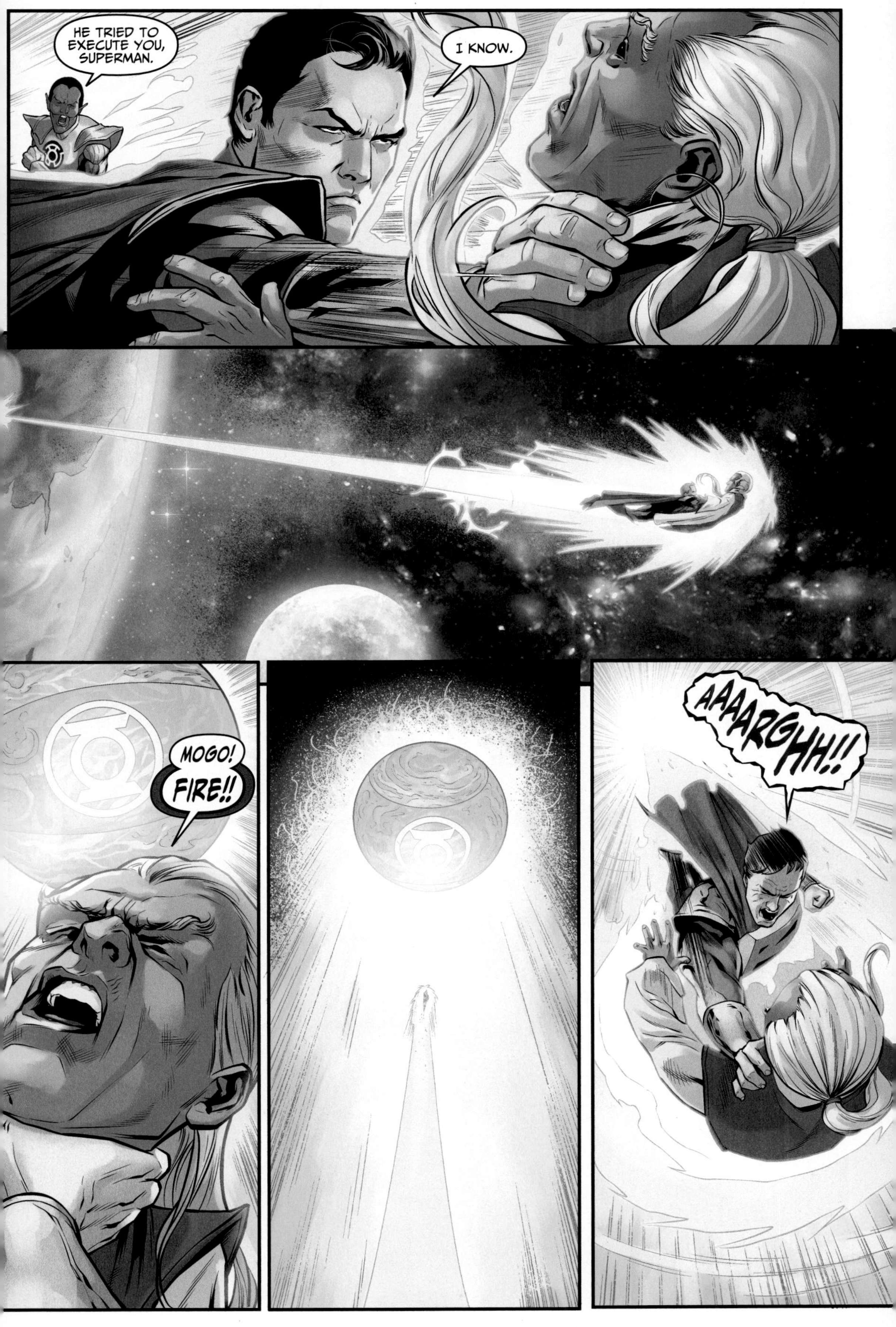
HE TRIED TO EXECUTE YOU, SUPERMAN.
I KNOW.
MOGO! FIRE!!
AAAARGHH!!

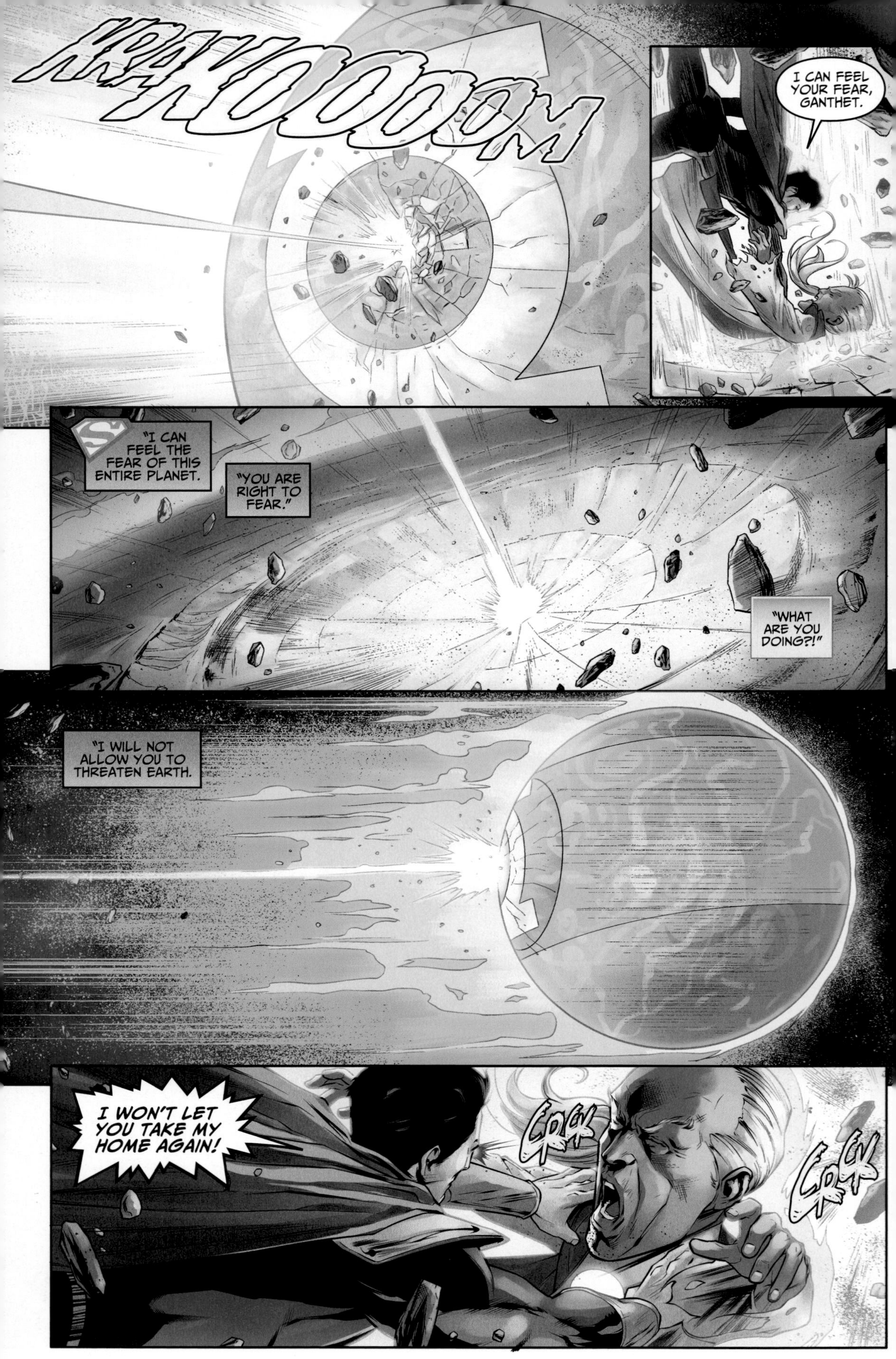
KRAKOOOOM
I CAN FEEL YOUR FEAR, GANTHET.
"I CAN FEEL THE FEAR OF THIS ENTIRE PLANET.
"YOU ARE RIGHT TO FEAR."
"WHAT ARE YOU DOING?!"
"I WILL NOT ALLOW YOU TO THREATEN EARTH.
I WON'T LET YOU TAKE MY HOME AGAIN!
CRACK
CRACK

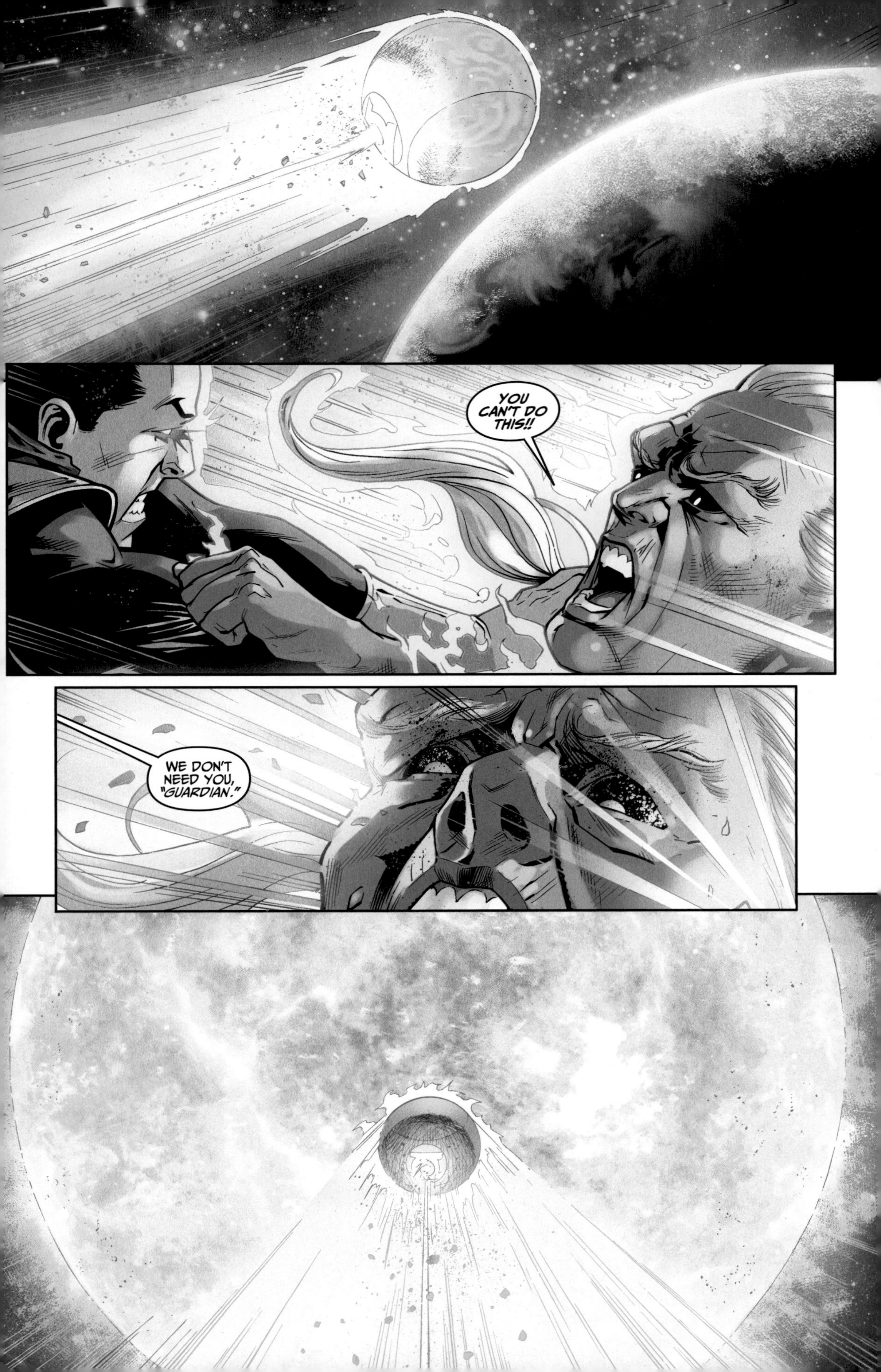
YOU CAN'T DO THIS!!
WE DON'T NEED YOU, "GUARDIAN."

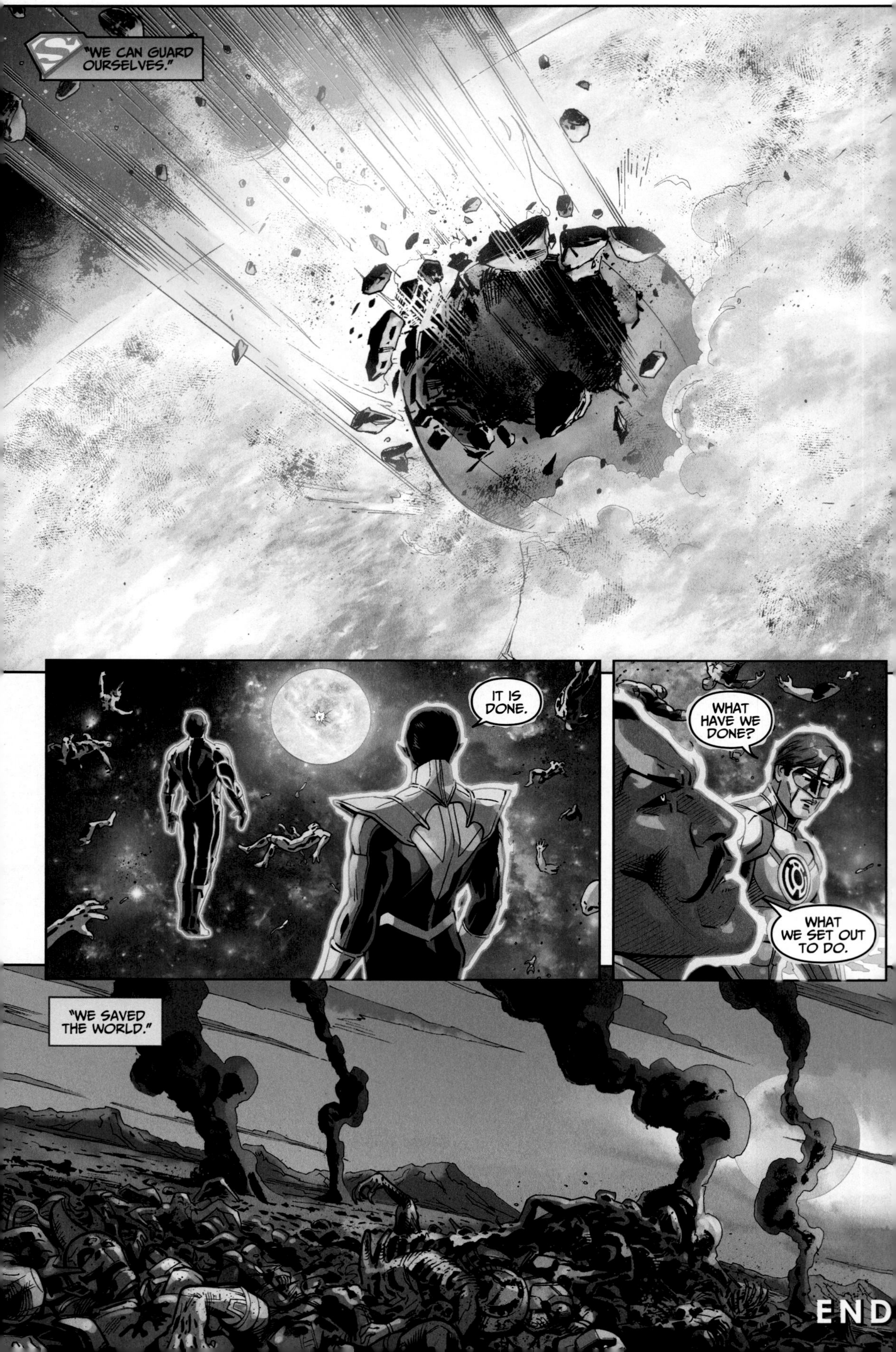
"WE CAN GUARD OURSELVES."
IT IS DONE.
WHAT HAVE WE DONE?
WHAT WE SET OUT TO DO.
"WE SAVED THE WORLD."
END

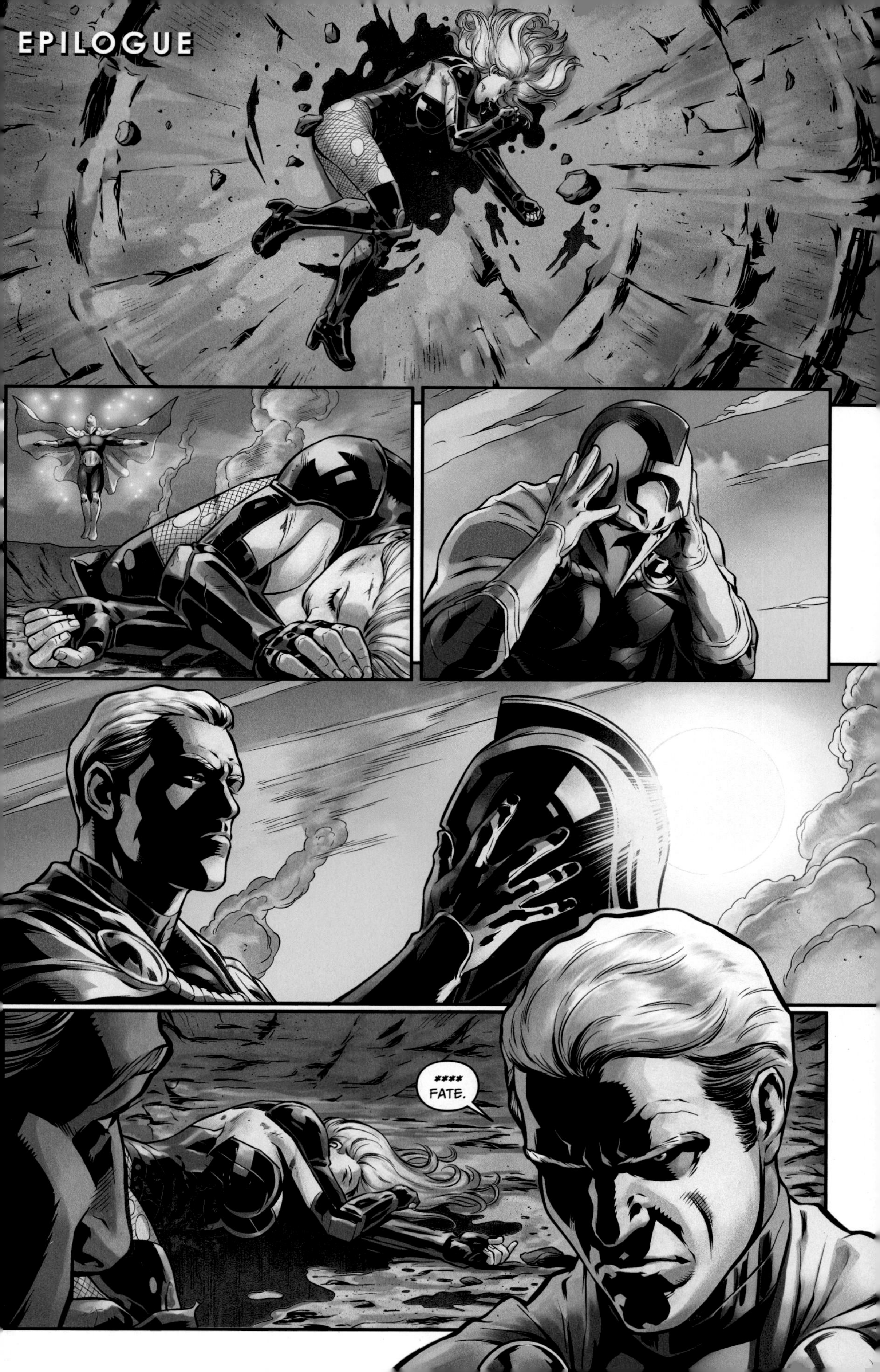
EPILOGUE
**** FATE.

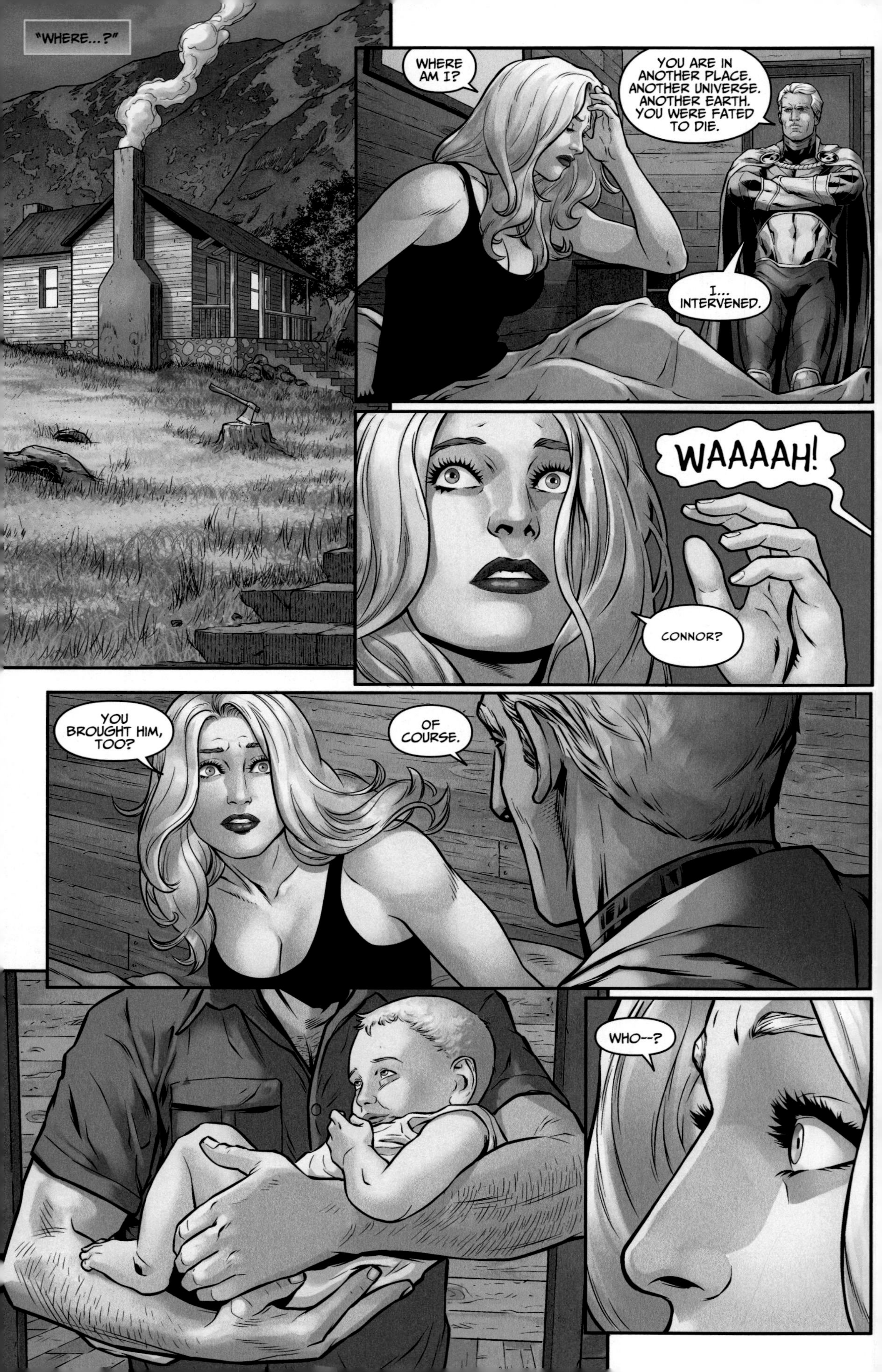
"WHERE...?"
WHERE AM I?
YOU ARE IN ANOTHER PLACE. ANOTHER UNIVERSE. ANOTHER EARTH. YOU WERE FATED TO DIE.
I... INTERVENED.
WAAAAH!
CONNOR?
YOU BROUGHT HIM, TOO?
OF COURSE.
WHO--?

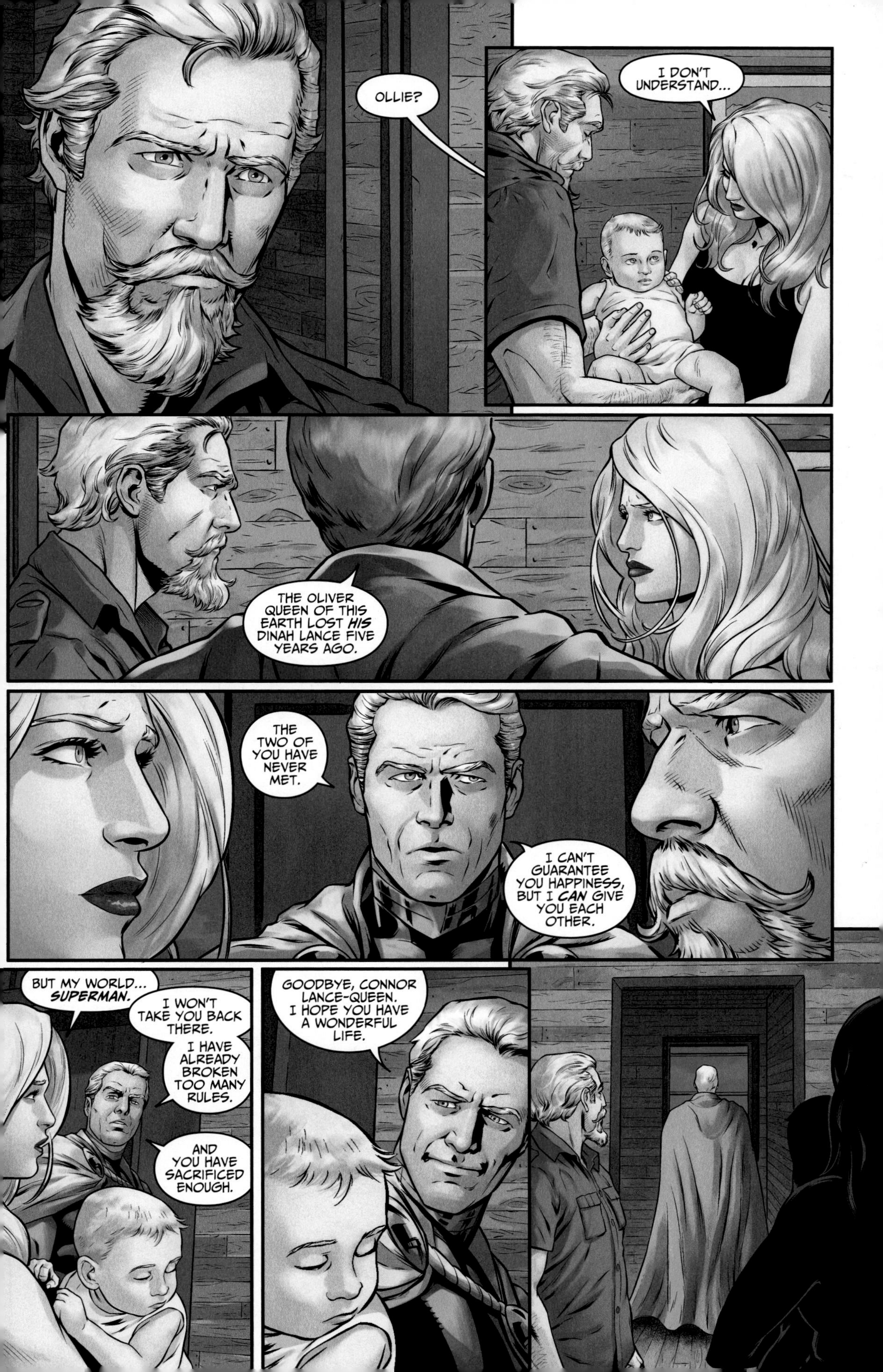
OLLIE?
I DON'T UNDERSTAND...
THE OLIVER QUEEN OF THIS EARTH LOST *HIS* DINAH LANCE FIVE YEARS AGO.
THE TWO OF YOU HAVE NEVER MET.
I CAN'T GUARANTEE YOU HAPPINESS, BUT I *CAN* GIVE YOU EACH OTHER.
BUT MY WORLD... *SUPERMAN.*
I WON'T TAKE YOU BACK THERE.
I HAVE ALREADY BROKEN TOO MANY RULES.
AND YOU HAVE SACRIFICED ENOUGH.
GOODBYE, CONNOR LANCE-QUEEN. I HOPE YOU HAVE A WONDERFUL LIFE.

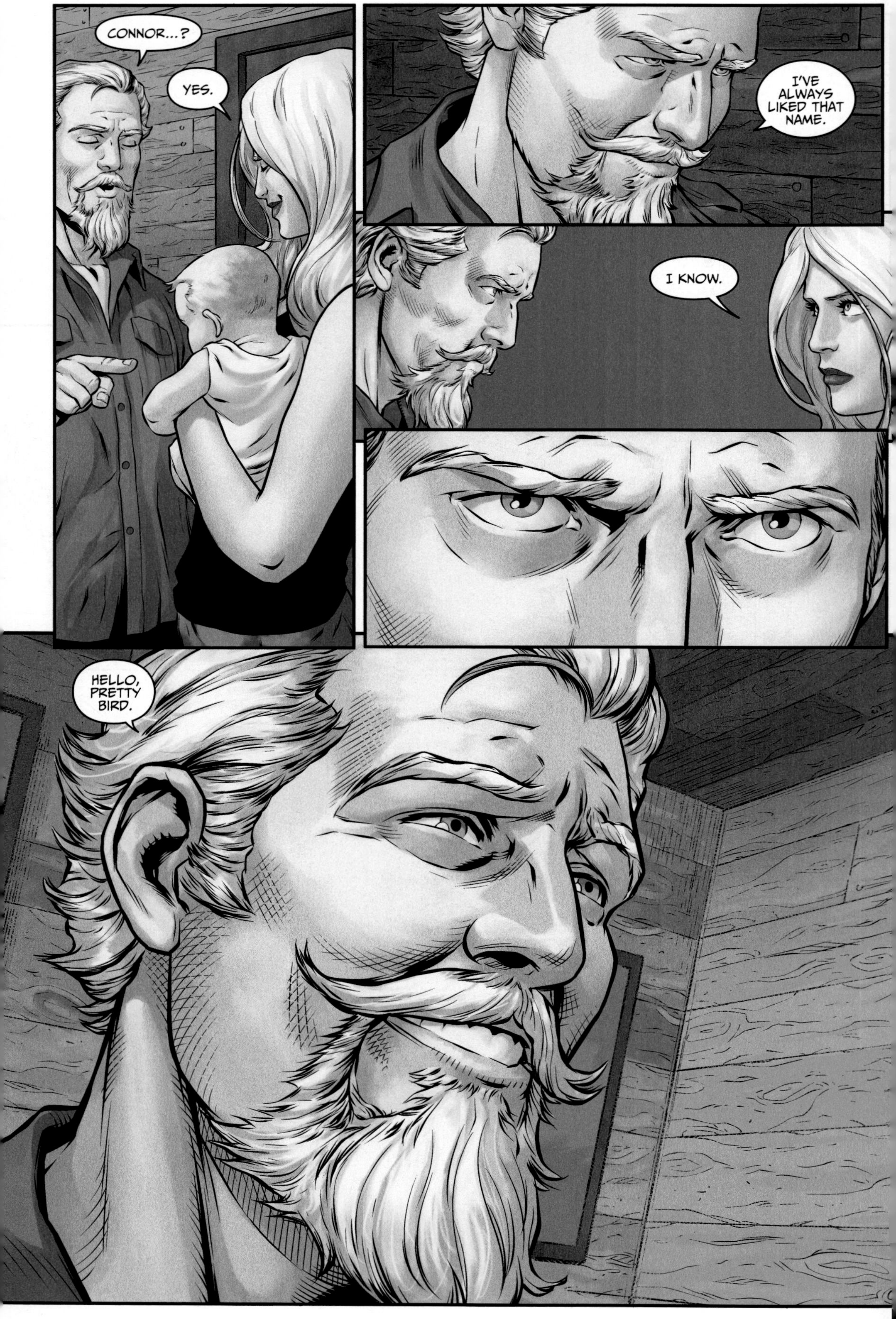
CONNOR...?
YES.
I'VE ALWAYS LIKED THAT NAME.
I KNOW.
HELLO, PRETTY BIRD.

Pencils from Injustice: Year Two #10 by Bruno Redondo

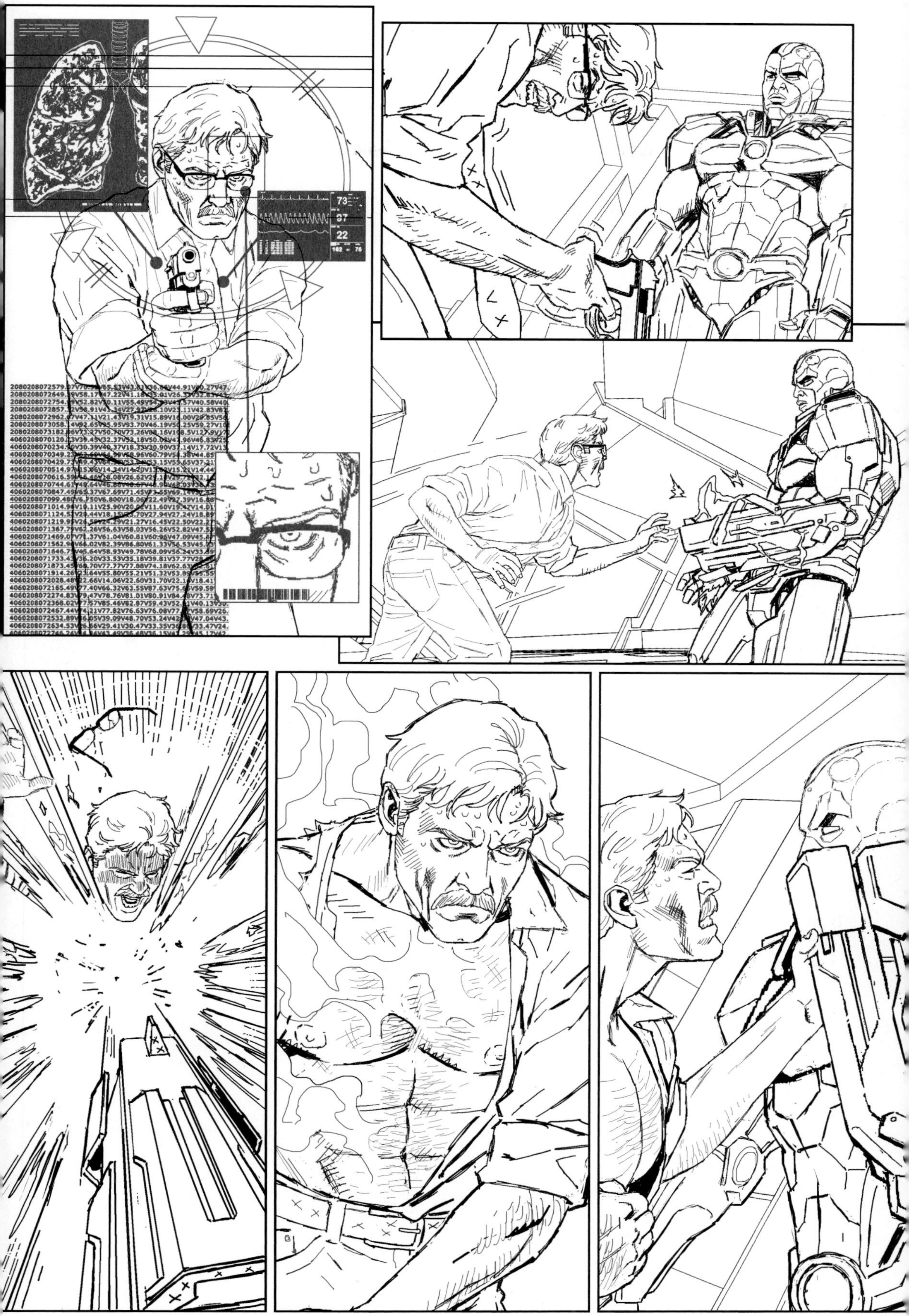

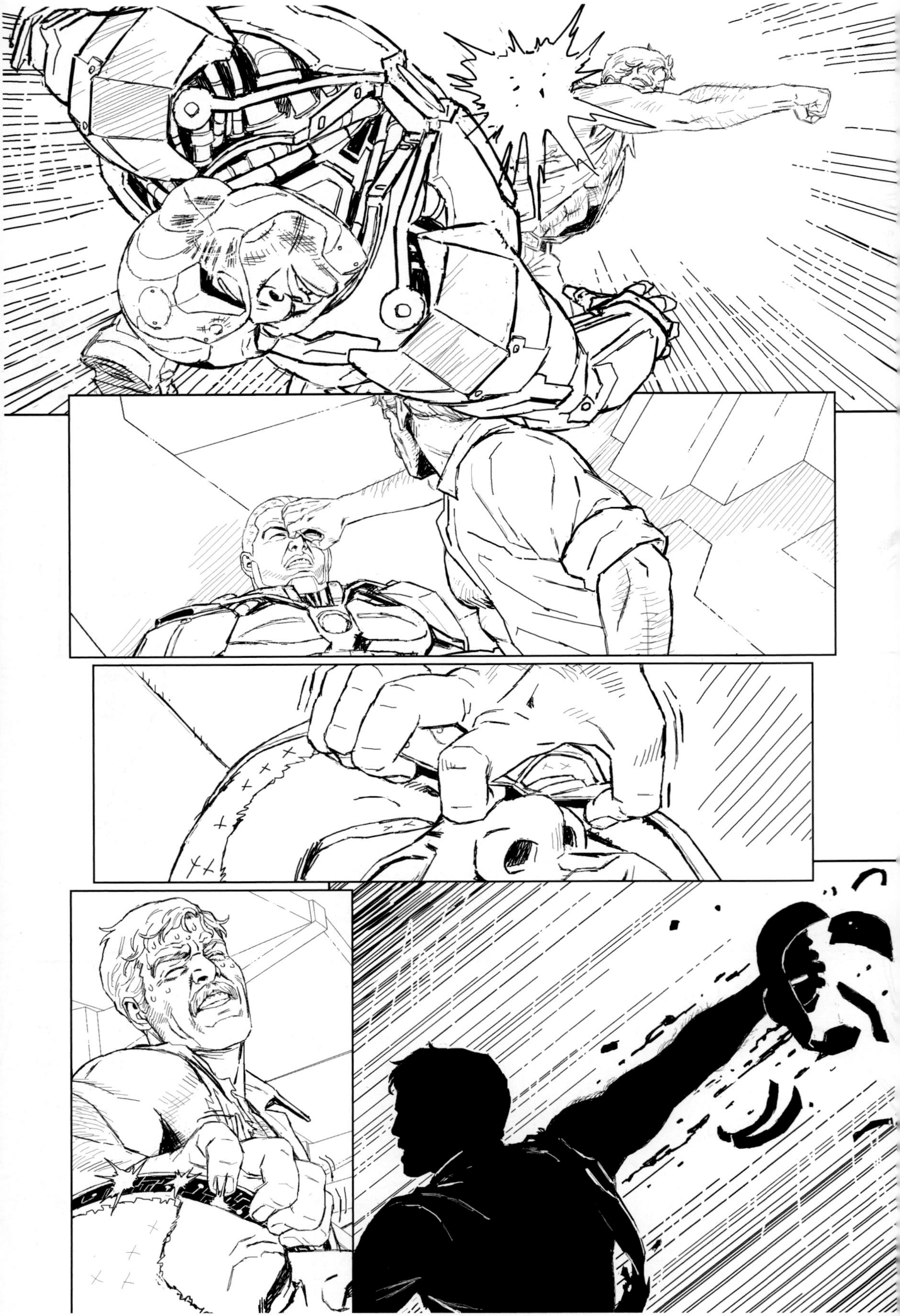

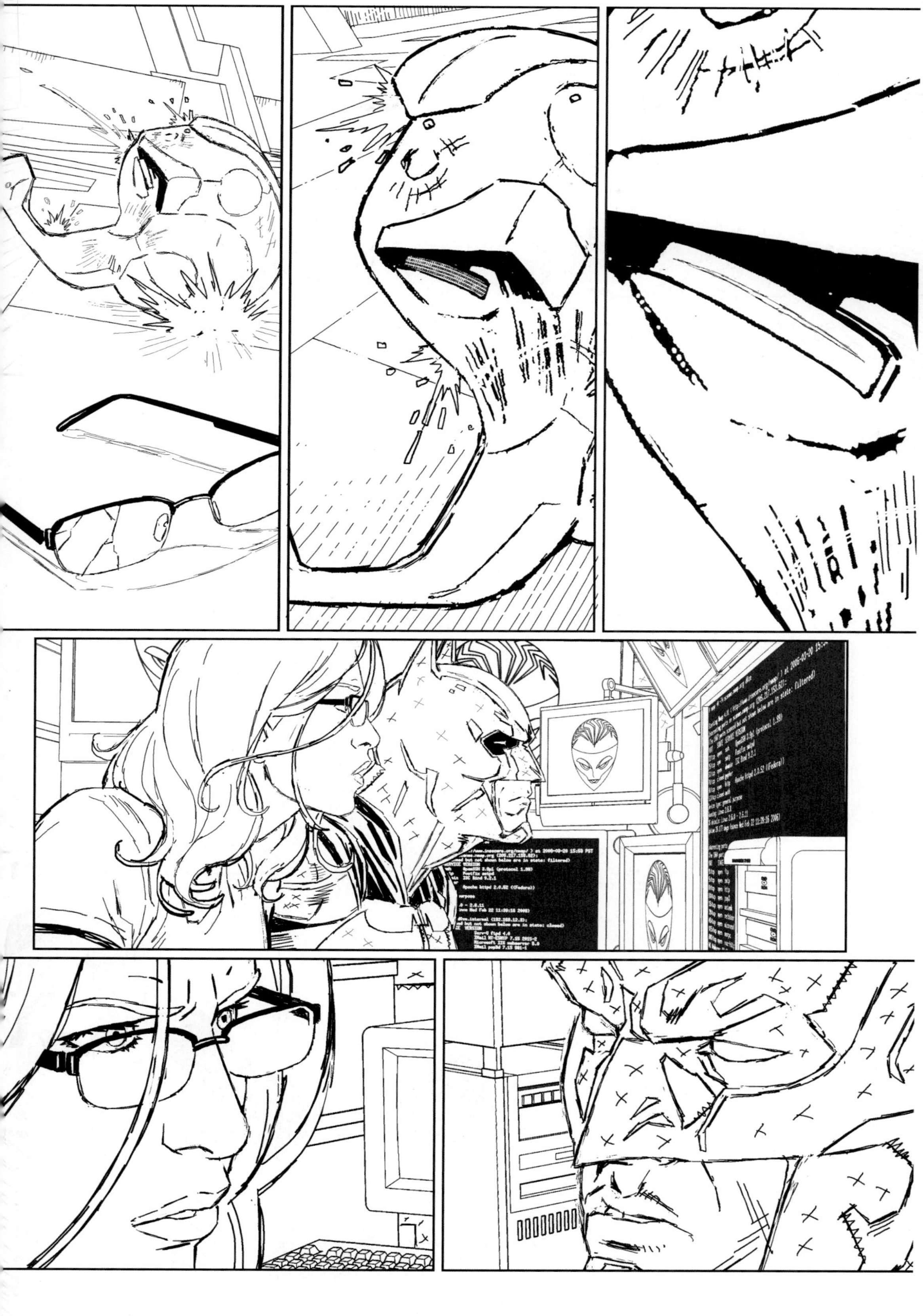

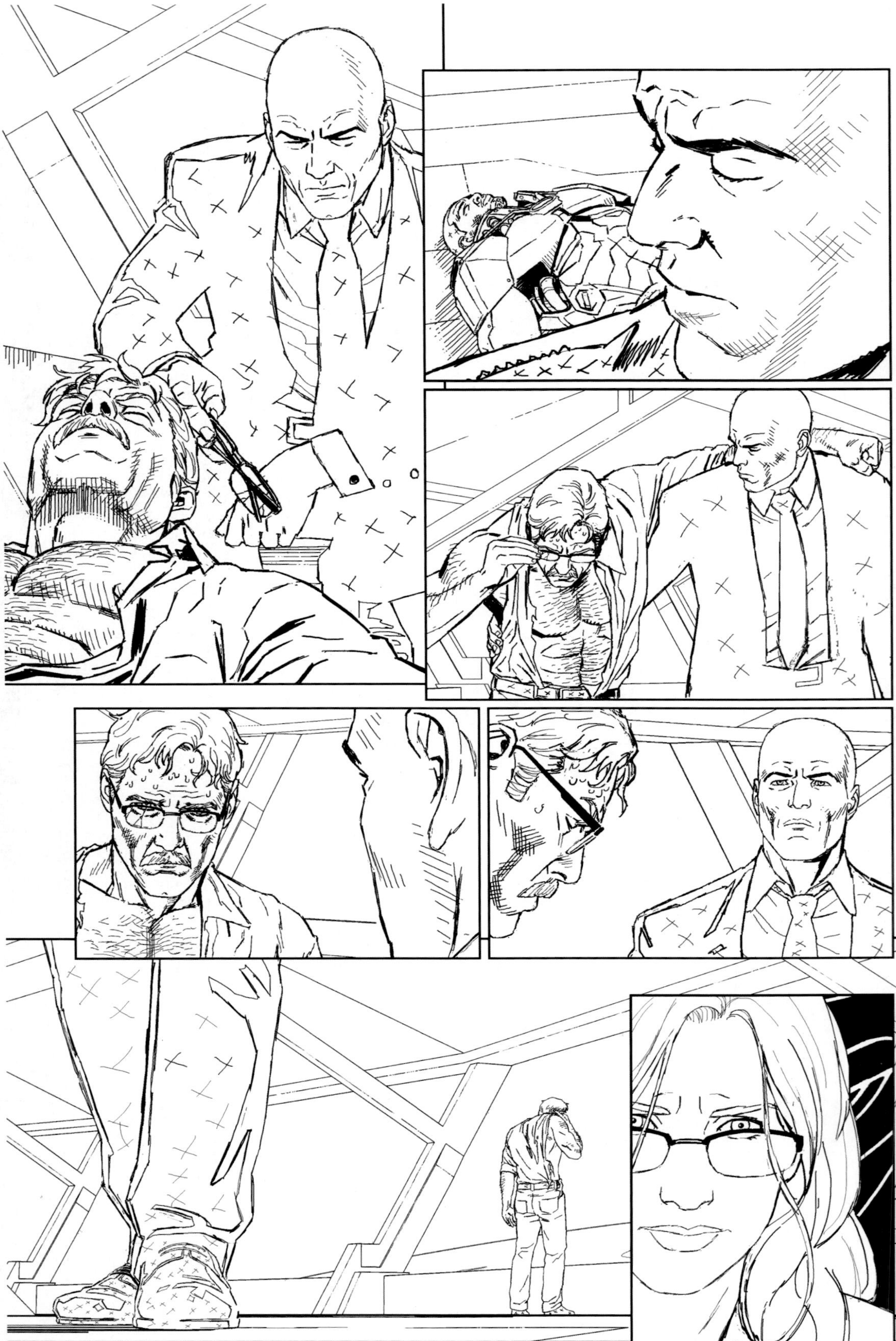